Textbook of
Pharmaceutical
Industrial Management

Textbook of
Pharmaceutical
Industrial Management

Biren N Shah
Associate Professor
Vidyabharti Trust College of Pharmacy, Umrakh

Bhavesh S Nayak
Associate Professor
Vidyabharti Trust College of Pharmacy, Umrakh

Vineet C Jain
Associate Professor
CK Pithawala Institute of
Pharmaceutical Science and Research, Surat

Dhiren P Shah
Associate Professor
CK Pithawala Institute of
Pharmaceutical Science and Research, Surat

CBS

CBS Publishers & Distributors Pvt Ltd
New Delhi • Bengaluru • Chennai • Kochi • Kolkata • Mumbai
Hyderabad • Jharkhand • Nagpur • Patna • Pune • Uttarakhand

Textbook of
Pharmaceutical
Industrial Management

ISBN: 978-93-54660-29-0

CBS Edition: 2021

Copyright © Authors and Publisher

Published by **Satish Kumar Jain** and produced by **Varun Jain** for

CBS Publishers & Distributors Pvt Ltd

4819/XI Prahlad Street, 24 Ansari Road, Daryaganj, New Delhi 110 002, India.
Ph: 011-23289259, 23266861, 23266867
Fax: 011-23243014

Website: www.cbspd.com
e-mail: delhi@cbspd.com;
cbspubs@airtelmail.in.

Corporate Office: 204 FIE, Industrial Area, Patparganj, Delhi 110 092
Ph: 011-4934 4934   Fax: 011-4934 4935   e-mail: publishing@cbspd.com;
publicity@cbspd.com

Branches

- **Bengaluru:** Seema House 2975, 17th Cross, K.R. Road, Banasankari 2nd Stage, Bengaluru 560 070, Karnataka, India
  Ph: +91-80-26771678/79   Fax: +91-80-26771680   e-mail: bangalore@cbspd.com
- **Chennai:** 7, Subbaraya Street, Shenoy Nagar, Chennai 600 030, Tamil Nadu, India
  Ph: +91-44-26680620, 26681266   Fax: +91-44-42032115   e-mail: chennai@cbspd.com
- **Kochi:** 42/1325, 1326, Power House Road, Opp KSEB, Ernakulam, Kochi 682 018, Kerala, India
  Ph: +91-484-4059061-65,67   Fax: +91-484-4059065   e-mail: kochi@cbspd.com
- **Kolkata:** 6/B, Ground Floor, Rameswar Shaw Road, Kolkata-700014 (West Bengal), India
  Ph: +91-33-2289-1126, 2289-1127, 2289-1128   e-mail: kolkata@cbspd.com
- **Mumbai:** PWD Shed, Gala no 25/26, Ramchandra Bhatt Marg, Next to JJ Hospital Gate no. 2, Opp. Union Bank of India, Noorbaug Mumbai-400009, Maharashtra, India
  Ph: +91-22-66661880/89   e-mail: mumbai@cbspd.com

Representatives

• Hyderabad	0-9885175004	• Jharkhand	0-9811541605	• Nagpur	0-9421945513
• Patna	0-9334159340	• Pune	0-9623451994	• Uttarakhand	0-9716462459

Printed at   Chaman Enterprises, Daryaganj, Delhi, India

Foreword 1

It is my pleasure to write a few words about the *Textbook of Pharmaceutical Industrial Management*. The textbook is written strictly in accordance with the current syllabus requirement for the subject of Industrial Management.

Management is a universal tool and is required for making judicious decisions, coordination of activities, effective communication and interpersonal relationships.

This textbook has covered principles and practices involved in pharmaceutical industry besides basic principles of accountancy and book keeping. All the topics have been explained in a simple language and are illustrated with good diagrammatic representation. The contents that merit attention are pointwise listed in the beginning of each chapter. At the end of each chapter, important exam-oriented questions have been provided. The book is a modest attempt by the author to present various pharmaceutical management principles ought to be known by a pharmacy graduate.

The book is useful for every pharmacy student for learning the tenets of management. I sincerely believe that this book will have a wider readership among the fellow pharmacists.

Dr B.N. Suhagia
Professor
L.M. College of Pharmacy, Ahmedabad

Foreword 2

It is my dispensation to write a few words about the *Textbook of Pharmaceutical Industrial Management*.

In the past, there have been isolated but enlightened attempts to categorize, analyze, and study this interesting discipline. Building on this platform, this book aims to shed light on all aspects of pharmaceutical industrial management, based on the day-to-day operating needs and the skills, and tools necessary to fulfil them. The book provides well-illustrated content, richly supported by caricatures and pictograms related to the subject.

The book aims to help pharmaceutical industry employees involved in management, product marketing, medical marketing, disease management, sales, distribution, pricing and regulatory affairs. Furthermore, it serves as a valuable educational tool for all industry stakeholders, namely, government regulators, trade association officials, pharmaceutical wholesalers, management consulting firms, marketing research professionals, over-the-counter drug marketers, public relation agencies, advertising agencies, sales training professionals, business and marketing editors, disease managers, and managed care executives. By studying this book the undergraduate and graduate students in management, marketing, and pharmaceutical and healthcare marketing may gain valuable insight into this dynamic industry and become better prepared for entering this challenging and rewarding field.

I strongly counsel this textbook to every pharmacy student for learning the doctrine of management principles. I am in no doubt that this book will have a wider readership among the fellow pharmacist brethren.

Kinnart Trivedi
M. Pharm., MBA
AGM, Marketing
Torrent Pharmaceuticals
Ahmedabad

Foreword 3

Information through books has played an increasingly discernible role over the past several years in improving the competitiveness in pharmacy education, management and business. More than just a tool, books should be used to guide and advance the knowledge in a way so that even a slow learner can be geared up effortlessly. The *Textbook of Pharmaceutical Industrial Management* is an integrated book consisting of the key areas of significant competitive advantage.

This textbook basically acquaints the reader with principles, practice and types of management involved in pharmaceutical industry and basic principles of accountancy and book keeping. All the topics have been explained in a simple language. The contents that merit attention are given in the form of Chapter Overview at the beginning of each chapter. At the end of each chapter, important questions have been provided to check the knowledge. The book is a modest attempt by the authors to present various pharmaceutical management principles ought to be known by a pharmacy graduate. The gorgeousness of the book is its concept of learning with fun by adding various caricatures and pictograms making the subject easy to understand. Other features of this book are also to be appreciated, like the whole chapter is divided in subtopics written in a very lucid language with supporting graphical representation and tables. At this juncture, I would like to congratulate the authors and the publisher for bringing out this book with outstanding quality. I am sure that it will immensely benefit not only pharmacy students but also the personnel working in pharmaceutical marketing and industries.

I extend my heartfelt compliments for such noble task of the authors and wish that they will continue this pace of academic exercise in the benefit of pharmacy education.

Dr A.K. Seth
Dean
Pharmacy & Allied Sciences
Sumandeep Vidyapeeth
Piparia, Vadodara (Gujarat)

Preface

This book is a unique effort devoted to the analysis and discussion of all aspects of pharmaceutical industrial management and basic accountancy. The discipline itself is a dynamic field, practised by all pharmaceutical companies and their collaborating partners—one of the largest industrial sectors in the world. Despite the size of the pharmaceutical/healthcare industry, its vitality and growth and the significant human resources contributing to its success, there is still a large gap between the management books, lecture hours and knowledge devoted to the management of consumer goods and those focused on the management of pharmaceutical products. This gap spans the globe.

In the past, there have been enlightened but isolated attempts to categorize, analyze and study this interesting discipline. Building on this platform, this book aims to shed light on all aspects of pharmaceutical industrial management, based on the day-to-day operating needs and the skills, and tools necessary to fulfil them. The book provides well-illustrated content, richly supported by caricatures and pictograms related to the subject.

The information gathered from the various sources has been painstakingly transformed into practical advice that focuses on all aspects of pharmaceutical management and solves most of the day-to-day pharmaceutical management dilemmas.

The book aims to help the pharmaceutical industry employees involved in management, product marketing, medical marketing, disease management, sales, distribution, pricing and regulatory affairs. Furthermore, it serves as a valuable educational tool for all industry stakeholders, namely, government regulators, trade association officials, pharmaceutical wholesalers, management consulting firms, marketing research professionals, over-the-counter (OTC) drug marketers, public relation agencies, advertising agencies, sales training professionals, business and marketing editors, disease managers and managed care executives. By studying this book, undergraduate and graduate students in management, marketing, and pharmaceutical and healthcare marketing may gain valuable insight into this dynamic industry and become better prepared for entering this challenging and rewarding field. In fact, this book has been designed using standalone educational/informational modules that may be used as course materials by interested educators and their audiences. Finally, this book is a document that may have limitations in areas of expertise practised by colleagues over years and decades. It cannot, possibly, remain up-to-date in such a constantly changing business environment around the globe. The authors appreciate any suggestions the readers may have and remain committed to updating its contents when the need arises.

Authors are thankful to Dr B.N. Suhagia, Professor, L.M. College of Pharmacy, Ahmedabad, Dr A.K. Seth, Dean, Sumandeep Vidyapeeth, Piparia, and Mr Kinnart Trivedi, AGM, Marketing, Torrent Pharmaceuticals, Ahmedabad, for writing the foreword for this book.

Last, but not the least, authors cannot forget to thank the Elsevier team for their efforts in bringing out this book.

Authors

Contents

Indian Pharmaceutical Industry

INTRODUCTION

Health is both the cause and the effect of economic development. Therefore, the pharmaceutical industry is specifically recognized in the UN Millennium Development Goals as an actor that can contribute to the economic development. In addition, the pharmaceutical industry provides significant socio-economic benefits to the society through the creation of jobs and supply chains, and through community development. The industry also plays an important role in the technological innovations that may reduce the cost of economic activity elsewhere in the economy. Various players in the pharmaceutical industry include branded drug manufacturers, generic drug manufacturers, firms developing biopharmaceutical products, nonprescription drug manufacturers and firms undertaking contract research. In addition, there are also enablers of the industry such as universities, hospitals and research centres that play an important role in the research and development (R&D) activities.

EVOLUTION OF THE INDIAN PHARMACEUTICAL INDUSTRY

Evolution of the Indian pharmaceutical industry can be classified into the following three periods:

1. Pre-1970s
2. 1970–95
3. 1995 onwards

Pre-1970s

During this period, the size of the Indian pharmaceutical industry was small, in terms of both the number of firms and the volume of production. Multinational companies (MNCs) dominated the market, in terms of both the volume of production and the patent holdings in India. The patent regime based on the Indian Patents and Designs Act, 1911, recognized both product and process patents. Due to the monopoly status enjoyed by the MNCs, the drug prices remained high during this period.

1970–95

The Government of India introduced a new patent act that came into effect in 1972, but it recognized only process patent and not product patent. The act enabled Indian firms to use the 'reverse engineering process' to manufacture drugs without paying royalty to the original patent holder. The act, along with the Drug Price Control Order, provided little incentive to the MNCs to introduce new pharmaceutical products in India. During this period, the number of domestic pharmaceutical firms increased considerably, from around 2000 units in 1970 to 24000 units in 1995. The production of bulk drugs increased from Rs 18 crore in 1965–66 to Rs 1518 crore in 1995, while that of formulations increased from Rs 150 crore to Rs 7935 crore during this period. The increase in production was more pronounced in case of formulations due to large-scale production of generic drugs by domestic firms. Low-cost and high-volume production has helped the Indian pharmaceutical industry in opening the export channels to many developed and developing countries. The share of exports as a percentage of total production has shown a significant increase—from 3.22% in 1980–81 to 24% in 1994–95.

1995 Onwards

The year 1995 recorded another milestone for the Indian pharmaceutical industry. One of the agreements under the World Trade Organization (WTO) was complying with the provisions of the Trade Related Intellectual Property Rights (TRIPS). The TRIPS agreement reintroduced product patent in India. Further, during this period, tariff and nontariff measures have come down. Such developments have worked in favour of the Indian pharmaceutical industry to undertake activities such as clinical research and new drug development. Indigenous producers dominated the market accounting for more than 70% of the market share. Exports also continued to increase during this period, due to strong R&D processes and low manufacturing cost.

INDIA'S PHARMACEUTICAL INDUSTRY IN THE SPOTLIGHT

In 2001, India's pharmaceutical industry became the focus of public debate when Cipla, the country's second-largest pharmaceutical company, offered an AIDS drug to the African countries for USD 300, while the same preparation cost USD 12000 in the United States. This was possible because the Indian company produced an all-in-one generic pill containing all the three substances required for the treatment of AIDS. This kind of production is much more difficult in other countries because there the patents for these three substances are held by three different companies. In the final analysis, the price slump was a result of India's lax patent legislation.

PRESENT STATUS OF THE INDIAN PHARMACEUTICAL INDUSTRY

The annual turnover of the Indian pharmaceutical industry is over USD 11 billion. Globally, it ranks fourth in terms of volume, with an 8% share in the world pharmaceutical market. In terms of value, it ranks 14th. The key therapeutic segments of the Indian pharmaceutical industry include anti-infective, gastrointestinal and cardiovascular drugs. Acute therapies make about 60% of the market. However, it is expected that with the changing lifestyle and aging population, sales of chronic therapies (i.e. diabetes, cardiovascular) are growing rapidly. The pharmaceutical industry is showing good performance in terms of exports also. It is one of the top export items from India, accounting for more than 4% of India's total exports in 2006–07. Exports that constitute around 50% of the industry's total production have grown at a compound annual growth rate (CAGR) of 14% in the last decade. Major export markets include the highly regulated markets such as the USA, Germany, the UK and Canada. Europe is the biggest export destination for Indian pharmaceuticals, accounting for more than 30% of the total exports, followed by the American region (25%). Government policies, viz. Drugs and Cosmetics Act (1940), Drugs Policy (1986), Indian Patents Act (1970), Drug Price Control Order (1995), Pharmaceutical Policy (2002) and the Indian Patents (Amendment) Act (2005) have played a major role in the growth of the Indian pharmaceutical industry. The government has also formulated a Draft National Pharmaceutical Policy (2006) that will be finalized after consultations with the stakeholders. Besides, the government has also facilitated the growth of the Indian pharmaceutical industry through institutional framework and by encouraging investments in R&D.

DISPROPORTIONATELY HIGH SALES GROWTH

Between 1996 and 2006 the nominal sales of pharmaceuticals on the Indian subcontinent were up 9% per annum (p.a.) and thus expanded much faster than the global pharmaceutical market as a whole (+7% p.a.). The Indian companies strongly expanded their capacities, making the country by and large self-sufficient. Nonetheless, with the total sector sales of roughly EUR 10 billion, India commands less than 2% share in the world's pharmaceutical market (1.5%). This puts the country in the twelfth place internationally—behind Korea, Spain and Ireland; and before Brazil, Belgium and Mexico. Among the Asian countries, India's pharmaceutical industry ranks fourth, at 8%, but has lost market share to China, as the sales growth there was nearly twice as high and the sales volume nearly four times higher than that of India. India's pharmaceutical industry currently comprises about 20 000 licensed companies employing approximately 5 00 000 staff. Besides many small firms, these also include internationally well-known companies such as Ranbaxy, Cipla and Dr. Reddy's. With sales of roughly EUR 1 billion, Ranbaxy is currently the world's seventh largest generic-drug manufacturer. Currently, the most important segment on the domestic market is the anti-infectives; they account for one quarter of the total turnover. Next in line and accounting for one-tenth each are cardiovascular preparations, cold remedies and pain killers. By contrast, medicines against civilization diseases (such as diabetes, asthma and obesity) or so-called lifestyle drugs (antidepressants, drugs to help smokers to quit and antiwrinkle formulations) are of little significance at present. All in all, the Indian pharma industry produces about 70 000 different drugs, which is higher than the number produced in Germany (60 000).

CHANGES IN DRUG PATENT LAW LEAD TO DEVELOPMENT OF ORIGINAL DRUGS

Since 2005 India's pharma sector has no longer been protected by the country's lax patent legislation. Hence innovation must come before imitation now. Large manufacturers, who already began to adjust their business models some time ago, put greater emphasis on drug research. In the long term, they do not want to limit themselves to the production of low-cost generic drugs. Even though a number of companies are well positioned in the generic-drug market, many of them are seeking to turn into research-based firms. However, they are facing fierce international competition in this segment, so it will take many years for India to become a serious competitor for the western pharmaceutical companies in the field of patent-protected drugs. According to the company's own information, approximately 40% of the turnover at the drugs manufacturer Ranbaxy stems from drugs developed in house that would still be about one-tenth lower than at similarly large western companies. In order to increase the speed of development and share the financial risk, there are likely to be more strategic alliances between the Indian and the foreign companies. India's leading pharmaceutical companies are currently spending nearly one-tenth of their revenues on research and development. At the large western companies, however, the R&D expenditure comes to 20%. Already in 1994, Dr. Reddy's launched a basic research programme, which was followed by Ranbaxy and Wockhardt in 1997. Last year, as many as 12 companies were engaged in the research for new pharmaceutical substances. The focus here is on drugs against malaria and AIDS, as the demand potential in these segments is particularly high. Malaria is the most common tropical disease, with about 300 to 500 new infections per year, according to the WHO. The number of people infected with HIV adds up to about 40 million worldwide.

However, compared with the large international players, the volume of research at the Indian pharmaceutical companies—especially basic research—is still very small. The average R&D spending of the Indian pharmaceutical companies comes to just under 4% of the total turnover, compared with 9% in Germany. However, one must bear in mind the different sizes of the pharmaceutical industries in the two countries. In this context, the Indian companies are likely to benefit from the liberalization process on the domestic capital market that began in the early 1990s and is not yet complete. The loosening of the financial market regulations has until recently led to an increasing presence of foreign investors, with the interest focusing mostly on the equity market. Since the early 1990s, Indian companies can also be listed on the foreign stock exchanges.

INCREASING R&D ACTIVITIES

Pharmaceutical industry is knowledge intensive and R&D investment plays a crucial role in the growth of this industry. R&D in pharmaceutical industry includes, directional search for solutions to existing medical problems and unmet medical requirements. In addition, pharmaceutical R&D may also be aimed at improving the existing solutions to improve the efficiency or safety of medicines. Thus the pharmaceutical R&D may be concentrated in the New Chemical Entities (NCEs), Novel Drug Delivery Systems (NDDS) or in generic products. Historically, research in Indian pharmaceutical firms was concentrated mainly on process engineering of bulk drugs and development of NDDS for formulations. Although research in the area of discovery of NCE has taken place, due to the heavy investment required in the clinical trial phase many companies have either licensed the molecules to players abroad or collaborated with the overseas players to conduct clinical research. However, the post-WTO patent regime has introduced new challenges for the Indian pharmaceutical industry. Now the pharmaceutical companies are increasingly becoming innovative rather than imitative. The industry is changing its R&D strategy from reverse engineering to patent-driven research. Although the product patent was introduced in 2005, many pharmaceutical companies have realized the need of increasing their R&D efforts only recently.

R&D EXPENDITURE OF SELECTED INDIAN PHARMACEUTICAL COMPANIES

Table 1.1 contains a list of pharmaceutical companies and their R&D expenditures:

Table 1.1. Pharmaceutical Companies and Their R&D Expenditures

Company name	R&D expenditure (in Rs crore)
Ranbaxy Laboratories Ltd.	639.33
Dr. Reddy's Laboratories Ltd.	253.95
Sun Pharmaceutical Industries Ltd.	161.49
Cipla Ltd.	155.40
Cadila Healthcare Ltd.	118.70
Nicholas Piramal India Ltd.	91.15
Torrent Pharmaceuticals Ltd.	87.36
Wockhardt Ltd.	81.08
Aurobindo Pharma Ltd.	77.01
Orchid Chemicals & Pharmaceuticals Ltd.	61.36
Panacea Biotec Ltd.	49.02
Glenmark Pharmaceuticals Ltd.	46.69
Jubilant Organosys Ltd.	39.38
Ipca Laboratories Ltd.	37.86

INORGANIC GROWTH STRATEGY—ACQUISITIONS OR JOINT VENTURES ABROAD

The global pharmaceutical industry has been undergoing, on the one hand, the consolidation mode driven by increasing competition and pressure on pricing and margins, while on the other, a desire for geographical diversification and growth in the market share. Indian companies have also adopted the inorganic growth strategy since recent times and have undertaken several mergers-and-acquisition (M&As) activities. There are various reasons that motivate companies to go for M&As or setting up of joint ventures abroad. These include the following:

1. A company may have a strong product portfolio, but it may lack access to the overseas distribution network. In such cases, a firm may acquire a foreign company to have a sound distribution network. Thus, acquisition helps the acquirer to explore new markets.

2. The reason for acquisition can also be firm specific. Acquisition can be made to gain control over new products, brands, technology and skills. Companies can acquire strong research expertise and boost their capabilities through consolidation.

3. The recent trend in acquisitions also shows an attempt for vertical integration by many firms that are specializing in generic-drug production to get into active pharmaceutical ingredients (API) production. This has been driven by sharp erosion of margins in the finished dosage products and the intense pressure on pricing experienced by generic-drug manufacturing.

Although the acquisition trend started in 1995, Indian firms have aggressively started acquiring foreign firms after the beginning of the decade. The year 2005 witnessed the highest number of overseas acquisitions by the Indian pharmaceutical firms. Ranbaxy, one of the largest Indian pharmaceutical firms, made 12 acquisitions during this period, in different countries like the USA, Germany, the UK, Japan and France. Other firms that have made considerable number of overseas acquisitions include Glenmark and Nicholas Piramal (five each); Dr. Reddy's Laboratories; Sun Pharmaceuticals and Jubilant Organosys (four each); Strides Arcolab and Matrix Laboratories (three each); and Wockhardt, Alembic and Aurobindo Pharma (two each).

The number of acquisitions by each company is listed in Table 1.2.

Table 1.2. Pharmaceutical Companies and Their Acquisitions

Company name	Number of acquisitions
Ranbaxy	12
Glenmark Pharmaceutical Ltd.	5
Nicholas Piramal	5
Dr. Reddy's Laboratories	4
Sun Pharmaceuticals	4
Jubilant Organosys Ltd.	4
Strides Arcolab	3
Matrix Laboratories	3
Aurobindo Pharma	2
Wockhardt	2
Alembic	2
Dishman Pharmaceuticals	1
Enzyme Technologies	1
Indegene Life systems	1
Ipca Laboratories	1
Lupin Ltd.	1
Malladi Drugs	1
Marksans Pharma	1
Natco Pharma	1
Solvay Pharma India	1
Suven Pharmaceuticals	1
Torrent pharmaceuticals	1
Wanbury Ltd.	1
Zydus Cadila	1

OUTLOOK FOR INDIA'S PHARMACEUTICAL INDUSTRY UP TO 2015

All in all we expect India to see a rise in the sale of drugs by an annual 8% to nearly EUR 20 billion between 2006 and 2015. To be sure, this growth rate is higher than those seen for Germany (+5% p.a.) and the entire world (+6% p.a.). Nonetheless, India's share in the world pharmaceutical sales will rise only marginally, to a good 2%. Growth of India's pharmaceutical industry and thus its share in the global drugs manufacturing could even be slightly higher if the infrastructure problems could be remedied quickly. While the pharmaceutical industries of China and Singapore will likely continue to show much higher growth, India looks set to lose market share even in Asia. Mainly affected by this development will be smaller Indian companies, with sales of up to EUR 10 million, that focus on traditional Indian medicines. It is likely that many of these companies will merge or altogether disappear from the market. By contrast, large pharmaceutical companies, with sales volumes of over EUR 50 million, will be able to increase their sales, as they will be better equipped to adjust their product ranges to the demands of the international markets. These firms will expand their capacities in India—mostly in the sector's clusters surrounding Delhi and Mumbai—but will also take over firms in the industrial countries. Medium-size businesses will benefit from increasing contract production for western firms.

All in all the share of pharmaceuticals in the total chemicals industry in India will come down to roughly 17% in 2015 (from 18% in 2006), compared with 28% in Germany (from 24% in 2006). For the world as a whole the ratio will likely be only slightly lower than the German level (25%).

Although India's pharmaceutical sector is growing strongly, the demand for drugs for the population cannot be met by the country's own production in all segments. At EUR 1.5 billion, India's total drug imports are comparable in size to Norway's entire pharmaceuticals market. Imports look set to continue to rise strongly. On a medium-term horizon, one-fifth of the world's pharma sales will be accounted for by the emerging markets. China will then be among the group of five largest manufacturers, while India will join the group of the ten largest suppliers.

The following figure depicts the rate of growth for Indian pharmaceutical industry as compared to the world till 2015:

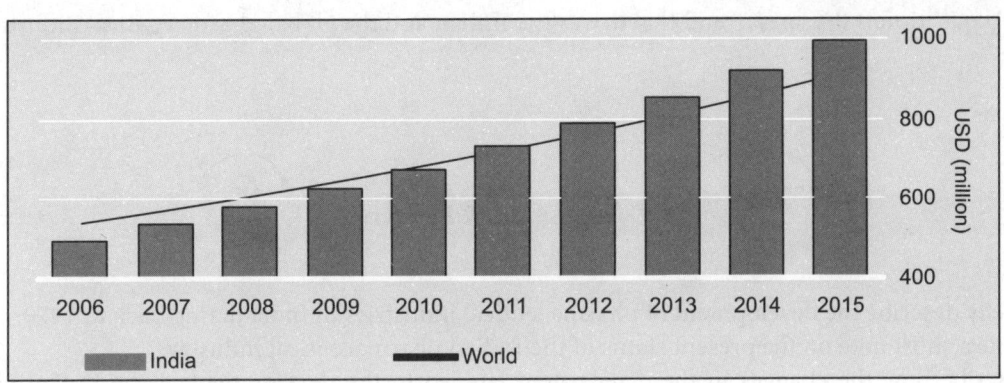

Figure 1.1. India's Pharmaceutical Industry up to 2015

HIGH EXPORT GROWTH OF INDIAN DRUG MAKERS

In the course of increasing contract production and low-cost manufacture of proprietary medicines, exports are expected to receive a major boost in future. However, Germany's very high export ratio of currently 55% will hardly be achieved by 2015, as this would imply more than trebling of total exports. In this context it should be considered that takeovers of foreign companies will lead to a strong increase in foreign production by Indian manufacturers and will have a dampening effect on exports, a positive impact on exports is expected from foreign investment in India, though. The competition between the Indian firms and western drug makers will probably be much fiercer as the companies from Asia are increasingly seeking to tap the global markets. The generic-drug market will grow in both the developed countries and the emerging markets. Most vital medicines are already exempt from patent protection today. The manufacture of generic drugs in that segment is growing strongly. In addition, patents for high-turnover drugs with a volume of EUR 100 billion will expire in the next few years. Of these drugs roughly one-third will likely be produced by Indian companies.

Points to Ponder

1. Good health leads to the economic development of the society and vice versa.
2. The Indian pharmaceutical industry has evolved over three phases namely
   a. Pre-1970s,
   b. 1970–1995 and
   c. 1995 onwards.
3. India has emerged as a production source of drugs at very low costs.
4. The current turnover of the Indian pharmaceutical industry is over USD 11 billion.
5. The important government regulatory policies include the Drugs and Cosmetic Act (1940), Drug Policy (1986), Indian Patents Act (1970), Drug Price Control Order (1995), Pharmaceutical Policy (2002) and Indian Patent Amendment Act, and the latest is the Draft National Pharma Policy (2006).
6. R&D is required in NCE, NDDS and the generic products for discovering new drugs to combat diseases.
7. Acquisition is the latest trend that drives the Indian and the global pharmaceutical industry.

 **Self-Assessment Exercises**

1. Briefly describe the development of pharmaceutical industries in India dating back to 1970.
2. Write a short note on the present status of the Indian pharmaceutical industry.
3. Describe how the changes in the drug patent law led to the development of the Indian pharma industries.
4. Describe the role of the R&D activities in the export market of pharma industries.

Introduction to Management

INTRODUCTION

The word *management* denotes the process of conducting and managing various business activities. It is the art of securing maximum results with minimum efforts, to secure maximum prosperity and happiness, for both the employer and the employees, and at the same time, to provide the best possible service to the public.

Management is the art and science of organizing and directing human efforts applied to control the forces and utilize the gifts of nature for the benefit of man. It is a science because it proves, predicts, defines, measures and utilizes knowledge. It is also an art because it feels, guesses, describes, expresses, communicates and practises. It is also a profession because it requires skill and knowledge, and the development of a positive attitude.

Management is principally a task of planning, coordinating, motivating and controlling the efforts of others towards a specific objective.

Management is the creation and maintenance of an internal environment in an enterprise where individuals, working in groups, can perform efficiently and effectively towards the attainment of their goals.

When the principles and practices of management are applied to the pharmaceutical industry and drug store, it is known as *pharmaceutical management*.

MEANING OF MANAGEMENT

The word *management* is used in different ways. Management as a collective noun means a group of people, but as a verb it refers to a process. Management is interpreted as an activity, a process, a discipline and as a group. These attributes are discussed below:

Management as an Activity

Management is the art of getting things done through informally organized groups of people. A manager is the person who accomplishes the objectives by directing the efforts of others in a team. As an activity, management means whatever the manager does to achieve the objectives of the group. A manager generally performs the following activities:

1. Interpersonal activities

Management involves achieving goals through other people. Therefore, a manager has to interact with his subordinates, his superiors and with others outside the organization. Interpersonal activities consist of attending social functions, motivating subordinates and maintaining contact with the clients.

2. Decisional activities

A manager has to take several types of decisions like initiating new projects, allocating resources and bargaining with clients. For example, the manager of the pharmaceutical factory decides the quantity and the quality of a pharmaceutical product to be manufactured. The decision of the manager serves the basis for actions of his subordinates.

3. Informative activities

In order to maintain relations and to take decisions a manager must regularly communicate with people inside and outside the organization. He receives and gives information concerning tasks, situations and people.

Management as a Process

Management is considered a process because it involves a series of interrelated functions. It consists of setting the objectives of an organization and taking steps to achieve these objectives. Management is a distinct process consisting of planning, organizing, staffing, directing and controlling. They are performed to determine and accomplish the stated objectives by using people and other resources.

Management as a process has the following implications

1. Social process

Management involves interaction among the people. Goals can be achieved only when there is a productive relation between people.

2. Integrated process

Management brings together human, physical and financial resources. It also integrates human efforts to maintain harmony among them.

3. Iterative process

All managerial functions are contained within each other. For example, when a manager prepares a plan, he also lays down the standards for control.

4. Continuous process

Management involves identifying and solving problems continuously.

Management as a Discipline

Management is now recognized as a formal discipline having an organized body of knowledge. Management is a distinct discipline because of two reasons. First, scholars and thinkers all over the world are researching on the principles and practices of management. They are disseminating this knowledge through books and journals. Secondly, the knowledge so generated is being formally imparted to others.

Management is comparatively a new discipline, but it is growing at a great pace. The popularity of management as a discipline can be judged from the heavy rush of admission to institutes imparting education and training in management. It is now being realized that managers are not necessarily born, they can be groomed through education and training.

Management as a Group

Management means a group of people occupying managerial positions. It refers to all those individuals who perform managerial functions. All the managers, e.g. chief executive (managing director), departmental heads, supervisors and so on are collectively known as *management*. There are three types of managers. They are as follows:

1. Family managers

Family managers are those that have become managers by virtue of their being owners or on being related to the owners of a company.

2. Professional managers

Professional managers are those that have become managers by appointment on account of their degree or diploma in pharmacy.

3. Civil servants

Civil servants are those managers who manage public sector undertakings.

Managers have become a powerful and a respected group in the modern society. The companies are run by senior managers, who enjoy a high standard of living and have become an elite group in the society.

CHARACTERISTICS OF MANAGEMENT

The salient features of management are as follows:

Management Is a Science and an Art

Management consists of a systematic body of knowledge as well as skills of applying that knowledge practically. The science and art of management are complementary. Scientific principles help to improve the technique of managing. With every improvement in the scientific principles of management, the art of management is bound to improve.

Management Is a Multidiscipline

Management has grown with the help of knowledge drawn from various disciplines like economics, sociology, psychology and anthropology. Much of the management literature is due to the result of the application of these social sciences.

Management Is an Integrated Process

Management integrates human effort with physical and financial resources. It creates an environment where people can perform their tasks efficiently. It also helps the organization to adapt to the changes in the environment.

Management Is Intangible

Management is an unseen force. Its functioning is not visible, but the results are apparent. People judge the effectiveness of management on the basis of the end result, although it cannot be observed during the operation.

Management Is Goal Oriented

Management means to achieve certain goals. Management goals are called *group goals* or *organizational goals*. The basic goal of management is to ensure efficiency and economy in the utilization of human, physical and financial resources. The success of management is measured by the extent to which the established goals are achieved.

Management Is Universal

Management is an essential element of every organized activity, irrespective of the size or the type of activity. Whenever two or more people are engaged in working for a common goal, management is necessary. All types of organizations like family, club, university, government, army or business require management. Thus management is universal.

Management Is a Social Process

Management is concerned with interpersonal relations and human behaviour. A manager has to create mutual understanding and cooperation among people. A manager is not answerable to the owners of the organization alone. He also has a social responsibility towards his workers, consumers and others.

Management Is an Activity

Management is a distinct class of activities. The knowledge and skills of its application can be acquired. Basically, it is a series of interrelated activities.

Management Is a Group Activity

Management is concerned with group efforts because it creates an effective cooperation among people working together in a group. It refers to all those individuals who perform managerial functions. So the groups of all managers, from the chief executives to the first-line supervisors, are correctly addressed as management.

IMPORTANCE OF MANAGEMENT

Management is indispensable for successful functioning of every organization. It is difficult to run any business enterprise without effective management. Every business needs repeated stimulus that can be provided by management only. The importance of management can be judged more clearly from the following points:

Achievement of Group Goals

A group consists of several people, each specializing in each part of the total task. Each person may be working efficiently, but the group cannot achieve its goal without mutual cooperation and coordination. The manager identifies and clearly defines the objectives that are to be fulfilled. Managers provide inspiring leadership to keep the members of the group working hard to achieve the desired goal.

Optimum Utilization of Resources

Management forecasts the need for material, machinery, money and manpower. It utilizes the resources more effectively to achieve the best possible results.

Reducing Cost

In the modern era of cut-throat competition, no business can succeed unless it is able to supply the required goods and services at the lowest possible cost per unit. Efficient management leads to reduced cost and increased output.

Survival and Growth

Modern businesses operate in a rapidly changing environment. An enterprise has to adapt itself to the changing demands of the market and the society. The management keeps in touch with the existing business environment and draws its predictions about the trends in future. It takes effective steps in advance to meet the challenges of the changing environment.

Generation of Employment

The management creates jobs during the course of expansion of the business enterprise. It creates an environment that helps to keep the economic and social needs of the employees satisfied.

Maintenance of the Discipline

Management helps to maintain discipline that is achieved by proper supervision at all levels in the organization.

Designing New Products

Management helps to design new products by adopting new techniques to give maximum satisfaction to the consumers and the society.

Development of the Nation

Efficient management is equally important at the national level. Management plays an important role in the economic and social development of the country. Management can design new products, adopt new technology, utilize the resources effectively and earn wealth. By producing wealth, the management increases the national income and the standard of living of the people. Due to this reason, management is regarded as a key to the economic growth of a country.

LEVELS OF MANAGEMENT

There are three levels of management, as shown in the figure below:

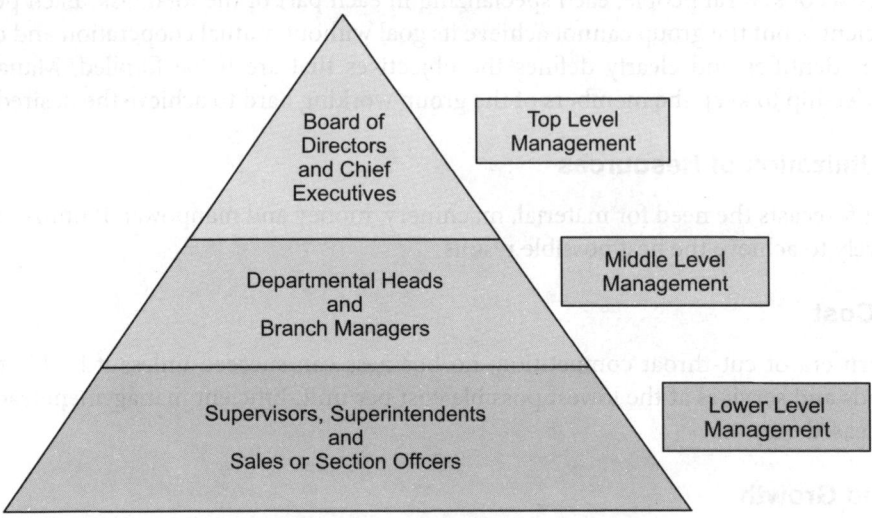

Figure 2.1. Levels of Management

The three levels of management are discussed below:

1. Top Level Management

The top level management of a company consists of the board of directors and the managing directors. The top management is the ultimate source of authority that frames the policies for the enterprise. The top level management generally performs the following functions:

   a.   Laying down the overall objectives and the broad policies of the enterprise

  b. Organizing the business into various departments and divisions
  c. Appointing department managers
  d. Issuing guidelines for the heads of the departments
  e. Coordinating the work of different departments
  f. Reviewing the work of departments and taking steps to ensure the achievement of objectives.

2. Middle Level Management

Middle level management generally consists of the head of departments. They are answerable to the top management for the efficient functioning of their departments. In small enterprises, there is one layer of middle management but in big enterprises, there may be senior middle level managers and junior middle level managers.

3. Lower Level Management

Lower level management is also known as the *supervisory management* because it is directly concerned with the control of performance of the operative employees. The level includes: supervisors, foremen, superintendents, sales officers, accounts officers etc. They issue orders and instructions, and guide the day-to-day activities. They also represent the grievances of the workers to the higher level management.

The lower level management performs the following functions:

  a. Planning of the day-to-day work
  b. Assignment of jobs and issuing orders and instructions
  c. Supervising and guiding workers
  d. Maintaining close personal contact with workers to ensure discipline and team work
  e. Evaluating operating performance
  f. Communicating the grievances and suggestions of workers to higher authorities.

FUNCTIONS OF MANAGEMENT

Figure 2.2 displays the main functions of management. The functions of management are discussed below:

1. Planning

Planning is an intellectual and a mental exercise requiring imagination and judgment. Planning helps to complete the tasks at hand in an orderly fashion. It increases the economy and efficiency by minimizing random action. Planning helps in the proper utilization of resources.

Planning aims at achieving the desired results. It involves forecasting of future problems and events, and selecting an appropriate course of action to handle such anticipations. For example, before starting a pharmaceutical industry, the following problems are anticipated:

  a. Selection of a proper site
  b. Items to be manufactured
  c. Obtaining the required license from drug administration to manufacture the selected items
  d. Arranging necessary finance for starting the business
  e. Sale of goods manufactured by the factory.

Figure 2.2. Functions of the Management

All these things are possible only through proper planning. Hence, proper management is required before starting a new pharmaceutical unit.

2. Organizing

Organizing is one of the important functions of management. It is to organize the enterprise by grouping similar activities together with a view to attain the planned objectives, define the responsibilities of the people in an organization, delegate appropriate authority to them to discharge their respective responsibilities, and establish relationships to enable coordination of the individual efforts to fulfil the objectives of the enterprise. For example, in order to start a pharmaceutical industry, classify the activities that will be involved in it, such as purchasing, production, quality control, stores, distribution, marketing, administration and finance. In order to run the factory smoothly, full authority must be given to the purchase manager as regards the purchase of raw materials. Inter-relate the other activities like quality control, production, marketing and finance departments for proper coordination, so that the final batch can be manufactured during the specified period in order to fulfil the objectives of the organization.

The process of organizing involves the following steps:

    a.   Identify the activities necessary to achieve the objectives
    b.   Grouping the activities into manageable units
    c.   Assigning duties or tasks to appropriate individuals
    d.   Delegating necessary authority to individuals and fixing responsibilities for results
    e.   Defining authority–responsibility relationships among individuals.

3. Staffing

The right person should be selected for the right type of job. The various activities, such as selection, communication, participation, counselling, training, compensation, dismissal, etc., come under it. For example, to run a syrup section of a pharmaceutical factory, a minimum of four people are required. One person is required for weighing the raw materials and mixing them in proper quantity in water to make syrup. Two people are needed for filling the syrup in bottles and then sealing and labelling it. One person is needed for testing, i.e. to analyse the prepared syrup. An honest and hardworking worker should be given due appreciation for his work. Suitable reward or compensation should be given.

Staffing consists of the following activities:

   a. Manpower planning, i.e. determining the number and quality of employees required in an organization
   b. Recruitment, selection and replacement of employees
   c. Training and their development
   d. Appraisal, promotion and transfer
   e. Employee remuneration, etc.

4. Directing

Management is the art and process of getting things done. Managers have the responsibility of guiding and supervising their subordinates in the following ways:

   a. By issuing orders and instructions
   b. By guiding and teaching the subordinates the proper method of work
   c. Supervising the subordinates to ensure that their performance conforms to the standards laid down by the company.

It becomes the responsibility of the management to motivate their subordinates to work and cooperate for the purpose of achieving the common objectives.

5. Controlling

Controlling means the steps taken by the management to ensure that the performance of the organization conforms to the plans. There should be adequate control, so that predetermined planned objectives are achieved. Strict control on the activities of the subordinates may sometimes lead to a loss of all initiative and enthusiasm on the part of workers. For example, the area manager of a pharmaceutical house can achieve his sales target if he calls for a meeting of his medical representatives, once in a week, to solve their problems and issue new instructions. But if he starts interfering with their day-to-day work, it will be difficult for him to achieve the fixed target since the medical representatives are likely to lose all initiative and enthusiasm due to unnecessary interference in their work.

6. Coordinating

In the management of an organization, coordination amongst various departments is important to achieve objectives.

There must be conscious effort on the part of the management to see that all activities are carried on by experts, and different departments contribute to the achievement of the objectives of the business. All other activities, not essential to the main objectives, must be discarded.

A well-coordinated enterprise must satisfy the following conditions:

    a.   Each department or division should be precisely informed of its share in the common task
    b.   Each department should work in harmony with other departments
    c.   The working schedules of various departments should be constantly attuned to circumstances.

The basic features of coordination are as follows:

    a.   It is a continuous process
    b.   It is an orderly arrangement of group efforts
    c.   The purpose of coordination is to secure unity of action towards common objectives
    d.   Coordination does not arise spontaneously. It has to be created through deliberate efforts.
    e.   It consists of the following three elements:
        i.   Timing
        ii.   Balancing
        iii.   Integrating

Timing means adjusting the time schedule of different departments. *Balancing* means ensuring that enough of one thing (e.g. machine) is available to support the other (e.g., materials). *Integrating* is the unification of objectives of the employees with those of the organization.

Coordination is the essence of management.

Points to Ponder

1.   Management is the art and science of organizing and directing human efforts applied to control the forces and utilize the gifts of nature for the benefit of man.
2.   There are three levels of management as follows:
    a.   Top level management
    b.   Middle level management
    c.   Lower level management
3.   The various functions performed by management are as follows:
    a.   Planning
    b.   Organizing
    c.   Staffing
    d.   Directing
    e.   Controlling
    f.   Coordinating

 **Self-Assessment Exercises**

1. Define the term *management*.
2. What do you mean by *pharmaceutical management*?

3. Explain the meaning of management as an activity.
4. What do you mean by management as a discipline?
5. Explain the meaning of management as a process.
6. Name the various levels of management.
7. Define the term *planning*.
8. Explain the term *organizing*.
9. What do you mean by *coordinating*?
10. Explain the term *controlling*.
11. Explain the main characteristics of management.
12. Describe the nature of management.
13. Discuss the importance of management.
14. Explain briefly about the various levels of management.
15. Name the various functions of management. Write in brief about any one function.
16. Define the term *management*. Describe its main characteristics.
17. What do you know about pharmaceutical management? Write the importance of management.
18. What are the different levels of management? Write the role of people at each level of management.
19. Describe the various functions of management in brief.
20. Discuss the nature and importance of management.
21. Explain the characteristics of management.
22. Name the fundamental functions of management and discuss each of them briefly.
23. Write short note on:

    a   Management
    b   Planning
    c   Organizing
    d   Controlling
    e   Staffing
    f   Coordinating
    g   Levels of managements

Principles of Management

INTRODUCTION

Management is a science. Management has to perform a number of functions, such as planning, organizing, coordinating, directing, controlling, etc., for the purpose of achieving its objectives. For a successful and effective functioning of any organization, the management has to observe certain guidelines.

The principles of management are statements of fundamental facts. These principles serve as guidelines for decisions and actions of managers. Management principles are derived through observation and analysis of events that managers face in actual practice.

Management principles are needed for the following reasons:

1. To increase efficiency
2. To highlight the true nature of management
3. To aid in the training of managers

4. To improve research
5. To attain social goals

SCIENTIFIC MANAGEMENT

Various thinkers have contributed to the development of modern management. F.W. Taylor and Henry Fayol are two outstanding names in the field of management. According to F.W. Taylor, 'Scientific management means knowing exactly what you want men to do and seeing that they do it in the best and the cheapest way'. His philosophy of scientific management is based upon the following principles:

1. Development of true science for each element of work
2. Scientific selection, training and development of workers
3. Close cooperation between workers and management
4. Equal division of work and responsibility
5. Maximum prosperity for both the employers and the employees
6. Mental revolution

Development of True Science for Each Element of Work

The first principle of scientific management requires scientific study and analysis of each element of the job in order to replace the old rule-of-thumb approach. Through scientific investigation, the best way of doing work can be developed. The decision should be made on the basis of facts rather than on opinions and beliefs.

Scientific Selection, Training and Development of Workers

The second principle requires that workers should be selected and trained in accordance with the requirements of the jobs to be entrusted to them. The physical, mental and other requirements should be specified for each job, and workers should be selected and trained to make them fit for the job. Systematic training and development programmes should be designed to improve their skill and efficiency.

Close Cooperation Between Workers and Management

The interests of the employer and the employees should be fully harmonized to create a mutually beneficial relationship. A close cooperation between the management and the workers should be created, so that work is done in accordance with the principles of scientific management. Maximum prosperity can be achieved only by mutual cooperation between the workers and their employer.

Equal Division of Work and Responsibility

The management should decide the methods of work, working conditions, time for completion of work, etc., instead of leaving it to the discretion of the workers. The management should take more responsibility for the planning and supervision of work, while the workers should be concerned with the execution of plans. The responsibility for planning and work should be equally divided between the management and the workers.

Maximum Prosperity for Both the Employers and the Employees

The aim of management should be to secure maximum prosperity for each employee and the employer. This can only be achieved when both efficiency and output are maximized. Maximum output and optimum utilization of resources will bring higher profits to the employer and thus higher wages or salaries for the employees.

Mental Revolution

Mental revolution means a complete change in the outlook of both the management and the workers with respect to their mutual relations, and in relation to the work effort. The management and workers should work together to increase the surplus, so that each can get more.

HENRY FAYOL'S PRINCIPLES OF MANAGEMENT

Henry Fayol was a French industrialist. He classified all business activities into six categories. These categories are as follows:

1. Technical (production or manufacturing)
2. Commercial (buying, selling and exchange)
3. Financial (search for optimum use of capital)
4. Security (protection of property and people)
5. Accounting
6. Managerial

According to Fayol, the first five groups of activities are quite well known and therefore, he concentrated his attention on the analysis of the sixth group, i.e. managerial activities. Fayol suggested the following 14 principles of management in order to make the job of managing more effective:

1. Division of work
2. Authority and responsibility
3. Discipline
4. Unity of command
5. Unity of direction
6. Subordination of individual interest to general interest
7. Remuneration of personnel
8. Centralization and decentralization
9. Scalar chain
10. Order
11. Equity
12. Stability of tenure of personnel
13. Initiative
14. Esprit de corps

Division of Work

The division of work helps to avoid the waste of time and effort caused by changes from one work process to another. The principle of the division of work implies that every employee should be assigned only one type of work. It applies to all types of work, technical as well as managerial.

Authority and Responsibility

Authority means the right or power of a superior to give orders to his subordinates. Responsibility means the duty of a subordinate towards his work as expected by his superior. Authority and responsibility are coextensive. Whenever authority is used, responsibility arises. Both must be clearly performed in an organization.

Discipline

Discipline is essential for the smooth functioning in all organizations. According to Fayol, discipline requires good supervisors at all levels, clear and fair agreements, and judicious application of penalties.

Unity of Command

According to this principle, an employee should receive orders only from one superior (boss) at a time. If the subordinate has more than one superior, it will undermine authority, weaken discipline, divide loyalty and lead to confusion or delay, etc. Therefore, dual subordination should be avoided.

Unity of Direction

According to this principle, in every category of work or any discharge of duties, there should be one plan of action and that action plan should be finalized and executed according to the mind and wishes of one particular supervisor (boss). The efforts of all supervisors of a group must be directed towards the achievement of common goals. A group with divergent plans and more than one head cannot function successfully.

Subordination of Individual Interest to General Interest

According to this principle, an organization is bigger than an individual. Therefore, the interests of the organization must prevail upon the personal interests of the individuals. If there is conflict between two superiors it will surely create indiscipline, disagreement and conflict between the employees hampering the cause, i.e. progress of the concern.

Remuneration of Personnel

The method of payment of remuneration to employees should be fair and reasonable. The remuneration must be given in good measured amount to keep the employees satisfied and happy, for them to work hard and honestly for the concern.

Centralization and Decentralization

Centralization means the concentration of authority at the top management. There should not be hard and fast rules to lay down the extent of authority to be retained at the top level or dispersed among the subordinates. Centralization and decentralization is a matter of proportion and this proportion (optimum ratio) should be decided, keeping in view the circumstances of a particular case.

Scalar Chain

Scalar chain refers to the chain of superiors ranging from the ultimate authority to the lowest rank. It is the unbroken line of command from the top to the bottom of the organizational structure. Normally all communications should flow through the established chain of command. However, to facilitate quick communication between two distinct links in the chain, direct contact may be created by passing the prescribed line of authority. Direct contact helps to minimize delays and difficulties in communication. Sometimes, on some particular events and actions, the scalar chain is bypassed and the order is passed from the top to the bottom. But this is done under vigilant and wise decisions of the superiors.

Order

There must be material and social order in an enterprise. Material order means 'a proper place for everything and everything in its right place'. Similarly social order means, 'a place for everyone and everyone in his appointed place'. The right man in the right job is very important for the successful functioning of an organization.

Equity

Management should treat the employees with justice and kindness. There should be equity of treatment in dealing with subordinates and no discrimination should be made between them. Nepotism and favouritism should not exist.

Stability of Tenure of Personnel

Stability of tenure of personnel means that every employee should always feel that his services are not going to be terminated without any substantial cause. Therefore, a reasonable security of service should be provided to all employees. The supervisors must be kind and justified towards their employees. Stability of tenure helps to develop loyalty and attachment on the part of the employees towards the firm. Unnecessary labour turnover or change of personnel increases the cost of selection and training. Moreover, it spoils the image of the firm.

Initiative

Employees at all levels should be encouraged to think out of the box and execute the assigned tasks in a better way. Initiative is a source of strength for an organization. Therefore, subordinates should be inspired to suggest improvements in the formulation and implementation of plans.

Esprit De Corps

There must be team spirit and coordination among the members of an organization. 'Unity is strength' and the strength of an enterprise lies in the cooperation and harmony in individual efforts. Group results are more than the aggregate of individual contribution on account of esprit de corps. There should be complete harmony and unity of the officers' staff and the employees. The management should not follow the policy of divide and rule.

COMPARISON BETWEEN MANAGEMENT OF F.W. TAYLOR AND HENRY FAYOL

The following table compares the management theories of F.W. Taylor and Henry Fayol:

Table 3.1. Comparison of Management Theories of F.W. Taylor and Henry Fayol

	F.W. Taylor	Henry Fayol
1.	F.W. Taylor looked at management from the supervisory point of view and tried to improve efficiency at the operating level.	Fayol analysed management from the angle of top management downward with emphasis on coordination.
2.	Taylor focused his attention on factory management and his principles are directly applicable at the shop floor.	Fayol concentrated on the functions of managers and his principles of management that are applicable to all spheres of human activity.
3.	The main aim of Taylor was to improve productivity of labour; to eliminate all types of waste through standardization of work and tools.	Fayol attempted to develop a universal theory of management. He gives stress on teaching the theory and the practice of management.
4.	Taylor called his philosophy *scientific management*.	Fayol described his approach as a *general theory of administration*.

FUNCTIONS OF MANAGEMENT

The process of management consists of certain basic management functions. The most commonly cited functions of management are planning, organizing, leading, staffing, controlling and coordination. The functions of management define the process of management as distinct from accounting, finance, marketing and other business functions (Figure 3.1).

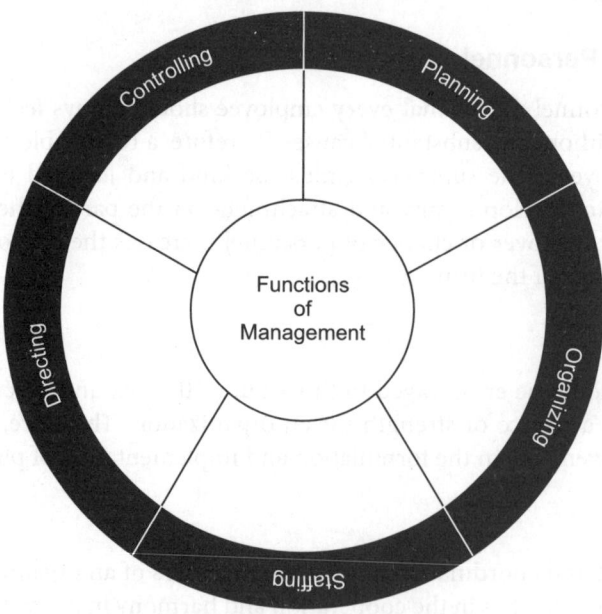

Figure 3.1. Functions of Management

The different functions of management are discussed below.

Planning

Planning involves selecting missions and objectives, and the actions to achieve them. It requires decision making that is, choosing future courses of action from alternatives. There are various types of plans, ranging from overall purposes and objectives to the most detailed actions to be taken, such as to order a special stainless steel bolt for an instrument or to hire and train workers for an assembly line. No real plan exists until a decision, a commitment of human or material resource, or reputation has been made. Before a decision is made, all we have is a planning study, an analysis or a proposal, but not a real plan. Planning includes identifying goals, objectives, methods, resources needed to carry out methods, responsibilities and dates for completion of tasks. Examples of planning are strategic planning, business planning, project planning, staffing planning, advertising planning and promotions planning.

Organizing

People working together in groups to achieve some goal must have roles to play, like the parts actors fill in a drama. These roles could be the ones they develop themselves or are accidental or haphazard, or are defined and structured by someone who wants to make sure that people contribute to the efforts in a group in a specific way. The concept of a *role* implies that what people do has a definite purpose or objective; they know how their job objective fits into the group effort; and they have the necessary authority, tools and information to accomplish the task.

Organizing, then, is that part of managing that involves establishing an intentional structure of the roles for people to fill in an organization. It is intentional in the sense of making sure that all the tasks, necessary to accomplish goals, are assigned and, it is hoped, assigned to people who can best perform those tasks. Imagine what would have happened if such assignments had not been made in the program of flying the special aircraft *Voyager* around the globe without stopping or refuelling. The purpose of an organizational structure is to help in creating an environment for human performance. It is, then, a management tool and not an end in and of itself. Although, the structure must define the tasks to be done; the roles so established must also be designed in the light of the workers' abilities and motivations; and organizing resources to achieve the goals in an optimum fashion. Examples of such organizing are organizing new departments like human resources, office, file systems, reorganizing businesses, etc.

Leading

Leading is influencing people so that they will contribute to the organization and to the group goals. It has to do predominantly with the interpersonal aspect of managing. All managers would agree that their most important problems arise from people, their desires and attitudes, their behaviour as individuals and in groups. Effective managers also need to be effective leaders. Since leadership implies followership and people tend to follow those who offer a means of satisfying their own needs, wishes and desires, it is understandable that leading involves motivation, leadership styles and approaches, and communication. Leading include setting direction for the organization, groups and individuals, and also influencing people to follow that direction. Examples of leading are establishing strategic directions like vision, values, mission and goals.

Staffing

Staffing involves filling, and keeping filled, the positions in the organizational structure. This is done by identifying workforce requirements, inventorying the people available, recruiting, selecting, placing, promoting, planning career, compensating and training or otherwise developing both the candidates and current job holders to accomplish their tasks effectively and efficiently.

Controlling

Controlling is measuring and correcting the activities of the subordinates to ensure that the events conform to plans. It measures the performance against the goals and plans; shows where the negative deviations exist; and puts in motion actions to correct deviations. Controlling also helps to ensure the accomplishment of plans. Although, planning must precede controlling, plans are not self-achieving. The plan guides the manager in the use of resources to accomplish specific goals. Then activities are checked to determine whether they conform to plans.

Control activities generally relate to the measurement of achievement. Some means of controlling, like the budget for expense, inspection records, and the record of labour hours lost are generally familiar. Each measures and shows whether plans are working out. If deviations persist, correction is indicated. But what is corrected. Nothing can be done about reducing scrap, for example, or buying according to specifications or handling sales returns unless one knows who is responsible for these functions. Compelling the events to conform to plans means locating the people, who are responsible for the results that differ from the planned action, and then taking the necessary steps to improve performance. Thus, controlling what people do controls the outcomes. Controlling the organization's systems, processes and structures is to effectively and efficiently reach goals and objectives. This includes the ongoing collections of feedbacks, and monitoring and adjustment of systems, processes and structures accordingly. Examples of controlling include use of financial controls, policies and procedures, performance management processes and measures to avoid risks.

Coordination

Some authorities consider coordination to be an additional function of management. It seems more accurate; however, to regard it as the essence of managership, for the purpose of managing is to harmonize individual efforts in the accomplishment of group goals. Each of the managerial functions is an exercise contributing to coordination.

Even in the case of a church or a fraternal organization, individuals often interpret similar interests in different ways, and their efforts towards mutual goals do not automatically mesh with the efforts of others. It thus becomes the central task of the manager to reconcile differences in approach, timing, effort, or interest and to harmonize individual goals to contribute to the organizational goals.

Points to Ponder

1. The principles of management serve as guidelines for decisions and actions of the managers. The management principles are derived through observation and analysis of events that managers face in actual practice.
2. F.W. Taylor and Henry Fayol are two outstanding names in the field of management.
3. According to F.W. Taylor, 'Scientific management means knowing exactly what you want men to do and seeing that they do it in the best and the cheapest way'.
4. Henry Fayol has classified all business activities into technical, commercial, financial, security, accounting and managerial categories.

 **Self-Assessment Exercises**

1. Define the term *scientific management*.
2. Explain the term *coordination*.
3. Why are management principles needed?
4. Explain the term *scientific management*. Discuss the various principles on which scientific management is based according to F.W. Taylor.
5. Define the term *management*. Discuss the principles of management by Henry Fayol.
6. Compare the concept of management as proposed by F.W. Taylor and Henry Fayol.

Communication

INTRODUCTION

Communication is the most vital element of any organization. Without communication an organization would only be an assembly of men, material and processes that are inoperative. Organizational effectiveness depends upon the quality of communication. Managers have to communicate with their subordinates and their superiors. They spend more than seventy-five per cent of their effective time in communicating. It is communication that gives life to the organizational structure. It is a thread that holds all the units, subunits, processes, systems and cultures together. If communication stops, the organization will cease to exist. Organizations have to communicate with external organizations and agencies and incorporate various inputs for survival and growth. Communication not only integrates various subunits but shifts the information of value acquired from the environment to various departments, groups and individuals. An effective communication is an essence of successful managers. As the organization grows, the role of communication becomes more critical. Therefore, there is a need for adjustment in the communication systems according to the shape, size, performance, location and the services that the organization offers.

Effective management is an output of effective communication. Poor communication or ineffective communication is a source of frustration, interpersonal conflict and stress. It plays an important role in strengthening relationships between friends, relatives and family members since we spend nearly seventy percent of our time interacting with them by way of speaking, listening, reading and writing. Poor communication leads to unpleasant situations and broken relationships. Oral and written communication is very important not only to get a job but to retain it. Oral communication is the most effective way of communication and considered to be a vital skill that an individual possesses. Effective communication is essential for the management to successfully perform its functions. It is an essential ingredient in the management–employee relationship. The best business plan is meaningless unless everyone is aware of it and are willing to put their energies together to achieve its objectives. Communication is essential to keep the entire organization functioning at optimum levels, and to achieve maximum output of our greatest management resource—the people.

Management needs to take employees in confidence and make them aware of the organizational policies, problems and vision. For a successful running of an organization, the following points need to be communicated to the employees:

1. Organization policy and future plans
2. Results achieved vis-a-vis the industry performance
3. Achievement of higher productivity
4. Industrial safety, health and welfare measures
5. Technical developments
6. Personal growth prospects

It is the responsibility of the management to keep their employees posted with the latest information about the above factors by resorting to greater interaction with them.

Chester Barnard (1930) highlighted communication as a dynamic force in shaping organizational behaviour. He considered it as one of the three important elements of an organization along with the common purpose and a willingness to serve. He also linked communication with the concept of authority that flows down through the channels of communication, in a classical organization. Authority can lose its meaning if the channels of communication are blocked or if the communication is misunderstood or if the strength of communication is diluted. Accordingly, he proposed seven communication factors that are indeed functions of objective authority. These are as discussed below:

1. The channels of communication must be clearly set and be known to all
2. Every member of the organization should be reached by some channel of communication
3. The line of communication should be as direct as possible
4. There should be no blockage in the line of communication and a formal line should be used
5. The communicator should be highly skilled in the art of communication
6. The line of communication should be constantly kept open
7. Every communication should be authenticated

OBJECTIVES OF COMMUNICATION

Following are the objectives of communication:

1. To keep the employees abreast with the external and the internal environment
2. To develop understanding and cordial relationship with the management

3. For the development of team spirit, group task resolution and the psychological bent of mind
4. To promote creativity and innovativeness
5. To develop social commitment among employees
6. To make them aware of their rights, entitlements and responsibilities
7. To prepare employees to accept and implement change
8. To prevent misinformation and counter rumours
9. To promote participative type of leadership model
10. To motivate employees by displaying an attitude of commitment
11. For knowledge management

COMMUNICATION PROCESS

Communication can be described as an impersonal process of sending and receiving symbols with meanings attached to them. When you communicate, there is a person called a *sender* (source) who sends the message to another person who receives it (the receiver). The message is sent through a medium. Medium can be (a) a written message, (b) a verbal message or (c) a message sent through some physical gestures or signs. When a message is sent, there is an element of disturbance called *noise*. Strictly speaking the receiver must receive a message as the sender thinks he should and then finally send the feedback. The communication process is shown in Figure 4.1 below:

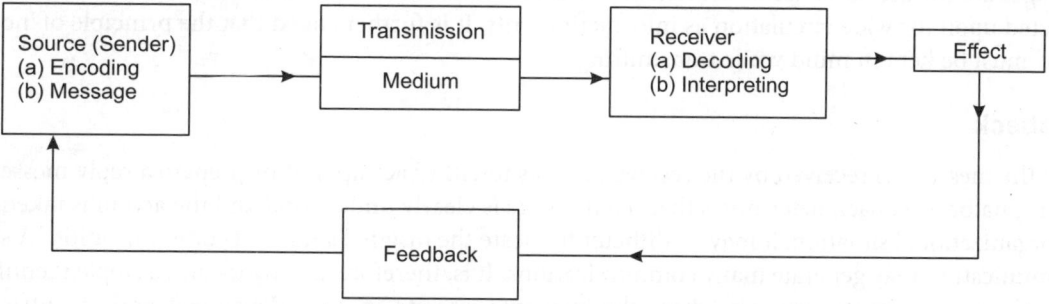

Figure 4.1. Communication Process

Source

Source is an initiator of a message. He may be an individual or a group or even an organization. A sender is a person who represents source. Message is an item of information. Message is required to be encoded that will depend upon the distance, the receiver, the available time (urgency) and the availability of channel.

Message

Message is information, and it may be in the form of a script. Message is what communication is all about. A message may be composed of symbols like $ (dollar). Encoding is a process of selecting an appropriate channel. Even today, messages sent to the Navy are in Morse code to maintain secrecy since they can be ciphered. When such messages are received, they are decoded by the receiver. Obviously, the sender and the receiver must have an identical code so that a correct meaning is assigned to the message by the receiver.

Medium

Medium is also called *channels* through which a message is transmitted. It is the path through which the message is physically sent to the receiver. It may be a face-to-face communication where the sender sends a message through gestures. Telephones, teleprinters, computer networks, mobile phones and radio sets are used as mediums for transmitting messages. What is important is the compatibility of the sender and the receiver to use the medium.

Receiver

The message is received by a person called a *receiver*. Receiver is an individual who receives the message individually if it is meant for him, or receives it on behalf of the group or the organization that he is working for. Receiver is also responsible for decoding the message and interpreting it in an appropriate manner. He must assign correct meaning to various symbols, gestures, words as are intended by the sender.

Effect

Effect is the change in the behaviour of the receiver. He may pass on the message to the department who is to take action. He may ignore it. He may store the information. This will depend upon the perception, attitude and the skill of the individual. A message may contain simple information or it may affect value that will lead to a reaction or a generation of new message for the sender. It must be remembered that messages are for action or for information. Action messages are acted upon and information messages are acted upon for wide circulation as information only. It is further stated that the principle of 'need to know' must be kept in mind while transmitting.

Feedback

Once the message is received by the receiver, he has to either act upon it or prepare a reply message to the originator. Feedback determines that the message is clearly understood and the action is taken. In a real organizational situation, it may be difficult to locate the original source of communication. A single communication may generate many communications. It is, therefore, a network and a single identifiable event. It is a synergistic process where the elements operate in an independent and an intricately, interwoven fashion. Communication generally takes a vertical or a horizontal pattern. It is dependent on the form of the organizational structure. Communication is superimposed on various appointments and related to the job. Psychological makeup of the sender and the receiver is important so that a positive outcome is achieved and thus the organizational objectives are fulfilled.

MODES OF COMMUNICATION

There are three primary methods of communication. These are written, verbal and nonverbal forms of communication. The choice of the method to adopt would largely depend on the location of the sender and the receiver, the ability, the nature of the message, the urgency with which the information is required to be passed on and the cost involved in passing or receiving the information.

Following is a discussion on the different modes of communication:

1. Written Communication

Written communication is generally in the form of standing orders, policy documents, orders, instructions, notes, memos, formal letters, official letters, etc. These contain information of a permanent nature. Employees refer to these instructions as a basic document. Written communication is important to ensure the uniformity of action and the future plans. It also provides a permanent record for further reference. Written documents can be saved and stored. Because of the introduction of computers and other electronic equipment, information of a very large size can be stored, and the required information can be retrieved in the fastest possible time. It is a great revolution. Volumes of information can just be stored in a single disc. Through electronic media, messages can be passed the world over in a fraction of a second with a hundred percent accuracy. Written communication is lengthy, time consuming and has a high probability of leakage in respect of confidential documents.

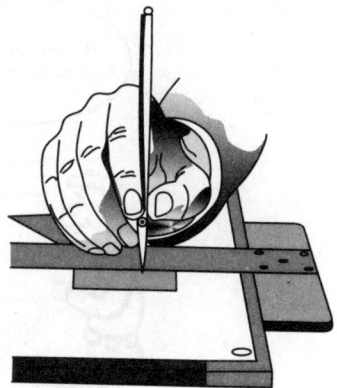

Advantages

The advantages of written communication are as follows:

1. It is taken more seriously.
2. It can be expressed more precisely after due thought.
3. It provides a record. The content of the message can easily be verified afterward.
4. It can be transmitted to several people at the same time. The message can be repeated at regular intervals.
5. It is more suitable when the message is long and a well-considered response is desired.

Disadvantages

The disadvantages of written communication are as follows:

1. It is time consuming and expensive, particularly for sending lengthy messages to distant places.
2. The necessary explanation and clarification cannot be given immediately.
3. It does not provide instant response or feedback.
4. It lacks personal touch and tends to be rigid. It does not carry feelings and emotions.

2. Oral Communication

Oral communication is the most common form of communication. Oral communication is used when both (sender and receiver) are present. It is a face-to-face communication. It is more effective than written communication because the receiver not only hears the contents of the message but is also influenced by the tone, speech, gestures, speed and even the volume of conversation. Oral communication is the best way of transforming an individual with particular reference to attitude, beliefs, trust and faith. Most of the education system uses oral communication in learning. Leaders use oral communication to address the public to convey their point of view. Oral communication can also be used by using electronic media like audiovisual conferencing, where people can converse with each other even when away. It is a direct, simple form of communication that is the least expensive and yet the most effective. Feedback is spontaneous and any error in the message is corrected immediately.

Oral communication promotes better relationship due to its personalized nature. However, oral communication suffers from various disadvantages like lack of records, misinterpretation of message by the receiver, filtration, distortions and giving a meaning to the communication that suits the receiver best. Oral communication, to be effective, must be specific, short, to the point and devoid of ambiguity of any sort. Grapevine is also a very powerful medium of communication where messages are passed by

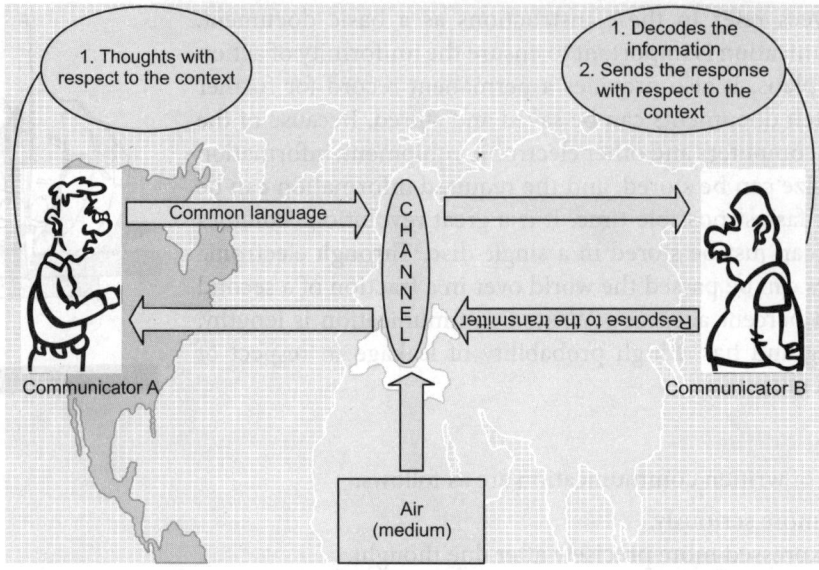

word of mouth. Grapevine is an informal way of transmitting information to the maximum number of employees in a minimum possible time. Grapevine travels like wild fire. Management can use grapevine in a productive manner to convey a particular message. The greater the quantity of information that passes through the grapevine, the less accurate it usually is.

Advantages

The advantages of oral communication are as follows:

1. It is fast and can be transmitted quickly if the message is brief.
2. It permits detailed explanation of the message and clarification of doubts.
3. It is more flexible as words can be changed to suit the situation.
4. It provides on the spot reaction on response.
5. It is more effective due to personal touch.
6. It is useful at the operational level. Supervisors issue oral instructions because workers may not be able to correctly interpret written instructions.

Disadvantages

Following are the disadvantages of oral communication:

1. The receiver of the message may not take the oral message seriously.
2. It is less reliable as there are chances of distortion of the message.
3. It does not provide authentic record.
4. It may be time consuming as in meetings and conferences.
5. It is influenced by time and situation.
6. It is not suitable when the message is lengthy.

3. Nonverbal Communication

Nonverbal messages are transmitted through gestures, facial expressions and through body language. It can also be expressed how one designs one's office and through official protocols. According to Tipkins and McCarter, facial expressions can be categorized as (1) interest—excitement, (2) enjoyment—joy, (3) surprise—startle, (4) distress—anguish, (5) fear—terror, (6) shame—humiliation, (7) contempt—disgust and (8) anger—rage.

Body language is known a *kinesics*. A handshake is probably the most common form of body language that conveys a lot about a person's personality. Eyes are the most expressive component of facial expressions. A glance, a stare, a smile or some provocative movement of the body conveys lot information. Facial expression can convey frustration, anger, arrogance, shyness, fear and other characteristics of a person that cannot be expressed through written or oral communication. Shrugging of shoulders expresses indifference, wink of an eye conveys intimacy and a palm on the forehead conveys forgetfulness. The knowledge of body language is very important and that should be carefully displayed. Managers should acquire adequate knowledge of nonverbal communication to enable them to know their subordinates.

STRUCTURE OF COMMUNICATION

The different structures of communication are discussed below.

Downward Communication

Communication has a structure that is based on two things. First, the organizational structure and secondly, the purpose intended through communication. In a hierarchical structure, where there are various organizational levels, the communication is from top to bottom. In this pattern, the communication flows from the superior to the subordinates. Such communication is in the written form in policy letters, standing orders, staff regulations, handbooks, procedure, manuals and the like. When it is verbal, it pertains to passing information about the day-to-day functioning and operations. Verbal communication is as important as written communication and should be weighed on an equal footing. The communication must be clear, simple and specific to be effective. Superiors should appreciate and understand the ability of the recipient and keep in mind the language and the level of perception.

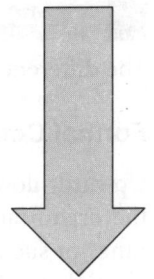

Upward Communication

Upward communication relates to the communication by a junior to his senior. This generally follows the reporting channel of command. The communication relates to reporting production levels, sales performance, reaction to certain orders and instructions. Communication reflects motivational condition of the employees. The flow of information from bottom to top helps the top management to know the actions, attitudes, opinions and feelings of people. Upward communication indicates the reaction of an employee to the policies of the organization. It is, therefore, necessary to ensure effective communication. Sharma suggests 'Research also notes the tendency, at times of subordinates or for fear of appraisals or for seeking undeserved rewards, place only that particular information before the superior which he would like. They try to check the flow of such information which goes against them or which the superior is not likely to appreciate'. Organizations must provide a climate and an incentive system that encourages upward communication. Management must evolve an open door system and employees should feel that their superiors are always

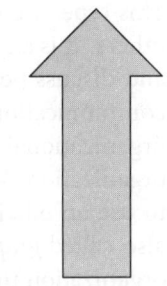

available to share their opinion, ideas and views that can be effectively used for decision making. Effective communication promotes the *we* feeling among workers.

Horizontal or Lateral Communication

Horizontal or lateral type of communication refers to the flow of information across departments or between people within different departments. It does not have a superior–subordinate relationship as in the downward and upward communication. It is more informal in nature and is necessary in promoting a supportive organizational climate. It provides the means by which 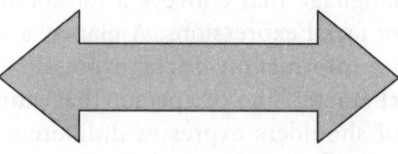 supervisors, grass root level workers and managers organize and coordinate their activities without referring the matters to their respective seniors. Generally, people prefer accomplishment of work smoothly and, therefore, like to refer laterally. Production managers and marketing managers have to be in constant touch with each other to know the consumer expectations, market share vis-à-vis production levels. In the present liberalized market scenario, lateral communication is not only restricted to the internal departments of a particular organization but spread to other organizations, government agencies who have to play a role in the business and may even extend to national and international levels.

TYPES OF COMMUNICATION

The different types of communications are as discussed below.

Formal Communication

Upward, downward and lateral communication follows the established routes of communication in the organization. Lateral communication is encouraged by organizations as it cuts down the delays. Lines of such communication are formally laid down. The communication may take written or verbal form that will depend upon the relationship, time available, importance of the issue, etc. This type of communication is called *formal communication*.

Informal Communication

Informal communication is not planned by the organization; hence no lines of communication exist. This type of communication takes place due to the sheer desire of an individual to communicate with others. It is an outcome of social interaction. Small groups are formed and they not only communicate and discuss personal issues, but also express their candid views on other official matters. This type of communication takes place during lunch or coffee or tea breaks and during social gatherings. If the organizational climate is healthy, this type of communication lends speed to solving problems in an organization. When the management wants to convey something to the employees and does not wish to use an official channel, it is passed on to the employees informally. This type of communication is also called *grapevine*. It is important to note that there is a likelihood of rumours being spread in the organization through informal communication channels. This should be guarded against.

Differences between formal and informal communication is mentioned in Table 4.1:

Table 4.1. Comparison Between Formal and Informal Communication

	Formal communication		Informal communication
1	It is preplanned	1	It is unplanned
2	It follows the officially established chain of commands	2	It is independent of the official chain of command
3	It is slow due to the prescribed path	3	It is fast due to no prescribed path
4	It consists mainly of work related messages	4	It consists of both work related and social messages
5	The direction of flow is orderly and systematic	5	The direction of flow is erratic and unsystematic
6	It is easy to fix responsibility for messages	6	It is not possible to fix responsibility
7	It stresses on authority and status	7	It stresses on interpersonal relations
8	It is generally in the written form	8	It is usually verbal
9	It is authentic, rigid and predictable	9	It is unofficial, flexible and inflexible
10	It does not carry rumours	10	It may carry rumours
11	It serves the needs of the organization	11	It serves the social needs of the members, as well as, the needs of the organization

EVOLUTION OF COMMUNICATION

In the earlier era communication was not so important. The management used to issue orders and instructions (downward communication) to various employees, who used to complete their day's work. Upward communication was either nonexistent or discouraged. Blind obedience to orders was expected. There was breakdown in communication when the subordinate crossed the channels of communication and the narrow span of the concept of management of the organizational structure was operative. Neoclassicists view communication as an important function of the organization. Communication should aim at satisfying the needs, for social interaction and as a tool for decision making. They recommend vertical and horizontal communication. Neoclassicists feel that informal communication is as important as the formal communication as it fills the gap that may occur in formal communication. The modernists view communication as the most important function of any organization. They adopt the behavioural view. Communication must aim at the improvement of human relations within the units and subunits, and also obtain, store, process and shift the required information for decision making, and interact with various agencies that exist in the external environment so that organizations not only survive but grow. They feel that overload, distortion and filtration are the basic drawbacks in the communication system that must be guarded against.

COMMUNICATION NETWORK

As stated earlier, it is the organizational structure that will, to a great extent, determine the communication network. In a typical centrally controlled organization, communication generally revolves around a pivotal person. Like in a production unit, the production manager would be a pivotal person and all communication will flow down to the supervisors (downward communication) and to the CEO or the president or the vice president (upward communication). Various types of communication are shown in Figure 4.2.

Chain, inverted Y and the wheel type of communication are used in centralized organizations. Chain type of communication is used when the information flows upwards and downwards in a hierarchical manner. There is no lateral communication. This type of communication is best suited for organizations

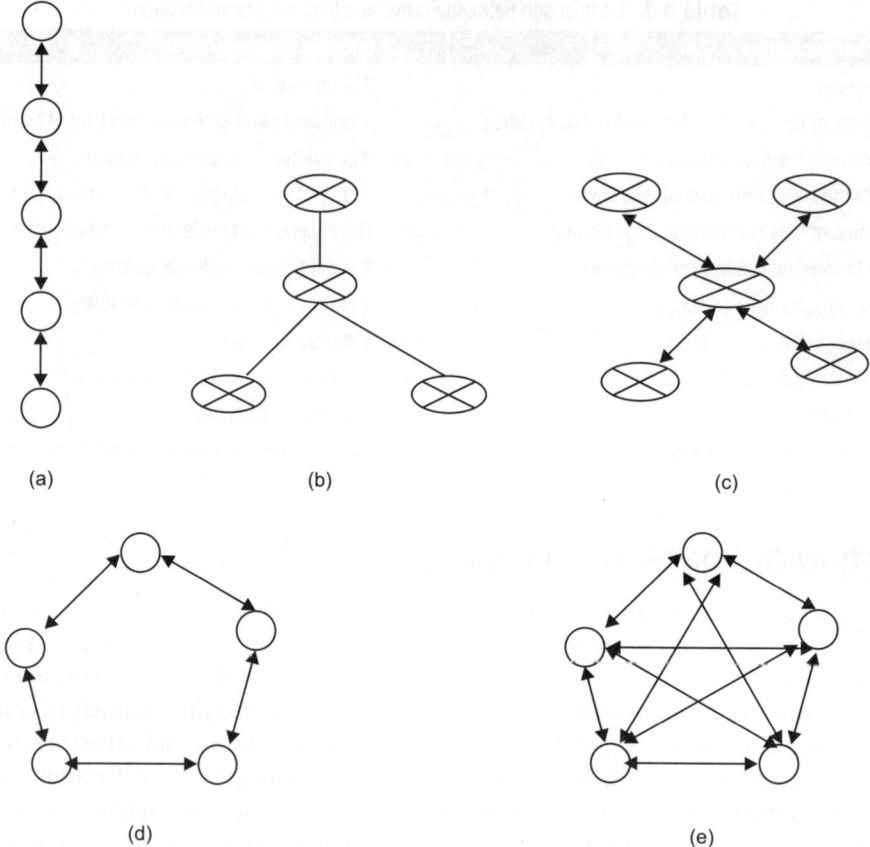

Figure. 4.2. Various Types of Communication

where reporting is strict and jobs are well-defined. Lot of written communication takes place in the form of orders, instructions, etc. The inverted Y type of communication represents one person having two subordinates. They report to the designated boss. The wheel type of communication represents a manager in the centre having control over two superior officers. Wheel type of communication is very commonly used in most of the organizations as it provides faster problem solving. This type communication displays lack of flexibility and shows the lowest job satisfaction.

The circle type of communication is used by a member to the adjoining member only. Communication is lateral in the circle type of communication. The all channel type of communication is used by a member of an organization to communicate with other members of the organization. There is no leader but a person may assume leadership. Members experience a greater level of satisfaction in this type of communication. This is prevalent in decentralized organizations. More centralized an organization is, poorer is the satisfaction of the employees.

Decentralized networks are suitable to the organizations where jobs are complex and members have to interact with various departments. When the tasks are comparatively simple and of routine nature, centralized communication is recommended.

BARRIERS TO EFFECTIVE COMMUNICATION

When a communication is made by a sender, it must be received correctly by the receiver. The message must be interpreted by the receiver as has been intended by the sender. There are various problems like the message does not reach the receiver, problems of encoding and decoding, faulty selection of channel, wrong language or the interpretation of the message. The list can be long and unending. These problems are called *noise in communication*. These problems can be classified as various barriers, such as physical distance, noise, attitude and sentiments of the sender and the receiver.

Following are the various kinds of barriers:

1. Physical barrier
2. Interpersonal barrier

Physical Barrier

Physical barrier occurs due to the following.

Poor timing

A person must evaluate the timing of sending a message. The receiver must get adequate time to implement the instruction given in the communication. If an action on the message is required to be taken in a distant future, there is a possibility that the receiver may forget the content of the message. Inadequacy of timing and a last minute communication is likely to put too much pressure on the receiver. Message, therefore, should be sent at an appropriate time.

Choice of channel

A message can be sent in written, verbal instruction (face-to-face) or conveyed by electronic media, online by telephone or by using combinations. The routine messages should be passed on verbally to the subordinates and to the boss. The important messages should be followed in writing as a confirmation to the verbal conversation. Face-to-face communication is more effective because of the body language of the sender and the receiver. It provides spontaneous solutions to misunderstanding.

Inadequate information

Too much or too little information is dangerous. Information must be of value, should be meaningful and be related to the job of the receiver. Volumes of information can be quickly sent anywhere around the globe. Information carries value if it is in the desired format and to the point.

Organizational structure

Every individual in the organization must know the channels of command and communication. They must also know the power centres. Authority and responsibility must be clearly defined so that the communication is directed towards the correct person and a quick decision is achieved at. Information overload is dangerous. The secretary to managers must maintain a log book where the incoming and the outgoing messages are recorded. Professional jealousy must not be allowed to interfere with various communications.

Information overload

Information may be passed to the concerned individuals as and when needed. Excessive information causes information overload. A lot of information can now be handled by an individual due to computers.

Excessive information causes confusion and may not be required. Network breakdown may also take place due to information overload.

Interpersonal Barriers

Effective communication largely depends upon the sender and the receiver, and their personal bent of mind, commitment to organizational effectiveness and the relationship they enjoy. Some of the important interpersonal barriers are discussed below:

Filtration

Filtration is a process when the sender deliberately wants to withhold information from the receiver. It is done by manipulating the information either, because the sender believes that all the information is not required or that the receiver is better off not knowing certain aspects of the information. Filtration takes place when subordinates send information to superiors based on the liking of the latter. A boss is told what he likes to hear. Therefore, the information may be far from the truth.

Perception

Perceptual process that operates in a situation may heavily influence the   communication process related to receiving the information from the environment and interpreting, and giving meaning to such information. It is human tendency to hear what he wants to hear and ignore the information that conflicts with his thought process. This type of communication totally distorts the intent and the contents of the message. Some of the perceptual situations are as under:

1. Stereotype effect: A manager may perceive people who belong to one category or another as stereotypes. It is a general perception that old employees are not hard working, even when some old employees work hard. Individuals, therefore, must be treated distinctly and their performance assessed accordingly.
2. Individuals generally assess their subordinates based on one particular trait that he likes. If an individual is punctual, he may create a favourable perception because he likes punctuality. The other employee may be efficient in his job but he is not considered favourably in his performance appraisal. It should be ensured that an individual is evaluated according to the standards laid down by the organization and not on individual liking.
3. It is human tendency that a person expects his subordinates to act, think and behave as he does. If a manager works overtime, he expects his subordinates to stay longer. This limits the ability of the manager to effectively deal with different situations and individuals.

It is important for managers to evaluate situations independently and take decision on the merit of the case. The perceptual skill must be applied carefully and each individual must be treated separately without any perceptual bias so that the credibility of the manager is increased. One must communicate facts, keep to the commitments made and eliminate negativity in perception.

Semantic barriers

Semantic barriers refer to the interpretation of words, abbreviations and symbols used by the sender and perceived by the receiver. If a receiver is likely to misunderstand symbol of a dollar ($), it is better that 'dollar' is spelt out in the script. Symbols that are accepted universally should generally be used in written communication. The choice of a wrong word or a comma at a wrong place can change the meaning of what is intended to be communicated and interpreted by the receiver. It is always desirable to repeat an important part of the message and ensure confirmation from the receiver.

Power position

Authority, power and status of an individual in an organization affect the communication with people interacting at various levels of hierarchy. While authority makes communication more authentic, but may create social distance and therefore, restrict communication due to a gap that may be created. Power centres may not allow views of less powerful individuals in the decision-making process. Thus free flow of information may not exist in the organization. This is counterproductive for growth.

Cultural barriers

Cultural differences can adversely affect the communication effectiveness. Multinational players are operating in India due to liberalization. It is, therefore, necessary to understand the ethnic backgrounds and cultures of various employees working in the organization. The religious sentiments of the employees must be protected while communicating. Norms play an important role like working on Fridays for Muslims, wearing white clothes by Hindu women in India, etc. In some countries punctuality is not considered important as long as the targets are met. Accordingly, the communicator must identify these barriers and identify the cultural differences so that an all out effort is made to ensure effectiveness of communication.

Sender credibility

If a sender's credibility is high, the receiver will take and interpret the message favourably. Conversely, if the sender is not trusted the receiver may try and interpret the message wrongly by deliberately giving hidden meaning to various words and may even distort the complete message. The communication of an expert is generally taken seriously and acted upon favourably. Emotions also play an important role in communication. If the receiver is happy and in a fine mood, he will receive and interpret the message as intended by the sender else the communication can be heavily distorted.

FEEDBACK

Feedback completes the total communication process. Feedback is important to ascertain if the message is understood and acted upon correctly. A lack of it or wrong feedback is counter productive to effective communication. In defence services there is a procedure to repeat the message by the receiver so that the sender knows that the message is being correctly received. Wrong reception of the message is instantaneously corrected and an acknowledgement sought. This is generally implemented when long distance weapon system is being used. The safety of one's troops and the maximum destruction of the enemy forces is sought. For example, the communication involved from ground to air for guiding strike aircraft in support of ground forces.

Wofford, Gerloff and Cummins point out that the greatest barrier to communication is the style of communication used by the manager. When a manager sends a message in a way that provokes defensiveness, he or she contributes to the poor interpersonal relationship. If relations are already strained, the chances of experiencing communication breakdown are greatly enhanced.

To conclude, the message must be received with the same spirit as is being sent. The message may be vitiated in many ways. It may be distortion, omission or filtration. Distortion takes place due to the motive, the attitude and the sentiments of both the sender and the receiver. Filtration takes place when a message is passed on by reducing it based on the liking of receiver, or by retaining information for bargaining purpose. Omission is related to the deletion of a part of a message.

OVERCOMING COMMUNICATION BARRIERS

Ways to overcome the communication barriers are discussed below:

Improve Listening Skills

An individual must be a good listener. Listening is half the communication. When one listens he also carries out concurrent mental interpretation of what he is hearing. Positive outlook goes a long way to ensure effective communication. Important points for good listener are as under:

1. Do not have preconceived ideas about a subject matter
2. Pay full attention to what the sender is saying
3. Think as the sender thinks
4. Check back as to what you have received
5. Give time to take feedback on the action taken on the message received
6. Keep the principle of 'need to know' in mind to avoid information overload
7. Do not jump to conclusions
8. Do not have a prejudiced mind and take every message independently

Improve Writing Skills

When a message is intended to be sent, it is necessary to identify the action and the information that is being addressed. The text of the message should be simple and should clearly indicate the actions that are required to be taken by the   receiver. A well-written communication in simple language has negligible chances of misinterpretation. Writing a good message is an art and it must be practiced overtime. The basic principles of a good written message are brevity, clarity and simplicity.

Maintain Unity of Command Principle

Most communication problems arise when channels of command and control are not followed strictly. One must receive orders from a specific authority and should be answerable to the same authority. In typical hierarchical organizations, chains of reporting are laid down and should be followed. Because of the multiplicity of organizational functions, lateral and diagonal communication is necessary; the same should be undertaken on an even level. Creation of power blocks should be discouraged. The object of communication is not only to carryout assigned tasks but also to create an atmosphere of trust and understanding among all members of the organization. It is only possible when the management is not only sensitive to the demands of the workers but also keeps their promises. According to Luft, openness and an atmosphere of trust builds healthy relationships and closes the credibility gaps thus contributing to the effectiveness and enhancement of communication.

Points to Ponder

1. Communication is the most vital element of any organization.
2. Communication can be described as an impersonal process of sending and receiving symbols with meanings attached to them.
3. There are three primary methods of communication. These are written, verbal and nonverbal forms of communication.
4. The different structures of communication are given below:
   a. Downward communication
   b. Upward communication
   c. Horizontal or lateral communication
5. The different types of communications are as follows:
   a. Formal communication
   b. Informal communication
6. Various kinds of barriers for communication are as follows:
   a. Physical barrier
   b. Interpersonal barrier

 **Self-Assessment Exercises**

1. Define communication. Why is communication important to an organization?
2. Explain in detail the communication process.
3. What is *noise* in communication?
4. What are the various communication barriers? How can they be eliminated?
5. What is a communication network? Explain.
6. The key to good communication is 'the principles of brevity, clarity and simplicity'. Explain the above statement.
7. Write notes on the following:
   a. Downward and upward communication
   b. Formal communication
   c. Informal communication
   d. Language barrier
   e. Communication channels

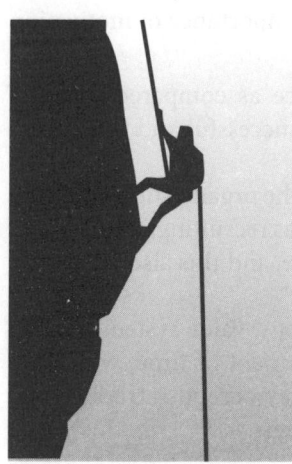

Motivation

INTRODUCTION

Motivation is a process of creating organizational conditions that will impel employees to strive to attain company goals. It is the stimulation of an emotion or a desire operating upon one's will and prompting or driving it to action.

Motivation is defined as a willingness to expend energy to achieve a goal or be rewarded. It is a force that activates dormant energies and sets in motion the actions of people. It is the function that kindles a burning passion for action among employees of an organization.

According to William G. Scott, motivation is defined as a process of stimulating people to action, to accomplish desired goals.

According to McFarland, motivation refers to the way in which urges, drives, desires, aspirations, strivings, needs, etc., transform the behaviour of human beings.

CHARACTERISTICS OF MOTIVATION

1. **Motivation is an internal feeling:** Motivation is a psychological phenomenon that is generated in an individual. Needs are feelings in the mind of a person, telling him that he lacks certain things. Such feelings affect the behaviour of the person.
2. **Person in total, not in plans, is motivated:** Each individual in an organization is self-contained and all his needs are interrelated. These affect the behaviour in different ways, depending upon the motivation given.
3. **Motivation causes goal-directed behaviour:** Motivation in different forms satisfies the urges and helps the employees to work towards the attainment of organizational goals.

IMPORTANCE OF MOTIVATION

Motivation is one of the most important factors determining the efficiency of an organization. All organizational facilities will go waste in the absence of motivated people. The importance of motivation in an organization can be summed up as follows:

1. **High performance level:** Motivated employees put higher performance as compared to other employees. High performance is a must for an organization to become successful and this comes through motivation.
2. **Low employee turnover and absenteeism:** Motivated employees stay in the organization and their absenteeism is quite low. High turnover and absenteeism create problems as recruiting, training and developing large number of new personnel into working teams takes time, and this also affects the reputation of an organization.
3. **Acceptance of organization change:** Because of the changes in technology, value system, etc., an organization has to incorporate those changes to cope with the requirement of time, which are resisted by people. However, if these people are properly motivated, they accept, introduce and implement these changes keeping organization on the right track of progress.

OBJECTIVE OF MOTIVATION

The purpose of motivation is to create conditions where people are willing to work with zeal, initiative, interest and enthusiasm with a high personal and group moral satisfaction, so that the goals of an organization are achieved effectively.

The two important elements of motivation are as follows:

1. An understanding of the fundamental drives, urges and needs of the people that are subject to emotional stimulation or motivation.
2. Communication with people so that they may have satisfactory stimulus to their urges.

FACTORS MOTIVATING PEOPLE IN AN ORGANIZATION

The various factors that motivate people can broadly be classified as below:

1. Money
2. Good working environment
3. Challenging work and responsibility

4. Personal accomplishment
5. Praise for good work
6. Communication system
7. Opportunity for growth and advancement
8. Need for satisfaction

Among all the above-stated factors, the most important is the need for satisfaction. The management must motivate employees to satisfy their needs, especially social and recognition needs, and the feeling of participation in a group effort.

TYPES OF MOTIVATION

Motivation can be of different kinds, as discussed below:

1. Self-motivation: Self-motivation is defined as the willingness to work on one's own. For this, one must overcome a certain amount of natural inertia. The barriers to human action include feeling of tiredness due to emotional reactions within oneself. The things that affect the conscious mind are collectively known as *anxiety*, and this is due to the following factors:

a. Monotonous work
b. Poor working conditions
c. Driven by boss
d. Does not get along with associates
e. Dissatisfied with work or achievements
f. Under constant strain
g. Gets no rest at home
h. Financial troubles

Other factors that affect the subconscious mind are known as *inner conflicts*. These factors also dissuade a person from working actively and indicate that a person is

a. unwilling to work,
b. wants to be tired and has an excuse for failure,
c. craves for sympathy,
d. thinks that the world owes him a living,
e. has some sort of inferiority complex or
f. hates his family and does not want to support his wife and children.

Anxiety and inner conflicts may be reduced by

a. making the job more interesting,
b. thinking constructively,
c. making the best possible use of one's strengths and not dwelling on weaknesses,
d. doing things one is afraid due to ignorance as ignorance causes fear,
e. being tough minded, particularly towards oneself,
f. adapting to the situation and
g. acquiring a sensible and worthwhile philosophy of life.

2. Group motivation: Group motivation is defined as the willingness to work in a group. People in a group can be well motivated when they are informed of the ideas, plans, inventions or systems. Communication of ideas, plans, etc., can be made effective when certain personal qualities have been developed. These qualities are honesty, fairness, integrity, truthfulness, loyalty, stability, tolerance, constructive criticism, orderliness in mind and action, sense of humour and broadmindedness. Groups can be motivated by improving human relations and dealing with people in a humane way by developing the will to do and by encouraging people to feel involved in their work.

MOTIVATION STEPS

The various steps involved in motivating people are as follows:

1. Sizing up situations
2. Preparing a set of motivating tools
3. Selecting and applying motivators
4. Following up the results of application

Sizing up situation: Sizing up situation involves ascertaining motivational needs. Every person needs motivation, but of varying kinds and in varying degrees; for example, one may take pride in producing quality work, another only in quantity. Therefore, lay stress on individual differences.

Preparing motivation tools: An executive draws up a list of devices that may motivate different types of people under different circumstances.

Selecting and applying motivators: An executive decides the words, tone of voice and gestures to be used for motivating people. He decides for their proper use, i.e. where and when (place and timing) to use them.

Following up results of application: Following up results of application requires finding out whether people have been motivated or not. If not, then other devices may be used.

RULES OF MOTIVATION

Following are the rules of motivation:

1. **Variability:** The motivation methods should not be the same but should change according to the circumstances. One set of motivator is not for everybody or for the same person for a period of time.
2. **Self-interest:** A person is selfish by nature. When he realizes that his own interests are best served by the attainment of goals for the organization, he is likely to be motivated.
3. **Attainability:** It is necessary to establish goals that are reasonable and attainable. When such goals are attained, employee satisfaction is achieved. Unattainable goals often frustrate people.
4. **Participation:** The desirability of participation of those to be motivated ensures their cooperation. This reduces suspicion of a management's motivational aims.
5. **Proportioning rewards:** Rewards should be in proportion to the efforts made.
6. **Human element:** Motivation appeals to the emotions. The executive who is most successful as a motivator can trace his success invariably to his skill in dealing with the feelings of others.
7. **Individual and group relationships:** Motivation must be based on group as well as individual stimulus.
8. **Situational:** Motivation must be based on a sound managerial theory.

CLASSIFICATION OF MOTIVATION

The universally accepted way of classifying motivation is as follows:

1. Extrinsic motivation: Extrinsic motivation occurs when things are done to or for people to motivate them. These include rewards, such as incentives, increased pay, praise or promotion; and punishments, such as disciplinary action, withholding pay or criticism.

Extrinsic motivators can have an immediate and a powerful effect, but will not necessarily last long. The intrinsic motivators that are concerned with the 'quality of working life' (a phrase and movement that emerged from this concept) are likely to have a deeper and a long-term effect because they are inherent in individuals and in their work. They are not imposed from outside in such forms as incentive pay.

2. Intrinsic motivation: Intrinsic motivation can arise from self-generated factors that influence the behaviour of people. It is not created by external incentives. Intrinsic motivation can take the form of motivation by the work itself—when individuals feel that their work is important, interesting and challenging, and provides them with a reasonable degree of autonomy (freedom to act); opportunities to achieve and advance, and scope to use and develop their skills and abilities. Deci and Ryan (1985) suggested that intrinsic motivation is based on the need to be competent and self-determining (that is, to have a choice).

Intrinsic motivation can be enhanced by job or role design. According to an early writer, Katz (1964), on the significance of the motivational impact of job design, 'The job itself must provide sufficient variety, sufficient complexity, sufficient challenge and sufficient skill to engage the abilities of the worker'. In their job characteristics model, Hackman and Oldham (1974) emphasized the importance of the core job dimensions as motivators, viz. skill variety, task identity, task significance, autonomy and feedback.

THEORIES OF MOTIVATION

From the very beginning, since human organizations have been established, people have tried to find answers to what motivates people to the maximum. However, all researches emphasize that due to the complex nature of human beings no generalization is possible. Moreover, the findings of research studies and theories are not universally applicable and they are affected by time, country and circumstances. The various theories of motivation based on different assumptions have been developed. They are put under certain distinct categories as follows:

1. **Prescription theories:** Prescription theories try to tell a management how to motivate employees. Taylor's Scientific Management Theory, Hawthorne's Human Relations Model and McGregor's X and Y theories come under this head. These theories are based on the trial and error experiences and popular beliefs.
2. **Content theories:** Content theories are concerned with the question of what causes behaviour to start and stop. It is based on the needs, motives or desires that drive employees to achieve job satisfaction. It includes Maslow's Needs Hierarchy Theory, Fredrick Herzberg's Two-Factor Theory and David McClelland's Need for Achievement Theory.
3. **Process theory:** Process theories talk about the origin of behaviour and its performance. It includes the Behaviourist Model.

4. **Cognitive theory:** Cognitive theories are based on the thoughts and feelings (i.e. cognition) of individuals. It includes the Vroom's Expectancy Theory.

There are a number of motivation theories that, in the main, are complementary to one another. The leading theories are listed and described in the following table:

Table 5.1. Leading Motivational Theories and Their Implications

Theorist(s)	Summary of theory	Implications
Taylor (1911)	People will be motivated to work if rewards and punishments are directly related to their performance.	Based on crude attempts to motivate people by incentives. Often used as the implied rationale for performance-related pay, although, this is seldom an effective motivator.
Hull (1951)	An experience is gained when needs are satisfied. People perceive that certain actions help to achieve goals while others are unsuccessful. The successful actions are repeated when a similar need arises.	Provides feedback that positively reinforces effective behaviour.
Maslow (1954)	A hierarchy of five needs exist: physiological, safety, social, esteem and self-fulfilment. Higher-level needs only emerge when a lower-level need is satisfied.	Focuses attention on the various needs that motivate people and the notion that a satisfied need is no longer a motivator. The concept of a hierarchy has no practical significance.
Alderfer (1972)	Three fundamental needs: existence, relatedness and growth.	A simpler and more convincing approach to Maslow's on motivation provided by needs.
McClelland (1973)	Managers have three fundamental needs: achievement, affiliation and power.	Draws attention to the needs of managers and the important concept of 'achievement motivation'.
Vroom (1964), Porter and Lawler (1968)	Effort (motivation) depends on the likelihood that rewards will follow effort and that the reward is worthwhile.	The key theory informing approaches to rewards, i.e. that there must be a link between effort and reward (line of sight). The reward should be achievable and should be worthwhile.
Latham and Locke (1979)	Motivation will improve if people have demanding but agreed goals and receive feedback.	Provides the rationale for performance management, goal setting and feedback.
Adams (1965)	People are better motivated if treated equitably.	Need to have equitable reward and employment practices.
Bandura (1977)	Emphasizes the importance of internal psychological factors, especially expectancies about the value of goals and the individual's ability to reach them.	Influences performance management and learning, and development practices.
Herzberg et al. (1957)	Two groups of factors affect job satisfaction: (1) those intrinsic to the work itself; (2) those extrinsic to the job (extrinsic motivators or hygiene factors) such as pay and working conditions.	Identifies a number of fundamental needs, i.e. achievement, recognition, advancement, autonomy and the work itself. Influences approach to job design (job enrichment). Underpins the proposition that reward systems should provide for both financial and nonfinancial rewards.
McGregor (1960)	Theory X is the traditional view that people must be coerced into performing; theory Y is the view that people will exercise self-direction and self-direction in the service of the objectives to which they are committed.	Emphasizes the importance of commitment, rewards and, integrating individual and organizational needs.

Some of the leading motivational theories are as follows:

1. McGregor's Theory X and Theory Y

The action of the management to motivate employees in an organization, according to McGregor, involves certain assumptions, generalizations and hypotheses relating to human behaviour and human nature. These assumptions may be neither consciously crystallized nor overtly stated, however, they serve the purpose of predicting human behaviour. McGregor has presented two opposite sets of assumptions about employees that are represented by theory X and theory Y. McGregor represent the extreme ranges of assumptions. The managerial attitudes and supervisory practices resulting from such assumptions have an important bearing on employee behaviour.

Theory X

Theory X is the traditional theory of human behaviour. This theory represents standard bureaucratic and authoritarian attitudes towards employees. The assumptions in theory X are as follows:

1. Most people prefer to be directed and prodded
2. They are lethargic
3. They want safety above all
4. The person dislikes work and, whenever possible, will avoid it
5. Most people are not ambitious and have little desire for responsibility
6. Most people have little capacity for creativity in solving organizational problems
7. To get people to work, it is necessary to use strict control, threats, constant pressure, persuasion and even punishment
8. Motivation occurs only at the level of the physiological and safety level

Theory X offers the management an easy rationalization for ineffective performance of the organization. It is due to the nature of human resources with which he must work.

Managers, who accept the assumptions of theory X attempt to structure, control and closely supervise their employees. They feel that external control is appropriate for dealing with unreliable, irresponsible and immature people.

McGregor, drawing heavily on Maslow's hierarchy of needs, concluded that assumptions about human nature in theory X, when universally applied are often inaccurate and that the management approaches that develop from these assumptions may fail to motivate many individuals to work towards the goal of the organization. Management by direction and control may not succeed. It is a questionable method for motivating those people whose physiological and safety needs are reasonably satisfied and whose higher level needs become predominant.

He developed an alternative theory of human behaviour called *theory Y.*

Theory Y

Theory Y represents the democratic approach and gives a scope for creativity and responsibility to the employee. The assumptions in theory Y are as follows:

1. People are not lazy and unreliable by nature.
2. They enjoy work, show initiative and imagination in self-direction and self-control in the service of the objectives to which they are committed, if they are properly motivated.

3. Work is a natural activity like playing and rest, if the conditions are favourable.
4. Close control and threats of punishment are not the only ways of getting people to do things.
5. A large percentage of population has a high degree of imagination and creativity that can be used in solving organization problems.
6. Commitment to objectives is determined by the rewards associated with this achievement.
7. Motivation occurs at the social, esteem and self-actualization levels, as well as at the physiological and security levels.
8. People can be self-directed and can be creative in work if properly motivated.
9. In the world of business, under the condition of modern industrial life, the intellectual potential of the average person is only partially used.
10. Under proper conditions, the average human being learns not only to accept but to seek responsibility.

In supervising human resources, the modern management realizes that theory Y offers a better description of people than theory X (Figure 5.1). There may be some indolent and lazy individual who need to be threatened or controlled and prodded very strictly, but most people respond to a manager who employs a leadership style based on theory Y.

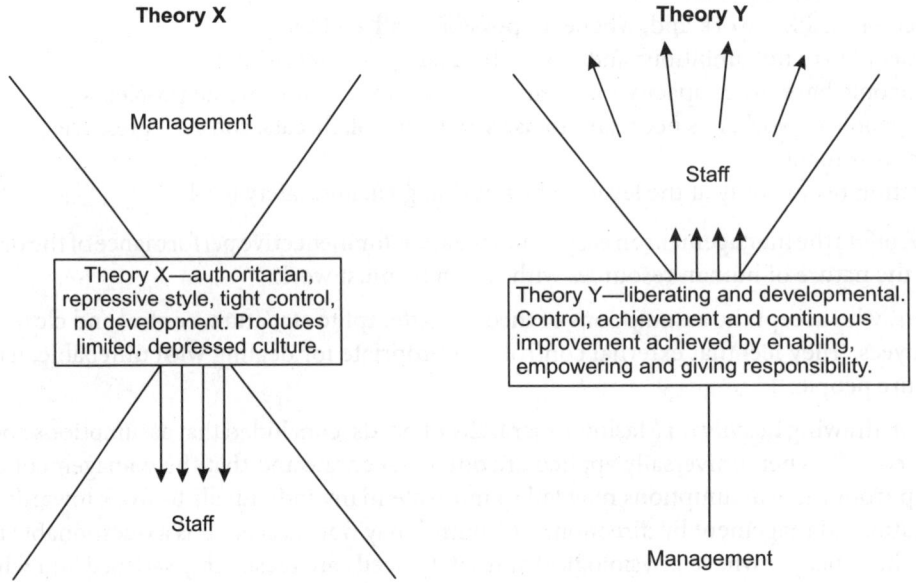

Figure 5.1. Schematic Representation of Theory X and Theory Y

Comparison of Theories X and Y

Both theories have certain assumptions about human nature. In fact they are the two side of the same coin—one representing head and the other representing tail. The differences between these two sets of assumptions can be summarized as below:

Theory X	Theory Y
Theory X assumes that human beings are inherently distasteful to work.	Theory Y assumes that for human beings work is a natural activity.
Theory X emphasizes that people are not ambitious and shirk away from responsibilities in a job.	Theory Y assumes that people take responsibility on themselves.
According to theory X, **most people** have little capacity for creativity.	According to theory Y, the capacity for creativity is widely present in the population.
In theory X, people **lack self-motivation** and are required to be extremely controlled and closely **supervised** to get maximum output from them.	In theory Y, people are self-directed, creative and self-controlled.

2. Herzberg's Two-Factor Theory

Herzberg's findings were obtained from a research that he conducted with a group of accountants and engineers in Pittsburgh. He and his associates sought answers to two questions:

   a.   what is about your job that you like?
   b.   what is about your job that you dislike?

The responses fell into two general categories as follows:

1.   The things people seemed to like about their job were directly related to the job itself. The elements when present, led to positive motivation such as achievement, recognition, creative and challenging work, responsibility, growth and advancement possibilities. These were called as *motivators* or *satisfiers* because they gave rise to job satisfaction. The absence of the satisfiers, however, do not cause dissatisfaction.
2.   The things people seemed to dislike about their work were related to the environment in which they performed their jobs and these included: supervision, salary, company policies and administration, benefits, job security, working conditions and relationship with superiors, colleagues and subordinates. These factors do not motivate people. If they are adequate and present, they only prevent dissatisfaction. They produce no improvement but are needed to avoid unpleasantness. If they are withdrawn, they create dissatisfaction. Herzberg called these factors as *dissatisfiers* or *maintenance factors* or *hygiene factors*.

Herzberg found that his hygiene factors, if given to the workers, helped in maintaining a zero level of motivation, and dissatisfaction if they were not given. Motivation factors are intrinsic to the job where as maintenance and hygiene factors are extrinsic to it. Motivators are job oriented as they relate to the job content; and maintenance factors are mostly environment centred as they relate to job context.

Hygiene factors have to be maintained to avoid damage to the efficiency or morale, but they are incapable of stimulating any effort. Various other studies have also confirmed the conclusions of Herzberg. The things that motivate employees are as discussed below:

1.   A challenging job that offers a feeling of achievement, responsibility, growth, advancement, enjoyment of the work itself and recognition.
2.   Factors that are peripheral to the job or work. Rules such as coffee breaks, titles and seniority rights, etc.

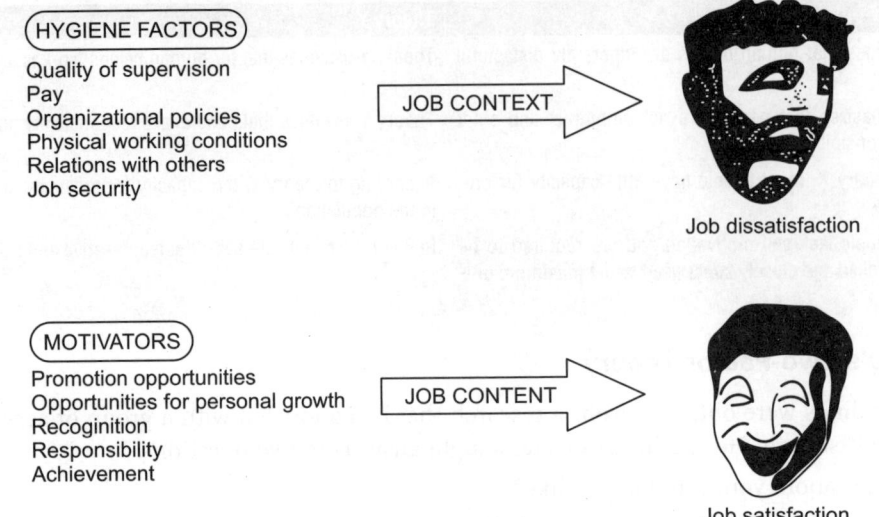

Figure 5.2. Herzberg's Two-Factor Theory

3. If opportunities for meaningful achievement are eliminated, workers become sensitized to their environment and begin to find fault with it.

If Herzberg's theory is applied to business, two important motivational ideas for managing human resources may be extracted from it. They are as given below:

1. There are some factors that simply do not motivate people. For some individuals, hygiene factors are actually motivators. But the important thing is that for each individual there are some items that fall under the heading of hygiene. As a result not everything a company does will motivate employees. Some will just stop them from becoming demotivated, like working conditions do not really motivate but without these people might do less work.

2. Herzberg's theory underscores the important fact of satisfying upper-level needs. Employees want recognition, increased responsibility, a chance for advancement and a more challenging work. In fact when comparing the same job in different companies, it is common to find people receiving identical pay and having similar working conditions. The differences occur at the psychological level and that accounts for the difference in the performance of the employees (Figure 5.2).

Herzberg has concluded that it is a mistake on the part of the management to emphasize on only hygienic and extrinsic factors that serve only to make the environment some what more tolerable. Management should seek to enrich a job so as to make it more interesting.

Drawbacks of Herzberg's Theory

Herzberg's theory has been criticized by many authors. Keith Davis has observed that a limited testing of the model on blue-collar workers suggest that some items normally considered as maintenance factors, like pay and security, are frequently considered motivational factors by them. Another study has indicated that the blue-collar workers lay greater stress on extrinsic job factors. It has been contended that achievement, recognition and responsibility are important for both satisfaction and dissatisfaction. Dimensions such as security, salary and working conditions are less important.

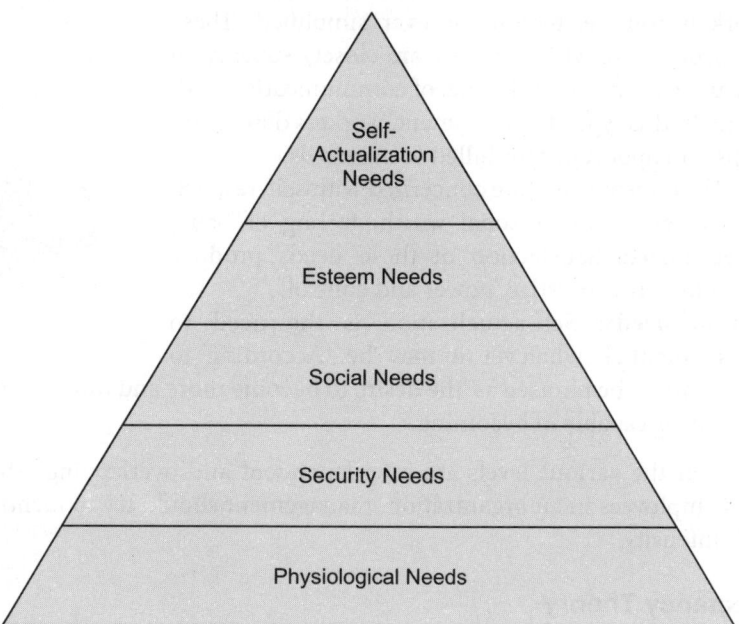

Figure 5.3. Hierarchy of Human Needs

Lastly Herzberg's study has been criticized as being methodology bound. It over simplifies the relationship between motivation and satisfaction, and is inconsistent with past evidence.

3. Maslow's Need Hierarchy Theory

The behaviour of an individual at a particular moment is usually determined by his strongest needs. Psychologists' claim that needs have a certain priority and when the basic needs are satisfied, an individual seeks to satisfy the higher needs. According to A.H. Maslow, there seems to be a hierarchy in which human needs are arranged as shown as below in Figure 5.3.

The human needs according to Maslow are discussed below:

1. **Physiological needs:** The physiological needs are located at the top of the hierarchy because they tend to have the highest strength. A person whose physiological needs (i.e., desire for food, water, clothing, shelter, etc.) are satisfied will work more efficiently as compared to the person whose needs are not fulfilled.

2. **Safety needs:** Once the physiological needs are satisfied to a reasonable level, then the safety needs come into picture. Safety needs are concerned with job security. In an industrial society, safety needs may take considerable importance depending upon the relationship of the employees to their employers. The organization can influence the safety needs either positively through pension plan, etc., or negatively by arousing fears of being fired, lay off or demoted.

3. **Social needs:** After the first two needs are satisfied, the social needs become important in the need hierarchy. Since man is a social being, he has a need to belong and be accepted by various groups. When social needs become dominant, a person strives for meaningful relationships with others. Social needs are concerned with giving and receiving affection, love, friendship, a sense of belongingness, etc. In an organization, workers form an informal group environment. Such environment develops

where the work is routine, tedious or over simplified. These situations are made worse when workers are closely supervised and controlled and have no clear channel of communication with the management. In this type of environment, workers depend on informal groups for support of unfulfilled social needs.

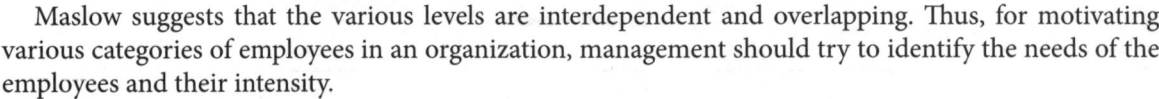

4. **Esteem needs:** The esteem needs are concerned with self-respect, self-confidence, a feeling of personal worth, feeling of being unique and recognized. Satisfaction of these needs produce feelings of self-confidence, prestige, power and control.

5. **Self-actualization needs:** Self-actualization is the need to maximize one's potential, whatever it may be. According to Maslow this need might be phrased as 'the desire to become more and more what one is, to become everything that one is capable of becoming'.

Maslow suggests that the various levels are interdependent and overlapping. Thus, for motivating various categories of employees in an organization, management should try to identify the needs of the employees and their intensity.

4. Vroom's Expectancy Theory

Vroom's Model is built around the concepts of value, expectancy and force. The basic assumption of the model is that the choice made by a person among alternative courses of action is lawfully related to the psychological events occurring, along with the behaviour. Vroom's concept of force is basically equivalent to motivation and may be shown to be the algebraic sum of the products of valences multiplied by expectations. Thus,

Motivation (force) = Valence × Expectancy

According to Vroom, valence means the strength of an individual's preference to a particular outcome. Other terms equivalent to valence used in different theories of motivation are incentives, attitude and expected utility. Expectancy is the probability that a particular action will lead to a particular outcome.

This theory was developed by Victor H. Vroom. It explains that motivation is a product of the values one seeks and one's expectation of the probability that a certain action will lead to those values. The assumptions of this theory are as follows:

1. Motivation is a force driving a person to achieve some level of job performance.
2. The force or effort depends upon his perception of the probability or likelihood of certain outcomes resulting from his effort as related to the values he places on these outcomes. For example, if an employee believes that high performance will yield higher income, and if this is of value to him, he will produce more. In achieving a high level of performance, he has the satisfaction which in turn influences his future effort. If he receives the higher income he expects, it will give him the satisfaction which in turn will tend to make future incomes appear more valuable.

Under this theory, two things can be done to motivate a person to work as discussed below:

1. The positive value of outcomes may be increased through means such as better communication about their values and actually increasing them (i.e. the rewards).

2. The expectancy may be increased that the work really will lead to the desired outcome through improved communication.

5. Behaviourist Theory

Behaviourist modification theory was evolved from the work of Skinner and is better known as the *organization behaviour modification* (OB Mod) theory. Behaviourist theory is also called Rat Man because Skinner, perhaps the most famous of all the behaviourist psychologists, did much of his work on rats. The theory assumes that the causes of behaviour are outside the person and in the environment. Behaviourist modification is achieved through operant conditioning. Operant behaviour is that which can be modified by its consequences. If the consequences of certain behaviour are favourable to a person, his behaviour will be strengthened. If they are unfavourable, the behaviour will be weakened. It is in this manner that operant conditioning occurs. Behaviour primarily is encouraged through reinforcement that provides a favourable consequence encouraging a repetition of behaviour. For example, if an employee finds that high-quality work earns him recognition in the shape of a reward, he may produce such quality work again. His behaviour is thus reinforced. Behaviour response for the removal of something undesirable is repeated when that undesirable state is encountered again. This is negative reinforcement.

6. Existence/Relatedness/Growth (ERG) Theory of Needs

Clayton Alderfer, in his existence/relatedness/growth (ERG), theory of needs, theorized that there are three groups of needs as shown in the figure below:

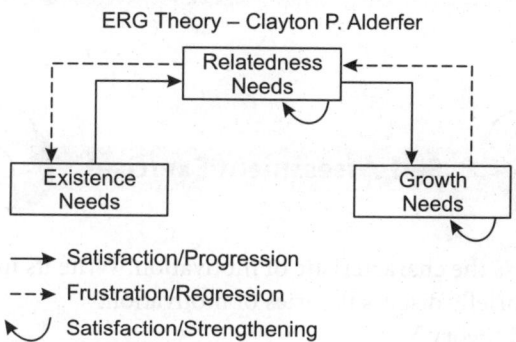

Figure 5.4. ERG Theory

The needs as illustrated above are discussed below:

1. **Existence:** This group of needs is concerned with providing the basic requirements for material existence, such as physiological and safety needs. This need is satisfied by money earned in a job to buy food, home, clothing, etc.

2. **Relationships:** This group of needs centres on or is built upon the desire to establish and maintain interpersonal relationships. Since one usually spends approximately half of one's waking hours on the job, this need is normally satisfied at least to some degree by one's co-workers.

3. **Growth:** These needs are met by personal development. A person's job, career or profession provides for significant satisfaction of growth needs.

Alderfer's ERG theory also states that more than one need may be influential at the same time. If the gratification of a higher-level need is frustrated, the desire to satisfy a lower-level need will increase. He identifies this phenomenon as the 'frustration and shypaggressiort dimension.' Its relevance on the job is that even when the upper-level needs are frustrated, the job still provides for the basic physiological needs upon which one would then be focused. If, at that point, something happens to threaten the job, the basic needs of a person are significantly threatened. If there are no factors present to relieve the pressure, the person may become desperate and panicky.

Points to Ponder

1. Motivation is a process of creating organizational conditions that will impel employees to strive to attain company goals.
2. Generally there are two types of motivation. They are as follows:
   a. Self-motivation
   b. Group motivation
3. The various theories of motivation can be summarized below:
   a. Prescription theories that includes McGregor's X and Y theories.
   b. Content theories that includes Maslow's Needs Hierarchy theory and Fredrick Herzberg's Two-Factor Theory.
   c. Process theory that includes the Behaviourist Model.
   d. Cognitive theory that includes Vroom's Expectancy Theory.

 **Self-Assessment Exercises**

1. Define *motivation*. Discuss the characteristic of motivation. Write its importance.
2. Classify motivation and briefly discuss theories of motivation.
3. Distinguish theory X and theory Y.
4. Write a note on ERG theory of needs.
5. Discuss Vroom's expectancy theory.
6. Explain Maslow's hierarchy of need.
7. Briefly explain Herzberg's Two-Factor Theory and discuss its drawbacks.
8. Write a short note on McGregor's theory X and theory Y.

Decision Making

INTRODUCTION

Decision making is an essential part of the management process. All the management functions demand effective decision making at all stages, if they are to be successful. For instance, in planning, the objectives and policies are laid down through a process of decision making. In organizing, decision making relates to the choice of structure, form and nature of the organization, division of work, delegating responsibilities, etc. In controlling, decision making helps in deciding the performance standards, strategic control points, control procedures and so on.

A decision needs judgment and a thorough understanding of the subject or matter. It is a point where plans, policies and objectives are translated into concrete action. The manner of decision making determines the success or failure in the business. It is, therefore, quite natural that the professionalized management has given so much importance to the techniques employed in taking correct decisions.

Today's management process is giving more attention to sharing decisions with subordinates. Extremely powerful mathematical models have also been built that can be applied to the process of decision making.

The purpose of decision making is to direct human behaviour towards a future goal. If there were no alternatives, there would be no need for a decision. Decision making is a systematic process involving diagnosis and the selection of the most appropriate course of action from the available alternatives. In an organization, managers make hundreds and varied types of minor as well as major decisions, viz. where to invest profits, where to open new office, when to launch new products, from where to source the raw materials, when to conduct employee trainings and so on. The minor decisions are taken almost subconsciously with the help of set rules and practices, whereas, the major decisions are taken very carefully and consciously.

A decision is a choice activity because there are alternatives to choose from. When managers make decision, they choose, i.e. they decide what to do on the basis of some conscious and deliberate judgments. Managers have alternatives when they make decisions. It does require wisdom and experience to evaluate several alternatives and select the best one.

CHARACTERISTICS OF DECISION MAKING

The basic characteristics of decision-making process are as follows:

1. It is a choice activity wherein the best course of action is selected from the available alternatives.
2. It is an intellectual activity wherein the application of intellectual abilities is a must for taking decisions.
3. It is always related to the environment that influences the process of decision making.
4. The act of decision making carries a certain purpose.
5. It involves a time dimension and a time lag.

TYPES OF DECISIONS

Decision making is an ongoing process and people working in the organization at different levels take many decisions of varied types, to their capacities. There are organizational and personal decisions, strategic and routine decisions, programmed and nonprogrammed decisions, and policy and operating decisions.

Organizational and Personal Decisions

Organizational decisions are those made by managers in their official capacity. For example, the setting of objectives, the approval of plans, etc. The implementation of such decisions can be delegated to others as the implementation of such decisions is a group effort.

Personal decisions relate to the manager as an individual not as a member of the organization. Such decisions are not delegated to others because their implementation does not require the support of organizational personnel. Deciding to retire, taking a job offer from a competitive firm, taking a leave of absence are some of the examples of personnel decisions.

Strategic and Routine Decisions

Strategic or basic decisions are more important and are taken by the top management and to some extent by the middle management. Strategic decisions can have major organizational effects. They are related to the policy matters and hence, need a lot of groundwork before making the decisions. Some of the examples are, selection of a new product, establishing new plant, joint ventures, collaborations etc.

Routine decisions are made repetitively following certain established rules, procedures and policies. They do not require special effort and are taken without much deliberation by the middle and the lower level management. They have a minor impact on the firm and they are often repetitive in nature.

Programmed and Nonprogrammed Decisions

A programmed decision is applied to structured or routine problems. These decisions are repetitive and are to be dealt according to specific procedures. On the other hand, nonprogrammed decisions arise because of unstructured problems. There are no specific procedures to solve such problems. They require a thorough study of the problem and analysis of the situation that has created a problem.

Most decisions are neither completely programmed nor completely unprogrammed; they are merely a combination of both. Most of the nonprogrammed decisions are made by upper level managers. Supervisors or lower level managers with the help of set procedure can take programmed decision. Programmed decisions being routine and repetitive, can be easily delegated.

The risks involved are not high. Assessment can often be made in quantitative terms and can be computerized. Nonprogrammed decisions, on the other hand, are few and involve high risks.

In the pharmaceutical industry, the decision of changing a supplier for sourcing a raw material, if the existing one refuses to supply, is a programmed decision; whereas if no supplier is ready to supply the desired material then the decision becomes nonprogrammed and needs a thorough study of the problem.

Policy and Operating Decisions

Policy decisions are of vital importance that affects the entire organization. Such decisions are taken by the top management only. Operating decisions are related with the implementation of policy decisions and are taken by middle and lower management.

For instance, in the pharmaceutical industry, deciding which medicine to be developed is a policy decision, whereas, decisions related to the execution of developing the molecule are operational decisions.

PROCESS OF DECISION MAKING

The decision-making process consists of the following:
1. Identifying the problem
2. Diagnosing the situation
3. Collecting and analysing data relevant to the issue
4. Developing solutions for solving the problem
5. Analysing these alternative solutions

6. Selecting the best among the available alternatives
7. Implementing the decision

Identifying the Problem

It is essential to identify the problem and the environment for the existence of the problem. There are many problems that the organizations face in day-to-day activities, like quality problems, employee problem, technological problems, customer problems, etc. Sometimes the results are not as per the scheduled plan. The projects get delayed or a competitor company launches new products and so on. It is the skill of the management on how they handle these problems. The decision makers have to thoroughly understand and analyse the problem.

Diagnosing the Situation

A correct diagnosis of the situation that has created the problem plays a very important role in the process of decision making. If the situation is diagnosed clearly, it helps in preventing the recurrence of the similar problem in future. A manager should follow a systematic approach in order to diagnose the situation correctly. He must make a thorough study of the situation and other related aspects.

Collecting and Analysing Data Relevant to the Issue

Managers should develop a scientific approach to reach correct decisions. They should collect and analyse the relevant data while diagnosing the problem in a situation.

Developing Solutions for Solving the Problem

After identifying the problem, diagnosing the situation, and collecting and analysing the data relevant to the problem, the next step is to develop alternative solutions to solve the problem. For every problem there are alternative solutions. For example, in the production department, there is a demand to install a new automated compression machine to increase the overall productivity. There are several alternatives that the management can consider like:

1. whether modification can be done in existing machine to improve the efficiency,
2. whether the existing process can be modified,
3. whether additional accessories can be attached to existing set up,
4. whether to buy a new machine as proposed,
5. whether to buy new machine other than what is proposed or
6. whether to continue with the same set up, etc.

It is always beneficial to develop more alternatives in order to make correct decisions.

Analysing these Alternative Solutions

Once the appropriate alternate solutions have been developed, the next step in decision making is to measure and compare their consequences. All the developed alternate solutions are analysed for their quality and acceptability. The tangible and intangible pros and cons are studied thoroughly.

Selecting the Best Among All Available Alternatives

Selecting the best of the alternatives is a very crucial step in the whole process of decision making. The best available solution is selected and communicated to all concerned in clear terms. The management tries to build consensus among all the decision makers while selecting the best alternative.

Implementing the Decision

It is very important to secure the acceptance of the employees while implementing the decision. If there is opposition or resistance, an effort should be made to remove the shortcomings. It is always important to take in confidence those concerned before implementing any decision. As all decisions affect the employees and their work, it is desirable to involve them in the process of decision making, else, even the best decisions may not be accepted by the employees.

 ## STEPS IN DECISION MAKING

The decision-making process consists of the following six steps:
1. Perception
2. Conception
3. Investigation
4. Deliberation
5. Selection
6. Implementation or promulgation

Perception

A state of awareness is known as *perception*. Out of perception, a consciousness of being arises. This consciousness of being gives tilt to the decision-making process. The executive first perceives and then moves on to choose one of the alternatives and thus takes a decision. Perception is, therefore, the first and an important step without which decisions relating to any problems in an organization cannot be taken. Other steps follow.

Conception

Conception relates to that power of the mind that develops ideas out of what has been perceived. Designs for action or programme for action may be known as *conception*.

Investigation

Perception is a location of the problem, whereas, conception is the preparation of design or programme for solving the problem. But only perception and conception cannot offer the solution. For investigating a solution, information relevant to a particular concept is to be sought, acquired and then analysed. Relative merits and demerits of the different analysed concepts are to be measured. Alternative courses of action are to be thought, analysed and compared. A manager should be able to carry this investigation either independently or with his coworkers.

Deliberation

Deliberations are strictly debates. Weighing the consequences of possible courses of action is called *deliberation*. The manager may either weigh the relative merits and demerits and the following consequences with himself or share it with others to equip him better. The deliberations remove bias, equip the manger with different ideas and alternatives, and help him arrive at a decision that may safely be ascribed as a good decision.

Selection

After deliberations one of the alternatives, the best possible in the circumstances, is selected. Selection is thus an act of choice, which in management terminology is known as a *decision*.

Promulgation

Perception, conception, investigation, deliberation and selection will carry weight only when the selected and the chosen alternative, that is, the decision, is properly and timely communicated to all those who are concerned and for whom the decision is meant. Only proper promulgation will help its execution.

Points to Ponder

1. The purpose of decision making is to direct human behaviour towards a future goal. If there were no alternatives, there would be no need for a decision.
2. The various types of decisions are categorized under the four main categories as follows:.
   a. Organizational and personal decisions
   b. Strategic and routine decisions
   c. Programmed and nonprogrammed decisions
   d. Policy and operating decisions
3. The decision-making process consists of the following:
   a. Identifying the problem
   b. Diagnosing the situation
   c. Collecting and analysing data relevant to the issue
   d. Developing solutions for solving the problem
   e. Analysing these alternative solutions
   f. Selecting the best among the available alternatives
   g. Implementing the decision
4. The decision-making process consists of the following six steps:
   1. Perception
   2. Conception
   3. Investigation
   4. Deliberation
   5. Selection
   6. Implementation or promulgation.

 **Self-Assessment Exercises**

1. What is *decision making*? Give its characteristics.
2. Describe in detail the different types of decisions.
3. Explain in detail the process of decision making.
4. Briefly discuss the various steps involved in decision making.

Leadership

INTRODUCTION

Any organization aspires to be successful, needs good leaders. But the pharmaceutical industry has not always been the best at producing leaders who can maximize the creativity and the effectiveness of the people working in various departments—and the industry is suffering as a result.

In today's fast changing business scenario, the only thing that has remained unchanged is change itself. Industries today are driven by change. The growth and success of industries depends on how they deal with change. Hence change management is a very crucial factor that influences the future of the organizations. To succeed in this competitive scenario and to take on the challenges, every organization needs leaders who will lead by example and will motivate the team towards the attainment of the organizational goals. The success of any industrial organization depends upon the quality of its leadership. Several important activities like determining the objectives, designing the methods to achieve them, forecasting the future trends, directing and coordinating organizational resources can be successfully performed only if there is able leadership. According to Peter Drucker, 'Leadership is the lifting of man's vision to higher sights, the raising of man's performance to a higher standard, the building of man's personality beyond its normal limitations'. In the words of Keith Devis, 'Leadership is the ability to persuade others to seek defined objectives enthusiastically. It is the human factor which binds a group together and motivates it toward goals'.

According to Mr Harry Truman, 'A leader is a man who has the ability to get other people to do what they don't want to do and make them like it'. History is full of such examples that signify the importance of leadership in the success of business organizations. The Tata group under the leadership of Shri J.R.D. Tata, Ford Motors with Henry Ford at the helm, General Electricals under the leadership of Jack Welch, Microsoft under the aegis of Bill Gates and Intel under the leadership of Andy Grove are some of the glaring examples of charismatic leadership.

The biggest challenge for organizations today is to convert their managers in to leaders. There is a big difference between management and leadership. Managers care about processes, whilst leaders care about the outcomes. A leader always creates informal power (through his ability to influence) in addition to the formal authorities that enable him to lead. A manager on the other hand survives only on the formal authority.

The development path of the managers working in various departments of the Pharma industry is a time-honoured progression, for example, in marketing, a person starts as a sales representative to junior product manager, then to brand manager and then to a marketing manager. Along the way, most of them pick up skills and experience that are required for the job and some of them perform well. But most of them fail when they progress to the point where they need to get the best out of other people. They lack in the quality of influencing people. Instead of leading from the front, they behave like bosses. They fail to motivate and direct their subordinates leading to poor performance and unsatisfactory results. Hence, leaders are required to guide and motivate people towards organization goals.

We always say that 'Leaders are born and not made' but because of the revolution in management in the recent past, we have to say that 'Leaders can also be made'. Many attributes make a good leader that can be learnt and practiced like self-confidence that is the key to leadership. As Mahatma Gandhi rightly said, 'The history of the world is with full of examples where many people rose to leadership with the sheer force of self-confidence'. Following are some of the tips for effective leadership:

Develop a Clear Vision

'Vision is the art of making future present.' Vision is the basic attribute of leadership. The leader must recognize the need for change and crucially help others understand this need. A leader must listen to his followers. Any vision has to be attractive, inspirational and motivational, and must clearly guide the team's behaviour going forward.

Develop Commitment and Trust

Commitment and trust go hand-in-hand. Without trust there is no commitment (and without commitment there is no success). Trust requires openness and honesty. Trust will enable a leader to maximize his team's performance by identifying strengths, dealing with weaknesses and building individual confidence. A leader must express his or her confidence in their team regularly and credibly, all of which, needs strong communications skills.

Use Symbolic Action

All effective leaders lead by example. Having set the vision, it is important to act in accordance with it. Everything the leader does and says has a symbolic significance. They need to avoid a descent into meaningless psychobabble. A leader must be aware of the power of words and should employ colourful and emotive language lacking metaphors, symbols and slogans.

Empower Employees

Empowering employees is what most managers know they have to do to become leaders but where most fail. It is not about avoiding the use of power—leaders must lead, not duck responsibility. If a team has adopted a vision, then an autocratic style will not be necessary, because each member of the team will know their role in fulfilling the vision. By creating such fully participating partners, the leader steers the team towards fulfilling the vision. The level of consultation and freedom will vary according to the needs of an organization, the experience of the team and their competence as they relate to the specific challenges it faces. The good leader will switch between different styles to meet different challenges—but individuals within the team will always feel the ownership of the desire to achieve the vision.

Clarify Roles and Responsibilities

This is very different from job description. Clarifying roles and responsibilities is about the roles in fulfilling the vision of a leader. A team member, who is clear about his role, will be confident and effective in delivering it. Too often we come across members of the Pharma marketing departments who cannot put into words their own expected contribution towards the success of the organization, over and above the merely operational elements. If they cannot express it, then clearly they cannot deliver it!

So it is important to create ownership not just for every objective, but even for every action and activity.

APPROACHES TO LEADERSHIP

The theory of leadership theory has evolved over the period through a number of different approaches. This progression is inevitable, and is a reflection of the changes in culture, so it will continue. But there is agreement that good leaders demonstrate transformational leadership rather than transactional leadership. Good leadership is no longer defined by *traits*, but rather by behaviours.

Transactional leadership is the classic leadership style of managers (not really the conventional leadership at all). It relies on extrinsic rewards for control, concentrating on process and creating bureaucratic behaviour.

The transformational leader does 'exactly what it says on the tin'—they transform and motivate followers by making them more aware of the importance of outcomes for the task they undertake, by inducing them to transcend their own self-interest for the sake of the team or the organization, and by activating their higher order needs—such as belonging, esteem and self-actualization.

SALIENT FEATURES

Following are the salient features of leadership:

1. Leadership is a process of influence exercised by the leader on the followers
2. Leadership involves the existence of followers

3. A leader and his followers make efforts to complete the common goals in the interests of the individuals as well as a group as a whole
4. Leadership is an ongoing process and it requires regular communication between the leader and his group
5. Leadership is related to a particular situation

A particular style of leadership may be successful in one situation but may fail in other situation

DIFFERENCE BETWEEN LEADERSHIP AND MANAGEMENT

The following table differentiates between leadership and management:

S. no.	Leadership	Management
1	It does not require managerial position	It requires managerial position
2	It mainly involves direction	It involves all the five functions
3	It is based on the acceptance of followers	It is based on the authority of positions
4	It is a narrow term	It is a wider term

IMPORTANCE OF LEADERSHIP

The importance of leadership is discussed below:

1. A leader interprets and explains the objectives of the group to his followers. As a result, the members of the group know the targets to be achieved and their individual contribution to achieve the common goal.
2. A good leader motivates his followers and creates an environment conducive to hard work.
3. A leader builds dedication and loyalty among the people in a group. He develops mutual cooperation and self-discipline among people. Thus, he helps to build morale of his followers.

4. The leader creates team spirit and coordination among members of the group. He resolves internal conflicts and differences of opinion.
5. Nowadays frequent changes are required in the structure and working of an organization. But change creates uncertainty and inconvenience. Therefore, people tend to resist change. A good leader persuades people to accept and carry out the desired changes.
6. A leader serves as the representative of his followers. He protects their interests and serves as their guardian.

QUALITIES OF A GOOD LEADER

A good leader should possess the following qualities:

1. He must have good health and sound physique so he can bear the stress and strain of leadership.
2. He should be intelligent enough to think logically and analyse the situation accurately.
3. He should have an emotional stability and a cool temperament. He should have a mature outlook.
4. He should have an open mind and should be able to look at problems from all angles.
5. He must have self-confidence and a strong will power.
6. He should have full knowledge of the work being performed by his subordinates.
7. He should be able to communicate clearly and precisely. This is necessary for persuading and convincing people.
8. He should be able to anticipate or visualize the future course of events. He needs a sound judgment and the ability to take the right decisions at the right time.
9. He should have a sense of responsibility. He should be trustworthy so that the subordinates can depend on him.
10. He must be able to win the confidence and loyalty of people. He should have the capacity to create team spirit among his followers.

Points to Ponder

1. Leadership is lifting the vision of man to higher sights, raising his performance to higher standards and building a man's personality beyond its normal limitations.
2. The salient features of leadership are as follows:
   a. Leadership is a process of influence exercised by the leader on his followers.
   b. Leadership involves the existence of followers.
   c. A leader and his followers make efforts to complete the common goals in the interests of the individuals as well as a group as a whole.
   d. Leadership is an ongoing process and it requires regular communication between the leader and his group.
   e. Leadership is related to a particular situation.
3. The main difference between leadership and management is that leadership does not require managerial position while the management requires the position.

 **Self-Assessment Exercises**

1. What do you mean by leadership?
2. Mention the qualities of a good leader.
3. Differentiate between leadership and management.
4. Explain the term *leadership*. Write its salient features and its importance. Describe the qualities of a good leader.

Administrative Management

INTRODUCTION

Management is a technique using which the purposes and the objectives of a particular group are determined, classified and effectuated. Management is forecasting, planning, organizing, commanding, coordinating and controlling. It is a social process entailing responsibility for the efficient planning and regulation of the operations of an enterprise.

ELEMENTS OF MANAGEMENT

The elements of management are the sole source of power and inspiration with the help of which all activities of the enterprise move and remain in purposeful positive action.

The six elements of management are as follows:

1. Determine objectives—planning

2. To setup an organization and assign responsibility—organizing
3. To interrelate and direct activities—command
4. To set standards and effect control accordingly—controlling
5. To motivate and socialize the employee groups—motivation
6. To cause cooperation among various factors of production and organized groups of personnel—coordination

Planning

Definition

Planning is an intellectual process, a conscious determination of the courses of action, basing the decisions on purpose, facts and considered estimates. Planning is deciding in advance what is to be done, when, where, how and by whom it is to be done. It is a mental process requiring the use of intellect, foresight, imagination and a sound judgment. It is concerned with the setting of organizational goals or objectives and determining the approach through which the goals and objectives are to be accomplished.

Elements of Planning

Planning coordinates the activities of the organization towards the objectives that are defined and agreed upon. The following are the important elements of planning:

    a. Objectives
    b. Policies
    c. Procedure
    d. Programme
    e. Budget

Objectives: The objectives determine the goals on the basis of which the action of an enterprise is projected. Goals are the foundation over which the whole structure of the plan is built.

Policies: Policies provide guidance to the subordinates and enlist their cooperation on the guided lines. Policies may either be written or oral but they must be stated in clear terms so that nothing should be left for interpretation, sometimes creating a very funny situation. Policies are mini plans since they also set out certain course of action to be followed for the attainment of the objectives.

Procedure: Procedure charts out the specific manner in which the actions are to be taken and the work accomplished. Procedures thus provide a charted course of action, deviation from which may be termed as setting an unhealthy trend and undisciplined action on the part of the subordinates. Procedures are generally rigid and gain a permanency during the course of time, while policies are flexible and are subject to change according to the demand of the situation and time.

Programme: Programmes are meant for assembling all plans into one in a workable form for a complete and an orderly course of action. Programmes may both be for repetitive and nonrepetitive actions. Repetitive action programmes are termed as *routine planning* while nonrepetitive action programmes are classified as *creative planning*.

Budget: Budgets too are part of plans. Budgets are said to be the statement of numerical facts designed to attain the desired results. Man hours, finances, production units, etc., are a few of the items that can only be stated in numbers. They are analysed and then plans are formulated with an aim to attain expected results.

Importance of Planning

Planning is the foundation of the most successful action of an enterprise. Without effective planning it is difficult to anticipate future uncertain events. Planning brings efficiency, stability and orderliness in managerial actions and decisions. It is a rational approach towards all the activities of a manager. The important benefits of planning are as follows:

1. **Improves competitive strength:** By proper planning the organization has a competitive edge. Planning enables to anticipate the tastes and fashions of the people, the technological changes, changes in work methods, etc.
2. **Improves motivation:** Planning improves the motivation of workers since they know exactly what is expected of them.
3. **Encourages innovations and creativity:** Planning generates thinking among managers, encourages them to come up with new ideas. It creates a positive attitude among the mangers.
4. **Planning offsets future uncertainty and change:** Without planning, a manger is forced to react to situations or problems. Planning permits a manager to act with initiative and to create situations to the organization's advantage.
5. **Planning helps in management by defining objectives:** Once the objectives are laid out, all efforts are directed towards those desired and well-defined objectives.
6. **Better coordination:** Well-defined objectives, well-developed programs and procedures lead to better coordination.
7. **Economy in operation:** Planning paves the way for proper utilization of resources. It develops the best and the most economical way of doing things in an organization.
8. **Helps in control:** With good control, effectiveness and smoothness is achieved.
9. **Executive development:** Planning helps in executive development.

Steps in Planning

Following are the important steps in the process of planning:

1. **Determination of objectives:** The first step in planning is to determine the enterprise objectives. These objectives set the pattern for the proposed course of action and shape the future policies.
2. **Establishment of planning premises:** The second step in planning is to establish the planning premises. Premises are planning assumptions, the future setting where the plan is to be commenced. Thus, it is a forecast of those business conditions under which a plan is to operate.
3. **Determination of alternative courses:** The third step in planning is to search for and examine the alternative courses of action. There is hardly a plan for which a number of alternatives cannot be found. In business, there exist a number of alternative courses of action for achieving the desired objectives. All possible alternatives should be found for their comparison and analytical evaluation.
4. **Evaluation of alternatives and selection of the course of action:** Following is the evaluation of alternative courses of action, and selecting the suitable and the best course of action.
5. **Preparation of derivative plans:** Formulating the derivative plans in support of the basic plan is the next step in the planning process. There are subplans or departmental plans. The basic plan prepared for the whole enterprise cannot be effectively operated in the absence of such plans. So within the framework of a primary or a basic plan, derivate plans are developed.
6. **Timing and sequence of operations:** Timing is an essential consideration in planning. After developing the plan, the subplans, deadlines for starting and finishing the plan should be fixed for each plan. Scheduling is very useful not only in the areas of sales and production but also in other functional areas.

7. **Securing participation of employees:** The execution of a successful plan depends to a large extent upon the loyalty and sincerity of the subordinates. It can be secured only when they are actively involved in planning. Plans must be communicated, explained and consulted thoroughly.

8. **Considering the strategy:** Strategy has a significant contribution towards the execution of a plan. So, a consideration of different strategies becomes an integral part of the planning process. A suitable strategy should be planned and followed for the success of planning.

9. **Providing follow-up to the proposed course of action:** Finally, a provision for follow-up measures should be made for the time when a plan is put into action. In the context of the current problems and situations, necessary adjustments in plans become imperative, so necessary provisions should be made for it beforehand.

Limitations of Planning

The following are the obstacles to the process of planning:

1. **A costly proposition:** Planning involves cost. It involves a loss of time, money and labour.

2. **Planning fails with big and regular changes:** Usually plans are made as flexible as possible so that they are adaptable to changes. But still the possibility of flexibility is very limited. Regular changes may waste the plan.

3. **Inelastic administration:** Planning beforehand makes the administration inelastic to a certain degree as people stop thinking and imagining. They are made to work just like a machine with no chance for them to think and rethink beyond a certain limit.

4. **Unreliable estimates:** Estimates are based on facts, data and information. Human prejudices cannot be ruled out while planning. Hence, this leads us to a conclusion that estimates based on the so called reliable data are really not that reliable.

5. **Initiative, originality and individuality yield to planned efforts:** Well planned out programs, policies and procedures lead to loss of initiative and original approach to the problem on the part of the employees. Individuality of the employees is lost because they are not a part of planning.

ORGANIZING

Definition

Organizing is a process of dividing and combining efforts of a working group to make the joint efforts more productive and fruitful. Organizing establishes a pattern of relationships among the efforts to be put, jobs to be done and work to be performed. Organizing creates teamwork. It is a framework for the fulfilment of common objectives.

An effective and efficient organizing process increases managerial efficiency and facilitates coordination. It ensures an optimum use of human efforts by balancing various activities. It provides for adequate training and helps in identifying the defects. It consolidates growth and expansion of the enterprise and discourages corrupt practices.

Organizing includes activities like grouping, assigning activities, allocation of duties, and responsibilities and delegation of authority in order to facilitate a smooth functioning of the organization.

Elements of organization: Organizing involves sharing the duties and responsibilities within a broad framework. There are three important elements of an organization. They are as follows:

1. Division of work
2. Interrelationship
3. Individual performances

Division of Work

An effective division of work between personnel selected to do a particular job(s) is the foremost function of an organization. If it is effective, it will bear fruits and the desired results may be achieved.

Interrelationship

Establishment of interrelationships between jobs, duties, responsibilities and authority either in a formal or in an informal way is also a primary function of an organization without which nothing tangible could be achieved.

Individual performances: Individuals do the assigned jobs. Whether an individual or a group of individuals is doing the assigned duties and carrying out the responsibilities in accordance with the instructions or not is to be observed and any deviation should have to be reported for an adequate action against the erring group or individual. The organization ensures it by preparing a scheme of inspection and supervision. It also makes one answerable for his work and conduct. It also aims at the strict adherence of the rules, etc., framed for the purpose. Unless it is done the very purpose of organization will be defeated.

Types of Organization (Patterns)

There are certain patterns of organizing the personnel in the organization. They are as follows:

1. Line organization
   a. Pure line organization
   b. Departmental line organization
2. Functional organization

Line Organization

It is also known as *vertical organization* or *departmental organization* or *scalar organization*. This organization is based on the superior–subordinate relationship. When a superior delegates authority to a subordinate, he in turn does so to another subordinate thus forming a line from the top to bottom of the organizational structure. The line of authority is known as *line authority*.

Pure line organization

Pure line organization is simple in form and seen in small units that produce only one item and where activities can be grouped according to their nature. In this organization, the activities at any one level are the same with each man performing the same type of work and the division is only for direction and control.

Departmental line organization

In departmental line organization, the business unit is divided into departments that are headed by department heads. These heads enjoy equal status and work independently. A department head receives orders from the general manager and passes them on to his immediate subordinate. The whole organization is under the charge of a general manager.

Advantages of Line Organization

Line organization is easy to establish and very simple for the employees. It leads to better coordination and stability. It ensures strong discipline because of the unity of command. The authorities of various personnel are well-defined hence, no conflict in their powers and authority. This type of organization is elastic and changes can be easily incorporated in the organization. Due to the unification of authority and responsibility, quick decisions can be taken.

Disadvantages of Line Organization

All the decisions are taken by the single boss and the success and growth of the whole department depends on his abilities only. The boss is overloaded with work and he may not direct the efforts of his subordinates properly. This type of organization suffers from lack of specialized skill of experts and inadequacy of a communication. There is a scope of favouritism by the boss. It is not suitable for large scale organizations. Creating so many departments becomes a problem.

Functional Organization

In functional organization, the whole task of management is classified according to the type of work involved. The normal operations performed in a business house are production, research, personnel, purchasing, finance, etc. These activities are assigned to various departments and functional experts are appointed to look after those activities.

Advantages of Functional Organization

It ensures higher degree of efficiency as the workers get instructions from experts and they have to perform a limited number of tasks. It ensures a greater division of labour. This type of organization is flexible and changes can be incorporated without disturbing the whole organization. It facilitates mass production through specialization and standardization of operations.

Disadvantages of Functional Organization

The disadvantages of functional organization are as follows:

Conflict in authority

This authority relationship violates the principle of 'unity of command'. It creates several bosses instead of a one line authority. It creates conflict for workers with regard to their loyalty to one particular authority. Their loyalty thus is divided.

Discipline is slackened

Due to the decentralization of control and the division of loyalty of the subordinates, the discipline of the enterprise slackens.

Lack of coordination

The use of several functional experts in an organization creates the problem of coordination.

Complication procedure

Functional organization is too complicated in operation because it entails the division of functions into a number of subfunctions.

Conflict in foremen

Functional organization may also lead to conflict among foremen or bosses of equal rank. This conflict mars their zeal and initiative. They work only as a machine in a routine manner. It harms the efficiency of subordinates also.

Impracticable and expensive

This pattern of organization is quite impracticable and expensive also. Therefore, small organizations cannot follow it.

Importance of Organization

The success of an organization depends on how the process of organizing has been carried out. The whole structure of management is built on the foundation of a well-planned organization. A well-planned organization has the following benefits:

1. It makes the management simple and efficient, and accelerates the progress.
2. It encourages specialization and promotes constructive thinking among the employees.
3. It increases productivity and boosts the confidence of the employees.

STAFFING

Definition

Staffing is the procurement of efficient people for the organization. It is a process of matching the jobs with the individuals. It is a function of manning the jobs. After organizing the enterprise, management is in a position to know the actual manpower requirement. Then by means of staffing, the management recruits, selects and trains the employees.

Staffing is a continuous process because existing employees may leave the organization and new employees may join it. Hence, a business organization has to recruit additional manpower to meet the growing requirements of the organization. Staffing is related to the following functions:

1. Forecasting the manpower requirements
2. Establishing job specifications and job descriptions
3. Determining the sources of recruitment
4. Recruitment
5. Selection and placement
6. Training and educating the employees
7. Coordinating, promotions, transfers etc.
8. Maintenance of necessary records for the efficient manpower management
9. Developing and following sound personnel policies

Importance of Staffing

The following points discuss the importance of staffing:

1. Staffing injects life into the organization by providing the right person for every job. The effectiveness of directing and the control functions also depend on staffing.

2. Employees in the organization are the most valuable asset of an organization. The quality of human assets largely determines the success and growth of an organization. Hence, staffing helps to build human resources as assets.

3. Staffing helps to build a healthy organization where the job performance and satisfaction for every employee is high. It identifies people with necessary skills and attitudes, induces them to join the organization, and ensures their continuous cooperation and association with the organization.

DIRECTING

Directing is a managerial function performed by managers at all levels of the organization. Managers have the responsibility of not only planning and organizing the operations but also of guiding and directing the subordinates.

Definition

Directing consists of the processes and techniques utilized in issuing instructions and making certain that operations are carried out as originally planned. In simple words, directing is guiding the subordinates in their work. Direction is a complex function that includes all those activities that are designed to encourage subordinates to work effectively and efficiently in both the short and the long run.

The function of direction has three essential components as discussed below:

1. **Function of command:** It is the issuing of instructions and orders.
2. **Guiding the people:** It is the responsibility of a manager to guide and teach the subordinates the proper methods of work.
3. **Supervising the people:** The management has to supervise the subordinates to ensure that their performance conforms to the plans. Directing is an executive function of guiding and observing subordinates.

Directing is the interpersonal aspect of managing where subordinates are led to understand and contribute effectively to the attainment of enterprise objectives.

Nature of Direction

The function of directing has the following characteristics:

1. It is an executive function that extends from the top to the bottom of the organization. It involves framing the scope, giving orders and instructions, and providing dynamic leadership.
2. Directing is a continuous activity. It is the basis of all future activities.
3. Directing is all pervading. It is not only concerned with issuing orders and instructions but also communication, supervision, motivation, and involves how an employee can contribute to the common objectives of the organization.
4. Directing is to have direct contact with the people. Since directing is related to the subordinates, it thus requires a direct contact with them.

Principles of Direction

There are certain principles of direction that should be observed by the management while directing the subordinates. These principles can be divided into two parts as follows:

1. Order
2. Supervision

Order

Order is a basic tool utilized by a manager to direct his subordinates. It is also called as *commanding*. An order initiates, modifies or stops an activity. A manager can by his order motivate, inspire or discourage his subordinates in their duties.

Definition

An order is a command by a superior requiring a subordinate to act or refrain from acting in a given circumstance. It is usually an instruction given by a superior to his subordinate. A direct line of command is required for giving orders. An order implies to do or not to do a certain thing in a given circumstance. An order is enforceable. A subordinate can be punished by his boss for not carrying out his orders.

Characteristics of a Good Order

A good order has the following characteristics:

1. The order must be reasonable and capable of immediate compliance by the subordinates.
2. The order must be compatible with the purposes and the objectives of the enterprise.
3. The order should be intelligible, complete and clear.
4. The tone of the order should be appropriate. It should stimulate ready acceptance.
5. It must specify the deadline of completing the instruction.

Techniques of Orders

Following are the important techniques of issuing orders:

1. **General or specific orders:** An order can be related to a general matter or a particular issue specifically. Whether an order is general or specific will depend on the preference of the superior and his ability to foresee the circumstances.
2. **Written or oral orders:** The written orders are more accurate, intelligible and well-considered. The subordinates get sufficient time to understand the order. It fixes the responsibility and accountability also. But written orders cannot be revised as oral orders. Moreover, they are expensive and time consuming and they are inflexible. For routine matters, oral orders serve the purpose. In emergencies also, oral orders can be used.
3. **Conformality:** The orders should be normal, informal and courteous. This type of orders motivates the subordinates to do their best.
4. **Timing:** The orders should be issued timely and should suit the situations and the circumstances. Only then can the enterprise and the subordinates achieve good results.
5. **Follow-up orders:** After the orders have been issued, a manager should find out whether his orders have been carried out or not. If necessary, he may cause some changes to his instructions.

SUPERVISING

Supervision is overseeing the subordinates at work. It is an important part of direction for every manager. It is observing to see if the subordinates are working according to the plans and policies of the organization, keeping the time schedule and also helps in solving their problems.

Definition

Supervision refers to the direct and immediate guidance and control of the managers over the subordinates in the performance of their task. Thus, supervision is the direction, guidance and the control of workforce to monitor whether they are working according to the plan, policy, program, instruction and keeping the time schedule. Supervision also helps the subordinates in their working and if they are in need of help of any kind in accomplishing their assigned tasks.

Functions of a supervisor

The supervisor has to perform the following important functions:

1. To schedule work for its even and steady flow
2. To assign work to different workers according to their abilities.
3. To provide proper working environment to the workers
4. To provide leadership to the workers
5. To elicit their willingness to work for the achievement of the group objectives
6. To control the performance of the workers
7. To motivate the workers by giving them various incentives
8. To take corrective action, whenever necessary

Qualities of a good supervisor

A good supervisor should possess the following qualities:

1. He should have a human approach to human problems. His attitude towards his subordinates should be sympathetic in dealing with their problems.
2. He should be mentally alert and he should never be caught unaware.
3. He should be competent to take quick decisions.
4. He should be honest in dealing with the subordinates so as to leave no scope in the minds of his subordinates about his integrity.
5. He should have patience and should not lose temper easily.
6. He should not depend upon his formal authority too much.
7. He should be a good leader so as to guide the subordinates towards organizational goals.
8. He should have sufficient technical skills to perform his job, to supervise and to get better quality output from the subordinates.

Requisites (essential qualities) of effective supervision

Following are the essential qualities of effective supervision:

1. **Knowledge of work and techniques of the supervision:** For a supervisor to be effective, he must have substantial knowledge of the different techniques of supervision, of machines, equipments, tools and materials that are under his control.
2. **Knowledge of rules and regulations:** A supervisor should be familiar with the organizational rules and regulations that are related to his organization. He should possess the knowledge of various labour laws that affect his organization.

3. **Skill in instructing:** A supervisor should have knowledge to issue instructions to his subordinates. Hence, he should have good communication skills.
4. **Skill in leading:** A supervisor should be a good leader. He should be able to guide the subordinates and promote harmonious relationship among them.
5. **Skill in dealing with current problems:** The supervisor is expected to make the best possible use of the resources available to him—men, material, machine and money.
6. **Human orientation:** A supervisor should treat his subordinates with equality and motivate them to achieve good results. He should adopt a helping attitude towards his subordinates.

Importance of a Supervisor

The ability of the workers and the success of an organization depends upon the supervisor's ability to plan and schedule within the framework of the organization. A position of a supervisor is very important in an organization because he is a conduit between the management and the workers. He functions as a specialist in human relations in the complete organizational structure. Because of his peculiar but significant position, he influences the work environment. He also influences the attitude, behaviour, conduct and even cooperative efforts of the workers in the organization. He is a morale booster. Hence, it is well said that 'even the best supervisor is no substitute for poor principles and practices in managing workers'. Thus it is the supervisor who brings either success or failure to an organization.

CONTROLLING

Definition

Control is checking the current performance against the predetermined standards contained in the plans with a view to ensure adequate progress and satisfactory performance. The objects of control are to point out the weakness and the error in order to rectify them and prevent occurrence. It operates on everything i.e. things, people and action.

The important features of controlling are:
1. It is an important managerial function
2. It is a step to ensure the performance according to the plans
3. It involves the management of actual performance and recording the deviations
4. It involves the preparation of plans, setting goals and objectives, and setting the standards
5. Controlling is positive and corrective, providing guidance for future steps. It is neither an order nor a command

Salient features (characteristics) of controlling

The salient features of control are as follows:
1. **An end itself:** Control is an end function of the process of management. It judges the performance of the different factors engaged in the attainment of the said objectives.
2. **A forward looking process:** Even though it lives in the present, it is related to the future. It is the present over which a control is exercised with a view to guard the future. Loss, deviation from plans, policies, programs and schedules, etc., are to be guarded against.

3. **A dynamic process:** Control is a dynamic process. Since the management functions are flexible and are required to adjust according to the needs and situations arising from time to time, the controlling process also acquires a flexible character.

4. **A continuous process:** Control is a continuous activity. It does not stop. A business manager should continuously monitor his organization for a steady development.

5. **Operation at all levels:** Controlling is done at all the levels of management. The chain of control is predetermined that runs through the whole organization.

6. **Identified with individuals:** The individuals in an organization are in charge of various operations and they are held responsible for any shortcomings and thus control is exercised over individuals performing their duties in an organization.

Steps in the Process of Control

The process of control can be split into various well-defined steps. The important elements of this process are as follows:

1. **Well-defined objectives and goals:** The organization has to define its objectives and goals first. The goals should be split into subgoals at the department level. The planned goals or objectives of an organization serve as a standard for performance measurement.

2. **Determination of strategic point of control:** The responsibility centres should be selected and fixed. In order to make the control process effective, the management should concentrate upon strategic points only.

3. **A predetermined criterion:** In this stage, the standards are established against which the actual results can be measured. Standards provide a way of stating what should be accomplished. These standards can be in the terms of money, time, physical units or some index. But there should be specific units so that comparison between the standard and the actual performance can be judged.

4. **Determination of controllable cost and control period:** A good control is one that establishes strategic points where corrective action will be the cheapest, the easiest and most effective.

5. **Strengthening the organization:** The process of control should be such that it overcomes the weakness and deviations, and establishes corrective steps that strengthen the organization.

6. **Measurement of performance:** It is the evaluation of actual performance. It involves the performance of the management with respect to work in terms of control standards and communicating to the concerned person the reason behind the deviations and then taking corrective actions. The measurement of performance must be clear, simple, rational, relevant and reliable. It must be understandable and inviting attention.

7. **Comparison of actual performance with standards:** This step helps to determine the extent of mistakes and enables a manager to predict the future results. Since all activities yield some variation, it is necessary to determine the limits within which this variation can be held and still be considered to be in control. When adequate standards are developed, it is very simple to compare the results of any major variations. Comparison of the performance can be done by means of control charts, pictorial presentation of data, ratios, indices and averages.

8. **Correction of deviations:** The final step is to correct deviations. The purpose of comparison of the planned with the actual performance is to make necessary corrections. The corrective measures may be based on any one of the following:

a. Review of plans and goals
b. Change in the assignment
c. Change in the existing techniques of direction and control
d. Change in the organizational structure
e. Incorporating new facilities.
9. **Review of control system:** It is necessary that periodically the process and procedure of control should be re-examined and modifications made according to the new plans and goals to fit realities as conditions change.

Elements of a Good Control system

The necessity, size and nature of the enterprise decide the control system on which depends the element of control. The following are the elements of a good management controlling system:

1. The control system should be according to the
   a. requirement,
   b. size,
   c. nature and
   d. necessity of the enterprise.
2. The system should be capable of detecting the deviations, etc., quickly and correctly.
3. The system should be flexible enough to incorporate the future changes, improvements, etc., in the system without much dislocation.
4. The system should be capable of defining the exceptions, if any, as clearly as possible.
5. The system should be objective oriented and should be in accordance with the organizational structure, plan, policies and programmes.
6. It should be simple and easy to follow.
7. It should be economical.

Points to Ponder

1. Management is a technique using which the purposes and the objectives of a particular group are determined, classified and effectuated.
2. The elements of management are the sole source of power and inspiration. The various elements of management are as follows:
   a. Planning
   b. Organizing
   c. Staffing
   d. Directing
   e. Supervision
   f. Controlling

Self-Assessment Exercises

1. Define the term *control*.
2. Explain the steps involved in the planning process.
3. Define order. Explain the characteristics of a good order.
4. Explain the limitations of planning.
5. Explain the requirements of an adequate control system.
6. Explain the term *organization*. Why is it regarded as the foundation upon which the whole structure of the management is built.
7. Explain the benefits of organizing.
8. Explain the scope of staffing.
9. Explain the direction function of management. What are the elements of the direction process?
10. 'Plans are selected courses along which the management desires to coordinate group action'. Discuss.
11. What do you mean by supervision? Discuss the position and importance of a supervisor in an industrial organization.
12. 'Managerial planning seeks to achieve a coordinated structure of operations'. Discuss.
13. What are the basic elements of control? Discuss its elements. How do managers exercise control?
14. Explain the concept staffing. State its salient features and its significance.

Managerial Control

INTRODUCTION

Control is one of the important functions of the management to measure progress. It is a very important process through which the management ensures that the actual activities conform to the planned activities. It involves three steps: establishing standards, comparing the actual performance against the standards and taking corrective actions.

According to E.F.L. Brech, 'Control is checking current performance against predetermined standards contained in the plans, with a view to ensuring adequate progress and satisfactory performance'. According to George R. Terry, 'Controlling is determining what is being accomplished, that is, evaluating the performance and if necessary applying corrective measures so that the performance takes place according to plans'.

TECHNIQUES OF CONTROL

Modern business enterprises use a large number of techniques for managerial control. These may be grouped into two categories as follows:

1. Traditional or conventional techniques such as budgetary control, ratio analysis, statistical data and reports, marginal costing, break-even analysis, standard costing, etc.
2. Modern or contemporary techniques such as management audit, PERT, CPM and management information system.

Some of the control systems like critical path method (CPM) or programme evaluation and review technique (PERT) are the techniques for production control, a specific functional area of an organization; whereas budgets, ratio analysis, break-even analysis and management audits are the control systems for the overall performance of the organization.

The different techniques of managerial control are discussed as under:

Budget

A budget is a plan expressed in quantitative and monetary terms. Budgets need to be prepared and approved in advance, before the period in which they are to be used. A budget is an estimate of future needs, arranged according to an orderly basis covering some or all the activities of an enterprise for a definite period of time. The Institute of Cost and Management Accountants of England has defined budget as a 'financial and/or a quantitative statement  prepared prior to a definite period of time of the policy to be pursued during that period for the purpose of obtaining a given objective'. A budget is an important device for managerial control. It provides a standard by which actual operations can be compared and variations can be measured and corrected.

A budget can be prepared for an entire organization or any department, sales territory, division, or for a significant activity such as the production and launch of a specific product.

Characteristics of a budget

1. It is prepared in advance and is derived from the long-term strategy of the organization.
2. It relates to the future period for which the objectives or goals have already been laid down.
3. It is expressed in quantitative form, physical or monetary units, or both.
4. Different types of budgets are prepared for different purpose, e.g. sales budget, production budget, administrative expense budget, raw material budget, etc. All these sectional budgets are later integrated into a master budget that represents the overall plan of the organization.

Advantages of budgets

A budget helps an organization in many ways:

1. It brings efficiency and improvement in the working of the organization.
2. It is a way of communicating the plans to the various units of the organization. By establishing the divisional, departmental and sectional budgets, the exact responsibilities can be assigned.
3. It is a way of motivating employees to achieve the goals set by the organization.
4. It serves as a benchmark for controlling the ongoing operations.

5. It helps in developing a team spirit, where participation in budgeting is encouraged.
6. It helps in reducing wastage and losses by revealing them in time for corrective action.
7. It serves as a basis for evaluating the performance of managers.
8. In short, for an organization, budgets are a multipurpose management tool supporting planning, control, coordination, communication, performance evaluation and motivation.

Types of Budgets

The different types of budgets are as follows:

Sales budget

The sales budget expresses a realistic sales forecast. It includes a forecast of the total sales during a period expressed in money and/or quantities. The forecast relates to the total volume of sales and also its break up, productwise and areawise. The responsibility for making the sales budget lies with the sales manager. The preparation of the sales budget is the key factor in any business enterprise.

The following factors are considered for preparing the sales budget:

1. Past sales figures and trends
2. Salesman's estimates
3. General economic conditions
4. Orders at hand
5. Seasonal fluctuations
6. Competition
7. Market research
8. Statistical methods (correlation analysis and examination of trends)
9. Sales force opinions
10. Government's control and policy

Production budget

Production budget includes a forecast of the output for a period analysed according to (1) products, (2) manufacturing departments and (3) period of production. It is generally based on the sales budget as it is the responsibility of the production department to schedule its production according to the sales forecast. It is prepared by the production manager by taking into account the following major factors:

1. The sales budget
2. Plant capacity
3. Inventory policy
4. Availability of raw materials, labour, power, etc.

Raw materials and purchasing budget

The purchasing budget is defined in two ways. The materials usage budget is expressed in quantities, whereas the materials purchases budget is expressed in both ways, i.e. quantitative and financial. The materials budget helps in scheduling the purchase of materials to produce a given volume of output, during a particular period, to meet the requirements of the customers during the period.

Factors influencing purchasing budgets are as follows:

1. Production requirements
2. Planning stock levels
3. Inventory control systems
4. Trends of material prices

Labour budget
Labour budget is both quantitative and financial. This is influenced by the following factors:

1. Production requirements
2. Man-hours available
3. Grades of labour required
4. Wage rates (union agreements)
5. Need for incentives

Cash budget
Cash budget defines a cash plan for a specific period of time. It summarizes the monthly receipts and payments. Hence, it highlights the monthly surpluses and deficits of the actual cash. Its main uses are as follows:

1. To maintain control over a firm's cash requirements, e.g. stock and debtors
2. To enable a firm to take precautionary measures and arrange in advance for the investment and loan facilities whenever the cash surpluses or deficits arise
3. To show the feasibility of the management's plans in cash terms
d. To illustrate the financial impact of changes in the management policy like the change of credit terms offered to customers.

Personnel budget
Personnel budget sets out manpower requirements of all departments for the budget period. It expresses labour requirements in terms of labour hours, cost and grade of workers. It helps the personnel manager in providing the required labour to the departments either by transfers or by new recruitments.

Administrative budget
Administrative budgets include the estimates of administrative expenses like expenses of all salaries of the managerial personnel. Such expenses form a significant part of the total cost of production. Preparation of this budget will help in keeping the administrative costs under control.

Selling and distribution expenses budget
The expenses budget includes the estimates of all the items of expenditure and promotion, maintenance and distribution of the finished products. The costs are divided into fixed, variable and semivariable categories, and estimated on the basis of past experiences. The various items of expenditure include sales office rent, salaries, depreciation and miscellaneous expenses, advertising, commission, bad debts, travelling expenses, etc.

Master budget
The Institute of Cost and Management Accountants, England has defined the master budget as the summary budget incorporating its component functional budgets, which is finally approved, adopted and employed. Thus, a master budget is prepared to incorporate all the functional budgets. It projects a comprehensive picture of the proposed activities and the anticipated results during the budget period. The master budget must be approved by the top management.

Fixed budgets
The fixed budget remains unchanged, irrespective of the level of activity actually attained. The main purpose of fixed budgeting is to coordinate sectional activities to attain the enterprise objectives. It is prepared for a given level of production and does not take into account the changes in circumstances. It becomes a rigid and unrealistic measuring yardstick in case the level of production actually accomplished does not conform to the one assumed for the purpose of fixed budgeting.

Flexible budget

Flexible budget facilitates the comparison of actual performance with budgeted performance at different volumes of activity. Such a budget is prepared after considering the fixed and the variable elements of cost, and the changes that may be expected for each item at various levels of activity. Flexible budgeting is of great help where it is not possible to predict accurately the sales forecast and where the level of production depends upon the availability of a factor, which is in limited supply.

Budgetary Control

No system of planning can be successful without having an effective and an efficient system of control. Budgeting is closely connected with control. The exercise of control in the organization, with the help of budgets, is known as *budgetary control*. Budgetary control involves the following three steps:

1. Preparation of budgets
2. Continuous comparison of actual results with the planned ones
3. Revision of plans or budgets in the light of changed circumstances

Budgetary control is a useful technique of management control that brings efficiency and economy in the working of the business.

Advantages of budgeting and budgetary control

There are a number of advantages to budgeting and budgetary control. They are as follows below:

1. It compels the management to think about the future, which is one of the most important features of a budgetary planning and control system.
2. It forces the management to look ahead, to set out the detailed plans for achieving the targets, for each department and each manager.
3. It promotes better coordination and communication.
4. It clearly defines the areas of authority and responsibility.
5. It provides a basis for performance appraisal (variance analysis).
6. It enables remedial action to be taken as variances emerge.
7. It motivates the employees by participating in the setting of budgets.
8. It improves the allocation of scarce resources.

Statistical Data and Reports

Statistical data are widely used for the purpose of managerial control. Statistical data may be presented in the form of statistical tables, graphical charts or special reports. The quality of presentation of the essential data will determine their efficiency for the purpose of managerial control.

A report is a form of systematic presentation of the information and statistical data relating to some aspect of the business. It may arise out of the available factual data, through enquiry, investigation or experiment. The information provided by the report may be used for the purpose of managerial control. It will help in knowing whether the policies of the management are being followed and if not, what steps should be taken to implement the same. The task of making reports is generally entrusted to a specialty group who will collect the desired information and present the same in the form of a report.

The pharmaceutical industries are subscribing to the data and reports generated by market research groups like ORG-IMS and many other companies that update pharma industries on the product movements.

Marginal Costing

Marginal costing is a very useful technique that guides the management in pricing, decision-making and assessment of profitability. Marginal costing is an important tool in the hands of the management for exercising cost control. Marginal cost is the amount of money at any given volume of output by which the aggregate cost is changed, if the volume of output is increased or decreased by one unit.

Usefulness of marginal costing

Since marginal costing is based on variable costs, the responsibility for controlling variable costs can be assigned to various departments. The reports by various cost centres include only those costs that can be controlled by them. The control of fixed costs is the responsibility of higher level managers.

Marginal costing facilitates the management by exception by focusing their attention to the results that are significantly moving out of control. It also helps the management in evaluating the performance of the individuals responsible for the variable costs. The impact of fixed costs is conveyed to the management in a more meaningful way under marginal costing. This helps the management to ensure better utilization of items that involve fixed expenditure such as plant and machinery, furniture, installation, etc. Finally, marginal costing helps the management in understanding the relationship between profit and the major factors affecting profit so it may exercise control over these factors to achieve higher profits.

Cost–Volume–Profit Analysis

Cost–volume–profit analysis is an attempt to study the relationship between the volume of output, cost incurred for such volume of output, revenue which becomes available from the sale of such output, and the profit likely to be available from producing and selling the output. The management of any organization is interested to know when it will start earning profits, the difference between the total revenue and the total cost. It assists the management in understanding which product is most profitable, what effect will the reduction in the sales price have on the final profit, what effect will a change in volume of the product mix have on the production costs and profits, etc.

The starting point of the cost–volume–profit analysis is the classification of all costs into fixed and variable costs. Fixed costs are those costs, which within certain limits and within a short term period remain fixed irrespective of any change in the volume of output. Fixed costs are also known as *period costs* as they are incurred for a certain period and remain constant even if production is increased or decreased in that period. Rent, salary of employees, taxes, etc., are some examples of fixed costs. On the other hand, variable costs are those costs, which vary in direct proportion and in the same direction as the changes in the volume of output. Material costs, labour costs (if paid on work basis), variable overheads, etc., are some examples of variable costs. The second step in cost–volume–profit analysis is to determine the ratio of the variable costs to the volume of sales. It is important to point out that profit is the function of the interplay of costs, prices and the volume of production. The important technique of cost–volume–profit analysis is the break-even analysis.

Break-Even Analysis

Break-even analysis is very widely used technique to present information to management for understanding the relationship between sales, variable costs, fixed costs and profit existing at different levels of the output. It also enables the management in taking strategic decisions. A concern is said to 'break-even' when it recovers the entire amount of the total costs from its sales revenue. In other words, a 'break-even' stage is reached when the total sales revenue becomes equal to the total costs incurred.

When the concern breaks even, there is neither any profit nor any loss to the concern. The output below the break-even point shows loss, whereas the output above this point shows profit. The break-even level changes with the change in the unit selling price or the unit variable cost or the changes in the fixed costs.

Break-even chart and break-even point

The break-even analysis information is presented in the form of break-even chart. For preparing the same, on X axis volume of output produced and sold is shown, and on Y axis the values of cost and sales are shown. As the fixed costs remain the same, a straight fixed cost line parallel to the X axis is drawn. The total cost line is also drawn for different levels of output, by calculating the variable costs and by adding it to the fixed costs. Similarly for different levels of output, the sales revenue is calculated and by joining the points of such sales values, the sales line is drawn.

The point at which the sales revenue line and total cost line intersects each other is known as the *break-even point*. The output at this point is called as *break-even output*, in terms of sales and volume.

The area below the break-even point is the loss area and the area above the break point is the profit area.

The angle formed by the sales revenue line and the total cost line above the break even point is called as the *angle of incidence*. If the angle is narrow, the profits are small and if the angle is broad, the profit area is large.

The chart also shows the margin of safety. It is in sales value as well as in units. In terms of sales value, it is the difference between the actual sales and the break-even point sales. In terms of units, it is the difference between the actual units sold and the break-even point units. The margin of safety should be large in order to absorb the shock of reduction in the sales.

The following break-even chart will help in understanding the break-even analysis. The data used is as under:

Variable cost per unit

- Materials   Rs 60
- Labour   Rs 40
- Variable expenses   Rs 20
- Fixed cost   Rs 80 000
- Selling price   Rs 200 per unit
- Actual units produced and sold   2200

Break-even chart

The above break-even chart shows that the total cost line and the sales revenue line intersect each other at a point which in terms of units is 1000 units, and in terms of sales value is Rs 2 00 000.

The margin of safety in units is 1200 (2200–1000) and in the sales value is 2 40 000 (4 40 000–2 00 000).

Formula for calculating the Break-Even Point (BEP)

1. BEP in units = fixed costs/contribution per unit.

   (Contribution per unit = selling price per unit – variable costs per unit)
2. BEP in sales value = Fixed costs/P/V ratio. (P/V ratio – contribution/sales × 100).

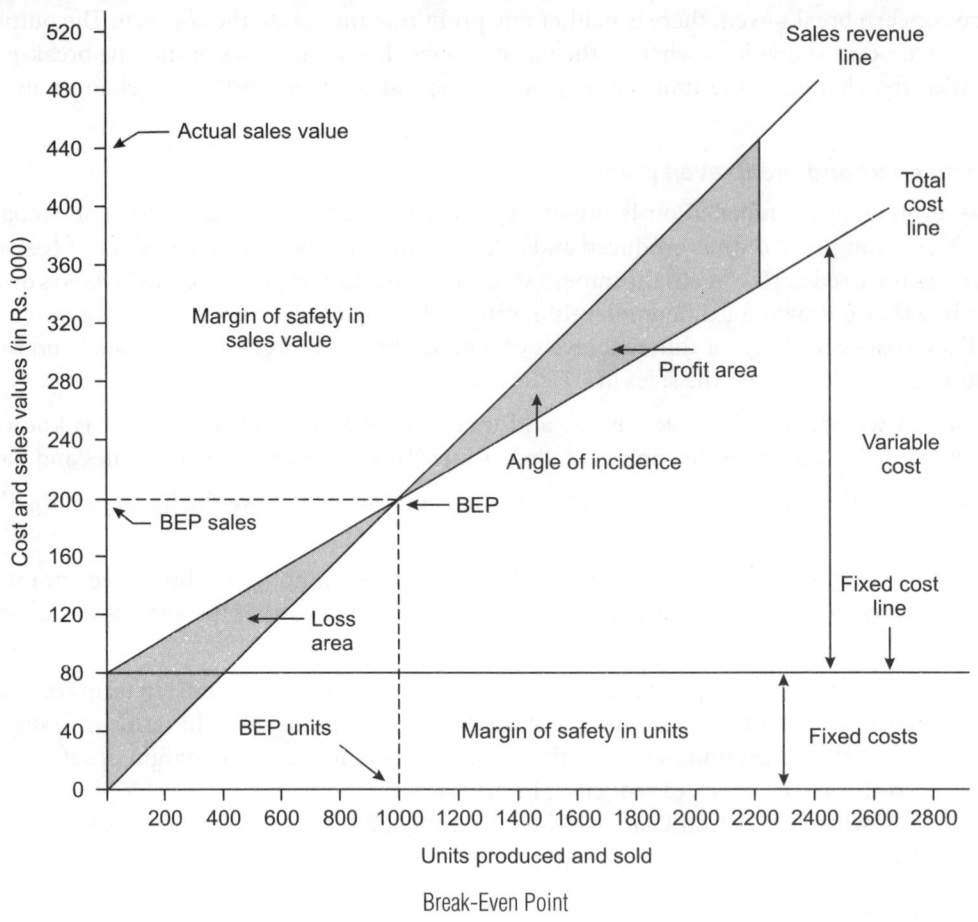

Break-Even Point

Management Audits

A management audit aims at detecting the potential managerial problems that are contributing to the negative growth of the organization. Management audit may be defined as a comprehensive and a constructive review of the performance of the management team of any organization. The management audit locates deficiencies in the performance of various functions and suggests possible improvements. This will help the management in managing the operations of the enterprise under its control in the most efficient manner.

The management audit is a more recent concept. It focuses on results, evaluating the effectiveness and suitability of controls by challenging the underlying rules, procedures and methods. The management audits that are generally performed internally are compliance audits plus the cause-and-effect analysis. When performed correctly, they are potentially the most useful of the evaluation methods because they result in change.

Some of the important characteristics of management audits are as follows:

1. It is conducted internally
2. Auditors challenge the requirements
3. More emphasis is on the results

4. Auditors assesses whether the requirements are effective and suitable

Advantages of management audit

There are many advantages of conducting a management audit. Some of them are as follows:

1. It would locate the present and the potential problems.
2. It would highlight the possible opportunities.
3. It would evaluate the performance of the control mechanisms.
4. It would reduce costs by suggesting how to reduce unnecessary waste and losses.
5. It would review the overall plans and policies of the business.
6. It would determine whether or not the enterprise is operating as efficiently as it should.
7. It would detect the cases where the organizational policies and procedures are not being complied with.
8. It would evaluate the progress made by the enterprise through the introduction of new technique and ideas.

Nowadays, many management consultancy firms have come to exist that offer to conduct management audits for organizations. But there is no central agency to regulate their code of conduct and practices, and procedures of management audit as in the case of financial and cost audits.

Management Information System (MIS)

The MIS is a system designed to gather the required information and provide it to the top management for an effective management of the organization. MIS is important because all businesses have a need for information. The task before businesses is to use information and technology as a tool for solving problems, and providing opportunities by increasing productivity and quality.

Information has always been important but it has never been so available, so current and so overwhelming. Great strides have been made in the collection, storage, and retrieval of information. The challenge remains in the selection, analysis and interpretation of the information to produce useful intelligence that will improve decision making and productivity.

As we step into the new millennium, we witness the growing importance of the computerized information systems. Increasingly, businesses are realizing the importance of computerized information systems simply to remain competitive.

A modern enterprise is managed by means of a variety of decisions made at various levels of its hierarchy. A wide range of information is needed to make such decisions. The quality of decisions will largely depend on the nature and the quality of information provided for making the decisions. Thus, installation of an efficient management information system is vital for the effective functioning of an organization.

Objectives of MIS

Some of the common objectives of MIS found in various enterprises are as follows:

1. To make the desired information available in the right form to the right person and at the right time

2. To supply the required information at a reasonable cost
3. To use the most efficient methods of processing data
4. To provide the necessary security and secrecy for important and/or confidential information
5. To keep the information up-to-date

Functions of MIS

Management information system can be broadly classified into two categories as discussed below:

1. Data collection
2. Data management

Data Collection

It is necessary to objectively determine who should collect what data, in what form and how often. The nature and the form of data will vary from one organization to another depending upon its nature of business and its objectives. The manner of data collection will depend upon the purpose for which the data is collected. After the collection of data, irrelevant data should be filtered out and the relevant data should be properly classified and tabulated so that it can be used easily when needed.

Data management

A good data management system involves following subfunctions:

1. Processing operations, viz. classifying, analyzing, summarizing and editing the data
2. Storage of data, viz. indexing, coding and filing of information
3. Retrieval of data, whenever required
4. Evaluation, i.e. judging the usefulness of the information in terms of its relevance and accuracy
5. Dissemination, i.e. providing the required data in the right form at the right time

The data management system should be capable of giving efficient service in terms of day-to-day processing of information. At the same time, the system design should not be rigid. With the changes in conditions, the demand on the information system may change. The same information may be needed in different formats or different levels of aggregation may be needed. An efficient system should be able to quickly respond to these types of demands from different sources.

Role of MIS in planning and control

It is an accepted fact that excessive, irrelevant or erroneous information can be highly dysfunctional. Information should help the management in the basic task of planning, decision making, performance evaluation, etc. Therefore, it can be said that the prime purpose of developing an information system is to supplement corporate planning and control systems. On the other hand, planning and control systems that are not served by effective information system may only be of marginal utility.

Network Techniques

Network analysis is an important management controlling technique widely used in industries. Under network analysis, a project is broken down to small activities or operations that are arranged, and the order in which they are to be performed is decided. A network diagram is drawn to present the relationship between all the operations involved. The network thus drawn shows the interdependence of various activities of a period and also points out the activities that have to be completed before the other activities are initiated.

The object of network analysis is to help management in planning, organizing and controlling the operations in accomplishing the project economically and efficiently. Among all other network techniques, PERT and CPM have gained wide popularity and are used largely in the industries. Both PERT and CPM recognizes the interrelated nature of elements within large work projects like construction of a building, construction of ships, preparation of satellites and launch vehicles, manufacture of aircrafts, etc. All these projects involve complex network of interrelated activities.

In network techniques, an activity is defined as an operation that is required to accomplish a particular goal. An activity requires a specific span of time for completion. An event is a point of time when an activity is begun or completed. In a project, some activities are sequential while the others are concurrent to each other.

PERT/CPM

PERT (Programme Evaluation and Review Technique)
PERT is an important technique in the filed of project management. This technique was developed in late 1950s in the USA as a tool of planning and controlling the 'Polaris Missiles Program' by Booz, Allen and Hamilton in association with the US Naval Department.

CPM (Critical Path Method)
CPM is the most versatile planning and control technique, widely used in managing complex projects. It was developed in 1957 by J.E. Kelly of Remington Rand and M.R.Walkar of Dupont.

PERT/CPM are very useful techniques in managing complex projects and forces the managers to plan the projects in explicit details. It gives the management the exact details like when will the project be completed, what are the critical and noncritical activities, how can resources be concentrated to speed up the project completion, etc.

Basic steps in PERT/CPM
1. Defining the project and all the significant activities
2. Determining the precedence relationship among the activities
3. Estimating the time required to complete each activity
4. Drawing a network connecting all activities and label it with time estimates
5. Computing a longest time path (critical path) through the network
6. Using the network to plan, schedule, monitor and control the project

Network
Nodes represent events (the start or completion of activity or activities). Arcs represent activities. A path is a sequence of connected activities from the start node to completion node.

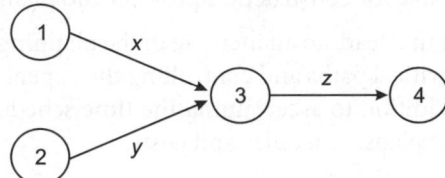

Activity z cannot begin before activities x and y have been completed. Event 3 marks the completion of activities x and y.

Programme evaluation and review technique (PERT)

In addition to its use in schedule planning and control, the network concept in PERT provides the framework for treating a wide range of product management problems. Recognizing this fact, the Navy Special Project Office of the USA extended the PERT to include the elements of cost and technical performance.

PERT is an integrated management system, designed to provide managers with the information they need in planning and controlling schedules, and costs in projects. Thus, PERT is directed towards the dynamic management of projects. It specifies the techniques and the procedures to assist project mangers in the following:

1. Planning schedulers and costs
2. Determining the time and cost status
3. Forecasting manpower skill requirements
4. Predicting schedule slippages and cost overruns
5. Developing alternate time–cost plans
6. Allocating resources among tasks

PERT uses the probability and linear programming for planning and controlling the activities. Probability helps in estimating the timings of various activities in the project, and linear programming is used to maximize the achievement of the project objective.

Application of PERT

PERT was developed as a research and development planning tool to estimate the timings of various activities with enough certainty. It helps in planning the time and the resources in the case of projects. It can be employed with great advantage in those cases (e.g. nonrepetitive project, research and development and defence projects) where a project cannot be easily defined in terms of time and resources required.

PERT is employed in the construction of ships, buildings and highways, the planning and launching of new products, the publication of books, and in the installation and debugging of the computer system. Frequently PERT systems are used in conjunction with computers. A computer programme is employed that permits calculations to be made without a reference to a flow chart or a diagram.

Critical Path Method (CPM)

Unlike PERT, it is applied in those projects where the activity timings are relatively well known. It is used for planning and controlling the most logical sequence of activities for accomplishing a project.

Under CPM, the project is analysed into different operations or activities and their relationships are determined and shown on the network diagram. It marks the critical activities in a project and concentrates on them. It is based on the assumption that the expected time is actually the time taken to complete the project. CPM is suitable for construction projects and plant maintenance.

CPM requires greater planning that leads to an increase in the planning cost, but this increase in cost is justified by concentrating on the critical paths and controlling the expenses on the strict supervision and control of the whole project. In addition to ascertaining the time schedules, it also provides a standard method of communicating project plans, schedules and costs.

The application of CPM leads to the following advantages:

1. It provides an analytical approach to the achievement of project objectives.
2. It identifies most critical elements and pays more attention to these activities.
3. It helps in ascertaining the time schedules.

4. It makes use of better and detailed planning.
5. It assists in avoiding waste of time, energy and money on unimportant activities.
6. It provides a standard method for communicating project plans, schedules and costs.

Points to Ponder

1. Control is checking the current performance against the predetermined standards contained in the plans, with a view to ensuring adequate progress and satisfactory performance.
2. A budget is a plan expressed in quantitative and monetary terms.
3. The different types of budgets are as follows:
   a. Sales budget
   b. Production budget
   c. Raw materials and purchasing budget
   d. Labour budget
   e. Cash budget
   f. Personnel budget
   g. Administrative budget
   h. Selling and distribution expenses budget
   i. Master budget
   j. Fixed budget
   k. Flexible budget
4. Break-even analysis is a very widely used technique to present information to management for understanding the relationship between sales, variable costs, fixed costs and profit existing at different levels of the output.

 **Self-Assessment Exercises**

1. Write a note on budget and budgetary control.
2. Write the characteristics of budget and give its advantages.
3. Describe in detail about the different types of budget.
4. What is *marginal costing*? Describe its usefulness.
5. Describe in detail the break-even analysis.
6. What is *managerial audit*? Enumerate its advantages.
7. Write a note on following:
   a. Management Information System (MIS)
   b. Sales budget
   c. Programme Evaluation and Review Technique (PERT)
   d. Critical Path Method (CPM)

Planning and Forecasting

INTRODUCTION

The process of management always starts with planning and ends with decision making, and implementing those plans is the first step leading to the attainment of the objectives.

According to Koontz, the great management thinker, 'Planning is deciding in advance what to do, how to do it, and who is to do it'. According to Hunt, 'Planning is setting objectives, devising means to those ends, harnessing effort and systematically feeding back against expectations'.

Planning, a prerequisite to other management functions, is a process involving managerial activities designed to attain desired organizational goals. In the absence of planning, managerial actions would become merely random activities producing nothing but chaos. Planning has been characterized as the process of thinking before doing. The process of planning involves thinking. It is simply an anticipation of the future activities and determining the appropriate course of action to achieve a desired result.

According to Fayol, the management thinker, 'The plan of action is the result envisaged, the line of action to be followed, stages to go through, and the methods to use. It is a kind of future picture and largely a mental process'. It is simply thinking before doing.

CHARACTERISTICS OF PLANNING

The various characteristics of planning are discussed below:

1. It is an intellectual activity that needs vision and foresight to decide and organize the things to be done in the future.
2. It is always governed by the objectives. Every plan specifies the objectives to be attained in the future and the steps necessary to achieve them.
3. It is a choice activity. It is about finding the various alternatives and selecting the best one. Thus decision making is an integral part of planning.
4. It is futuristic in nature. It is forward looking and always deals with forecasting future events, e.g. customer demands, competition, market trends, etc.
5. It is the most basic of all management functions.

BENEFITS OF PLANNING

Following are the benefits of planning:

1. Planning ensures operational effectiveness and efficiency.
2. It always helps the managers to remain focused on the objectives.
3. Planning helps in reducing the uncertainties of the future because the events are already anticipated.
4. Planning helps in performing the function of control. It lays down objectives and standards of performance that are essential for the performance of control function.
5. Planning always encourages innovation and creativity in managers. Many new ideas are generated during the planning process that creates a forward-looking attitude in managers.
6. A good planned activity ensures the participation of the entire staff, thus enhancing their motivation.
7. Effective planning gives a competitive edge to the organization over other competitors.
8. Planning helps in achieving the best coordination and always secures unity of direction towards the organizational objectives.

LIMITATIONS OF PLANNING

Sometimes planning fails to achieve the desired results. Some of the causes of the failure of planning are as follows:

Lack of Initiative

Planning is a forward-looking process. If the managers believe in just following instead of leading, then they will not be able to design good plans. Therefore, planners must take the required initiative and the responsibility to execute the plans.

Lack of Reliable Data

Planning always fails if not based on reliable data, figures or information. It is important to ensure that the plans are based more on reliable information than on assumptions.

Rigidity in Organizational Working

Internal inflexibly in the organization sometimes compel the planners to make rigid plans. This may deter the managers from doing innovative thinking. It is important that planners must have sufficient flexibility in the organization for the plans to be successfully executed.

Reluctance to Change

It is a commonly experienced phenomenon in business organizations. People are reluctant to change and this is a major limitation of planning.

External Limitations

The effectiveness of planning is sometimes limited because of external and unforeseen factors that are beyond the control of the planners. Sudden change in the government policies, natural calamities, war, etc., makes the execution of plans difficult.

Psychological Barriers

Psychological factors also limit the scope of planning. Few people consider the present to be more important than the future and don't like to plan for the future thus limiting the planning process.

CLASSIFICATION OF PLANS

We can classify planning on the basis of the following dimensions:

Organizational Level

Corporate planning (Top level)

Corporate planning is strategic in nature and covers the entire spectrum of organizational activities. It is defined as a systematic and comprehensive process of planning taking into account the resources and capabilities of the organization as well as the environment within which it has to operate.

Plans at the corporate level are formulated by the top-level managers and they integrate various divisional and functional plans of the organization.

Divisional planning (Middle level)

Divisional planning relates to a particular division or a department. It sets the objectives, plans, procedures, policies, rules, programmes of a particular division or department in tune with the corporate plans. These are operational within the confines of the division or department and are set to achieve goals limited to that division or department.

Sectional planning (Lower level)

Sectional planning is highly specific and lays down the detail plan for a particular section or unit mainly for the day-to-day activities. The first line managers are responsible for designing the plans for their units in the light of the divisional plans.

Focus Level

Strategic planning

Strategic plans are designed by the top management of the organization after a proper SWOT analysis (study of strength, weaknesses, opportunities and threats). Strategic planning is the process of designing the objectives of the organization and deciding the manner in which the resources are to be allocated to realize the objectives. Strategic plans generally relate to the long-term goals.

Operational planning

Operational planning is about developing a control mechanism to ensure efficient operations through efficient use of the allocated resources. Operational plans provide details on the accomplishment of the strategic plans.

Tactical planning

Tactical plans are made for short-term moves in order to meet the challenges of the sudden changes influencing the organization and where the impact on the business status is foreseen.

Time Period

Long-range planning

Long-range planning sets long-term goals and formulates strategic plans to attain these goals. In today's organizational scenario, due to the rapid changes in the business environment, the planning period has been compressed. It covers a period ranging from three years to ten years.

Middle-range planning

Middle-range plans are made to support the long-term plans. They may relate to the development of new markets, promotional strategies, etc. It covers a period ranging from one year to three years.

Short-term planning

Short-term plans are made to achieve the short-term goals or to deal with sudden changes in the business environment and covers a period up to one year. They are very specific in nature like changing a product design, training the workforce to meet the current changes, reducing the inventory controls, etc.

PLANNING PROCESS

The basic process of planning comprises of five tasks as discussed below:

1. Formulating goals
2. Determining the availability of resources
3. Forecasting trends

4. Choosing the best course of action among all available alternatives
5. Formulating the activities required by the selected course of action

In any type of an organization, planning is necessarily a responsibility of the management. In general, the more complex the organizational structure, the more difficult becomes the process of planning.

Planning is a function of every manager, although, the character and scope of planning will vary with his level, responsibility and authority. Generally, the following procedure is followed in planning:

1. The manager must clearly identify the problem that calls for planning and action.
2. The second step is to establish objectives. Objectives indicate the end points of what is to be done, where the primary emphasis is to be placed and what is to be accomplished by networking the policies, procedures, rules, budgets, programmes, etc.
3. The third step is to establish and obtain an agreement to utilize the future setting where planning takes place—the environment of plans in operations.
4. The next step is to search for and examine the alternative course of action. After finalizing and evaluating the alternative courses, the next step is to select the most appropriate course of action. This is the point where managerial decision making plays a very important role.
5. The last step is to construct the derivative plans to support the basic plan. Managers of each segment have to make plans necessary for converting the basic plan to reality.

It is very important that managers must be trained to develop the confidence, the forward looking attitude, and the analytical and decision-making abilities required for the planning element in the job.

The planning process involves the development of objectives, policies, programmes, procedures, schedules, budgets, competitive strategies, projects and forecasts. These are discussed below:

Objectives

Objectives are the established goals towards which the activities of the organization are directed. Objectives may be long term or short term. Essentially, objectives are fundamental to the control of the organizational activity, and are vital for the construction of policies, programmes and derived rules.

Policies

Policies are generally statements of understanding that guide or channel the thinking process in managerial decision making. Policies are usually the result of the top management's formal deliberations, but they may also result from informal processes and customary modes of operations.

Procedures

Procedures are the guidelines mentioning the instructions necessary for carrying out the activities successfully. Procedures are often utilized when high degree of accuracy in performance is needed. If the policies are to be executed effectively, it is very important to review and revise procedures at regular intervals.

Rules spell out specifically required actions or nonactions allowing no discretion. They are usually the simplest types of operational plans. Rules differ from procedures in that they guide action without specifying a time sequence. Again, rules are different from policies. The purpose of a policy is to guide the decision making. Rules allow no discretion in their application.

Programmes

They involve policies, procedures, rules, task assignments, steps to be taken, resources to be employed and other elements necessary to carry out a given course of action and they are ordinarily supported by the necessary capital and operating budgets. Programmes can be major as well as minor. It should be noted that the key to success of a programme is the skill in coordinated planning.

Budgets

A budget, as a plan, is a statement of expected results expressed in numerical terms. It is a statement, in quantified terms, of the future expenditures and revenues, reflecting the resources allocated to specified activities within a stated period of time (usually one year). Budgets vary considerably in accuracy, detail and purpose.

Competitive Strategies

Competitive strategies may be regarded as plans made to counter the strategies and plans of the competitors. A complete knowledge of the competitor's plan is necessary.

Project

Project is a detailed activity encompassing planning, execution, supervision and stage-by-stage assessment of certain specific work. Generally, jobs involving multiple disciplines of work, their interdependency in execution and a time-bound completion are taken up on project basis.

Forecasting

A successful planning process is an outcome of sound forecasting. Forecasting helps greatly in understanding and organizing the requirements of the future. It provides management with the relevant information that helps in planning and decision making.

Forecasting is drawing prior conclusions about the probables of production, sales, profits, etc. in the future, on the basis of research, study and surveys. A forecast is tomorrow's expectation, based on yesterday's achievements and today's plans.

Definition

According to Henry Fayol, 'Business forecasting includes both assessing the future and making provision for it'. According to Allen, 'Forecasting is a systematic attempt to probe the future by inference from known facts'.

Methods of Forecasting

Usually, forecasting is done by analysing past trends, studying the current trends (present situation) and taking into account the emerging trends. Some of the methods of forecasting are as follows:

Direct versus indirect methods

In case of direct method, one can arrive at the requirements of a company by summing up all the estimates submitted by its different units. In the indirect method, first, the requirement of the entire trade or industry is estimated and then the share of a particular unit is ascertained.

Empirical versus scientific methods

Empirical method attempts to view the future in terms of the past, while the scientific method tries to use scientific methodology in establishing causal relationship.

Historical, deductive and joint-opinion methods

The historical method mainly deals with the analysis and interpretation of past events for understanding problems and forecasting future.

The deductive method is based on assumptions that past events do not fully determine the future, as with the change in economic conditions, some factors may become insignificant, while others may become important.

The joint-opinion method is a committee type of approach. It is principally based on a well-organized survey of views and opinions of people who are directly concerned with forecasting. This method sometimes degenerates into more chaos and confusion.

Forecasting methods and procedures are many; some simple others more sophisticated. Some emphasize quantification, statistical analysis and mathematic models, others are based heavily on guesses and opinions.

The correctness of the management decisions depends upon sound forecasting. Most managers claim that short-term forecasting is more accurate than long-term forecasting and that forecasts are not foolproof and condition proof. However, it has been observed that successful forecasting results in higher profits and developing the team spirit, morale and motivation.

Points to Ponder

1. Planning is deciding in advance what to do, how to do, and who is to do it.
2. Planning can be classified on the basis of the following dimensions:
   a. Organizational level
   b. Focus level
   c. Time period
3. The process of planning comprises of five tasks. They are as follows:
   a. Formulating goals
   b. Determining the availability of resources
   c. Forecasting trends
   d. Choosing the best course of action among all available alternatives
   e. Formulating the activities required by the selected course of action

Self-Assessment Exercises

1. What is *planning*? Give its characteristics.
2. Enumerate the benefits and limitations of planning.
3. Describe in detail the classification of plans.
4. Write a note on the planning process.
5. Define forecasting.
6. Describe in details the methods of forecasting.

Personnel Management

INTRODUCTION

Personnel management is that phase of management that deals with the effective control and use of manpower as distinguished from other sources of power. It is that part of management function that is primarily concerned with the human relations within an organization.

It is the recruitment, selection, development, utilization and accommodation of human resources by the organizations. The human resources of an organization are individuals who are engaged in any of the organizational activities regardless of their role.

Personnel management is a field of management that is concerned with the management functions (planning, organizing, directing and controlling) and various operative functions (procurement, development, maintenance and utilization) with a view to attaining the organizational goals economically and effectively and meeting the individual and social goals.

Personnel management is concerned with managing people at work. It covers all levels of personnel, including blue-collared employees (craftsmen, foremen, operatives and labourers) and white-collared employees (professional, technical managers, officials, clerical workers and sales workers). It helps the employees to develop their capacity and potential to the best of their ability, so they may derive great satisfaction from their job.

OBJECTIVES OF PERSONNEL MANAGEMENT

The main objectives of personnel management are as follows:

1. To achieve an effective utilization of human resources in the achievement of the organizational goals.
2. To establish and maintain an adequate organizational structure and a desirable working relationship among all members of an organization by dividing the tasks of an organization into functions, positions, jobs and by defining clearly the responsibility, accountability and authority for each job.
3. To generate maximum individual or group development within an organization by offering opportunities for advancement to employees through training and job education.
4. To recognize and satisfy individual needs and group goals by offering an adequate remuneration, economic and social security in the form of monetary compensation and protection against hazards of life.
5. To secure the integration of the individuals and groups with an organization, by reconciling an individual or group with those of an organization in such a manner that the employees feel a sense of involvement, commitment and loyalty towards it.
6. To maintain a high morale and better human relations inside an organization by sustaining and improving the conditions as have been established so that the employees may stick to their jobs for a longer period.

FUNCTIONAL AREAS OF PERSONNEL MANAGEMENT

On the basis of the various functions that personnel management generally undertakes, the functional areas of personnel management may be set forth as below:

1. Organizational planning and development
2. Staffing and employment
3. Training and development
4. Comparison, wage and salary administration
5. Motivation and incentives
6. Employee services and benefits
7. Employee records
8. Labour or industrial relations
9. Personnel research and personnel audit

Organizational Planning and Development

Organizational planning is concerned with the division of all the tasks to be performed into manageable and efficient units (the departments division) and with providing for their integration. Both differentiation and integration are vital for the achievement of predetermined goals.

Staffing and Employment

The staffing process is a flow of events that results in a continuous manning of organizational positions at all levels from the top management to the operative level. This process includes manpower planning, authorization for planning, developing sources of the applicants, evaluation of the applicants, employment decisions (selections), offers (placements), induction and orientations, transfers, demotions, promotions and separations (retirement, lay-off, discharge, resignation, disability and death).

Training and Development

It is a complex process and is concerned with enhancing the capabilities of individuals and groups so they may contribute effectively to the attainment of the organizational goals. The training needs of the company are identified, suitable training programmes are developed, operatives and executives are identified for training, motivation is provided for joining these training programmes and the services of the specialists are enlisted. The effectiveness of training programmes have to be evaluated by arranging follow-up studies.

Compensation, Wages and Salary Administration

It is concerned with the process of compensation, directed towards remunerating employees for services rendered and motivating them to attain the desired levels of performance. This includes job evaluation, wage and salary programme, performance appraisal.

Motivation and Incentives

Motivation is concerned with motivating employees by creating conditions where they may get social and psychological satisfaction. For this purpose, a plan for nonfinancial incentives (such as recognition, privileges and symbols of status) is formulated. These incentives are administered and reviewed from time to time with a view to encourage the efficiency of the employee.

Employee Services and Benefits

These are concerned with the process of sustaining and maintaining the workforce in an organization. They include safety provision inside the workshop, employee counselling in solving their work problems, medical services, the recreational, and their welfare facilities and fringe benefits. These benefits are usually given to employees in order to tempt them to remain in the organization to provide them with social security.

Employee Records

The employee record is completed and up-to-date information is maintained about the employees. These records may be utilized at the time of making transfers or promotions, giving merit pay or sanctioning leave.

Such records include information related to personal qualifications, special interests, aptitude, results of tests and interviews, job performance, promotions, rewards and punishments.

Labour Relations

Labour relations mean the maintenance of healthy and peaceful labour management relations, so the production or work may go on undisturbed. This includes the rules and regulations that are framed for the maintenance of discipline in the organization, removing grievance by finding its causes and to observe as well as comply with labour laws of the country.

Personnel Research and Personnel Audit

This includes a systematic study of finding a way to make an organization's personnel programme more effective. The data relating to quality, wages, productivity, grievances, absenteeism, labour turnover, strikes, lock-outs, accidents, etc., that are collected and supplied to the top management so they may review, alter or improve the existing personnel policies, programmes and procedures.

ORGANIZATIONAL STRUCTURE OF THE PERSONNEL DEPARTMENT

The internal organizational structure of the personnel department varies widely in different companies, depending upon their size. In a big company, where the personnel activities are generally of a complex nature, a separate department is organized for the purpose. This department is generally known as the *personnel department* or the *industrial relations department* and is headed by the personnel manager or personnel director or vice-president personnel or by the industrial relations director or labour relations officer or employment officer depending upon the nature of duties assigned to him.

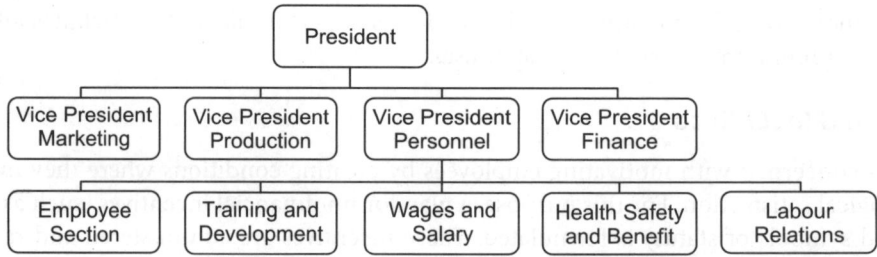

Figure 11.1. Organizational Chart of Personnel Department

From Figure 11.1, it is clear that the personnel manager has under him subordinates, who look after the employee section, the training and development section, the wages and salary administration section, the health, safety and benefits section and the labour relations section. The personnel in charge of these sections are generally known as *employment officer, training officer, wages and salary administrator, labour welfare officer, security officer, health officer, labour relations officer,* etc.

RECRUITMENT AND SELECTION PROCESS

Recruitment is the process of exploring the source of supply of the required personnel and stimulating the prospective employees to apply for jobs in the organization. Its purpose is to create a pool of candidates from which the most suitable persons may be selected for the job.

Sources of Recruitment

There are two sources of recruitment as discussed below:

Internal Sources

These include personnel already on the payroll of an organization. Whenever any vacancy occurs, somebody from within the organization is upgraded, transferred, promoted or sometimes demoted. This source is used by many organizations but a majority of them ignore this source especially for the middle management jobs.

Advantages

The advantages of internal recruitment are as follows:

1. It improves the morale of the employees because they are assured of the fact that they would be preferred over outsiders when vacancies occur.
2. It promotes loyalty among the employees because it gives them a sense of job security and opportunities for advancement.
3. The employer is in a better position to evaluate those presently employed than candidates outside the organization.
4. It is less costly than recruiting outside the organization.
5. They are tried people and can be relied upon.

Disadvantages

The disadvantages of recruiting internal candidates are as follows:

1. It often leads to inbreeding and discourages fresh ideas from entering an organization.
2. A promotion is based on seniority, so there is danger that a really capable person may not be chosen.
3. There are possibilities that the internal sources may dry up and it may be difficult to find the requisite personnel from within the organization.

External Sources

These sources lie outside the organization. They usually include young, mostly inexperienced potential employees, trained unemployed and retired experienced personnel.

Advantages

The advantages of recruiting from external sources are as follow:

1. It provides the requisite type of personnel for an organization having skill, training and education up to the required standard.
2. Since people are recruited from a large market, the best selection can be made without any distinctions of caste, sex or colour.
3. In the long run, this source proves economical because the potential employees do not need extra training for their jobs.

Disadvantages

The disadvantages of recruiting from external sources are:

The system suffers from brain drain especially when experienced people are hunted by sister concerns.

Methods of Recruitment

The following methods are used for recruitment of the employees in an organization:

1. **Direct methods:** In this method, the recruiters are sent to colleges and technical institutions. Most college recruitments are done in cooperation with the placement office of a college. The placement office usually provides help in attracting students, arranging interviews and providing student résumés. For managerial, professional and sales personnel, campus recruiting is very commonly used.

2. **Indirect methods:** In this method, an advertisement is generally given in the leading daily newspapers, popular magazines, trade and professional journals. The detailed description of the post is given and the interested candidates are required to submit their applications giving their complete bio data on a prescribed proforma before the last date. The application form should provide the following information:

    Biographical data: Name, father's name, date and place of birth, age, sex, nationality, height, weight, identification marks, physical disability, if any, marital status, and number of dependants.

    Educational attainment: Education (subjects offered and grades secured), training acquired in special fields and knowledge gained from professional or technical institutions or evening classes or through correspondence courses.

    Work experience: Previous experience, the number of jobs held with the same or other employers, including nature of duties and responsibilities, and the duration of various assignments, salary received and reasons for leaving the present employer.

    Salary: Demanded and other benefits expected.

    Personal items: Association memberships, extracurricular activities, sports, hobbies and other pertinent information supporting a candidate suitable for a post.

    Other items: Name and address of previous employer, reference, etc.

3. **Third party methods:** Third party methods include the use of commercial or private employment agencies, state agencies, placement offices of schools, colleges and professional associations, recruiting firms, management consulting firms, friends and relatives.

SELECTION

A well-organized selection procedure has to be adopted to select suitable candidates for various jobs. The selection procedure is concerned with securing relevant information about an applicant. The information is secured in a number of steps or stages. The objective of the selection process is to determine whether the applicant meets the qualifications for the specific job and to choose the applicant who is most likely to perform in that job. The selection procedure involves various stages. At each stage, facts may come to light that may lead to the rejection of the applicant.

The following selection procedure is generally followed:

1. **Scrutiny of applications:** The applications received up to the due date are carefully scrutinized. The incomplete applications and applications of candidates who do not fulfil the required eligibility conditions are rejected.

2. **Preliminary interview:** The candidates considered suitable on the basis of their applications are called for a preliminary interview. This is generally a brief interview and its purpose is to eliminate those candidates who are either unqualified or unsuitable for the job.

3. **Selection test:** It may be a written or an oral test. The technical knowledge and the administrative capability can be judged from these tests. The psychological tests are very popular these days to judge the human behaviour in actual work situations. The following tests are commonly used in the selection process:

   a. **Intelligence tests:** Intelligence tests are used to estimate the IQ or the mental alertness of the candidate. It also helps to know whether he has the mental capacity to deal with new problems.

   b. **Aptitude tests:** Aptitude tests help to measure a candidate's capacity to learn particular skills and his potential abilities. These tests are generally used for the selection of personnel in lower positions, who are entrusted with the jobs of operating machines.

   c. **Trade tests:** Trade tests are designed to measure the applicant's level of knowledge and the skill already achieved in a particular trade or occupation. These tests are also known as *performance tests* or *proficiency tests.*

   d. **Personality tests:** Personality tests are employed to find the emotional balance, maturity, temperament, etc., of the candidate. These tests also help find the ability of a person to adjust himself to the stresses of everyday life and his capacity for interpersonal relations and self-image. These tests are generally done to select supervisors and higher executives.

      The personality tests are of four types:

      i. Objective tests: The objective tests measure the neurotic tendencies, self-sufficiency, dominance-submission and self-confidence.

      ii. Protective tests: In protective tests, a candidate is asked to project his own interpretation into certain standard stimulus situations. The way in which he responds to these stimuli depends on his own values, motives and personality.

      iii. Situation tests: Situation tests measures an applicant's reaction when he is placed in a peculiar situation, his ability to undergo stress and his demonstration of ingenuity under pressure.

      iv. Interest tests: Interest tests help to find the type of work that a candidate is interested in.

4. **Selection interview:** A face-to-face dialogue between the employer or his representatives and the interested candidate is the most popular tool of selection. The main purpose of a selection interview is:

   To find out the suitability of the candidate

   To cross check the information revealed in the application and the tests

   To give to the candidate an accurate picture of his job and the enterprise

   An interview is a time consuming and an expensive process, and its conclusions may be distorted due to the bias of the person conducting the interview.

5. **Physical examination:** Physical examination of the candidate is conducted to ensure that he is physically fit for the job. If he is suffering from any disease or disability, he is rejected.

6. **Reference check:** Usually the candidates are required to write in their application form the names and address of two important people who know the candidate. These persons are contacted to collect information about the character, ability and background of the candidate. But the information supplied by them may be biased in favour of the candidate.

7. **Final selection and placement:** The candidates who have been found suitable in all respects are appointed by issuing appointment letters to them. They are generally appointed on probation for one or two years. After successful completion of the probationary period, they are made permanent employees. The selected candidates are assigned specific jobs. This is known as *placement.*

SERVICE CONDITIONS

The promotion and maintenance of the employee discipline is essential for the proper growth of an enterprise. The selected person is governed by the service rules and regulations that help the employee cope with various situations in an enterprise. Promotions, demotions, transfers, separation, absenteeism and turnover are some such situations.

Promotion

A promotion may be defined as an upward advancement of an employee in an organization to another job, which commands better pay or wages, better status or prestige, higher opportunities and challenges, higher rank with responsibilities and authority, better working environment, hours of work and facilities.

Promotion provides incentives to initiatives, minimizes discontent and unrest. It attracts capable individuals, necessitates logical training of advancement and forms an effective reward for loyalty and cooperation.

All promotions should be done by adopting certain uniform criteria. The promotion is generally based on seniority or on merit. In every organization, the rules are framed for regulating the seniority of employees in different service cadres and promotions are made from the seniority list. In private sectors, however, promotions are generally done considering the efficiency of an employee.

Demotion

Demotion means lowering down the status, salary and responsibility of an employee. It is used as a punitive measure when there are serious breaches of duty on the part of an employee and it is often a preliminary to a dismissal from service. Demotion is used as a disciplinary measure.

Demotion serves as a useful purpose in keeping the employees alert and alive to their responsibilities and duties. Demotions should be made infrequently because such actions will not improve the performance of the individual.

Transfer

Transfer is a horizontal or a lateral movement of an employee from one job, section, department, shift, plant or position to another at the same or another place where his salary, status, and responsibility are the same. Every organization should have an impartial transfer policy and it should be known to each employee.

Transfers are generally affected to build a more satisfactory work team and to achieve the following purposes:

1. To satisfy the needs of an organization that may arise out of a change in the quantity of production, fluctuations in work requirements and changes in the organizational structure.
2. To meet an employee's own request.
3. To properly utilize the services of an employee.
4. To adjust the workforce of one plant with that of another.
5. To replace a new employee by an employee who has been in the organization for a sufficiently long time.

6. To help employees work according to their convenience so far as timings are concerned, i.e. transferring the employee from one shift to another shift.
7. To penalize the employee.
8. Transfer for the maintenance of a tenure system.
9. To increase the versatility of the employee.

Transfers may be intradepartmental (i.e. within the same section or department) or interdepartmental (from one department to another). Transfer from one place or unit to another place or unit involves a considerable change in the working conditions and cost to the organization. Transfer orders should be given in writing after giving due notice to the employees.

Separation

Separation means cessation of service of agreement with the organization for one or the other reason. The employee may be separated from the payroll of a company as a result of:

1. Resignation
2. Discharge and dismissal
3. Suspension and retrenchment
4. Lay-off
5. Redeployment
6. Absenteeism

Resignation

Resignation may be put involuntarily by the employee on grounds of health, physical disability, better opportunities elsewhere or maladjustment with the company policies and officers, or they may be compulsory when an employee is asked to put in his resignation if he wants to avoid termination of his services on the grounds of gross negligence of duty on his part or some serious charges against him.

Discharge and dismissal

A discharge involves permanent separation of an employee from the payroll for violation of company rules or for inadequate performance. A discharge becomes necessary in the following circumstances:

1. When the volume of business does not justify the continuing employment of the person involved.
2. When a person fails to work according to the requirements of the job either because of his incapacity or because he has deliberately slowed down on work due to carelessness, laziness or lack of cooperation.
3. When an individual forfeits his right to a job because of his violation of basic policy often involving the safety of others, the morale and discipline of a group.

To avoid unnecessary grievances arising from discharges, proper rules should be framed to govern them. Discharge is generally made with standing orders. The action taken should be bonafide and is neither a punitive measure nor a case of victimization. The reason for discharge should be clearly stated to the concerned employee. A discharged employee needs a reasonable notice or an equivalent of pay in lieu of notice.

A dismissal is the termination of the services of an employee by way of punishment for some misconduct or for unauthorized and prolonged absence from duty.

Before the termination of services of an employee, an opportunity should be given for him to explain his conduct and to justify why he should not be dismissed. The general rule is that in the process of dismissal, there should be no violation of the principle of natural justice, which ensures that punishment is not out of all proportion to the offence.

Suspension and retrenchment

This is a serious punishment and is generally awarded only after a proper enquiry has been conducted. For reasons of discipline, an employee may be suspended without prejudice during the course of an enquiry. During suspension, the employee receives a subsistence allowance.

Retrenchment means a permanent termination of the services of an employee for economic reasons in a going concern. Retrenchment is generally done, when a part of the workforce is found to be superfluous.

On retrenchment, an employee is entitled to both retrenchment compensation and gratuity. The retrenchment compensation is equivalent to fifteen days average pay for every completed year of continuous service or any part thereof in excess of six months.

According to the retrenchment procedure, the last person employed in each category must be the first person to be retrenched, i.e. last come first go. For this purpose, the employer prepares a list of all the employees in the category where retrenchment is contemplated. The list is required to be displayed on the notice board at least seven days before the actual date of retrenchment.

When vacancies arise after retrenchment, the employer gives an opportunity to the retrenched workers to offer themselves for reemployment and they are given preference. Such vacancies are generally notified at least ten days before they are filled up.

Lay-off

A *lay-off* refers to an indefinite separation of the employee from the payroll due to factors beyond the control of the employer. It involves a temporary or permanent removal from the payroll of people with surplus skills. The purpose of a lay-off is to reduce the financial burden on an organization when human resources cannot be utilized profitably.

The general principle to be followed is to lay-off last in first out. A lay-off worker is paid fifty per cent of the basic wages and dearness allowance for every working day on which he reports for work. Lay-off compensation need not be paid for more than forty-five days during any period of twelve months. In order to receive his lay-off compensation, the workman must present himself on each working day at the appointed time.

Redeployment

When a redeployment of employees becomes necessary on account of a reorganization of production, modernization of equipment or expansion of an enterprise, then redeployment should be effected with minimum hardship for affected employees. There should be no reduction in the remuneration for any one. If, on redeployment, employees need further training then that should be arranged at the employer's cost.

Absenteeism

Absenteeism is the practice or habit of being an absentee and an absentee is one who habitually stays away from work. It is very significant, if an employee is absent from work when he is scheduled to be present at work. Any employee may stay away from work, if he has taken leave to which he is entitled, or on the ground of sickness or some accident or without any previous sanction of leave. Thus, absence may be authorized or unauthorized, wilful or caused by circumstances beyond one's control.

PERFORMANCE EVALUATION

Performance evaluation is an important tool of personnel management. Once the employee has been selected, trained and motivated, he is then appraised for his performance. Performance appraisal is the process of evaluating the performance and qualifications of the employee in terms of the requirements of the job for which he is employed; for purposes of administration including placement, selection for promotions, providing financial rewards and other actions that require differential treatment among the members of a group.

The process of evaluation begins with the following steps:

1. Establishment of performance standards. These standards should be clear and indicated on the appraisal form.
2. Communicate the performance expectations to the employees.
3. Measure actual performance.
4. Compare actual performance with standards.
5. Discuss the appraisal with the employees periodically where the good points, weak points and difficulties, are indicated and discussed so that the performance is improved. The information that is received by a subordinate about his assessment has a great impact on his self-esteem and on his subsequent performance.
6. Initiate corrective action if necessary. Immediate corrective action can be of two types—one is immediate and deals predominantly with symptoms. The other is basic and goes deep into the causes. Immediate corrective action is often described as putting out fires, whereas, basic corrective action gets to the source of the deviation and seeks to adjust the difference permanently. Coaching and counselling may be done.

Methods of Performance Evaluation

The following two methods are used for performance evaluation of employees:

Traditional methods

1. Straight ranking method
2. Man to man comparison method
3. Grading
4. Graphic rating scales
5. Forced choice description method
6. Forced distribution method
7. Checklists
8. Free form essay method
9. Critical incidents
10. Group appraisal
11. Field review method

Modern methods

1. Appraisal by results
2. Assessment centre method
3. Human asset accounting method

Traditional methods of evaluations

1. Straight ranking method: The straight ranking method is the oldest and the simplest method of performance evaluation, by which the man and his performance are considered as an entity by the one who rates. The performance of an individual is compared with other individuals in a workgroup and the ranking is done against that of another, i.e. people are tested in order of merit and placed in simple grouping. This is the simplest method of separating the most efficient from the least efficient person.

2. Man to man comparison method: By this method, certain factors are selected for the purpose of analysis (such as leadership, dependability and initiative) and a scale is designed by the one who rates for each factor. Each man to be rated is compared with the man in the scale and certain scores for each factor are awarded to him. This method is used in job evaluation.

3. Grading method: Under this system, the person in charge of rating selects certain features and marks them according to a scale. The selected features may be analytical ability, cooperativeness, dependability, self-expression, job knowledge, judgment, leadership and organizing ability, etc. They may be—A – outstanding; B – very good; C – good; D – average; E – below average; and F – very poor.

The actual performance of an employee is compared with these grade definitions and he is allotted the grade that describes his performance.

4. Graphic rating scales: Graphic rating scale is the most commonly used method. Under it, a printed form, one for each person to be rated is prepared according to two factors:

    a. Employee characteristics that include qualities, such as, initiative, leadership, cooperative's dependability, attitude, enthusiasm, loyalty and ability.
    b. Employee contributions that include quantity and quality of work, the responsibility assumed, specific goals achieved, regularity of attendance, attitudes towards superiors and associates.

These distinguishing features are then evaluated on a continuous scale wherein the individual rating then places a mark somewhere along a continuous scale. The rating scale method is easy to understand and easy to use. A ready comparison of scores among the employees is possible. These scores indicate the worth of every individual. It is the most common evaluation tool in use nowadays.

5. Forced choice description method: Under this method, the rating elements are several set of pair phrases or adjectives (usually sets of four phrases, two of which are positive and two are negative) relating to job proficiency or personal qualifications. In individual rating, the employee is asked to indicate which of the four phrases is the most and least descriptive of the employee.

The following statements are illustrative of the type of statements that are used:

    a. Make little effort and individual instruction,
    b. Organizes the work well,
    c. Lack the ability to make people feel at ease,
    d. Has a cool even temperament?
    e. Is punctual and careful?
    f. Is a hard worker and is cooperative?

g.   Is dishonest and disloyal?

h.   Is overbearing and disinterested in work?

In each of above illustration, two of the above phrases are relatively favourable terms, while the other two are relatively unfavourable. The favourable terms earn a plus credit, while the unfavourable terms get no credit.

6. Forced distribution method: Forced distribution method is a simple method to understand and very easy to apply in organizations. Under this method, the two factors, viz. job performance and promotability is used for rating. Employees are placed between the two extremes of *good* and *bad* job performances. For example, 10% are placed at the top end of the scale (given outstanding merit), 20% good rating (i.e. above the average) 40% satisfactory (or average) 20% fair and 10% unsatisfactory (or below average or poor). This forced distribution method assumes that, of the total personnel, 10% must go to the top grade, 20% to the second grade, 7% to the middle grade, 20% to the grade next to the lowest end of the scale and 10% of the lowest grade.

The system is used to eliminate or minimize any biasing by the one who rates so that all personnel may not be placed at the higher end or the lower end of the scale.

7. Checklist: Under this method, there is no employee performance evaluation but the person in charge of rating supplies report about it. The final rating is done by the personnel department. A series of questions are presented concerning an employee's behaviour. The person in charge checks to indicate if the answer to a question about an employee is positive or negative. The value of each question may be weighed equally or certain questions may be weighed more heavily than the others. An example of a checklist is given below:

a.   Is the employee really interested in his job? Yes/No

b.   Is he regular on his job? Yes/No

c.   Is he respected by his subordinates? Yes/No

d.   Does he show uniform behaviour to all? Yes/No

e.   Does he follow instructions properly? Yes/No

f.   Does he ever make mistakes? Yes/No.

The method suffers from bias on the part of the one who rates because he can distinguish positive and negative questions. The method is expensive and time consuming because a separate checklist must be developed for different classes of jobs.

8. Free essay method: Under this method, the superior makes an open ended appraisal of an employee in his words and puts down his impressions about the employee. The description is always as factual and concrete as possible. No attempts are made to evaluate an employee in a quantitative manner.

The method is advantageous because an essay can provide a good deal of information.

9. Critical incident method: In this method, the performance of the worker is measured in terms of certain events or episodes that occur in the performance of the rate's job. These events are known as *critical incidents*. The supervisor keeps a written record of the events (either good or bad) that can easily be recalled and used in the course of a periodical or formal appraisal evaluation. Feedback is provided about the incidents during performance review session.

The critical incidents are discovered after a thorough study of the personnel working on a job. The collected incidents are then ranked in order of frequency and importance.

This method provides an objective basis for conducting a discussion of an individual's performance. Vague impression and general remarks are avoided. But this method has certain limitations. Negative incidents are generally more noticeable than positive ones. Very close supervision is required to narrate incidents which may not be liked by the employees.

10. Group appraisal method: Under this method, the employees are rated by an appraisal group, consisting of their supervisor and three or four other supervisors who have some knowledge of their performance. The supervisor explains to the group, the nature of the duties of his subordinates. The groups then discuss the standards of performance for that job, the actual performance of the job holder, and the causes of their particular level of performance, and offers suggestions for future improvement, if any.

The advantage of this method is that it is thorough, very simple and is devoid of any bias because it involves multiple judges. But it is very time consuming.

11. Field review method: Under this method, a trainer employee from the personnel department interviews the line supervisors to evaluate their respective subordinates. The evaluator puts definite test questions to the supervisor. The supervisor is required to give his opinion about the progress of his subordinates. The level of the performance of each subordinate includes his weakness, good points, outstanding ability, promotability and the possible plans of action in cases requiring further consideration. The questions are asked and the answers are given verbally. The evaluator takes notes of the answers that are then approved by the supervisor and placed in the employee's personal folder. The success of this system depends upon the competence of the interviewer. This system is useful for a large organization.

Modern methods of evaluation

1. Appraisal by results or management by objectives (MBO): Management by objectives is a process whereby the superior and subordinate managers of an organization, jointly identify its common goals, define each individual's major areas of responsibility in terms of the results expected of him and use these measures as guides for operating the unit and assessing the contributions of each of its members.

Under the MBO programme, an employee and his supervisor meet and together define, establish and set certain goals or objectives that the employee would attempt to achieve within the prescribed time period.

They also discuss the ways and methods of measuring employee progress. The set goals are work related and career oriented. The employee periodically meets his supervisor to evaluate the employee's goal progress. Frequent feedback and supervisor–subordinate interaction helps to enhance performance. These goals may be revised, if it is necessary. This method is largely applied to technical, professional, supervisory or executive personnel.

MBO can be an effective technique for performance evaluation and for motivating subordinates, by developing communication between the executives at all levels. Those at the bottom must be willing to listen to the voice of experience and those at the top willing to accept fresh ideas from lower level employees.

2. Assessment centre method: In this method, many evaluators join together to judge the employee performance in several situations with the use of a variety of criteria. Assessments are made to determine employee potential for the purpose of promotion. The assessment is generally done with the help of a couple of employees and involves a paper and pencil test, interviews and situational exercise.

The assessment centres generally measure interpersonal skills and other aspects such as organizing and planning, interpersonal competence, quality of thinking, resistance to stress, motivation to work and dependence on others.

The duration of assessment centre programme varies with the person. For example, centre designed for selection of first line supervisors, sales personnel and management trainee generally last for a day or less, while those used for higher level managers may run for two to three days or longer if used for development and not for selection purposes.

3. Human asset accounting method: This method is not yet very popular. The method refers to the activity devoted to attaching money estimates to the value of a firm's internal human organization and its external customer goodwill. If able, well-trained personnel leave a firm, the human organization is worthless and if they join it, its human assets are increased. If distrust and conflict prevail, the human enterprise is devaluated and if teamwork and high morale prevails, the human organization is a very valuable asset.

Periodic measurement of two variables, i.e. key causal and intervening variables provide the needed data for the computation of the human asset accounting. The key causal variables include the structure of an organization's management policies, decisions, business leadership, skill and behaviour. The intervening variable reflects the internal state and health of an organization. They include loyalties, attitudes, motivation and collective capacity for effective interaction, communication and decision making.

4. Behavioural anchored rating scale (BARS): This is new appraisal technique. It involves five steps:
   a. Generate critical incidents
   b. Develop performance dimensions
   c. Reallocate incidents
   d. Scale of incidents
   e. Develop final instrument.

BARS technique is more time consuming and expensive than other appraisal tools, yet it is more accurate gauge.

Points to Ponder

1. Personnel management is the recruitment, selection, development, utilization of and accommodation to human resources by the organizations.
2. There are two sources of recruitment as follows:
   a. Internal sources
   b. External sources
3. Two methods are used for the performance evaluation of employees. They are as given below:
   a. Traditional methods
   b. Modern methods

Self-Assessment Exercises

1. Define the term *personnel management*
2. Explain the term *recruitment.*
3. Define the term *selection.*
4. Define the term *absenteeism.*
5. Explain the term *separation.*
6. What do you know about *retrenchment*?
7. Name the various sources of recruitment.
8. Name the various methods of recruitment.
9. Write the objectives of personnel management.
10. What are the different sources of recruitment?
11. Give the various service conditions of an employee.
12. Write the names of the various methods of performance evaluation.
13. Write the various steps that are involved in the evaluation process.
14. Write the various steps that are involved in the selection process.
15. Give in brief the various tests that are done in the selection test.
16. Define the term *personnel management.* Discuss the functions of personnel management.
17. Define the term *recruitment.* What are the different sources of recruitment? Describe the various methods of recruitment.
18. Explain the term *selection.* Discuss in brief about the selection procedure which is generally adopted for the recruitment of employees.
19. Explain the term *performance evaluation.* Discuss the different methods of performance evaluation.
20. Write in brief about the various service conditions of employees in an organization.
21. Write short notes on the following:
    a. Sources of recruitment
    b. Selection procedure
    c. Service conditions
    d. Selection tests
    e. Organizational structure of personnel management

Production Management

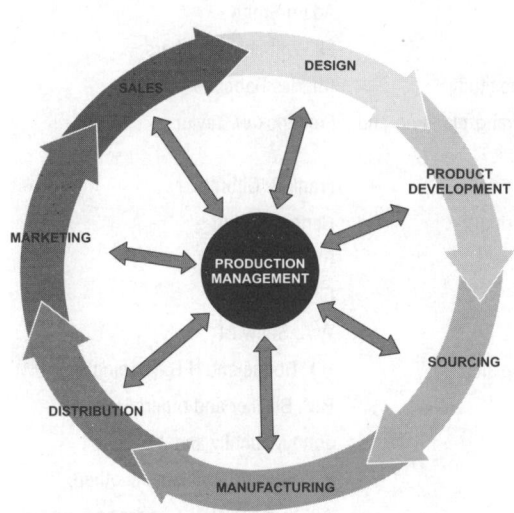

INTRODUCTION

Production or operations management is a process that combines and transforms various resources used in the production or operations subsystem of the organization into value-added products or services, in a controlled manner, as per the policies of the organization. Therefore, it is that part of an organization that is concerned with the transformation of a range of inputs into the required (products or services) having the requisite quality level.

The set of interrelated management activities that are involved in the manufacturing of certain products is called *production management*. If the same concept is extended to services management, then the corresponding set of management activities is called *operations management*.

HISTORICAL EVOLUTION OF PRODUCTION AND OPERATIONS MANAGEMENT

For over two centuries, the operations and production management has been recognized as an important factor in a country's economic growth. The traditional view of manufacturing management began in the eighteenth century when Adam Smith recognized the economic benefits of specialization of labour. He recommended breaking the jobs into subtasks and recognizing workers to specialized tasks in which they would become highly skilled and efficient. In the early twentieth century, F.W. Taylor implemented the theories of Smith and developed scientific management. From then till 1930, many techniques were developed prevailing the traditional view. Brief information about the contributions to manufacturing management is shown in the Table 12.1 below

TABLE 12.1. Historical Summary of Operations Management

Date	Contribution	Contributor
1776	Specialization of labour in manufacturing	Adam Smith
1799	Interchangeable parts, cost accounting	Eli Whitney and others
1832	Division of labour by skill, assignment of jobs by skill, basics of time study	Charles Babbage
1900	Scientific management time study and work study developed, dividing planning and doing of work	Frederick W. Taylor
1900	Motion of study of jobs	Frank B. Gilbreth
1901	Scheduling techniques for employees, machines jobs in manufacturing	Henry L. Gantt
1915	Economic lot sizes for inventory control	F.W. Harris
1927	Human relations, the Hawthorne studies	Elton Mayo
1931	Statistical inference applied to product quality: quality control charts	W.A. Shewart
1935	Statistical sampling applied to quality control: inspection sampling plans	H.F. Dodge and H.G. Roming
1940	Operations research applications in World War II	P.M. Blacker and others.
1946	Digital computer	John Mauchlly and J.P. Eckert
1947	Linear programming	G.B. Dantzig, Williams & others
1950	Mathematical programming, nonlinear and stochastic processes	A. Charnes, W.W. Cooper and others
1951	Commercial digital computer: large scale computations available	Sperry Univac
1960	Organizational behaviour: continued study of people at work	L. Cummings, L. Porter
1970	Integrating operations into overall strategy and policy, computer applications to manufacturing, scheduling and control, material requirement planning (MRP)	W. Skinner J. Orlicky and G. Wright
1980	Quality and productivity applications from Japan: robotics, CAD-CAM	W.E. Deming and J. Juran

The term *production management* became acceptable from the 1930s to the 1950s. As the works of F.W. Taylor became more widely known, managers developed techniques that focused on the economic efficiency in manufacturing. Workers were studied in great detail to eliminate wasteful efforts and achieve greater efficiency. At the same time, psychologists, socialists and other social scientists began to study people and human behaviour in the working environment. In addition, economists, mathematicians and computer socialists contributed newer, more sophisticated analytical approaches.

With the 1970s emerged two distinct changes in our views. The most obvious of these, reflected in the new name *operations management,* was a shift in the service and manufacturing sectors of the economy. As the service sector became more prominent, the change from 'production' to 'operations' emphasized the broadening of our field to service organizations. The second, more suitable change was the beginning of an emphasis on synthesis, rather than just analysis, in management practices.

Planning, implementation and control of industrial production processes are used to ensure a smooth and an efficient operation. The techniques of production management are used in both manufacturing and service industries. The responsibilities of production management include the traditional 'five M's': men and women, machines, methods, materials and money. The managers are expected to maintain an efficient production process with a workforce that can readily adapt to new equipment and schedules. They may use industrial engineering methods, such as time-and-motion studies, to design efficient work methods. They are responsible for managing both the physical (raw) materials and the information materials (paperwork or electronic documentation). Inventory control is most important of their duties involving money. This involves tracking all the component parts, work in process, finished goods, packaging materials and general supplies. The production cycle requires that the sales, financial, engineering and the planning departments exchange information—such as sales forecasts, inventory levels and budgets—until detailed production orders are dispatched by the production control division. Managers must also monitor operations to ensure that planned output levels, cost levels and quality objectives are met.

Production management, alternatively referred to as *manufacturing management*, is required for transforming raw materials and partly fabricated materials into finished products. Production management does not imply management of productive processes alone, but it covers all the activities that go into the making of production. To make production a concrete reality, one must pay heed to the factors of production like land, labour, capital and organization, or to speak in the language of business— materials, man, money, machines and methods. Production management, thus, calls for the work of planning and control pertaining to each of these factors of production.

Production management does not involve a mechanical assemblage of relevant factors. In contrast to mere transformation of raw materials into finished products, it aims at transmuting and permuting resources of higher productivity so that the greatest outputs are obtained from the least inputs. With its end in view, production management embraces the productive process too and involves planning, directing and controlling operations till their successful completion. Quality, quantity, cost and time of production have an important bearing on the productivity of the manufacturing enterprise. Accordingly, it is the task of the production management to see that the effective utilization of resources is made, time is shortened, wastes and scrapings are avoided, and harmonious working is made to prevail in the plant. For an effective managerial performance, the work of the production department is required to be organized on sound lines. All the principles and practices of organizing are to be applied in building a sound structure for improving the result of production management. Successful production management is not practicable without the existence of an appropriate organization structure. Consequently, managerial efforts are to be directed in designing an organizational structure that conforms to the needs of the product, size of the enterprise and availability of production facilities. Organizing for production may be conceived, in a broader sense, to include some aspects of works engineering or works organization like plant layout and factory building. The problems of production management differ from one case to the other and are mainly related to the system of production. There are several systems of production that determine the magnitude of production work and the problems to be tackled in the manufacturing operations. Hence, a familiarity with the different systems of production is required for understanding the intricacies of production management. Of course, the system of production is dictated in a particular case by the volume of sales and the nature of the products. The quantity to be produced is nothing but an answer to the question of 'what can be sold'. In the ultimate analysis, therefore, sales are the regulator of a system of production.

The management of transformation process, of inputs into outputs, is the essence of production management. In the present competitive world, the production process in every enterprise needs some effective and scientific planning as well as proper control. Thus, production management can be defined as the 'Management which by scientific planning and regulation sets into motion the part of an enterprise to which it has been entrusted the task of actual transformation of inputs into output'. In the words of Mr E.L. Brech, 'Production management then becomes the process of effectively planning and regulating the operations of that part of an enterprise which is responsible for the actual transformation of materials into finished products'. This definition appears to be incomplete as it does not include the human factors involved in a production process. It lays stress only on the materialistic features. In a broader sense, production management actually deals with decision making related to production processes, so that the resulting goods and services are produced in accordance with the quantitative specifications and demand schedule with minimum cost. To attain these objectives, the two main activities of production management are the design and control of production systems.

In production management, effective planning and control are essential. In the absence of effective planning and regulation of any production activity, the goals cannot be achieved, the customers may not be satisfied and ultimately certain activities may be closed that may lead to social evils.

CONCEPT OF PRODUCTION

Production function is that part of an organization that is concerned with the transformation of a range of inputs into the required outputs (products), having the requisite quality level. Production is defined as 'the step-by-step conversion of one form of material into another form through chemical or mechanical process to create or enhance the utility of the product to the user'. Thus production is a value-addition process. At each stage of processing, there will be value addition.

Edwood Buffa defines production as 'a process by which goods and services are created'.

Some examples of production are: manufacturing custom-made products like boilers with a specific capacity, constructing flats, some structural fabrication works for selected customers, etc., and manufacturing standardized products like car, bus, motor cycle, radio, television, etc.

PRODUCTION SYSTEM

The production system is that part of an organization that produces products of the organization. It is that activity whereby resources, flowing within a defined system, are combined and transformed in a controlled manner to add value in accordance with the policies communicated by the management.

The production system has the following characteristics:

1. Production is an organized activity, so every production system has an objective.
2. The system transforms the various inputs to useful outputs.
3. It does not operate in isolation from the other organization systems.
4. There exists a feedback about the activities that is essential to control and improve the system performance.

PRODUCTION METHODS

One activity of the administrative side of production is concerned with finding and stating the one best way to do all jobs. No longer is this left to the skilled and interested operators, proceeding by trials and errors, successive operators making the same, or sometimes a different result. As more machines, tools and equipments, some of them highly specialized, have been designed and become available, new materials and process materials and processes developed, it has become increasingly a skilled technical job to keep abreast of the developments and always to be up-to-date or know the best way to do a job. It would be quite impossible today for the craftsman at the bench or the machine to keep himself so informed and do a job of producing. Skilled men are still required, but increasingly today they become setters, minders or maintenance men. The old type of foreman is apt to think that the appointment of a production engineer, process engineer or a chemist reduces his usefulness or his value to the company or his status. It does nothing of the kind, of course. It is true that, before the development of production engineering and the use of chemists in the works as well as in the analytical laboratory, the work manager and his foreman supplied the production 'know-how', and decided how a job should be done. But it is now recognized that the training and supervision of people is a much more complex job than it once was and to relive a foreman of a large amount of administrative work makes it possible for a higher general performance and his job more valuable, not less. It is essential to separate planning from doing, administration from execution.

When a new material is developed or a new product designed, the method of production is obviously either known or worked out. But from then onwards all is change. Better methods of production are being discovered continually. Furthermore, in many factories, particularly those engaged in engineering, the detailed method of production for each part to be manufactured, the machines to be used and equipment required, is decided subsequent to the design. The task of deciding the best method of production, of saying how a job shall be produced and of finding new and better ways of doing so, should be the responsibility of a method of the production engineering department. Similarly, in a company where the technical knowledge is supplied by chemists, the production method would be the responsibility of the works laboratory.

In deciding the one best way of doing a job, the production engineer or a chemist must have regard for the costs of production, and therefore for the time to do the job. He must also have some say in the new tools or equipment required. These are the three divisions into which the activities of the production or the methods engineer usually fall that is to say, work study or methods, work measurement or time study, and tool design. These three aspects all call for close collaboration with the designer and the works departments. The design of the jigs and tools might be thought to be a logical development of the design or the drawing office work and in some works it is done in the drawing office. But it cannot be effectively developed without a detailed study of methods and work being done in the factory and, as will be shown later, this study forms the basis of the standards for time and hence for the payment by results, production planning and costs. This study work calls for a specialized technique and training quite different from the drawing office work. The outlook required is different too. It is more successful in practice if it is recognized as a separate activity and combined with the design of tools and equipment. To avoid it becoming too remote from or independent of the drawing office, design department, or technical department the new drawings, designs or technical developments should always be referred to, and discussed with, the production engineers before the final issue. The development of production engineering as a special skill and the extensive use of specially designed tools and equipment have contributed largely to a greater output per man-hour. There is no doubt that it is through such development, adding horse-power to man-power and taking out the manual efforts from the jobs, there lies a way to reduce man-hour requirements.

Because the production engineers tend to get machine or gadget minded, they are apt to forget or neglect the human factor. Machines cannot yet operate without human agency and men should not be made into robots. The foremen may have something to say if the division of labour, for example, is carried too far or if new methods are forced on them without consultation. Continued and close cooperation between the production engineers and works departments is absolutely essential.

The function of the production engineering or methods department is to determine, in collaboration with the design and works departments, the most effective, economical and the suitable method of production and to design special tools and equipment required.

PRODUCTION PLANNING

Planning may be defined as 'Any information which either specifies or guides the taking of future actions by its members geared towards overcoming existing or anticipated problems'. Billy E. Goetz has rightly remarked planning as 'fundamentally choosing', and 'a planning problem arises when an alternative course of action is discovered'. So, in the simplest way, we may define production planning as the planning of production. But production planning requires a careful and elaborate study of coordinating the related activities that are necessarily performed by different departments. Messrs. Bethol, Smith and others in their book *Industrial Organization and Management* have defined the production planning as 'It is a series of related and coordinated activities performed by not one but a number of different departmental groups, each activity being designed to systematize in advance the manufacturing efforts in its area'.

Conclusively, production planning may be defined in the words that 'It is the predetermination of manufacturing requirements such as available materials, money men, order, priority, production process, etc., within the scope of Industrial unit for efficient production of goods to cope with its sale requirements'.

Production planning mainly depends on the type of manufacturing plants that can be divided into two categories:
1. Continuous type of manufacturing plants such as rayon, yarn, shoes, paper plants, etc., and
2. Intermitted type of manufacturing plants such as the engineering type of plants and also repetitive type of industries—automobiles, typewriters, etc.

Planning in the continuous type of plant is somewhat easy as we have to only decide what and when, and not to decide how and where. In the intermittent type of plant, planning becomes difficult by the entry of a number of complex factors into the picture. The same machine is engaged for production of different parts at different times, the machine is kept busy to meet the requirements for various parts to the customer's best satisfaction. In the repetitive type of plant, such as automobiles, the process appears to be continuous but we have depend on many parts meeting the schedule before we can move on to the next; thus planning becomes complex. For example, in an automobile plant, a subassembly process cannot be said to be complete unless all the various parts, whether manufactured on the plant or sub-contracted form outside, are available as complete.

CLASSIFICATION OF THE PRODUCTION SYSTEM

The production systems can be classified as job shop, batch, mass and continuous production systems. They are discussed as follows:

Job Shop Production

Job shop productions are characterized by manufacturing of one product or quantity of products in few numbers designed and produced as per the specification of customers within the prefixed time and cost. The distinguishing feature of this is low volume and high variety of products. A job shop comprises of general purpose machines arranged into different departments. Each job demands unique technological requirements, demands processing on machines in a certain sequence.

Characteristics

The job shop production system is followed when there is

1. high variety of products and low volume,
2. use of general purpose machines and facilities,
3. highly skilled operators who can take up each job as a challenge because of uniqueness,
4. large inventory of materials, tools, parts and
5. detailed planning is essential for sequencing the requirements of each product or capacities for each work centre and order priorities.

Advantages

Following are the advantages of job shop production:

1. Because of general purpose machines and facilities, a variety of products can be produced
2. Operators will become more skilled and competent, as each job gives them learning opportunities
3. Full potential of operators can be utilized
4. An opportunity exists for creative methods and innovative ideas

Limitations

Following are the limitations of job shop production:

1. Higher cost due to frequent setup changes
2. Higher level of inventory at all levels and hence higher inventory cost
3. Production planning is complicated
4. Larger space requirements

Batch Production

Batch production is defined by the American Production and Inventory Control Society (APICS) 'as a form of manufacturing in which the job passes through the functional departments in lots or batches and each lot may have a different routing'. It is characterized by the manufacture of limited number of products produced at regular intervals and stocked awaiting sales.

Characteristics

Batch production system is used under the following circumstances:

1. When there is shorter production runs

2. When the plant and machinery are flexible
3. When the plant and machinery setup is used for the production of an item in a batch and a change of se up is required for processing the next batch
4. When the manufacturing lead time and cost are lower as compared to the job order production

Advantages

Following are the advantages of batch production:

1. Better utilization of plant and machinery
2. Promotes functional specialization
3. The cost per unit is lower as compared to the job order production
4. Lower investment in plant and machinery
5. Flexibility to accommodate and process a number of products
6. Job satisfaction exists for operators

Limitations

Following are the limitations of batch production:

1. Material handling is complex because of irregular and longer flows
2. Production planning and control is complex
3. Work in process inventory is higher as compared to continuous production
4. Higher setup costs due to frequent changes in setup

Mass Production

The manufacture of discrete parts or assemblies using a continuous process is called *mass production*. This production system is justified by very large volume of production. The machines are arranged in a line or product layout. The product and process standardization exists and all outputs follow the same path.

Characteristics

Mass production is used under the following circumstances:

1. Standardization of product and process sequence
2. Dedicated special purpose machines having higher production capacities and output rates
3. Large volume of products
4. Shorter cycle time of production
5. Lower in process inventory
6. Perfectly balanced production lines
7. Flow of materials, components and parts is continuous and without any back tracking
8. Production planning and control is easy
9. Material handling can be completely automatic

Advantages

Following are the advantages of mass production:

1. Higher rate of production with reduced cycle time
2. Higher capacity utilization due to line balancing
3. Less skilled operators are required
4. Low process inventory
5. Manufacturing cost per unit is low

Limitations

Following are the limitations of mass production:

1. Breakdown of one machine will stop an entire production line
2. Line layout needs major change with the changes in the product design
3. High investment in production facilities
4. The cycle time is determined by the slowest operation

Continuous Production

In continuous production, the production facilities are arranged as per the sequence of production operations from the first operations to the finished product. The items are made to flow through the sequence of operations through material handling devices such as conveyors, transfer devices, etc.

Characteristics

Continuous production is used under the following circumstances:

1. Dedicated plant and equipment with zero flexibility
2. Material handling is fully automated
3. Process follows a predetermined sequence of operations
4. Component materials cannot be readily identified with the final product
5. Planning and scheduling is a routine action

Advantages

Following are the advantages of continuous production:

1. Standardization of product and process sequence
2. Higher rate of production with reduced cycle time
3. Higher capacity utilization due to line balancing
4. Manpower is not required for material handling as it is completely automatic
5. Person with limited skills can be used on the production line
6. Unit cost is lower due to the high volume of production

Limitations

Following are the limitations of continuous production:

1. Flexibility to accommodate and process number of products does not exist
2. Very high investment for setting flow lines
3. Product differentiation is limited

PRODUCTION MANAGEMENT

Production management is a process of planning, organizing, directing and controlling the activities of the production function. It combines and transforms various resources used in the production subsystems of the organization into value-added products in a controlled manner as per the policies of the organization.

E.S. Buffa defines production management as 'Production management deals with decision-making related to production processes so that the resulting goods or services are produced according to the specifications, in the amount and by the schedule demanded and out of minimum cost'.

Objectives of Production Management

The objective of the production management is 'to produce goods services of right quality and quantity at the right time and the right manufacturing cost'. These objectives are discussed below:

Right quality

The quality of a product is established based upon the customers needs. The right quality is not necessarily the best quality. It is determined by the cost of the product and the technical characteristics as suited to the specific requirements.

Right quantity

The manufacturing organization should produce the products in the right number. If they are produced in the excess of the demand, the capital will block up in the form of inventory and if the quantity is produced in short of demand, it will lead to shortage of products.

Right time

Timeliness of delivery is one of the important parameters to judge the effectiveness of the production department. So, the production department has to make the optimal utilization of input resources to achieve its objectives.

Right manufacturing cost

Manufacturing costs are established before the product is actually manufactured. Hence, all attempts should be made to produce the products at pre-established cost, so as to reduce the variation between the actual and the standard (pre-established) cost.

OPERATING SYSTEM AND OPERATIONS MANAGEMENT

The operating system converts inputs in order to provide the outputs required by the customer. It converts physical resources into outputs, the function of which is to satisfy customer wants that is, to provide some utility for the customer. In some organizations, the product is a physical good (hotels) while in others it is a service (hospitals). The bus and taxi services, tailors, hospital and builders are some examples of an operating system.

Everett E. Adam and Ronald J. Ebert define operating system as 'An operating system (function) of an organization is the part of an organization that produces the organization's physical goods and services'.

Ray Wild defines operating system as 'An operating system is a configuration of resources combined for the provision of goods or services'.

Operations management is an area of business that is concerned with the production of goods and services, and involves the responsibility of ensuring that the business operations are efficient in terms of using as little resource as needed, and effective in terms of meeting the customer requirements. It is concerned with managing the process that converts inputs (in the forms of materials, labour and energy) into outputs (in the form of goods and services).

Operations, traditionally, refer to the production of goods and services separately, although, the distinction between the two main types of operations is increasingly difficult to make as manufacturers tend to merge product and service offerings. More generally, operations management aims to increase the content of value-added activities in any given process. Fundamentally, these value-adding creative activities should be aligned with market opportunity for optimal enterprise performance.

According to the US Department of Education, the operations management is (the field concerned with managing and directing) the physical and/or technical function of a firm or an organization, particularly those relating to the development, production and manufacturing. The operations management programs typically include, instructions in principles of general management, manufacturing and production systems, plant management, equipment maintenance management, production control, industrial labour relations and skilled trades' supervision, strategic manufacturing policies, systems analysis, productivity analysis and cost control, and materials planning.

Operations management focuses on carefully managing the processes to produce and distribute products and services. Usually, small businesses do not talk about 'operations management', but they carry out the activities that the management schools typically associates with the phrase 'operations management'. Major overall activities often include product creation, development, production and distribution. (These activities are also associated with the product and service management. However, product management is usually in regard to one or more closely related products—that is, a product line. Operations management is in regard to all the operations within the organization). Related activities of operations management include, managing purchases, inventory control, quality control, storage, logistics and evaluations. A great deal of focus is on the efficiency and effectiveness of the processes. Therefore, operations management often includes substantial measurement and analysis of internal processes. Ultimately, the nature of how the operations management is carried out in an organization depends very much on the nature of the products or the services in the organization, e.g. retail, manufacturing, wholesale, etc.

Nowadays, operations management is of critical importance to business and the organization. It is the management of manufacturing, production and services operations. Operations management is diverse. It may be defined as the design, operation and improvement of the production system that creates the firm's primary products or services. However, the role of information technology is the most effective tool, strategy, and technique of the operations management functions and it supports the decision making process of operations management. Information technology is increasing in every business functions, especially in the operations management function. This research supports how information technology affects the operations management from many perspectives such as decision-making process, communication, production systems and management.

What Is Operations Management?

Operations management deals with the design and management of products, processes, services and supply chains. It considers the acquisition, development and utilization of resources that firms need to deliver the goods and services to their clients' expectation.

The survey of OM ranges from strategic to tactical and operational levels. The representative strategic issues include determining the size and location of manufacturing plants, deciding the structure of services or telecommunication networks and designing technology supply chains.

Tactical issues include, plant layout and structure, project management methods, and equipment selection and replacement. Operational issues include production scheduling and control, inventory management, quality control and inspection, traffic and materials handling, and equipment maintenance policies.

Concept of operations

An operation is defined in terms of the mission it serves for the organization; the technology it employs; and the human and managerial processes it involves. Operations in an organization can be categorized into manufacturing operations and service operations. Manufacturing operations is a conversion process that includes manufacturing and yields a tangible output—a product, whereas a conversion process that includes service yields an intangible output—a deed, a performance or an effort.

Distinction between manufacturing operations and service operations

The following characteristics can be considered for distinguishing manufacturing operations with service operations:

1. Tangible or intangible nature of output
2. Consumption of output
3. Nature of work (job)
4. Degree of customer contact
5. Customer participation in conversion
6. Measurement of performance

Manufacturing is characterized by tangible outputs (products) that the customers consume overtime, jobs that use less labour and more equipment, little customer contact, no customer participation in the conversion process (in production), and sophisticated methods for measuring production activities and resource consumption as product are made.

OBJECTIVES OF OPERATIONS MANAGEMENT

The objectives of operations management can be categorized into customer service and resource utilization.

Customer Service

The first objective of operating systems is customer service, the satisfaction of customer wants. Therefore, customer service is a key objective of operations management. The operating system must provide something to the specification that can satisfy the customer in terms of cost and timing. Thus, the primary objective can be satisfied by providing the 'right thing at a right price at the right time'.

Table 12.2. Aspects of Customer Service

Principal function	Principal customer wants	
	Primary considerations	Other considerations
Manufacture	Goods of a given or requested acceptable specification	Cost, i.e. purchase price or cost of obtaining goods Timing, i.e. delivery delay from order or request receipt of goods
Transport	Management of a given or requested requested acceptable specification	Cost, i.e. cost of movements Timing, i.e. 1. Duration or time to move 2. Wait or delay from requesting its commen-commencement
Supply	Supply of a given or requested acceptable specification	Cost, i.e. purchase price or cost of obtaining goods Timing, i.e. delivery delay from order or request receipt of goods
Service	Treatment of a given or requested or requested acceptable specification	Cost, i.e. cost of movements Timing, i.e. 1. Duration or time required for treatment 2. Wait or delay from requesting treatment to its commencement

These aspects of customer service—specification, cost and timing—are described against four functions in Table 12.2. They are the principal sources of customer satisfaction and must, therefore, be the principal dimension of the customer service objective for operations managers.

Generally an organization will aim for reliability and consistency to achieve certain standards and the operations manager will be influential in attempting to achieve these standards. Hence, this objective will influence the operations manager's decisions to achieve the required customer service.

Resource utilization

Another major objective of the operating systems is to utilize the resources efficiently for the satisfaction of the wants of the customer, i.e. the customer service must be provided with the achievement of effective operations through efficient use of resources. Inefficient use of resources or inadequate customer service leads to commercial failure of an operating system.

Operations management is concerned essentially with the utilization of resources, i.e. obtaining maximum effect from the resources or minimizing their loss, under utilization or waste. The extent of the utilization of the resources potential might be expressed in terms of the proportion of available time used or occupied, space utilization, levels of activity, etc. Each measure indicates the extent to which the potential or capacity of such resources is utilized. This is referred as the *objective of resource utilization*.

Operations management is also concerned with the achievement of both satisfactory customer service and resource utilization. An improvement in one will often give rise to the deterioration in the other. Often both cannot be maximized, and hence a satisfactory performance must be achieved on both objectives. All the activities of operations management must be tackled with these two objectives in mind, and many problems will be faced by operations managers because of this conflict. Hence, the operations managers must attempt to balance these basic objectives.

The role of the operations manager

Some people (especially those professionally involved in operations management) argue that operations management involves everything an organization does. In this sense, every manager is an operations manager, since all managers are responsible for contributing to the activities required to create and deliver goods or services to an organization. However, others argue that this definition is too wide, and that the operations function is about producing the right amount of a good or service, at the right time, of the right quality and at the right cost to meet customer requirements.

So, operations managers are responsible for managing activities that are part of the production of goods and services. Their direct responsibilities include, managing the operations process, embracing design, planning, control, performance improvement and operations strategy. Their indirect responsibilities include interacting with those managers in other functional areas within the organization whose roles have an impact on operations. Such areas include marketing, finance, accounting, personnel and engineering.

Following are the responsibilities of an operations manager:

1. **Human resource management**—the people employed by an organization either work directly to create a good or service or provide support to those who do. People and the way they are managed are a key resource of all organizations.
2. **Asset management**—an organization's buildings, facilities, equipment and stock are directly involved in or support the operations function.
3. **Cost management**—most of the cost of producing goods or services are directly related to the cost of acquiring resources, transforming them or delivering them to the customers. For many

organizations in the private sector, driving down cost through efficient operations management gives them a critical competitive edge. For organizations in the not-for-profit sector, the ability to manage cost is no less important.

4. Decision making is a central role of all operations managers. Decisions need to be made in:
   a. designing the operations system
   b. managing the operations system
   c. improving the operations system.

The five main kinds of decision in each of these relate to the following:

1. the processes by which goods and services are produced
2. the quality of goods or services
3. the quantity of goods or services (the capacity of operations)
4. the stock of materials (inventory) needed to produce goods or services
5. the management of human resources

THE TRANSFORMATION MODEL

The discussion above has highlighted the role of operations in creating and delivering the goods and services produced by an organization for its customers. This section introduces the transformation model for analysing operations. This is shown in Figure 12.1., which represents the three components of operations: inputs, transformation processes and outputs. Operations management involves the systematic direction and control of the processes that transform resources (inputs) into finished goods or services for customers or clients (outputs). This basic transformation model applies equally in manufacturing and service organizations and in both the private and not-for-profit sectors.

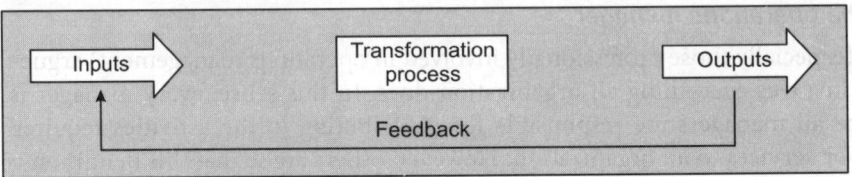

Figure 12.1. The Transformation Model

Inputs

Some inputs are used in the process of creating goods or services; others play a part in the creation process but are not used up. To distinguish between these, input resources are usually classified as:

1. **Transformed resources**—those that are transformed in some way by the operations to produce the goods or services that are its outputs
2. **Transforming resources**—those that are used to perform the transformation process.

Inputs include different types of both transformed and transforming resources.

There are three types of resource that may be transformed in operations that are discussed below:

1. **Materials**, the physical inputs to the process
2. **Information** that is being processed or used in the process
3. **Customers**, the people who are transformed in some way

Many people think of operations as being mainly about the transformation of materials or components into finished products, as when limestone and sand are transformed into glass or an automobile is assembled from its various parts. But all organizations that produce goods or services transform resources. Many are concerned mainly with the transformation of information (e.g. consultancy firms or accountants) or the transformation of customers (e.g. hairdressing or hospitals).

Galloway (1998) defines operations as all the activities concerned with the transformation of materials, information or customers.

The two types of transforming resource are as follows:

1. **Staff**—the people involved directly in the transformation process or supporting it
2. **Facilities**—land, buildings, machines and equipment

The staff involved in the transformation process may include both kinds of people, those who are directly employed by the organization and those contracted to supply services to it. They are sometimes described as 'labour'. The facilities of an organization—buildings, machinery and equipment—are sometimes referred to as 'capital'. Operations vary greatly in the mix of labour and capital that make up their inputs. Highly automated operations depend largely on capital; others rely mainly on labour.

Outputs

The principal outputs of a doctor's surgery are cured patients; the outputs of a nuclear reprocessing plant include reprocessed fuel and nuclear waste. Many transformation processes produce both goods and services. For example, a restaurant provides a service, but also produces goods such as food and drinks.

Transformation processes may result in some undesirable outputs (such as nuclear waste in the example above) as well as the goods and services they are designed to deliver. An important aspect of operations management in some organizations is minimizing the environmental impact of waste over the entire life cycle of their products up to the point of final disposal. Thus, protecting the health and safety of employees and that of the local community is also the responsibility of operations management. In addition, the operations function may be responsible for the ethical behaviour in relation to the social impact of the transformation processes, both locally and globally. For example, in the United States, manufacturers of sports footwear have come under fire for employing child labour and paying low wages to workers employed in their overseas factories.

Transformation processes

A transformation process is any activity or group of activities that takes one or more inputs, transforms and adds value to them, and provides outputs for customers or clients. Where the inputs are raw materials, it is relatively easy to identify the transformation involved, as when milk is transformed into cheese and butter. Where the inputs are information or people, the nature of the transformation may be less obvious. For example, a hospital transforms patients who are ill (the input) to healthy patients (the output).

The transformation processes include the following:

1. Changes in the physical characteristics of the materials or customers
2. Changes in the location of the materials, information or customers
3. Changes in the ownership of materials or information
4. Storage or accommodation of the materials, information or customers
5. Changes in the purpose or form of the information
6. Changes in the physiological or psychological state of the customers

Often all three types of input—materials, information and customers—are transformed by the same organization. For example, withdrawing money from a bank account involves information about the customer's account, materials such as cheques and currency, and the customer. Treating a patient in the hospital involves not only the customer's state of health, but also any materials used in the treatment and the information about the patient.

One useful way of categorizing different types of transformation is into the following:

1. **Manufacture**—the physical creation of products (e.g. cars)
2. **Transport**—the movement of materials or customers (e.g. a taxi service)
3. **Supply**—change in the ownership of goods (e.g. in retailing)
4. **Service**—the treatment of customers or the storage of materials (e.g. hospital wards, warehouses)
5. Several different transformations are usually required to produce a good or service. The overall transformation can be described as the *macro operation* and the more detailed transformation within this macro operation as *micro operations*.

Feedback

A further component of the transformation model in Figure 12.1 is the feedback loop. Feedback information is used to control the operations system, by adjusting the inputs and the transformation processes that are used to achieve the desired outputs. For example, a chef relies on the flow of information from the customer, through the waiter, about the quality of the food. Adverse feedback might lead the chef to change the inputs (e.g. by buying better quality potatoes) or the transformation process (e.g. by changing the recipe or the cooking method).

Feedback is essential for operations managers. It can come from both the internal and external sources. Internal sources include testing, evaluation and continuously improving goods and services; external sources include those who supply products or services to end customers as well as take feedbacks from the customers themselves.

The boundary of the operations system

The simple transformation model provides a powerful tool for looking at operations in many different contexts. It helps us to analyse and design operations in many types of organization at many levels. This model can be developed by identifying the boundaries of the operations system through which the goods and services of an organization are provided to its customers or clients. In this model, there are three components located outside it. They are as follows:

1. Suppliers
2. Customers
3. Environment

Suppliers: Suppliers provide inputs to the operations system. They may supply raw materials (e.g. a quarrying company providing limestone to transform into glass); components (as in car assembly); finished products (e.g. a pharmaceutical company providing drugs to a hospital, or an office supplies company providing it with stationery); or services (as in the case of a law firm providing legal advice).

Customers: Customers (or clients) are the users of the outputs of the transformation process. The boundary drawn around the transforming process can be thought of as the boundary of the organization, so that the whole organization is viewed as an operations system, with its customers external to it. This may be an appropriate way of viewing a small organization, whose outputs go directly to its external customers.

However, most macro operations are made up of a number of micro operations, or sub systems. Only the outputs of the final micro operation go directly to a customer or client who is not part of the organization that is carrying out the macro operation. The final users or the clients of the goods or services are the organization's external customer, and the users or clients of the outputs of the other micro-operations are the internal customers. Most of the operations in a large organization serve internal, rather than external customers. For example, if you are the manager of a human resources department, a printing unit or a building maintenance section within a large organization, your customers are internal: they are the other sub systems within the larger organization that are external to your operations system but internal to the organization as a whole.

Environment: All operating systems are influenced by the organization's environment. This environment includes both other functional areas within the organization, each with its own policies, resources, forecasts, goals, assumptions and constraints; and the wider world outside the organization—the legal, political, social and economic conditions within which it is operating. Changes in either the internal or the external environment may affect the functions of operations.

Traditionally, organizations have kept the functions of operations separate from both its customers and its suppliers, in order to protect it from environmental disturbances. This can lead to a closed system mentality, in which the operations function loses contact with external customers and suppliers, and focuses only on the transformation process that it controls. A closed system tends to limit flexibility and result in a loss of competitiveness. An open system mentality, in which communication with the customers and suppliers is encouraged, seeks to reduce the barriers between the operations function and its environment, in order to enhance the organization's competitiveness.

An added complication is that, as organizations become more complex, it becomes increasingly difficult to draw neat boundaries around the operations function. Operations management must, therefore, focus its attention on the key interfaces within the organization as well as on the interfaces between the organization and its external customers and suppliers. Most operations systems are part of a supply chain that involves materials, information and customers, and the distribution of finished goods or services to customers or clients. It is, therefore, the responsibility of the operations function to coordinate the flow of information that links these activities through the supply chain. Thus, while some operations managers are concerned only with the transformation process within a single organizational unit, such as a factory or service outlet, many are involved in managing operations across several organizational units or even across separate organizations.

SCOPE OF PRODUCTION AND OPERATIONS MANAGEMENT

The concern of the production and operations management concern is with the conversion of inputs into outputs, using physical resources, so as to provide the desired utilities to the customer while meeting the other organizational objectives of effectiveness, efficiency and adoptability. It distinguishes itself from the other functions such as personnel, marketing, finance, etc., by its primary concern for 'conversion by using physical resources'. Following are the activities that are listed under production and operations management functions (Figure 12.2):

1. Location of facilities
2. Plant layout and material handling
3. Product design
4. Process design

5. Production planning and control
6. Quality control
7. Materials management
8. Maintenance management

Location of facilities

Location of facilities for operations is a long-term capacity decision that involves a long-term commitment about the geographically static factors that affect a business organization. It is an important decision making at the strategic level for an organization. It deals with questions such as 'where our main operations should be based?'

The selection of the location is a key decision as a large investment is made in building plant and machinery. An improper location of the plant may lead to a waste of all the investments made in the plant and machinery equipments. Hence, the location of the plant should be based on the company's expansion plans and policies, the diversification plans for the products, the changing sources of raw materials and many other factors. The purpose of the location study is to find the optimal location that will result in the greatest advantage to the organization.

Plant layout and material handling

Plant layout refers to the physical arrangement of the facilities. It is the configuration of departments, work centres and equipment in the conversion process. The overall objective of the plant layout is to design a physical arrangement that meets the required output quality and the quantity most economically.

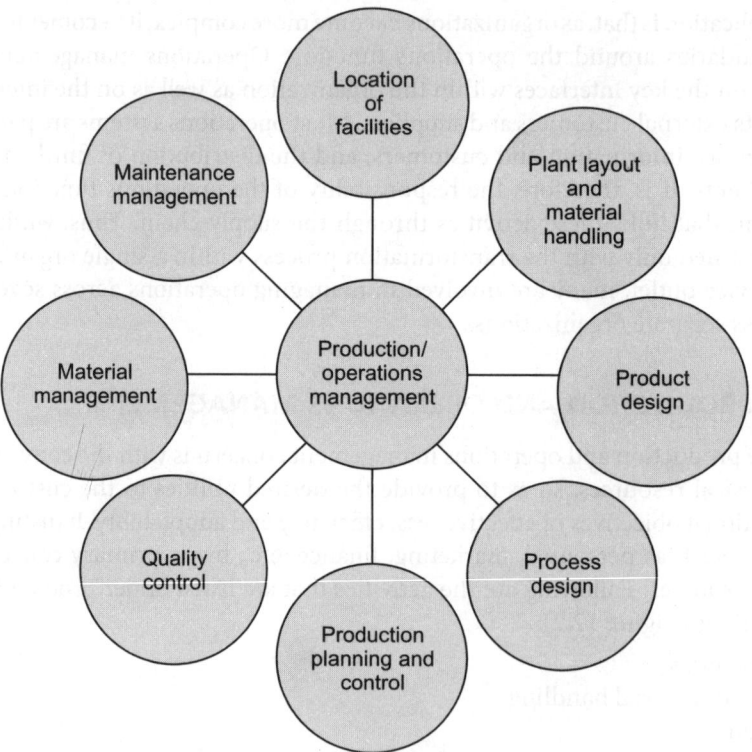

Figure 12.2. Scope of Production and Operations Management

According to James Moore, 'Plant layout is a plan of an optimum arrangement of facilities including personnel, operating equipment, storage space, material handling equipments and all other supporting services along with the design of best structure to contain all these facilities'.

Material handling refers to the 'moving of materials from the store room to the machine and from one machine to the next during the process of manufacture'. It is also defined as the 'art and science of moving, packing and storing of products in any form'. It is a specialized activity for a modern manufacturing concern, with fifty per cent to sevety-five per cent of the cost of production. This cost can be reduced by proper section, operation and maintenance of the material handling devices. Material handling devices increases the output, improves quality, speeds up the deliveries and decreases the cost of production. Hence, material handling is a prime consideration while designing a new plant and also for several existing plants.

Product design

Product design deals with the conversion of ideas into reality. Every business organization has to design, develop and introduce new products as a survival and growth strategy. Developing the new products and launching them in the market is the biggest challenge faced by the organizations. The entire process of need identification to physical manufactures of the product involves three functions: marketing, product development and manufacturing. Product development translates the needs of customers given by the marketing into technical specifications, and then designing the various features into the product to these specifications. Manufacturing has the responsibility of selecting the processes by which the product can be manufactured. Product design and development provides a link between marketing, the customer needs and expectations, and the activities required to manufacture the product.

Process design

Process design is a macroscopic decision making of an overall process route for converting the raw materials into finished goods. These decisions encompass the selection of a process, the choice of technology, the process flow analysis and the layout of the facilities. Hence, the important decisions in process design are to analyse the workflow for converting raw material into finished product and to select the workstation for each included in the workflow.

Production planning and control

Production planning and control can be defined as the process of planning the production in advance, setting the exact route of each item, fixing the starting and finishing dates for each item, to give production orders to the shops and to follow up the progress of the products according to the orders.

The principle of production planning and control lies in the statement 'First plan your work and then work on your plan'. The main functions of production planning and control include, planning, routing, scheduling, dispatching and follow-up.

Planning is deciding in advance what to do, how to do it, when to do it and who is to do it. Planning bridges the gap from where we are, to where we want to go. It makes it possible for things to occur that would not otherwise happen.

Routing may be defined as the selection of the path that each part of the product will follow to being transformed into the finished product from the raw material. Routing determines the most advantageous path to be followed from one department to another and from one machine to another till the raw material gets its final shape.

Scheduling determines the programme for the operations. Scheduling may be defined as 'the fixation of time and date for each operation' as well as it the sequence of operations to be followed.

Dispatching is concerned with the commencement of the processes. It gives necessary authority so as to start a particular work that has already been planned under routing and scheduling. Therefore, dispatching is the 'release of orders and instructions for the starting of production for any item in acceptance with the route sheet and the schedule charts'.

The function of **follow-up** is to report the daily progress of work in each shop in a prescribed performa and to investigate the causes of deviations from the planned performance.

Quality control

Quality Control (QC) may be defined as 'a system that is used to maintain a desired level of quality in a product or a service'. It is a systematic control of various factors that affect the quality of the product. Quality control aims at prevention of defects at the source, relies on effective feedback system and the corrective action procedure.

Quality control can also be defined as 'that industrial management technique by means of which the product of uniform acceptable quality is manufactured'. It is the entire collection of activities that ensures that the operation will produce the optimum quality products at minimum cost.

The main objectives of quality control are as follows:

1. To improve the company's income by making the production more acceptable to the customer, i.e. by providing long life, greater usefulness, maintainability, etc.
2. To reduce the company's cost through the reduction of loss due to defects.
3. To achieve interchangeability of manufacture in large scale production.
4. To produce optimal quality at a reduced price.
5. To ensure the satisfaction of the customer with the production or service of high quality; to build customer goodwill, confidence and reputation of the manufacturer.
6. To make an inspection prompt to ensure quality control.
7. To check the variation during manufacturing.

Materials management

Materials management is that aspect of management function that is primarily concerned with the acquisition, control and use of materials needed, and the flow of goods and services connected with the production process having some predetermined objectives in view. The main objectives of materials management are a follows:

1. To minimize material cost
2. To purchase, receive, transport and store materials efficiently, and to reduce the related cost
3. To cut down costs through simplification, standardization, value analysis, import substitution, etc.
4. To trace new sources of supply and to develop cordial relations with them in order to ensure a continuous supply at reasonable rates
5. To reduce the investment tied in the inventories for use in other productive purposes and to develop high inventory turnover ratios

Maintenance management

In modern industry, equipment and machinery are a very important part of the total productive effort. Therefore, their idleness or downtimes are very expensive. Hence, it is very important that the plant machinery should be properly maintained. The main objectives of maintenance management are:

1. To achieve minimum breakdown and to keep the plant in good working condition at the lowest possible cost
2. To keep the machines and other facilities in such a condition that permits them to be used at their optimal capacity without interruption
3. To ensure the availability of the machines, buildings and services required by other sections of the factory for the performance of their functions at optimal return on investment.

FUNCTIONS OF OPERATIONS MANAGEMENT

A Framework for Managing Operations

Managing operations can be enclosed in a frame of general management functions. Operations managers are concerned with planning, organizing and controlling the activities which affect human behaviour through models. They are discussed below:

Planning

The activities that establish a course of action and guide the future decision making is called *planning*. The operations manager defines the objectives for the operations subsystem of the organization, and the policies, and procedures for achieving those objectives. This stage includes, clarifying the role and focus of operations in the overall strategy of the organization. It also involves product planning, facility designing and using the conversion process.

Organizing

Operations managers establish a structure of roles and the flow of information within the operations subsystem. They determine the activities required to achieve the goals and assign authority and responsibility for carrying them out.

Controlling

Activities that assure the actual performance in accordance with planned performance. To ensure that the plans for the operations subsystems are accomplished, the operations manager must exercise control by measuring actual outputs and comparing them to planned operations management. Controlling cost, quality and schedules are the important functions here.

Behaviour

Operations managers are concerned with how their efforts to plan, organize and control affect the human behaviour. They also want to know how the behaviour of the subordinates can affect the planning, organizing, and controlling actions of the management. Their interest lies in the decision-making behaviour.

Models

As operations managers plan, organize and control the conversion process, they encounter many problems and must make many decisions. They can simplify their difficulties using models like *aggregate planning models* for examining how best to use existing capacity in short term; *break even analysis* to identify break even volumes; *linear programming and computer simulation* for capacity utilization; *decision tree analysis* for long-term capacity problem of facility expansion; *simple median model* for determining best locations of facilities, etc.

NEWER TECHNIQUES IN PRODUCTION MANAGEMENT

Following are the new techniques in production management:

1. Just-in-time (JIT) production
2. Kanban production control system

Just-In-Time (JIT) Production

Just-in-time (JIT) is defined in the APICS dictionary as 'a philosophy of manufacturing based on planned elimination of all waste and on continuous improvement of productivity'. It also has been described as an approach with the objective of producing the right part in the right place at the right time (in other words, 'just in time'). The waste results from any activity that adds cost without adding value, such as the unnecessary moving of materials, the accumulation of excess inventory or the use of faulty production methods that create products requiring subsequent rework. JIT (also known as *lean production* or *stockless production*) should improve profits and return on investment by reducing inventory levels (increasing the inventory turnover rate), reducing variability, improving product quality, reducing production and delivery lead times, and reducing other costs (such as those associated with machine setup and equipment breakdown). In a JIT system, underutilized (excess) capacity is used instead of buffer inventories to hedge against problems that may arise.

JIT applies primarily to repetitive manufacturing processes in which the same products and components are produced over and over again. The general idea is to establish flow processes (even when the facility uses a jobbing or batch process layout) by linking work centres so that there is an even, balanced flow of materials throughout the entire production process, similar to that found in an assembly line. To accomplish this, an attempt is made to reach the goals of driving all inventory buffers towards zero and achieving the ideal lot size of one unit.

The basic elements of JIT were developed by Toyota in the 1950s, and became known as the *Toyota Production System (TPS)*. JIT was well-established in many Japanese factories by the early 1970s. JIT began to be adopted in the US in the 1980s (General Electric was an early adopter), and the JIT or lean concepts are now widely accepted and used.

Some key elements of JIT

Following are some key elements of JIT:

1. Stabilize and level the MPS with uniform plant loading (*heijunka* in Japanese): Create a uniform load on all work centres through constant daily production (establish freeze windows to prevent changes in the production plan for some period of time) and mixed model assembly (produce roughly the same mix of products each day, using a repeating sequence if several products are produced on the same line). Meet demand fluctuations through end-item inventory rather than through fluctuations in production level. Use of a stable production schedule also permits the use of back flushing to manage inventory: an end-item's bill of materials is periodically exploded to calculate the usage quantities of the various components that were used to make the item, eliminating the need to collect detailed usage information on the shop floor.

2. Reduce or eliminate setup times: Aim for single digit setup times (less than ten minutes) or 'one-touch' setup--this can be done through better planning, process redesign and product redesign. A good example of the potential for improved setup times can be found in autoracing, where a NASCAR pit crew can change all four tires and put gas in the tank in under twenty seconds. (How long would it take you to change just one tire on your car?) The pit crew's efficiency is the result of a team effort using specialized equipment and a coordinated, well-rehearsed process.

3. Reduce lot sizes (manufacturing and purchase): Reducing setup times allows economical production of smaller lots; close cooperation with suppliers is necessary to achieve reductions in order lot sizes for purchased items, since this will require more frequent deliveries.

4. Reduce lead times (production and delivery): The production lead times can be reduced by moving workstations closer together, applying group technology and cellular manufacturing concepts, reducing queue length (reducing the number of jobs waiting to be processed at a given machine), and improving the coordination and cooperation between successive processes; delivery lead times can be reduced through close cooperation with suppliers, possibly by inducing suppliers to locate closer to the factory.

5. Preventive maintenance: Use machine and worker idle time to maintain equipment and prevent breakdowns.

6. Flexible work force: Workers should be trained to operate several machines, to perform maintenance tasks, and to perform quality inspections. In general, JIT requires teams of competent, empowered employees who have more responsibility for their own work. The Toyota Production System concept of 'respect for people' contributes to a good relationship between the workers and the management.

7. Require supplier quality assurance and implement a zero defects quality program: Errors leading to defective items must be eliminated, since there are no buffers of excess parts. A quality at the source (*jidoka*) program must be implemented to give workers the personal responsibility for the quality of the work they do, and the authority to stop production when something goes wrong. Techniques such as 'JIT lights' (to indicate line slowdowns or stoppages) and 'tally boards' (to record and analyse causes of production stoppages and slowdowns to facilitate correcting them later) may be used.

8. Small-lot (single unit) conveyance: Use a control system such as a *kanban* (card) system (or other signalling system) to convey parts between workstations in small quantities (ideally, one unit at a time). In its largest sense, JIT is not the same thing as a kanban system, and a kanban system is not required to implement JIT (some companies have instituted a JIT program along with a MRP system), although, JIT is required to implement a kanban system and the two concepts are frequently equated with one another.

Kanban Production Control System

A kanban or pull production control system uses simple, visual signals to control the movement of materials between work centres as well as the production of new materials to replenish those sent downstream to the next work centre. Originally, the name *kanban* (translated as signboard or visible record) referred to a Japanese shop sign that communicated the type of product sold at the shop through the visual image on the sign (e.g. using circles of various colours to indicate a shop that sells paint). As implemented in the Toyota production system, a kanban is a card that is attached to a storage and transport container. It identifies the part number and container capacity, along with other information, and is used to provide an easily understood, visual signal that a specific activity is required.

In Toyota's dual-card kanban system, there are two main types of kanban as follows:

1. **Production kanban:** signals the need to produce more parts
2. **Withdrawal kanban** (also called a *move* or a *conveyance kanban*): signals the need to withdraw parts from one work centre and deliver them to the next work centre.

In some pull systems, other signalling approaches are used in place of kanban cards. For example, an empty container alone (with appropriate identification on the container) could serve as a signal for replenishment. Similarly, a labelled, pallet-sized square painted on the shop floor, if uncovered and visible, could indicate the need to go get another pallet of materials from its point of production and move it on top of the empty square at its point of use.

A kanban system is referred to as a pull system, because the kanban is used to pull parts to the next production stage only when they are needed. In contrast, an MRP system (or any schedule-based system) is a push system, in which a detailed production schedule for each part is used to push parts to the next production stage when scheduled. Thus, in a pull system, material movement occurs only when the work station needing more material asks for it to be sent, while in a push system the station producing the material initiates its movement to the receiving station, assuming that it is needed because it was scheduled for production. The weakness of a push system (MRP) is that the customer demand must be forecast and production lead times must be estimated. Bad guesses (forecasts or estimates) result in excess inventory and the longer the lead time, the more room for error. The weakness of a pull system (kanban) is that following the JIT production philosophy is essential, especially concerning the elements of short setup times and small lot sizes, because each station in the process must be able to respond quickly to requests for more materials.

Dual-Card Kanban Rules

1. No parts are made unless there is a production kanban to authorize production. If no production kanban are in the 'in box' at a work centre, the process remains idle, and workers perform other assigned activities. This rule enforces the 'pull' nature of the process control.
2. There is exactly one kanban per container.
3. Containers for each specific part are standardized, and they are always filled with the same (ideally, small) quantity. (Think of an egg carton, always filled with exactly one dozen eggs.)

Decisions regarding the number of kanban (and containers) at each stage of the process are carefully considered, because this number sets an upper bound on the work-in-process inventory at that stage. For example, if 10 containers holding 12 units each are used to move materials between two work centres, the maximum inventory possible is 120 units, occurring only when all 10 containers are full. At this point, all kanban will be attached to the full containers, so no additional units will be produced (because there are no unattached production kanban to authorize production). This feature of a dual-card kanban system enables systematic productivity improvement to take place. By deliberately removing one or more kanban (and containers) from the system, a manager will also reduce the maximum level of work-in-process (buffer) inventory. This reduction can be done until a shortage of materials occurs. This shortage is an indication of problems (accidents, machine breakdowns, production delays, defective products) that were previously hidden by excessive inventory. Once the problem is observed and a solution is identified, the corrective action is taken so that the system can function at the lower level of buffer inventory. This simple, systematic method of inventory reduction is a key benefit of a dual-card kanban system.

Points to Ponder

1. Production management deals with decision making related to the production processes so that the resulting goods or services are produced according to the specifications, in the amount, by the schedule demanded and out of minimum cost.

2. The term *production management* became acceptable from the 1930s to the 1950s. With the 1970s emerged two distinct changes. They were as follows:

   a. The most obvious of these reflected in the new name *operations management*.

   b. The second more suitable change was the beginning of an emphasis on synthesis, rather than just analysis, in management practices.

3. The production systems can be classified as job shop, batch, mass and continuous production systems.

4. Production and operations management performs the following functions:

   a. Location of facilities

   b. Plant layout and material handling

   c. Product design

   d. Process design

   e. Production planning and control

   f. Quality control

   g. Materials management

   h. Maintenance management

Self-Assessment Exercises

1. What do you mean by *production*?
2. What do you mean by *production system*?
3. Mention the different types of production systems.
4. What is *job shop production*?
5. What is *batch production*?
6. What is *mass production*?
7. What is *continuous production*?
8. Mention any four advantages of the job shop production.
9. Mention any four limitations of job shop production.
10. Mention any four advantages of batch production.
11. Mention any four limitations of batch production.
12. Mention any four advantages of mass production.
13. Mention any four limitations of mass production.
14. Mention any four advantages of continuous production.

15. Mention any four limitations of continuous production.
16. Define *production management*.
17. Mention any four objectives of production management.
18. Define *operating system*.
19. How do you manage operations?
20. What do you mean by *operations*?
21. What do you mean by *manufacturing operations*?
22. What do you mean by *service operations*?
23. Briefly explain the production system and its characteristics.
24. Describe the characteristics, advantages and limitations of job shop production?
25. Describe the characteristics, advantages and limitations of batch production?
26. Describe the characteristics, advantages and limitations of mass production?
27. Describe the characteristics, advantages and limitations of continuous production?
28. Explain in brief the objectives of production management.
29. Explain in brief the objectives of operations management.
30. Distinguish between manufacturing operations and service operations.
31. Explain the key issues to be considered for managing global operations.
32. Explain the different types of production systems.
33. Explain the framework of managing operations.
34. Explain the scope of production and operations management.

Materials Management

INTRODUCTION

Raw materials and semifinished goods are of great significance for the success of an enterprise. These can directly affect the efficiency of a system. Materials management is a basic function of a business that adds value directly to the product itself. Materials management is the planning, directing, controlling and coordinating those activities that are concerned with the materials and inventory requirements from the point of their inception to their introduction into the manufacturing process. Materials management deals with controlling and regulating the flow of materials in relation to the changes in variables like demand prices, availability, quality, delivery schedule, etc.

Materials management deals with procurement of raw materials, machines and equipment that are necessary for the production process and spare parts for the maintenance of the plant.

OBJECTIVES OF MATERIALS MANAGEMENT

The objectives of materials management is discussed below:

1. It helps to provide regular uninterrupted supply of raw materials to ensure the continuity of production
2. It provides economy in purchasing and minimizing waste that leads to high productivity
3. It helps to minimize the cost of production to increase profits
4. It helps to minimize the storage and stock control costs
5. It helps to purchase items of best quality at the most competitive price

Materials management involves the following functions:

1. Planning and programming for materials purchase
2. Stores and stock control
3. Receiving and issuing of the materials
4. Transportation and materials handling of the material
5. Disposal of scrap and surplus materials

ORGANIZATION OF MATERIALS MANAGEMENT DEPARTMENT

In order to facilitate the planning, directing, control and coordination of various activities related to the materials in an enterprise, there should be separate department of materials management.

The organizational structure of the department can be as shown in Figure 13.1 below:

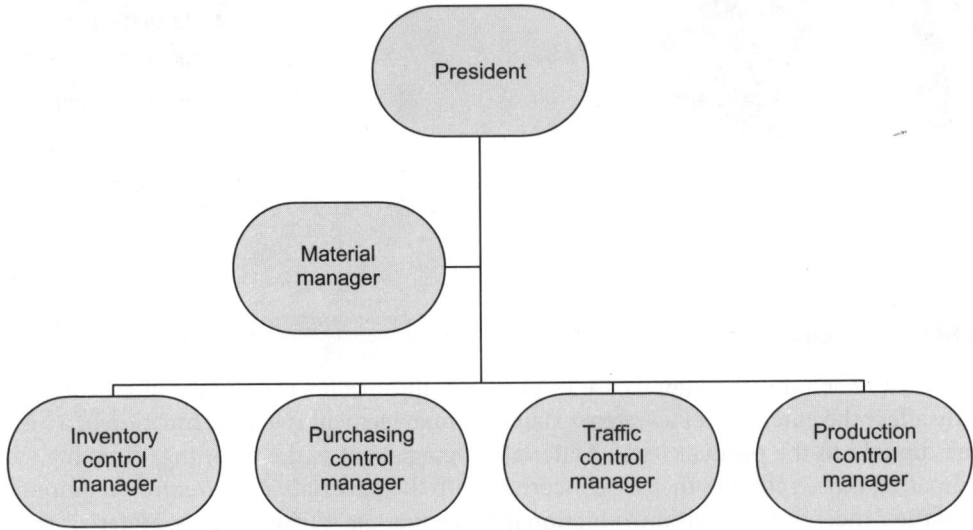

Figure 13.1. Organizational Structure of the Materials Management Department

IMPORTANCE OF MATERIALS MANAGEMENT

The materials management department plays a vital role in the success of an enterprise. Around 70% of the capital is invested in purchase of materials. A well-designed materials management operation can lead to a considerable saving in the capital expenditure. An effective materials management has the following advantages:

1. The regular supply of the materials is ensured, reducing the chances of any interruption in the production process.
2. There is a check on the procurement costs and transportation costs associated with the materials.
3. It minimizes waste of materials due to efficient store and stock control.
4. It assures timely supply of raw materials and other inputs.
5. It helps to avoid congestion in stores at different stages of production.
6. It helps to eliminate shortages.
7. The inspection of materials at the time of their procurement minimizes the possibility of the finished product being rejected by the consumers.
8. It helps in the better utilization of labour, capital and equipment.
9. It helps to reduce the length of the manufacturing cycle to the minimum.
10. A slight change in the cost of materials will exert a great impact on the profit of a firm.

PURCHASING

Purchasing is the first phase of materials management. Purchasing means procurement of goods and services from some external agencies. The object of the purchasing department is to arrange the supply of materials, spare parts and services or semifinished goods required by the organization to produce the desired product. Purchasing is the procuring of materials, supplies, machines, tools and services required for the equipment, maintenance and operation of a manufacturing plant.

Importance and Objectives of Purchasing

The purchase of materials is one of the important functions of materials management. A proper purchase of materials and merchandize, and the control of stock are of great importance in any business, i.e. manufacturing, wholesale or retail trade. In a trading business, the merchandize purchased must be of proper quality at an appropriate price, in proper quantities and at the proper time.

The objective of purchasing is not only to procure the raw material at the lowest price but also to reduce the cost of the final product.

The following points are taken into consideration while purchasing the materials:

1. **Right source:** The source from where the materials are procured must be dependable and capable of supplying items of uniform quality. The buyer has to decide about the proper source for the procurement of materials.
2. **Right quality:** Before purchasing the materials, a sample should be procured and its quality determined. After verifying the right quality, the order may be placed with the supplier for its purchase.
3. **Right quantity:** It is an important factor in buying. While deciding the right quantity, factors such as price structure, discounts and availability of items are to be taken into consideration.

4. **Right price:** The items should be purchased at the right price. The right price does not mean the lowest price. To determine the right price, the cost structure of the product is to be taken into consideration.

5. **Right time:** For determining the right time of purchase, the lead time information is taken into consideration. The lead time means the total time consumed between the recognition of the need of an item till its receipt for use.

6. **Right place of delivery:** The supplier should supply the items at the premises of the business.

7. **Right mode of transportation:** The goods may be supplied by road, rail or air. The mode of transportation is to be decided between the supplier and purchaser.

Organization of the Purchase Department

The organization of the purchase department varies according to the size of the enterprise, its comparative significance towards the procurement and the capability of the purchase personnel.

In an organization engaged in the procurement of smaller range of items from a number of suppliers, the purchase officer is attached to the controller of accounts. In an organization with a batch system of production, purchasing becomes a complicated exercise and needs regular and thorough coordination with the production department. In such cases the purchase manager is directly attached to the production manager.

The size of the purchasing department depends on the nature of the products manufactured by the organization, size of the production runs and type of the manufacturing system.

The composition of the purchasing department is shown in the figure below:

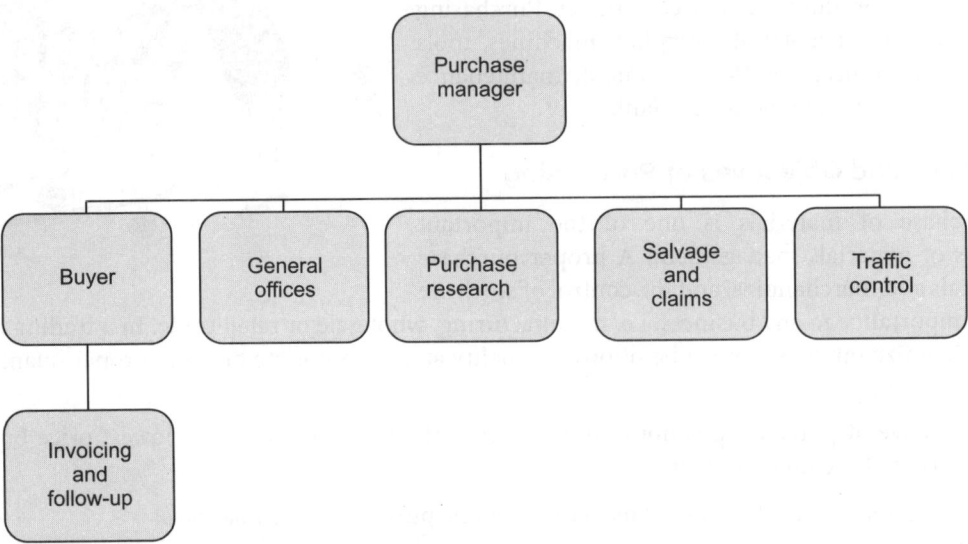

Figure 13.2. Organization of the Purchase Department

Typical Organization of a Purchase Department

In the organization, the purchase manager occupies an important position. He should be a man with quick decision-making skills, should have a pleasing personality, should have good leadership skills and a foresighted approach.

Centralized or Localized Purchasing

The centralized or localized purchasing policy depends upon the nature of the manufacturing organization. In an organization with only one plant, there is mostly centralized purchasing system. In a multi plant organization, sometimes centralized purchase system can be adopted on the basis of homogeneity in terms of product produced, location of plants and suppliers of the material required, etc.

Generally, in case of multi plant organizations, decentralized (localized) purchasing units are preferred in each plant. This system is more appropriate in cases where plants are situated at far away places and are producing different kinds of products.

Advantages

The advantages of a central or localized purchasing unit are as follows:

1. There is undivided responsibility. The officials can concentrate in their operations more efficiently.
2. The purchasing is done in bulk that can be more economical as it increases the bargaining power of the department and can encourage quantity discount.
3. It reduces the inventory carrying cost as well as investment in inventories.
4. The more specialized personnel in purchasing can be employed.
5. There is more economy in the maintenance of records, easy adaptability of the market conditions. All this leads to a most efficient and effective use of the resources.

Disadvantages

The disadvantages of a central or localized purchasing unit are as follows:

1. Localized purchasing can have more flexibility in purchases.
2. It cannot have close liaison with suppliers as well as other departments of the organization.
3. It cannot properly deal the demand and supply problems to avoid misunderstanding and possibility of wrong purchases.

Purchasing Procedure

The purchasing procedure means the sequence of steps through which a purchase transaction takes place. The purchasing procedure starts when it is felt that further supply of an item is required. The purchasing procedure generally involves the following stages:

1. **Purchase requisition:** Whenever the existing stock of an article approaches a minimum limit or the reorder level, the person in charge of the stores ledger, fills the requisition form and sends it to purchase department. The purchase requisition indicates the type, quantity and quality of the item to be purchased.
2. **Selection of the suppliers:** A list of the items to be purchased is sent to various suppliers or a tender is invited through leading newspapers. On receiving the quotations from different suppliers, the comparative statement of all the quotations received is prepared. The supplier who quotes the lowest rate is generally selected. However, apart from the price, other relevant considerations like his ability to supply the required volume, maintenance of the quality of goods, ability to deliver the goods as per the schedule and terms of payment are also taken into consideration.
3. **Placing the order:** After the selection of the supplier, the order is placed on the standard purchase order form commonly known as the supply order. The supply order gives the detailed specification of the items, quantity required, the price and other terms and conditions of the supply. It is signed by the authorized persons. The supply order is a legal document. Generally five or six copies of the

supply order are prepared. Two copies are sent to the suppliers, who are expected to sign one copy as an acknowledgement and return it to the supply department. One copy is sent to the store incharge. One copy goes to the accounts department and one copy remains with the purchase manager.

4. **Receiving and checking of material:** The material that is supplied by the supplier is received and inspected for its quantity and quality. The goods are compared with the *challan* form or invoice or the bill sent by the supplier. If the goods received do not conform to the specifications on the purchase order, the goods are rejected and defects or deficiency, if any, recorded on the invoice or the *challan* form.

5. **Checking of invoice or bill:** If the goods are received in a satisfactory condition, the invoice or bill is checked before it is approved for payment. The rates of the various items charged in the bill and the other terms and conditions are thoroughly checked and compared with the supply order.

6. **Recording of bills in books:** The bills are then sent to the accounts section, where the bills are entered into the account books. The receipt of the damaged materials, excess materials, a short supply or a supply of inferior quality of materials, if any, is reported to the concerned authority for further action.

7. **Releasing the payment to the supplier:** According to the terms and conditions of the supply order, the payment is released by the accounts section to the supplier. However, in small organizations, the payment is released by the purchase department itself.

Methods of Purchasing

There are a number of methods used by different purchase departments.   Following are some popular methods of purchasing:

1. **Purchasing according to requirement:** In such cases, an order is placed only when there is some need for the product. This method is appropriate for those items that are not of regular and common use in the production process. These items are not stored in the inventories. The purchase department always keeps a record of the reliable and trustworthy suppliers who can supply the materials, whenever it is needed to be purchase.

2. **Market purchasing:** The policy of making the purchases at a time when the fluctuations in price of the items provide an advantage to the purchaser is known as *market purchasing*. The method provides procurement at lower price and saving in purchase expenses. The method is useful in situations where the major price variations are prominent.

3. **Speculative purchasing:** The excessive purchases are made when the market is low for the item, with the hope of earning profit by selling such items at a higher price. The merit of this method lies in more profits and more protection against shortages.

4. **Contract purchasing:** The purchase department enters into an agreement with various suppliers to supply the items at some future period or periodically. Generally, the organization tries to enter into a contract when the prices are comparatively low. By this method, the supply is ensured as per the scheduled requirements as well as there is protection against frequent price fluctuations. The method is suitable to both the purchaser and the supplier because the purchaser is able to reduce the size of the inventory and the supplier is assured of a stable demand.

5. **Scheduled purchasing:** It is a scientific method of purchasing. The purchasing is scheduled according to the requirements of various departments of the organization. A proper balance is maintained between the amount procured and the amount required. In fact, scheduled purchasing is closely related to a carefully controlled production.

STOREKEEPING

It is a servicing facility, inside an organization, responsible for the proper storage of the material and then issuing it to the respective departments on proper requisition. The custodian of the stores is generally known as a *storekeeper*. Those items that are not in use for some specific duration, for example, spare parts and the raw materials are called as *store* and the building or space where these are kept is known as a *storeroom*. Storekeeping is that aspect of the materials control that is concerned with the physical storage of goods.

It is an established fact that more than seventy per cent of the capital of an enterprise is invested in stores. Therefore, it is necessary that the management of stores should be entrusted to the experienced, sincere and efficient personnel and the location of stores should be at some proper and safe place.

Objectives of Storekeeping

The objectives of storekeeping are as follows:

1. Easy location of the items in store
2. Proper identification of the items
3. Speedy issue of the materials
4. Efficient utilization of space
5. Reduction in the need of materials handling equipment

Functions of Storekeeping

The functions of storekeeping are as follows:

1. Receiving, handling and speedy issue of material
2. Custodian of goods in store against damage and pilferage
3. To establish regular supply of materials
4. Effective utilization of store space
5. To provide service to the organization in the most economic way
6. To keep the details of the items available in store up-to-date
7. Proper identification and easy location of items
8. Physical checking of stocks

Location of Stores

The location of stores in an enterprise should be at a place where handling, transportation and the movement of materials is minimum. If there is only a single plant or many plants situated at the same area, then it is profitable to have one centralized store to serve all the production operations. But in case of plants located at distant places, it is desired to have separate stores for each plant. Sometimes a policy of maintaining centralized stores for common category of items and decentralized stores for individual items is followed by the management. The choice of a centralized or a decentralized system of stores depends on the degree of control, convenience, reduction in cost of storing, transportation, nature of items, etc. Following are some of the advantages and disadvantages of centralized storing.

Advantages

The advantages of centralized storing are as follows:

1. Economy in investments

2. Reduction in incidental expenses
3. Less storage space. Better security arrangements to safeguard against pilferage and theft
4. Less manpower required thus reducing the administrative costs
5. Economy in transportation costs
6. More bargaining power due to buying in bulk
7. The variety of items in the inventory can be reduced due to a larger scope of standardization of items

Disadvantages

The disadvantages of centralized storekeeping are:

1. More materials handling operations
2. More exposed to loss due to natural calamities like fire, rain, dust, etc
3. The chances of delay are likely to be more

Working of a Stores Department

The stores department performs the following functions:-

1. Receiving: The items ordered by the purchase department are received by this section. The supplier delivers the items along with other documents to the receiving section of the stores department. The consignment is properly checked and entered in the 'goods inward note'. The discrepancy, if any, is also recorded in this note.

The receiving section in the stores department can be centralized, semicentralized or decentralized. The building where the receiving section is located should have sufficient space for loading, unloading and inspection of consignments.

2. Stores section: The stores section is a place where all materials received by the stores department are kept with a protection against deterioration and pilferage. They are stored in such a way that their location is easily identified at the time of issue.

Stores are to provide space to the materials till these are issued to the respective departments of the enterprise. Stores are in the form of covered sheds, building and open space. The stores in charge receive the materials from the receiving sections along with the 'goods inward note'. The material is classified and coded according to their nature and use. The coded sign is inscribed on the items for identification. Items may also be identified by different colours. The items are then stored at assigned shelves or places inside the store. For a quick and easy identification of an item's category, a bin card is tagged with each shelf. The bin card contains up-to-date information about the receipt, issue and balance of the respective items in the stock. The materials from the store section are issued to the respective departments on the instructions from the dispatch section.

A good store is equipped with various types of tools or equipment for handling, measuring, and weighing the materials.

3. Issue section: The issue section handles the issue of materials to departments of the enterprise when required. A storeroom does not always issue a material in the same unit where it is purchased. The materials lying in the store carry some money value and in order to avoid malpractices and to curb the tendency of waste, the items should be issued against proper requisition. The requisition gives details of the type and quantity of the material and is duly signed by some authorized person.

The requisition should be properly checked and scrutinized before the issue of the material. The store clerk puts the identification number of the desired materials on the requisition and passes it to the stock record clerk. The record clerk subtracts the amount of the material issued from the record card, calculates the balance in stock and sends it to the accounting department. The accounts clerk subtracts the value of the account for the issued material.

On the basis of the requisition, the store staff finally collects the items from the stores and sends them to the requisitioning department. All the requisitions must be posted daily on the bin cards and stock register. The fresh balance is struck on every receipt or issue.

Duties of a Storekeeper

The following are the main responsibilities of a stores controller in an organization:

1. The items in stores should be placed in such a way that these can be easily located
2. To maintain cleanliness in the store premises
3. To provide an efficient and effective service to the organization
4. To ensure that materials are issued against authorized requisition only
5. To keep an up-to-date record of the materials issued, received and the balance in stock
6. To maintain an efficient and effective material handling system
7. To communicate the requirements to the purchase department
8. To plan and execute the stock checking activities

INVENTORY CONTROL

An inventory shows the major current assets of a business enterprise. An inventory can be described as the sum of the value of raw materials, fuels and lubricants, spare parts, maintenance consumables, semiprocessed materials and finished goods, the stock of a business firm at any given point of time. Inventories are primarily maintained for a smooth running of the business. On an average, a business has about thirty per cent of its working capital tied up in inventories.

Inventory management is essential to maintain a large size inventory for an efficient and smooth production, and also for sales operation. It also minimizes a firm's investment in inventory with a view to gain maximum profit. For a smooth running of the business enterprise, it is evident that it should keep neither excessive nor inadequate inventories. The inventories should be maintained at a level lying between the excessive and the inadequate. This level is known as *the optimum level of inventories.*

Objectives of Inventory Control

The main purpose of having an inventory control is discussed below:

1. Maximum customer service
2. Minimum inventory investment
3. Low-cost plant operation

Customer service is improved if the inventories are raised to a very high level and the production schedules are kept flexible to meet the changing demands. The inventories block the capital of a business enterprise. They generate storage cost or become obsolete in storage. So, a minimum investment is required to raise inventory. Any interruption of production raises cost. The overall plant costs are kept low by a stable production that is possible only by having sufficient inventories. Apart from the other main objectives discussed above, inventory control is also to keep a balance.

Functions of Inventory Control

The main functions of inventory control are as follows:

1. To keep the inventories as low as possible to be consistent with the market conditions
2. To minimize 'out of stock' danger that results in crash purchase at uneconomical rates
3. To maintain a sufficient stock of the finished products and to meet the reasonable expectations of customers for a prompt delivery of goods
4. To maintain proper records so as to supply an accurate and regular material reports to the management
5. To forecast the market and economic conditions of supply as regards the availability of the materials

Techniques of Inventory Control

The following are the different techniques commonly used to control the inventory:

1. ABC analysis
2. Economic order quantity
3. Perpetual inventory system
4. Review of slow and nonmoving items
5. Input-output ratio analysis
6. Setting of various levels
7. Materials budgeting
8. Establishing an effective purchase procedure

ABC Analysis

In big drug stores, large inventory items are stocked. In order to maintain a proper control of inventories, the ABC (Always Better Control) technique is used. In this technique, the materials are divided into three groups A, B and C according to the cost of the materials and the money value of consumption. These three groups of materials are discussed below:

A items: In the whole of the inventory, there are a few costly items that come under this group. These items may not be more than 10% of the total items, but these consume about 70% of the total budget of inventories. So these items require proper storage and handling. Overstocking is avoided for these items. Only necessary quantities of these inventories are purchased and stocked, so as to minimize the investment on these items.

B items: Those items come under this group that are neither costly nor cheap. These items constitute 20% of the total quantity of the inventories and 20% of the total expenditure of inventories is spent on these items.

C items: C items are comparatively cheaper in cost and represents 70% of the total quantity of the inventories. 10% of the total expenditure of inventories is spent on these items.

Table 13.1 given below gives, in a summary of how an organization treats the various categories of items according to their consumption value.

Table 13.1. Summary of the Various Categories of Items According to their Consumption Value

	A items	B items	C items
1	It covers 10% of the total inventories	It covers 20% of the total inventories	It covers 20% of the total inventories
2	It consumes about 70% of total budget	It consumes about 20% of total budget	It consumes 10% of the total expenditure of inventories
3	It requires very strict control	It requires moderate control	It may require loose control
4	It requires either no safety stocks or low safety stocks	It requires low safely stocks	It requires high safety stocks
5	It needs maximum follow up	It needs periodic follow up	It needs a close follow up
6	It must be handled by senior officers	It can be handled by middle management	It can be handled by any official of the management

Advantages of the ABC analysis

The main advantages of the ABC analysis are discussed as under:

1. The investment in inventory can be regulated and funds can be utilized in the best possible manner.
2. There is a close and strict control on those items that represent a major portion of total stock value.
3. It helps in maintaining enough safety stock of C category of items.
4. The scientific and selective control helps in the maintenance of high stock turnover rate.

Economic order quantity (EOQ)

The technique of EOQ is used to find out how much of the inventory is to be ordered at a time. The correct quantity to buy is the quantity at which the ordering cost and the inventory carrying cost will be the minimum. The ordering cost consists of the cost of paperwork involved in placing an order like the use of paper, typing, posting, filing, etc. It also includes the cost of the salaries of staff involved in this work, the costs incidental to placing an order like follow up, receiving or inspection. The ordering cost is more or less fixed. The inventory carrying cost is represented by items like the rent of storage, the cost of insurance and taxes, the salaries of a storekeeper and the losses in stores due to pilferage, wastage, breakage, etc.

Methods for the determination of economic order quantity

The following methods are generally used for determination of economic order quantity:

1. Tabular determination of EOQ
2. Graphic presentation of EOQ
3. Determination of EOQ by an algebraic formula.

Tabular determination of EOQ: A tabular arrangement of data relating to the items of the materials helps in the determination of an approximate EOQ. This arrangement may help the company to find the number of orders that need to be placed weekly, quarterly, monthly or yearly. The following Table 13.2 helps to determine the EOQ.

Table 13.2. Determining EOQ

	Number of orders per year (1)	Annual ordering cost (2)	Annual inventory carrying cost (3)	Total annual cost (2+3)
1.	12	48	8.33	56.33
2.	6	24	16.66	40.66
3.	4	16	25.00	41.00
4.	3	12	33.33	45.33
5.	2	8	50.00	58.00
6.	1	4	100.00	104.00

For example, the order cost is Rs 4 per order. The inventory carrying cost is 10% of the rupee value of annual usage. The rupee value of the annual usage is Rs 1000.

Suppose an item was ordered once in every month, the order cost per year would be Rs 48.00. Similarly, if the items were purchased once every two months, i.e. 6 times in a year then the cost of ordering for the year would be Rs 24.00 (Rs 4 × 6 = 24). In this manner the annual ordering cost can be calculated for other frequencies.

The annual inventories carrying cost is then calculated by the following method:

The items that were purchased once every month, the annual inventory carrying cost will be (10/100 × 1000/32 = Rs 8.33).

If it were purchased once every two months, the inventory carrying cost would be (10/100 × 1000/6 = Rs 16.66).

Similarly, the inventory carrying cost for other frequencies can be calculated.

The total annual cost of purchasing the items at different order frequencies per year can be calculated by adding the ordering cost and the inventory carrying cost.

From Table 13.2, it is observed that the total annual costs for purchasing the items are the lowest when it is bought six times per year. The total annual cost at this frequency is Rs 40.66 per year.

Graphic presentation of EOQ

The economic order quantity can also be determined graphically. If a graph is plotted between the order quantity and the cost to order and carry, the ideal order size is the point where the sum of both the costs is the minimum. The point occurs at A, where the line representing the annual carrying cost intersects the line representing the ordering cost (Figure 13.3).

Determination of EOQ by algebraic formula

EOQ can also be computed by using the following formula:

$$EOQ = \sqrt{\frac{2ab}{cs}}$$

where,

a = Annual consumption

b = Buying cost per order

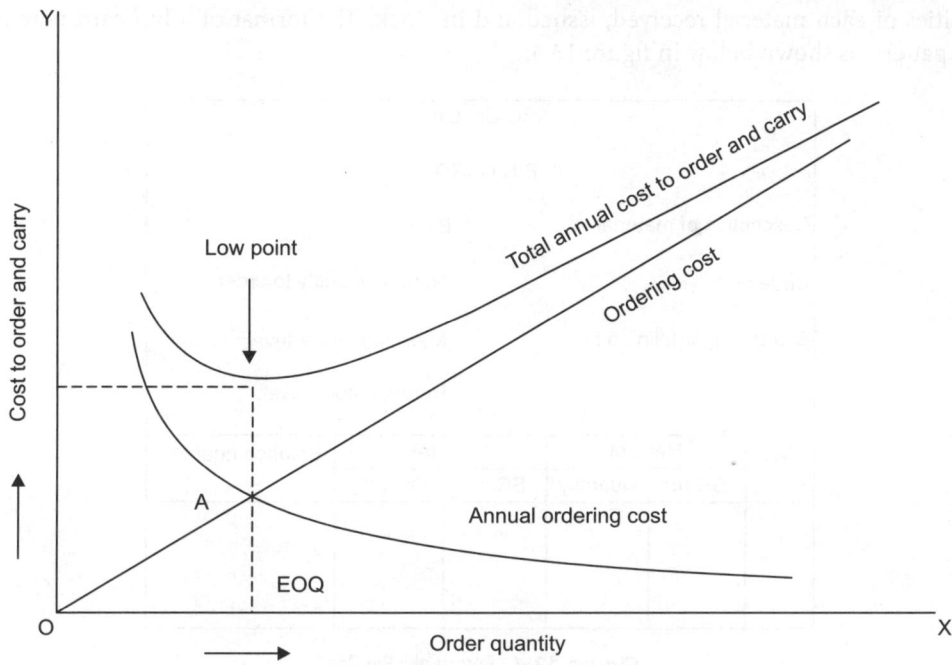

Figure 13.3. Graphical Determination of the EOQ

c = Cost per unit of material

s = Storage and other inventory carrying cost

For example, the annual usage of a material is 1200 units and the cost to handle an order of this material is Rs 10. The price is Rs 1.00 per unit regardless of the quantity purchased and the carrying cost of the inventory is 24% per year. Then,

  EOQ = 316 units

Perpetual inventory system

Perpetual inventory system is a method of recording the store balance after every receipt and issue, to facilitate a regular checking and to prevent the closing down for stocktaking. After every receipt or issue, the entry is made in the bin card and the balance is adjusted. Thus, the bin card becomes a perpetual inventory record and the store balance is recorded continuously after every receipt and issue. All errors detected are adjusted both in the bin card as well as in the stores ledger under proper authority.

The perpetual inventory system comprises:

1. Bin card
2. Stores ledger
3. Continuous stocktaking

Bin card

Bin card is a document maintained by the storekeeper in his store to keep record of all the items of the materials and goods in his store. So, a bin card serves the purpose of providing ready references. It shows the quantities of each material received, issued and in stock. The format of a bin card may be on the following pattern as shown below in figure 13.4:

| ABC Co. Ltd. |
| BIN CARD |

Description of material	Bin no.:
Code no.:	Normal quantity to order
Stores ledger folio no.:	Maximum stock level:
	Reorder stock level:

Date	Receipt		Issue		Balance quantity
	GR no	Quantity	SR no	Quantity	

Figure 13.4. Format of a Bin Card

A bin card is used for each material. Each receipt, issue or return is recorded in the bin card in a chronological order and the latest balance is shown after each receipt and issue.

Stores ledger
The stores ledger is kept in the cost accounting department. It is generally maintained in the form of loose leaf cards because they can be easily removed and inserted. The format of a stores ledger is shown as under in Figure 13.5.

Continuous stocktaking
Under this system of continuous stocktaking, only a limited number of items are verified on a day. The selection of the items of materials should be such that each 'tern of material gets checked up at least a certain number of times in a year and the checking of a particular item is evenly distributed during the period. The selected number of items are counted daily or at frequent intervals and compared with the bin card and stores ledger by the storekeeper. The bin card and the stores ledger record the balances, and their correctness can be verified by means of physical verification. In case of any difference between the recorded and the actual balances, it has to be pointed out to the management.

Advantages of perpetual inventory system
The advantages of a perpetual inventory system are as follow:

1. It helps in detection and immediate rectification of clerical errors oe discrepancies
2. It ensures a reliable checking of the store items in a methodical manner without disturbing the routine work of the enterprise
3. Timely action can be taken on serious shortages
4. It serves as a moral check on the staff, thus serving as a deterrent to dishonesty
5. It helps in the compilation of a profit and loss account and the balance sheet on interim dates if so required

ABC Co. Ltd.

STORES LEDGER ACCOUNT

Description of material   Maximum stock:

Code no.:   Minimum stock:

Bin no: Reorder level:

Location: Ordering quantity:

Unit:

Date	Receipts					Issue			Balance			Stock verified		
	GR no.	Qty.	Rate	Amt.		Qty.	Rate	Amt.	Qty.	Rate	Amt.	Date	Initial	Remarks

Figure 13.5. Format of the Stores Ledger Account

6. Overstocking and under stocking is avoided because the perpetual inventory system covers the verification of stocks with regard to the maximum and minimum stock level

Review of slow and nonmoving items

Inventory is an important constituent of the total cost and as such a proper system of inventory control leads to a significant economy in the total cost of production. So a proper system must be enforced to detect and control the slow moving items, obsolete items and dormant stocks. The slow moving materials are those items that are moving at a slow rate. Dormant materials are those items that are moving temporarily because of the seasonal production. Obsolete items are those that have become useless due to a change in the design, the method of manufacture, product or process, etc. The slow moving items are to be valued at cost, replacement price or net realizable value, whichever is less.

The following steps may be taken to detect the slow and nonmoving items:

1. Periodic report
2. Obsolete items
3. Moving ratios

Periodic report: A monthly or quarterly report on the stocks of nonmoving items is prepared that indicates its purchase, consumption and balance in hand. These reports are given to the management.

Obsolete items: Many of the slow and nonmoving items may become useless with the passage of time. A well-designed information system has to be devised to locate such obsolete items, so that these can be utilized and their further purchase can be stopped.

Moving ratios: In order to isolate slow moving items, dormant and dead stocks, moving ratios may be calculated periodically. These ratios show the turnover of these items for presentation to the management.

SCRAP AND SURPLUS DISPOSAL

Scrap is the residue incidentally obtained from the manufacturing processes. It is usually of small value and is recoverable without further processing, e.g. powder and fine granules obtained in processing of tablets, nonreturnable containers and packing cases. The surplus items are those items that are not required by the organization. It is generally spoiled raw materials, rejected components, defective parts, obsolete material and equipment. In a drug store, an expiry date goods comes under this category.

The scrap may be classified into the following types:

Legitimate scrap: The scrap that can be predetermined or anticipated in advance due to the manufacturing operations. For example, the material obtained in the form of fine granules and powder in the granulation process during tablet manufacturing.

Administrative scrap: The administrative scrap results when materials, etc., become obsolete due to the change in design.

Defective scrap: Defective scrap results from substandard raw materials and poor workmanship in handling such materials.

There are two methods for the disposal of scrap and surplus material. They are as follows:

1. The scrap and surplus material is sold if it cannot be recycled into useful material for subsequent production of the basic product.
2. The scrap and surplus can be reprocessed into useful raw materials for subsequent production of basic products.

Control of Scrap

The scrap can be controlled by effective management of raw materials during its manufacture. The following measures are helpful:

1. By providing proper attention during the designing stage of the product
2. By selecting the right materials and equipment during production of finished goods
3. By selecting the right type of personnel with proper training and experience, so that they can handle the materials properly

PRICING OF STOCK

Various methods are used for pricing the materials issues that are based on different principles. The following are the important methods of pricing the materials issues:

First in first out method (FIFO)

Under the first in first out method, the materials that are received first are issued first. The issues are priced at the cost price of the oldest consignments till it gets exhausted. As soon as the oldest lot is exhausted, the issues are priced at the cost price of the next of the oldest lot in the sequence. The closing stock is valued at the latest purchase price. For example, the following transactions occurred during the first week of April 2009.

April 1	200 units purchased @ Rs 5 per unit
April 5	500 units purchased @ Rs 6 per unit
April 10	300 units issued to job no.102
The issue of 300 units will be priced as under:	
From the first lot 200 units @ Rs 5	Rs 1000.00
Remaining 100 units from 2nd lot @ Rs 6	Rs 600.00
	Rs 1600.00

The value of the closing stock of 400 units (i.e. the second lot 500 units less 100 units issued) will be @ Rs 6, i.e. the value of closing stock would be Rs 2400.

Last in first out method (LIFO)

In this method the price of the latest consignment in stock is used for calculating the value of issue until that consignment is exhausted, then the next lot of pricing is used and so on through the successful lots. For example, the following transactions occurred in stores department during the first week of April 2009.

April 1	500 units purchased @ Rs 5 per unit.
April 5	300 units purchased @ Rs 6 per unit
April 10	400 units issued to Job order no. 102
The issue of 400 units on April 10 will be priced as under:	
First 300 units @ Rs 6	Rs 1800.00
Remaining 100 units @ Rs 5	Rs 500.00
	Rs 2300.00

The closing stock of 400 units will be price @ Rs 5, i.e. Rs 2000.

Highest in first out method (HIFO)

In this method, the materials received at the highest price in the stock are issued first. This method is good, when it is desired to keep the inventory value of the materials at the lowest possible price.

Base stock price method

In this method, a minimum quantity of stock is always held at a fixed price as a reserve in stock. The minimum stock is known as *base stock* or the *safety stock* and is used only in case of an emergency. This stock is valued at normal price, at the long run, while the stock in excess of this stock is priced on some other basis, usually the FIFO or the LIFO basis.

This method is usually applied in industries where the raw materials used are basic and homogeneous. The finished product is made of basic raw materials and the processing takes a long time. So it is desirable to maintain a base stock.

Average cost method

In this method, when a new stock of goods is received the total value of goods in stock is divided by the total quantity in hand and this will give the average price. All issues of goods will be made at this price until a new consignment is again received. Then a new price will be calculated. This method has an advantage when the prices are subject to constant change.

It should be noted, that instead of the simple average, wherein only the unit cost is considered for calculating the average cost to be charged to the issues, weighted average cost can also be used. Under the weighted average cost, along with the unit cost the quantity of the units is also considered. For example, the following two lots were purchased during April 2003.

    (1) 1000 units @ Rs 3
    (2) 5000 units @ Rs 5

$$\text{The simple average cost} = \frac{3+5}{2} = \text{Rs } 4$$

Replacement price method

The replacement price method is also known as *market price method*. In this method, the materials are priced at the prevailing market price on the date of issue. According to this method, the replacement price is determined each time when the material is issued. The main advantage of this method is that it considers the current market price that is more significant for the purpose of pricing policies.

Standard price method

In the standard price method, the material issues are charged at a predetermined or estimated price that reflects a normal or an effected future price. The standard price is generally fixed after careful examination of the current market price, trend of the price and market conditions, etc. The standard price is made applicable for a definite period, say a month or a quarter or a year. The standard price should be revised periodically to avoid discrepancies that go beyond a particular limit.

The material pricing is to be done on the basis of the acquisition cost of the materials. The acquisition cost should include the net invoice price of the supplier and the transport charges. Besides that, charges, such as cost of ordering, receiving, unpacking, inspection, insurance, storing, etc., may also be included.

Nowadays compounding of drugs or prescription has almost become obsolete in retail sale. The readymade drug formulations are available for retail sale and the price to be charged from the patients are also stated on the label as the maximum retail price, inclusive of all taxes.

Inflated price method

The inflated price method is used for those goods that are subject to some wastage. The total amount paid is divided by the quantity expected to be finally available for use and that rate is used for the sale of goods.

There are certain types of normal wastages that are incidental to the material usage, like loss on breaking the bulk, evaporation, etc. The cost of such normal wastage is included while charging the price when such material is sold.

Actual price method

In this method the material issues are priced at the actual acquisition cost of the respective materials. This method is applicable, where the purchases are made for the specific jobs and are kept physically separate in the store room. Each material receipt is recorded in separate stores ledger card and the material issues are costed at the actual acquisition cost. This method is relatively awkward; however, it is advised where few costly items are used in processing and where nonstandardized materials are purchased to meet the customer's specification.

Points to Ponder

1. Materials management is the planning, directing, controlling and coordinating those activities that are concerned with the materials and inventory requirements from the point of their inception to their introduction into the manufacturing process.
2. The various phases included in material management are as follows:
   a. Purchasing
   b. Storekeeping
   c. Inventory control
   d. Scrap and surplus disposal
   e. Pricing of stock
3. Different techniques commonly used to control the inventory are as follows:
   a. ABC analysis
   b. Economic order quantity
   c. Perpetual inventory system
   d. Review of slow and nonmoving items
   e. Input-output ratio analysis
   f. Setting of various levels
   g. Materials budgeting
   h. Establishing an effective purchase procedure

 **Self-Assessment Exercises**

1. Define the term *materials management*.
2. Explain the term *purchasing*.
3. Name the various stages of purchase procedure.
4. Define the term *storekeeping*.
5. Define the term *inventory*.
6. Name the various techniques used for inventory control.
7. Explain the term EOQ.
8. What is the full form of EOQ?
9. What do you know about the bin card?
10. Write the algebraic formula for finding EOQ.
11. What is the full form of ABC?
12. What is the primary function of a store?
13. Explain the term *perpetual inventory system*.
14. Define the term *danger level*.
15. Explain the term *input–output ratio*.
16. Write the objectives of materials management.
17. Name the various factors to be considered while purchasing the materials for a store.

18. What are the objectives of purchasing?
19. Write the objective of storekeeping.
20. Describe the various functions of inventory control.
21. Give a brief account of ABC analysis.
22. What are the different methods of finding EOQ?
23. Write the formula to find minimum stock level of inventory.
24. How is the reorder level of inventory calculated?
25. Write in brief about maximum stock level.
26. Name the various method of pricing of stock.
27. Define the term *materials management*. Describe its objectives and importance.
28. What are the various points to be taken into consideration while purchasing materials for the store?
29. Discuss the various stages in purchasing procedure for procurement of materials for the store.
30. What are the different methods for determining the price of materials issued from a store?
31. Define the term *inventory control*. Write the different techniques that are used to control the inventories. Describe in detail about economic order quantity technique of inventory control.
32. Explain the term *inventory control*. What are its functions? Discuss the ABC analysis. Write the main differences between A, B and C types of inventories.
33. What do you know about EOQ? Discuss the various methods for determining the EOQ.
34. What is perpetual inventory system? How is this helpful in inventory control? Write the advantages of this system.
35. Write in detail about various levels of inventory that are required to be maintained to control it.
36. Define the term *storekeeping*. What are the objectives of storekeeping? Write its importance.
37. Discuss in brief about important methods of pricing the materials issues.
38. Write short notes on the following:
    a. Localized purchasing
    b. Purchase procedure
    c. Maximum stock level
    d. Minimum stock level
    e. Bin card
    f. Input output ratio
    g. Reorder level
    h. Danger level
    i. First in first out method
    j. Last in first out method
    k. Replacement price method
    l. Inflated price method

Pharmaceutical Marketing

INTRODUCTION

The term *market* has been derived from the Latin word *marcatus* that means a place where business is conducted. Marketing consists of those efforts that affect the transfer in ownership of goods and care for their physical distribution. It is the process by which products are made available to the ultimate consumers from their point of origin. In short, marketing means the performance of business activities that direct the flow of goods and services from the producers to the consumers. The modern concept of marketing is consumer oriented. Marketing involves the design of products that are acceptable to the consumers, and the conduct of those activities that facilitates the transfer of ownership between the seller and the buyer.

Pharmaceutical marketing is defined as 'the performance of pharmaceutical business activities that direct the flow of pharmaceutical goods and services from producer to the consumers'.

The old concept of marketing was simple selling and sales promotion. Nowadays, there is lot of competition in the market. The production of goods cannot be made possible without the knowledge of its demand in the market. The producer is very conscious to fulfill the needs and desires of the consumers.

Differentiation Between Pharmaceutical Marketing and General Marketing

The major differences between pharmaceutical marketing and general marketing are as follows:

1. The consumer does not have the choice to buy the pharmaceutical product. He has to purchase the drug that is prescribed by the physician. Similarly, the seller is also bound to sell the same drug which is prescribed by the physician.
2. A proper drug license is required to deal in the pharmaceutical marketing.
3. The person dealing in pharmaceutical marketing must be qualified in the pharmacy profession, because he has to deal with potent drugs. Little carelessness can prove to be harmful for the consumer.

FUNCTIONS OF MARKETING

The following are the functions of the marketing:

1. Buying and assembling
2. Selling
3. Transportation
4. Storage
5. Grading
6. Packing and packaging
7. Financing
8. Risk bearing
9. Feedback information

Buying and Assembling

Buying is one of the fundamental functions of marketing. It can be considered as the first step in the process of marketing. The manufacturers buy raw materials and equipment to manufacture its pharmaceutical products. Similarly, merchants or middlemen (wholesalers and retailers) have to buy the goods or products from various sources of supply to sell it at a profit to the consumers. The economical and efficient buying by the manufacturer or the merchant will naturally enable him to earn profit. For this purpose, goods of the best possible quality are to be purchased at the most reasonable price from those sellers offering the best terms and conditions. The supply orders of the required items are prepared after having negotiated with the suppliers on terms of sale, the mode of delivery, etc. In the supply order, the detailed description of the item, quantities, terms and conditions of the supply are given. On receiving the supply order by the supplier, the goods are supplied.

There are four methods of buying as discussed below:

1. **By inspection:** In the method of by inspection, the buyer or his agent visits the premises of the seller for the inspection of the goods that is proposed to be purchased. The purchases are made after the buyer is satisfied with the quality of the goods on actual examination.

2. **By sample:** By sample is a very common method of purchase of goods. The sample of goods is supplied by the supplier for its approval from the buyer. The buyer examines the sample and places the supply order for the supply of goods as per the quality of the sample approved.
3. **By description:** By description refers to the purchases of goods made on the basis of the description of goods in the catalogue or price-list of the supplier.
4. **By grade:** The goods that are standardized and graded are purchased in required quantity simply by mentioning their grades, e.g. ISI, Agmark, IP, BP, USP, etc.

Assembling means the collection of commodities required at a central place. Assembling is not the same as buying, but it can be regarded as an important aid to it. Goods are generally produced in small quantities at numerous centres. They cannot be economically processed by the manufacturers unless they are made available in large quantities. It is also not economical to transport them, if they are not moved in bulk. For these reasons, it becomes necessary to bring together, collect and concentrate goods from various sources of supply at centrally located places.

Goods are assembled chiefly for two purposes as discussed below:

1. For meeting the demand of the buyer
2. To provide sufficient volume of business to the middlemen like wholesalers and retailers

In general, the purchasing should be done of proper quality, in proper quantity, at proper time, at proper price and from the proper supplier.

Selling

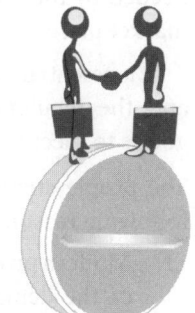

Selling is another important function of marketing. Selling and buying are interlinked with each other. It is the process whereby the goods and the services finally flow to the consumers who need them, and the firm performs its functions of distributing its products among the consumers. Sales are the lifeblood of business, and selling is the heart of marketing. Selling is the process of creating demands, finding buyers, negotiating the terms of sale, transferring title, credit and collection, and servicing sale.

In pharmaceutical marketing, the sale of a particular brand of the medicine mainly depends on the physicians. So, the pharmaceutical manufacturers approach the physicians through its medical representatives. They try to convince the physicians to prescribe the medicines manufactured by its firm.

Transportation

Transportation means the movement of goods and people from one place to another by a systematic conveyance. Transportation performs the essential function of marketing. Mass selling and mass production are impossible without efficient and economical transport.

Railways, roads, waterways and airways are the chief modes of transport. Each has its own advantages and disadvantages and is suitable under particular conditions.

Rail transportation is the most effective means of movement of both men and materials. Materials are moved from one place to another by the goods train. Goods are carried from the pharmaceutical house to the railway station by road transport, and packed it into wagons of goods train. Rail transport is owned by the government, whereas road transport is owned by private companies. Some big pharmaceutical houses have their own carriers such as trucks, tempo, station wagon, etc. to transport its goods from one place to another. Air transport is not commonly used except at the time of emergency. Airways are always used for import and export of goods from one country to the other.

Transportation has the following advantages:

1. Effective transport facility has made possible trade within and between countries.
2. Transportation helps in the stabilization of prices of the commodities by movement of supplies from the surplus to the deficient areas.
3. It helps in the promotion of several industries producing perish able articles like fishing, dairying, farming, poultry farming, foods and vegetables, etc.
4. It is indispensable for the assembling and dispersal of raw materials and goods, and helps in the production of goods without any interruption.

Storage

Storage is another essential function of the marketing process. It involves the making of proper arrangements for retaining the goods in a perfect state till they are needed by the consumers and are to be taken to the market place.

It is essential for the manufacturers, the wholesalers and the retailers to maintain a sufficient stock of goods to meet the demands of their consumers.

The proper storage of goods is necessary due to the following reasons:

1. Modern production is carried out in anticipation of the demand rather than in response to the specific order of consumers. So the manufacturers need proper storage of their products to ensure continuous availability of the goods in the market.
2. It helps to maintain the stability of prices.
3. It helps to ensure the availability of goods throughout the year in spite of the fact that the same grows or is produced only during a particular season. For example, Tincture Orange is manufactured when oranges are available, but it is available in the market throughout the year.
4. Storage helps to maintain an adequate reserve of stock and to eliminate the possibility of delay in receiving further stocks of goods in time as a result of delay in transportation.
5. Certain goods such as drugs, chemicals, perishable foods, etc., are required to be properly stored to prevent their destruction or damage.
6. Storage facilities are provided by three types of warehouses as follows:
    a. **Private warehouses:** Private warehouses are owned by the big business concerns or wholesalers who use them for storage of their own stocks.
    b. **Public warehouses:** Public warehouses are operated by business firms that provide storage facilities to the general public for a certain charge. It may be owned and operated by an individual,

a cooperative society, a dock authority, etc. These warehouses are required to work under a license from the government and under prescribed rules and regulations. These warehouses are also known as *commercial* or *duty paid warehouses*.

c. **Bonded warehouses:** Bonded warehouses are licensed to accept imported goods for storage until the payment of custom duties are made. These are situated at ports. These warehouses are either owned or operated by the government or work under its control. These warehouses are of great use to the businessmen as they are required to pay the custom duties immediately after the arrival of the ship. Instead the goods can be stored in a bonded warehouse. These goods can be removed in instalments by paying the custom duty on the portion that is removed. Thus, import duty has not to be paid on the whole lot of goods all at once but is charged only on the goods actually taken out by the owner.

Grading

Grading is an important process in the function of standardization. A standard is a measure or a designation of a particular quality that is decided on the basis of the size, colour, shape, strength, chemical content and taste, etc. In the case of pharmaceutical products, grading is done as IP, BP, USP, depending upon the standards maintained as per that pharmacopoeia. In the case of manufactured goods, standardization in the process of marketing is not generally required, because they are usually standardized in the process of production itself. The function of sorting out the different types of commodities in accordance with the particular established standards and then classifying them into different group is known as *grading*.

Advantages

The advantages of grading are as follows:

1. It assures goods of standard quality to the consumers.
2. It enables the manufacturer to produce standardized goods.
3. It enables the seller to sell by sample and description. This helps in widening the market for a particular commodity.
4. It facilitates the distribution of goods at every stage.
5. It facilitates hedging and future trading because the price quotations and the market reports accurately convey the demand and the supply position. Hence, the price comparison becomes easier.
6. The standard goods eliminate uncertainty in purchasing and enable the seller to get a better price for the product.
7. It helps in making claims easily from the insurance companies and the railway authority in the event of loss or damage because the standardized and the graded commodities can be easily valued.
8. It reduces the cost of advertisement and the sales promotion.

The advantage of grading will depend on the people who are entrusted with this task. If the drug inspectors and other people on the checking and grading staff are honest, grading will be really useful. But if they are dishonest or corrupt, it will be a mere absurd and futile proceeding, and the consumers may only be cheated.

Packing and Packaging

The products after their manufacture are required to be packed properly to protect the same from spoilage, breakage and leakage during handling and transportation.

Packing refers to the wrapping, crating, filling and compression, etc., of goods. Whereas packaging is concerned with the creation and designing of proper packages for different products.

Proper packaging is needed for the following purposes:

1. It protects the products from deterioration, exposure, pilferage, etc., during transportation, storage and use of the product.
2. It facilitates handling and use of the product.
3. It ensures the supply of products of right quality, quantity and weight to the consumers.
4. It promotes sales as aesthetic packaging attracts the attention of the consumers.
5. It helps in branding and advertising of the product.
6. It reduces the cost of transportation and storage.
7. It helps in the identification of the product as a trademark is fixed on the packing. The package indicates the nature, weight, content, etc., of the product.
8. It has a repack and resale value for the consumer after the use of the product.
9. It can be easily stocked in retail drug stores that may not be very spacious.
10. It helps to pass on the informative literature (packed inside the package), regarding the uses of the product, to the consumers.

Financing

Financing is an important function of marketing. The provisions of funds are essential for the meeting of the various requirements of marketing. The marketing concerns require both fixed and working capital.

The wholesaler, retailer, commission agent, broker, cooperative undertakings or sales department of a manufacturer need relatively large amount of capital for the purchase of goods, for resale, paying of wages and salaries, extending credit facilities to the consumers and other operative expenses. The capital required for this purpose is called the *working capital*. Similarly, fixed capital is required for the purchase of land, building, machinery, furniture and other office appliances. The fixed capital required for this purpose may be small because land and building are generally taken on rent.

Finance is needed for the following purposes:

1. To maintain a minimum level of inventories in the anticipation of demand.
2. To meet the buying, selling and transport expenses.
3. To regulate the production and storage of goods that is in demand during a particular season.
4. To provide credit facility to the consumers.
5. To meet the changes in style, fashion and competitive products.
6. To meet temporary needs during the off seasons or low sales, etc.

Sources of Finance

Basically, there are two methods of raising capital for any business enterprise explained below:

1. Owned capital
2. Loan capital

Owned capital is contributed by the owner, i.e. the sole proprietor, partners, shareholders, etc., whereas loan capital is raised from individual banks or financial institutions. The loan capital is available only against mortgage or the pledge of property of the borrower.

The sources of finance can be classified into three parts on the basis of the duration for which it is required in the business. These are as follows:

1. **Long-term finance:** Long-term finance is often invested in fixed assets, such as land, building, machinery, etc. It remains invested in the business for a considerably long period, i.e. ten years and more. It may be raised through shares, debentures, ploughing back of the profit and loan from financial institutions.
2. **Medium-term finance:** Medium-term finance is generally used to implement expansion, extension or modernization programmes of a business. It remains invested in business for a period of three to ten years. It may be raised through shares, debentures, public deposits and loans from the banks or financial institutions.
3. **Short-term finance**: Short-term finance is used to meet the seasonal or current expenditure such as purchase of raw material, payment of wages and other recurring expenditure. It is raised for a period of less than two years. The short-term finance is raised by trade credit, bank credit, instalment credit and customers advances.

Risk Bearing

Risk means the possibility of loss likely to occur due to some unforeseen events such as theft, fire, hoods, cyclones, earthquakes, etc. The loss arising due to these risks can be protected through the insurance contracts. But there are certain other risks, such as leakage, spoilage, bad debts and fluctuation in prices that cannot be insured, and hence the owner himself will have to bear the losses arising from such risks.

The marketing risk can be divided into four types. These are as under:

1. **Economic risks:** Economic risks arise from the changes in the market and other economic conditions. These risks are of the following types:

   a. **Time risk:** Time risk arises due to the time gap between the purchase and the sale of a commodity. During this period, there maybe a fall in prices or demand due to the changes in fashion, style or taste, etc.

   b. **Place risk:** Place risk arises due to the differences in prices of the same commodity at different places. The risk is also caused by spoilage, leakage or breakage, etc., during the transportation of goods from one place to the other. The risk has been reduced to the minimum due to the modern means of transportation.

   c. **Risk of changes in demand:** These days, goods are produced in the anticipation of the demand. If the demand does not come to the expectations of the producer at the time of marketing of the products, the profit of the producer may be reduced.

d. Risk of competition: A producer and a merchant, both have to face the risk of losing the demand of its product due to the activities of its competitors. The competitor may reduce the cost of its product by improving the method of production or may improve the quality of the products. This may reduce the sales and the profits of the competitors. Sometimes competitors may also adopt unfair or unethical trade practices to gain profit.

2. **Natural risks:** Natural risks arise due to the natural forces such as fire, flood, storm, earthquake, lighting, hail storm, disease etc. These risks are largely beyond the control of man.

3. **Human risks:** Human risks arise due to social hazards and manmade factors such as theft, pilferage, fire, accidents, riots, strikes lock outs, dishonesty, etc. Sometimes the risks also arise due to technological changes.

4. **Political risks:** Political risks are caused by the changes in the government and its policies. The changes made by the government in taxation, licensing, labour laws, industrial policies are some of the important causes of business risks. Risks may arise due to the disputes between nations or adverse public opinions.

The above risks can be reduced or prevented by using the following measures:

1. The business can be insured against human risks and risks due to natural calamities.
2. The industrial machinery may be thoroughly examined before its operation in order to prevent the accident.
3. The labour problems may be solved to avoid strikes and lockouts.
4. The market research may be done to avoid risk of price changes and the reduction in value.
5. The fire proof risk may be avoided by constructing a fire proof building or observing all the norms of fire fighting.
6. The inventories may be frequently checked in order to avoid time risk.
7. Proper packing of goods may be done to avoid risk of spoilage, leakage or breakage during the transportation.

Effective advertisements or sale promotion methods may be adopted to avoid risk of competition.

Feedback Information

Feedback information is needed for the proper running of a business. The management collects information regarding demand, supply, latest trend of the market, package size preferable and the future demand of their items through proper market research. Market research is defined as a systematic, objective and exhaustive research, and study of the facts relevant to any problem in the field of marketing.

There are two sources from where the required information of market trends can be collected.

1. **Internal sources:** The internal sources, such as statistics of sales turnover, advertising expenditure, transport cost, etc., can be analysed to get the desired information regarding the market trend.
2. **External sources:** There are two external sources from where the required information can be collected. They are as follows:

a. Primary sources
b. Secondary sources

The primary sources of market information are salesman, dealers and consumers. The secondary sources include trade press, trade associations, published surveys and the government as well as the international publications.

Advantages

Following are the advantages of the feedback information:

1. It supplies information regarding the consumer's response to a particular product introduced by the organization in the market.
2. It helps to introduce new products in the market after a proper survey of the market.
3. It helps the manufacturer to find other similar products available in the market.
4. It gives an idea about the future trends regarding the particular products.
5. It helps in finalizing the various plans to boost sales.
6. It helps in the discovery of a potential market.
7. It reveals the defects and thus makes a corrective action possible on the part of the manufacturer.
8. It helps to discover the reasons for resistance on the part of the consumers.
9. It indicates whether the product is in constant demand throughout the year so as to adjust its production accordingly.
10. It helps in earning higher profits after adjusting the price structure of the product.
11. It gives an indication about the latest government policies concerning a particular business.

Points to Ponder

1. Pharmaceutical marketing is the performance of pharmaceutical business activities that direct the flow of pharmaceutical goods and services from the producers to the consumers.
2. The functions of the marketing are as follows:
    a. Buying and assembling
    b. Selling
    c. Transportation
    d. Storage
    e. Grading
    f. Packing and packaging
    g. Financing
    h. Risk bearing
    i. Feedback information

Self-Assessment Exercises

1. Define the term *market*.
2. Explain the term *marketing*.
3. Name the main marketing functions.
4. Define the term *assembling*.
5. Explain the term *grading*.
6. What is meant by risks in business?
7. Name the different methods of protection against risks in marketing,
8. Define the term *buying*. Name the different methods of buying.
9. Define the term *packing*.
10. Name the various sources of collecting market information.
11. Differentiate between the pharmaceutical marketing and the general marketing.
12. Write the different methods of buying goods from the market.
13. Write the advantages of transportation.
14. Why is proper storage of goods necessary?
15. Discuss the various types of warehouses.
16. What are the advantages of grading?
17. Write the advantages of proper packing.
18. What are the different sources of finance?
19. Discuss the various types of marketing risk.
20. Explain the various measures by means of which the risk can be reduced or prevented.
21. Write the various sources from which the required information of market trends can be collected.
22. Define the term *marketing*. Name the various marketing functions. Explain any three functions in detail.
23. Name the various marketing functions and describe in brief the importance of each function.
24. What do you mean by marketing functions? Name them and explain in detail any three functions.
25. Define the term *grading*. What are its advantages?
26. Explain the term *packing*. Discuss the importance of proper packing.
27. What do you know about the risks in business? Discuss the various types of risks. Write the different measures by which risks can be reduced or prevented.

Marketing Research

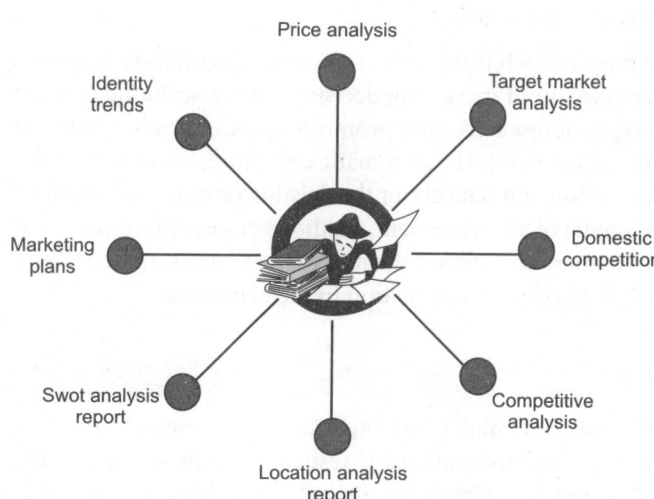

INTRODUCTION

Definition

'Consumer is the king' is the theme of all the marketing activities these days. It follows that all the marketing activities of all the businesses and industrial enterprises today go around satisfying the needs of the consumer. All efforts are made to provide the goods and services to the consumer at the right time and place, and keeping in view their tastes, income, fashion, etc. Marketing research is a tool to achieve this objective. Marketing research is the collection, summary and analysis of the data regarding the goods and services so that the behaviour of the consumers may be understood and maximum satisfaction may be provided to them. The term *marketing research* has been defined by many eminent scholars. Some of the important definitions are as follows:

Philip Kotler: 'Marketing research is the systematic problem analysis, model building and fact finding for the purpose of improved decision making and control in the marketing of goods and services'.

American Marketing Association: 'The systematic gathering, recording and analysis of all facts about the problems relating to the marketing of goods and services is called *marketing research*'.

Tousley, Clark and Clark: 'Marketing research is the careful and objective study of the product design, markets and such transfer activities as the physical distribution, warehousing, advertising and sales management'.

Luck, Wales and Taylor: 'Marketing research may be defined as the application of scientific method to the solution of marketing problems'.

Lorei and Roberts: 'Marketing Research is any systematic attempt to get information useful in solving marketing problems (making marketing decisions)'.

Prof. Rechard D. Crisp: 'Marketing Research is the systematic objective and exhaustive search for, and the study of, facts relevant to any problem in the field of marketing'.

The definitions above make it clear that marketing research is the collection, analysis and the interpretation of relevant data to help a marketing manager take sound marketing decisions. It is a scientific method of solving the marketing problems. It includes all types of research, sales promotion research, advertisement research, etc. It may also be concluded that marketing research is the systematic collection, recording, analysis, interpretation and reporting of necessary information and data about the existing or potential consumers, marketing methods, channels of distribution, media of advertisement, methods of sales promotion and competitors. The object of marketing research is to prepare and amend the marketing policies, strategies and programmes in such a manner that they may provide maximum satisfaction to the consumers.

SCOPE OF MARKETING RESEARCH

The scope of marketing research is very wide. Prof. M.J. Baker has included sales research, product research, advertisement research, motives research, exports marketing research, business economies, etc., in the scope of marketing research. Prof. Richard D. Crisp has included products and services research, markets research, sales policies and strategies research, advertisement research, etc., in the scope of marketing research. Thus, it is clear that marketing research is a very wide term that embraces all the research activities in connection with the management and performance of the marketing activities. The scope of marketing research may be explained as follows:

1. Research of products and services
2. Research on markets
3. Research on sales methods and policies
4. Advertising research
5. Research on miscellaneous activities

ADVANTAGES OR IMPORTANCE OF MARKETING RESEARCH

Marketing research is a gift of the modern concept of marketing (consumer-oriented concept). All the activities of a business and industrial enterprise start and end with the maximum satisfaction of the consumer needs. The satisfaction of consumer needs necessitates the study of their behaviour, tastes, habits and attitudes. The study of these attributes is a difficult problem in itself. This problem can be solved if the marketing decisions of the enterprise are based on marketing research. Marketing research helps in the study and analysis of the above attributes of the consumers.

Production at large scale, ever increasing competition, improving the standard of living of the consumers, frequently changing habits and attitudes of the consumers, frequently changing fashions, frequently changing conditions of the economic world and the ever developing techniques and methods of production have increased the need and importance of marketing research. No business and industrial enterprise can achieve its marketing objectives in the absence of marketing research. The importance of marketing research can be explained as under:

Production of New Products

Marketing research explores the possibility of selling a new product into a market and, thus, provides an opportunity to the enterprise to start the production of this product. Production of a new product helps the enterprise in capturing the market substantially.

New Uses of Products

Marketing research explores the new uses of the products of the enterprise. The enterprise can widely publicize these alternative uses of its product among the customers and, thus, can create a new market and new demands for its products.

Important Information About Customers

The most important role of marketing research is the study of habits, tastes, attitudes and behaviour of consumers. This study helps the enterprise in understanding its customers—who are the customers? Why do they purchase the products of the enterprise? When and where do they purchase the products? For what do they purchase the products? This information helps the enterprise in deciding its marketing policies, strategies and programme.

Selection of the Channels of Distribution

Marketing research makes a comparative study of the terms of conditions, way of working, popularity among consumers and effectiveness of different channels of distribution. It helps the enterprise in the selection of a particular channel of distribution for distributing its products. It also helps in changing these channels, if necessary.

Existence in Competitive Situation

Marketing research collects and analyses the data in respect to the products and services offered by the competitors to the consumers. It also studies their marketing policies and programmes. It evaluates the effectiveness of their policies in the market. It helps the enterprise in deciding its marketing policies and programmes. It also helps in making the necessary changes from time to time in these policies and programmes so that the enterprise may face the competition successfully.

Knowledge of Demand

Marketing research makes a thorough study of the demand of products of the enterprise. It helps in deciding the nature and trend of demand. It also helps in deciding the elasticity of demand. Such study helps an enterprise in planning for the distribution of goods and services at the right time and at the right place.

Planned Production

As marketing research helps in making sales forecasts, the enterprise can establish harmonious adjustment between the demand and supply of its products.

Improvement in the Quality of Products

Change in the need and want of the consumers is a regular feature of the market. The consumers may discard the product tomorrow which they prefer today. Therefore, it is imperative to be in continuous touch with the changes in the habits, tastes and attitudes of consumers. It is also necessary to be in continuous touch with the changes in fashion and the marketing policies of the competitors so that necessary improvement in the quality of products may be made at the right time. Marketing research helps in this target.

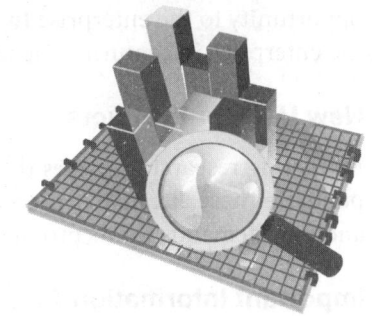

Discovery of Potential Markets

Marketing research makes an intensive and extensive search for new markets for the products of an enterprise. It helps the enterprise in developing new markets, in turn, increasing the demand for its products.

TYPES OF MARKETING RESEARCH

The different types of marketing research are discussed as follows:

Product Analysis

Product analysis is a detailed and a thorough study of the popularity of products among consumers of an enterprise. This analysis helps the enterprise in the study of the extent to which the quality, characteristics, utilities form, design, colour, packing and price, etc., of its products meet the expectations, habits, tastes, attitudes, and the standard of living of its consumers. Such study helps the enterprise in deciding the improvements and the changes to be made in its products so that maximum satisfaction may be provided to the consumers and maximum demand may be created for its product. In addition to this, the decision of the development of a new product is also taken on the basis of product analysis.

Market Analysis

Market analysis is the study of markets available for a particular product of an enterprise. Market analysis determines the quantity that can be sold of a product in a market. It helps in determining the quota of different mediaries. It helps in determining the channels of distribution, selection of mediaries and salesmen, and the determination of their sales territories. Market analysis tries to explore the possibility of selling the products of the enterprise in new markets. It also determines the market or the areas where special efforts are necessary to make the products of the enterprise more popular.

Distribution Analysis

Distribution analysis is related with the analysis of different problems related to the physical distribution of goods and services, such as storage, transportation, advertisement, sales promotion, pricing policy, etc. The main aim of distribution analysis is to control the costs of distribution and to provide the goods and services to the consumers at the right place and at the right time.

Competition Analysis

Competition analysis is the analysis of the competitive situations prevailing in the market. It makes an analytical study in respect to the characteristics, qualities, form, design, uses, packing, labelling, etc., of the products of competitors. It also makes a study of the policies of the competitors in respect to the prices, physical distribution, advertisement, sales promotion and after sale services, etc. Such study is perhaps the most important gift of marketing research to the enterprise. It helps the enterprise in deciding its marketing policies and strategies, and in making the necessary changes in these policies and strategies.

Consumer Research

Consumer research is the research on the present and the potential consumer of the enterprise. It makes a study of the different aspects of the consumers, such as who are the consumers? Where do they live? Why do they purchase? Where do they purchase? When do they purchase? In what quality do they purchase? What are their buying motives? What impression do they have about the products of the enterprise? In addition to this, the consumer research also makes a study of the consumers of the enterprise, by dividing them on the basis of their age, education, sex, income, caste, etc. Consumer research collects the options of different consumers regarding the products and marketing image of the enterprise.

Sales Analysis

Sales analysis is an important tool to measure the effectiveness of the sales organization of an enterprise. Sales analysis includes collection of actual sales performance of a salesman, determination of sales territories, analysis of the trend of sales, analysis of the market segmentation analysis of the uses of products, analysis of the cost of sales, etc. Such study helps in evaluating the results of the performance of selling force of the enterprise so that necessary amendments may be made in the policies of the enterprise in this respect.

Motivational Research

Motivational research is the study of the reaction of consumers or society towards the products of an enterprise or the enterprise itself. It is a very difficult task in itself because sometimes the consumers are not in a position to express their wants or feelings or why they feel so. The marketing manager tries to understand the behaviour of his consumers with the use of psychological techniques. Such study is very helpful for directing the activities of the salesmen.

Advertisement Research

The importance of advertisements is increasing day-by-day. No business and industrial enterprise can think of success in its marketing efforts without advertisement. It is not enough to advertise, even through the best available media. The evaluation of the effectiveness of advertising programmes and sales promotion campaign is much more important. Advertising research undertakes this responsibility. It analyses and evaluates the success productivity and effectiveness of the advertising campaign of the enterprise. It helps in making the necessary modifications in the advertising policy of the enterprise.

NEED OF MARKETING RESEARCH

Marketing research is not only desirable but has become a necessity of all the business and industrial enterprises of today. It is the time of large scale production and cut throat competition. The maximum satisfaction of the needs and wants of consumers is the only key for achieving marketing objectives for all the enterprise. Satisfying the consumers' needs and wants is a very difficult task because the habits, tastes, attitudes and behaviour of the consumers always keep on changing. Therefore, it becomes necessary that an enterprise must keep itself in continuous touch with day-to-day changes in the behaviour of the consumers and the policies of the competitors. All this is possible only through marketing research. Marketing research collects and makes an analysis of all such information that helps the enterprise in planning, organizing, directing, motivating, coordinating and controlling its marketing activities. Market research is necessary in the following conditions:

1. When a new product is to be launched into the market
2. When adequate data are not available with respect to the demand of a product
3. When there are fast changes in the habits, tastes and attitudes of the consumers
4. When there are fast changes in fashion
5. When the sale of a particular enterprise goes on declining
6. When adequate data is not available about the consumers of a particular group
7. When adequate data is not available about a particular market segment
8. When the data of consumer reactions to the packing or utility or price of a product are to be collected
9. When the effectiveness of an advertising campaign is to be evaluated
10. When the possibilities of developing a new products are to be explored

PROCEDURE OF MARKETING RESEARCH

Marketing research is the most important tool in the hand of the management for taking managerial decisions in the field of marketing. Marketing research analyses and defines the problems in marketing, develops the possible alternatives to solve these problems, evaluates and analyses the merits and demerits of these alternatives so that a best possible alternatives may be selected and the problem is solved.

William J. Stanton, in this regard, states, 'Marketing research is fundamental tool which is used by the management in making decisions and solving the problems in the field of marketing'. The procedure of marketing research may be different in different enterprises but the procedures commonly adopted may be explained as under:

Defining the Problem

The very first step of marketing research is to define the problem. It is not possible to take a right decision unless and until the problem is specifically identified and properly defined. While defining a problem, a careful study of all the internal and external factors must be made. After this, the problem must be analysed. For example, if an enterprise wants to take a decision on the question whether to continue the production of a particular product or to stop it, the questions may be further analysed on different grounds, such as:

1. What is the demand of the product in the market?
2. If the production is discontinued, what will be its effect on the total sale of the enterprise?
3. Whether the demand of the product can be increased or not?
4. If the production is discontinued, will it affect the other activities of the enterprise also?
5. Fall in the sales of any other product of an enterprise?
6. Whether the idle capacity of the enterprise on the discontinuation of the product can be used or not?

Situation Analysis

The second step in the process of marketing research after the problem has been defined is the study of relevant factors affecting the problem. It includes the analysis of the situation prevailing in the enterprise, markets and the whole industry. The competitive situations are also analysed. Attempts are made to revise the problem so that important aspects to be concentrated may be recognized and understood. Situation analysis limits the scope of problem and sometimes it offers a solution to the problem itself.

Checking the Available Sources of Information

After this, attempts are made to know the sources of information that may be used to solve the problem. These sources must be thoroughly checked so that the right information can be made available for the solution of the problem.

Collection of Data

After preparing a plan of marketing research, a collection of the required data is a very important step. The sources of collection of data can be divided into two parts as follows:

1. Internal sources
2. External sources

Internal sources include the records of the company, reports of the salesmen, correspondence with customers, etc. External sources include the data collected by one enterprise and published by another enterprise.

Tabulation of Data

After collecting the data, these are tabulated so that a comparative and an analytical study of the data can be made.

Analysis and Interpretation of Data

After collecting and tabulating the data, they are analysed and interpreted. Such analysis and interpretation leads to important decisions. After this, the decisions are arrived at in the light of the problem. This is a very important step in marketing research because a marketing manager gets relevant information for the solution of a problem only through such analysis and interpretation.

Preparation of Research Report

After arriving at the conclusions, a research report must be prepared by the research scholar. This report should neither be very lengthy nor very short. This report must contain all the facts and conclusions of the research undertaken. The research scholar should consult the marketing manager before preparing such a report so that the report may contribute in the process of decision-making. This report must clearly specify the objectives and the scope of research so that no doubt may arise at any stage.

Follow up of the Report

Though the process of marketing research is completed with the preparation of the research report but it is also important that an effective implementation of the decisions arrived at during the course of the marketing research must be ensured and chased by the marketing manager so that the research may produce the best results for the enterprise.

Points to Ponder

1. Marketing research is the systematic problem analysis, model building and fact finding for the purpose of improved decision making and control in the marketing of goods and services.
2. The different types of marketing research are as follows:
   a. Product analysis
   b. Market analysis
   c. Distribution analysis
   d. Competition analysis
   e. Consumer research
   f. Sales analysis
   g. Motivational research
   h. Advertisement research
3. The various steps involved in marketing research are as follows:
   a. Defining the problem
   b. Situation analysis
   c. Checking the available sources of information
   d. Collection of data
   e. Tabulation of data
   f. Analysis and interpretation of data
   g. Preparation of research report
   h. Follow up of the report

 **Self-Assessment Exercises**

1. Indicate whether the following statements are TRUE or FALSE:
   a. Consumer is the king.
   b. Marketing research is a scientific method of solving the marketing problems.
   c. Important information about the customers is obtained through marketing research.
   d. The importance of marketing research is declining day-by-day.
   e. The main aim of distribution analysis is to control the costs of distribution.
   f. Marketing research has become a necessity of all the business enterprise of today.
   g. The procedure of marketing research is similar in every organization.
   h. Internal sources include the data collected by one enterprise and published by another enterprise.
2. What is marketing research? Outline the important areas of research and describe the benefits it is expected to confer.
3. Discuss the various kinds of marketing research. State when the marketing research is necessary?
4. Explain the procedure and the limitations of marketing research.

Recruitment, Selection and Retention of Pharmacy Personnel

INTRODUCTION

This chapter is intended to assist pharmacy managers in the recruitment, selection and retention of qualified employees. The pharmacy manager working in an organized health care system will usually have to work with the system's human resources department and within the framework of the specific recruitment, selection and hiring policies of the organization.

RECRUITMENT

The following points are to be looked at during the recruitment process:

Position Description

Well-developed job descriptions are extremely important in addressing many personnel issues. They are often used to establish salary ranges, define performance expectations and write performance evaluations, but they can also be crucial tools in a successful recruitment effort. The position description should contain detailed information on the knowledge, skills, experience and abilities that an acceptable candidate should possess. The following information may be included in a position description:

1. Position title and position control number (if applicable)
2. Duties, essential job functions and responsibilities of the position
3. Education, training, experience and licensure required
4. Knowledge, skills and abilities required to perform assigned duties
5. Reporting relationships
6. Pay grade and salary range (optional)
7. Education and training required to maintain competence
8. Other specifications of the position that may be required to meet the legal requirements (e.g. the Americans with Disabilities Act) or the objectives of the organization (e.g. residency or certification requirements).

A revised position description should be reviewed with staff members currently in that position and with the supervisor of that position. In many workplaces, human resource departments maintain a file of position descriptions and may require approval of all position descriptions in the organization. Procedures specific to the workplace should be followed. The staff with legal expertise should review the revised position descriptions to determine compliance with the organizational and legal requirements.

Recruitment Sources

Recruitment processes will depend on the type of position being filled. The strategies for filling a support staff position may not be appropriate when searching for a management candidate and vice versa. A recruitment plan should be developed for each position being filled. This plan should incorporate strategies that have worked in the past while allowing for innovative ideas. Organizations that recruit frequently or have very limited candidate pools should consider a continuous recruitment plan so that a list of prospective candidates is available even before an opening occurs.

The recruitment of individuals from within the department or the organization (e.g. from another department) creates internal growth opportunities and may result in greater employee retention and staff loyalty. Internal recruitment may also be less disruptive and expensive. To facilitate internal recruitment, a notice of a vacant position can be posted within the organization before the information is made available to candidates outside of it. The posting of the vacancy can be accomplished by various means including memoranda, email, voice mail, newsletters, announcements at staff meetings and bulletin boards.

Recruitment of outside candidates expands the number of potential candidates and the experience available to the organization. It brings in new talent and discourages a reliance on seniority as the primary basis for promotion. Budgetary constraints and the urgency to fill a position may affect the recruitment method selected for external candidates. When recruitment of individuals outside the organization becomes necessary, the following methods should be considered:

1. Advertisements in professional journals, newspapers, state professional society newsletters and electronic bulletin boards
2. Personnel placement services provided by the national or state professional societies
3. Oral and written recommendations from colleagues. Some organizations offer a finder's fee for hires that result from an employee referral
4. Personal discussion or correspondence with potential candidates

5. Recruitment visits to colleges of pharmacy or to facilities that conduct technician training programs
6. Professional recruiting firms that typically charge the organization a percentage of the position's annual salary. In addition, recruitment advertising companies offer access to a list of job seekers for a fee
7. Familiarizing students with the organization by offering summer jobs or participating in college of pharmacy experiential rotations
8. Tuition assistance programs for students in exchange for future work commitments
9. A prospect list of individuals applying for previous job openings, which can often be supplied by the human resources department
10. Internet jobsite postings
11. Community job fairs and local or state welfare-to-work programs
12. Organization-sponsored events such as the continuing education sessions, award presentations or community outreach programs.

The ability to recruit qualified candidates will depend on a multitude of factors, including the financial stability and location of the organization, the area's cost of living, the organization's compensation program (including salary, fringe benefits and raise structure), the position's schedule and reporting structure, opportunities for professional growth and advancement, and the reputation and scope of pharmaceutical services offered. Only some of these factors are within the pharmacy manager's control.

Preinterview Information

The applicant's correspondence, résumé or curriculum vitae, letters of recommendation, academic records and completed application form (if any) should be carefully evaluated on the basis of the position description to determine the suitability of the candidate for an interview.

There are certain legal restrictions on the type of information that may be requested from the candidates on an application form. In general, an application form may request only that information that relates directly to the evaluation of the applicant's ability to perform the job for which he or she is applying. If an application form is different from that the organization uses, it is advisable to have the human resources and legal departments review it before its distribution to potential candidates.

SELECTION

The following points have to be considered while selecting a candidate:

Initial Screening Interview

An initial screening interview may be necessary if several qualified candidates have been identified. The screening interview is generally a brief interview conducted by the human resources department or the direct supervisor of the position. It offers a quick assessment of the suitability of the candidate for the position. This interview is often conducted by telephone, especially if the candidate lives far away. The screening interview should be documented and included in the applicant's file.

The Interview Process

A successful interview process is one that matches the best available candidate with a specific position. The process should allow the interviewers to predict the future performance of the candidates as accurately as possible. One style of interview is the individual interview with one interviewer and one interviewee. Individual interviews offer the advantages of simplicity, ease of scheduling and consistency of perspective. Because they are less intimidating to the candidate than group interviews, individual interviews may allow the interviewer to more accurately evaluate the applicant and provide the applicant with more opportunities to ask questions. The disadvantage of an individual interview is that it does not allow for multiple viewpoints and therefore, increase the chances of something being overlooked.

Another style, team interviewing, involves a group of interviewers. Members of the team may interview the candidate individually and then pool their results or they may interview the candidate as a group. The well-prepared team approach offers multiple perspectives within a standardized evaluation scheme. The disadvantages of a team interview are extra time consumed to train the team and conduct interviews, and the intimidating effect it may have on candidates. However, the advantage of the same is that it incorporates more individuals into the process of analysing a candidate's qualifications.

Team interviews foster the ideal of teamwork and the involved employees share responsibility for the success or failure of the person hired. They also provide an opportunity to observe the candidate's ability to interact with groups that may be important if the position will require that type of activity.

The composition of the interview team will depend on the position being filled. The team should include people with a common interest in the outcome of the selection process and people who have been in the organization long enough to share with the applicant some history of the organization and the department.

The characteristics of an effective interview process include the following:

1. Prior to the interview, the manager should provide the following to the candidate: information about the health-system institution, department, city and state (if the applicant is not from the area) an agenda for the interview, the position description, travel directions to the facility and clarification of expenses that will be incurred or reimbursed.
2. The interview should be carefully planned. Consider the availability of those who need to participate in the process and allow adequate time for each event, including a tour of the facility (if needed).
3. Interviewers should be well prepared. Preinterview information submitted by the candidate should be distributed to and reviewed by participants in advance of an interview.
4. Carefully planned, open-ended questions should be developed in advance. Literature can be consulted to obtain sample questions, and questions that are inadvisable or prohibited by law. The human resources departments can usually assist in developing questions.
5. To the extent possible, a core group of questions should be asked of all candidates as a means of comparing them. This does not negate the need to investigate different areas for each candidate or to pursue specific questions that surface during the interview.
6. Questions should focus on predetermined criteria for the position and the qualifications of the candidates. The goal is to match the best candidate with the vacant position. The questions should focus on the past performance, which is often a good indicator of the future performance. In

addition to questions regarding professional competency, the interview should contain questions that will help determine whether the applicant's behaviour and attitudes and will be suitable for the job. Behaviour-based selection criteria should be used whenever possible.

7. The interviewer should give the candidate a realistic view of the position, including both favourable and unfavourable information. If the candidate is oversold on the position, dissatisfaction may set in when the truth becomes apparent.

8. Performance standards and methods used for evaluation should be fully explained, and opportunities for professional growth should be presented.

9. A description of employee benefits (like medical insurance, vacation, sick leave, retirement benefits and holidays) should be provided, either by the manager or by the human resources department.

10. The initial salary and the salary range for the position should be discussed with the candidate.

11. The employee work schedule should be reviewed with the candidate.

12. Any additional services or covered expenses the department offers should be outlined. Examples of these services of covered expenses include serving as a provider of continuing education programs, travel expenses and time off for continuing-education programs, payment of professional membership fees and any other benefits that would attract the candidate to the position.

13. A tour of the department should be provided.

14. If the candidate is not from the area, a tour of the region should be given. The employees of the department or a real estate agency may show a candidate the area and describe the housing market and local schools.

15. A follow up letter is sent to the candidate after the interview to express thanks for the interest in the position and the organization, and to advise the candidate of the next steps. Timely and well-organized communication between the recruiters and the candidates is essential to a successful recruitment effort.

16. Each interview should be documented to keep track of each candidate's responses and to avoid confusion later. Documentation could include interview questions and the candidate's responses or simply a rating of the candidate's responses to specific questions. One person may be designated to collect and collate comments from a group interview. Documentation should occur immediately after the interview. When considering a potential employee, the interviewer should examine punctuality, completeness and accuracy of the résumé or curriculum vitae, communication skills, compensation expectations, skills and knowledge pertinent to the position and the optimal fit with coworkers. The recruitment team should agree in advance on a systematic method for selecting the successful candidate.

Background Verification

The accuracy of the information provided by the candidate should be verified by the human resources department. Information may be obtained from the following sources:

1. Personal letters of reference provided by the applicant
2. Letters of reference provided by the previous employers or preceptors (with the applicant's permission)
3. The state board of pharmacy records
4. Academic records
5. Legal background searches (when permitted by law and/or by the applicant).

Job Offer

The job offer should be made as quickly as possible after the interview process is completed. Offers should be made to candidates with enthusiasm and should include a deadline for the response. Information about candidate selection should be kept confidential until the offer has been accepted. The organization may have specific policies and procedures regarding job offers.

The salary offered to a candidate will usually be competitive with the salaries for similar jobs in other organizations in the same market and compatible with the organization's existing salary structure. The market may vary, depending on the position. For example, the market for a pharmacy technician may be local, whereas the market for a pharmacist or pharmacy manager may be regional or national. To preserve equity within the organization, the salary offered to a candidate generally should be consistent with the salaries of the staff currently in that position. When exceptions are considered, it may become necessary to reassess the compensation of the existing staff.

In addition to the salary, other commitments made to a candidate should be expressed in writing as part of the formal job offer. These may include the following:

    a.   Date on which the employment will begin
    b.   Supervisor's name and position
    c.   Position description
    d.   Performance standards and evaluation system
    e.   Next performance review date
    f.   Next compensation increase date
    g.   Expected work schedule and whether it is subject to change depending on future needs of the department
    h.   Employee benefits (e.g. insurance, vacation, tuition assistance, sick leave, holidays and retirement and pension benefits)
    i.   Miscellaneous commitments (e.g. employment bonus, relocation expenses, licensure reimbursement, payment for professional association memberships and payment for attendance at professional education programs)
    j.   Potential drug screening (as applicable and in keeping with the law) or employee physical examination and the dates of these activities.

RETENTION

Staff turnover is costly. The time required to recruit and train new employees has been shown to cause a temporary loss of productivity in the workplace. Staff turnover also has a negative impact on staff morale that may further reduce productivity and increase the turnover. Because individuals have varied needs and wants that may change over time, there is no consistent formula for application by managers to ensure employee retention. Each organization's experience will depend on such factors as the age of employees, the stage in life and career of the employee, the organizational structure, the work environment and the work itself.

Retention may compete with recruitment. For example, creating staff positions with exclusively morning shifts may help retention but hurt recruitment, because fewer candidates are interested in evening shifts. When the competing issues arise, pharmacy managers must balance them with the short and long-term departmental goals and the current demand for employment.

Each organization should identify and assess retention factors by examining the unique aspects of the respective department and the organization. For example, a committee broadly representing the organization could be established to determine major retention factors. On the basis of this assessment, a retention plan should be developed. The plan should be reviewed periodically as the needs of employees change; employee surveys may help determine these. The following factors may be considered in analysing staff retention:

1. **Training period:** The department should devote sufficient time and attention to training the employee. Prepare for the new employee's first day by providing him or her with the key material in advance and by developing an organized training schedule. Introduce the new employee to key people on the first day and have everyone in the department introduce themselves during the orientation period. Communicate with the new employee regularly during the training period and throughout the first three months.

   Sufficient training time ensures that the new employee is comfortable in the new work environment and decreases the likelihood that he or she will become frustrated in the new position. Some organizations have developed a structured mentoring program in which a new employee is paired with a senior employee during the training period.

2. **Intent to stay:** In several studies, this factor was the best predictor of staff retention. Employees can simply be asked whether they intend to stay. Replies will reflect the employee perceptions and should be considered in the light of the behaviour (i.e. the actual turnover rate). Replies may also be influenced by the employees' fear of reprisal.

3. **Job satisfaction:** Job satisfaction is a measure of the degree to which the individuals like their jobs, their work environment and relationships with their coworkers. Job satisfaction is important to retention, although, the relationship may be direct or indirect. Employees can be asked how satisfied they are with their jobs; there are many survey instruments to assist pharmacy managers and directors in performing this task. Job dissatisfaction does not necessarily lead to staff turnover, if other factors are more important to the individual.

4. **Pay and benefits:** Pay benefits refer to the remuneration for work performed and the organization's overall benefit plan. The pay may be hourly (a wage) or salaried and may include overtime premiums or bonuses and incentive plans. A benefit plan may include life, medical, dental, disability and liability insurance; tuition payments; retirement packages; paid organizational membership dues; sick leave; paid vacation; child care and prescription benefits. The value of specific benefits to an employee will likely change over time. Many organizations offer a benefits plan that gives the employee the option of choosing benefits individually suited to his or her stage in life and career.

5. **Performance management:** Performance appraisal is a periodic assessment of an employee's performance throughout the year. Performance appraisal is only one step in a performance management process that includes appraisal, ongoing feedback, goal setting and development. This process is important to the success of the manager, the employee and the organization. The goal of performance management is to share information that will help the employee grow, both personally and professionally and improve the organization. Periodic discussions with the employee are necessary to provide and receive feedback, and to avoid surprises at the time of the scheduled performance appraisal. Direct observation and evaluation by supervisors and coworkers can contribute to a meaningful appraisal.

6. **Recognition and awards:** Employees often feel that recognition is lacking in the workplace. New supervisors or managers should receive training in employee recognition that includes both formal and informal feedback mechanisms, from structured employee of the month (or year) programs

to a simple thank you given in private or at a department meeting. Managers should identify how employees want to be recognized through employee surveys or informal discussions.

The methods of employee recognition include the following:

a. Thank you notes
b. Commendations
c. Acknowledgment at department meetings
d. Organization-wide events during National Pharmacy Week
e. Employee of the month, quarter or year
f. Support for attendance at a professional meeting
g. Small awards such as movie tickets or gift certificates for coffee.

7. **Promotion opportunities:** Opportunities in promotion may be in the form of formal promotions, career advancement programs, training opportunities, or special project or committee appointments. Flat organizational structures provide few formal opportunities for staff promotion. Employees who have made personal investments in the organization—through expanded responsibilities associated with promotion—may have stronger feelings of loyalty that translate into increased retention. The succession planning is a key organizational strategy that ensures the availability of future leaders.

8. **Job design:** Job design refers to the general tasks that an employee performs—the content of the work. Job design includes autonomy, the complexity of tasks, and the support and tools provided to the employee. Studies have found that job content is more highly correlated with retention as the level of an employee's education increases. Motivational theories suggest that the job itself can motivate intrinsically and that success in the job can lead to increased employee satisfaction.

9. **Peer relations:** Peer relations refer to the working relationships with peers, nurses, physicians and technical support staff. Peer relations are often highly rated as a reason for staying with an organization. It is difficult to predict during the interview process how a candidate's peer relations will develop, but past behaviours and discussion of hypothetical scenarios can provide some insight.

10. **Kinship responsibilities:** Kinship responsibilities refer to family considerations, such as childcare needs, spouse-employment transfers and care for elderly relatives. Child and elder care needs are important for working parents. These considerations are also difficult to screen for during the interview process, and they will change over time. Legal restrictions prevent recruiters from asking some questions; the organization's human resources department should be able to offer advice on this issue.

11. **Opportunity:** Opportunity refers to other options in the job market. Obviously, tight job markets (a relative lack of alternative positions) increase retention, whereas, open job markets (those with many other open positions) may increase the turnover. Managers should always be attentive to retaining good employees, but in the open job markets they need to be especially attentive.

12. **Staff-development opportunities:** Staff-development opportunities refer to the job training, educational opportunities, and tuition reimbursement or other educational and personal growth opportunities for staff. Training and educational opportunities can affect recognition and awards, promotion opportunities, job design and peer relations. So they can have a big impact on employee retention.

13. **Management style:** The management style refers to the organizational structure and the prevalent management style in the organization (e.g. on the spectrum from autocratic to participatory). The accessibility of the management staff may be a factor, as well as, the extent to which the staff input is encouraged. Each employee will prefer a particular management style, no one style will work equally

well for all employees. Managers must be sensitive to the management styles that are effective for their staff.

14. **Employee coaching:** Employee coaching refers to the manager's mentorship role. Managers should provide feedback to employees regarding performance, teach specific job related skills, hold formal and informal career discussions with employees, help employees achieve greater self-awareness, advise employees on how best to prepare for career options and assist employees in preparing a yearly career development plan. In addition, it is important that managers recognize and acknowledge the contributions of the employees to the health system.

15. **Management survey:** Management survey refers to the organization's commitment to identifying opportunities for improving management. Such opportunities can be identified by surveying employees about the performance of their manager. The survey should be conducted by each manager's supervisor. Managers should also complete the survey to see how their rating compares with that of their staff. Action plans should be established on the basis of the survey results. Such 360-degree surveys should be managed with caution, however, they may create animosity and foster unhealthy relationships between the management and staff.

16. **Physical working conditions:** The physical working conditions refer to the physical characteristics and safety of the workplace, such as space, equipment, noise levels, parking accommodations and cleanliness.

17. **Scheduling:** Scheduling refers to the opportunities for varied scheduling, vacation time, shift rotation, job sharing, flexible hours and part-time work.

18. **Motivation:** Extrinsic motivators for change (such as salary, promotion and recognition) can affect behaviour, but they cannot change values and attitudes. In the workplace, change occurs most readily when people are motivated by the desire to bring their professional activities inline with their personal and professional values and beliefs. The living vision and value statements offer the employees an opportunity to shape an inspiring organizational culture. Although, motivations of each employee will be different, some theories of motivation can help managers understand what contributes to job satisfaction. Maslow's hierarchy of needs, e.g. states that employees will be happiest when they are working toward self-actualization that requires that their more basic needs for security, esteem, belonging and knowledge be satisfied first. Herzberg et al. motivation/hygiene theory explains that employees cannot be motivated by the hygiene aspects of their work (organization policies, supervision, salary, peer relations and working conditions), but that dissatisfaction with those aspects can interfere with the motivating factors (the work itself, responsibility, achievement, recognition and advancement).

19. **Exit interview:** An interview should be scheduled with a director of the department, the human resources department and the exiting employee. The director should ask in depth questions to identify why the employee is leaving. The exit interview should explore the employee's opinion of the company, department, his or her direct manager, as well as, any other issues the employee may have for leaving. Pharmacy managers should validate and share this information with the appropriate management staff to decrease the likelihood that another employee may leave for a similar reason.

SAMPLE QUESTIONS TO BE ASKED OF JOB CANDIDATES

Questions for Experienced Pharmacists and Technicians

1. How did you become interested in pharmacy?

2. What skills or traits do you think a pharmacist needs to have to be successful?
3. What is the single greatest contribution you have made in your present (or most recent) position?
4. What is something you have recommended or tried in your present (or most recent) position that did not work? Why did it not?
5. How are you evaluated in your present (most recent) job?
6. What would your present (most recent) employer say are your strong points? Your weak points?
7. Why did you (do you want to) leave your last (present) job?
8. Do you prefer working on a team or alone? Why?
9. What part of the job did you like the best and the least?

Questions for Recent College-of-Pharmacy Graduates

1. What was your most rewarding college experience?
2. Why did you want to study pharmacy?
3. What would you change about your college experience if you could?
4. Do you think your grades accurately reflect your academic achievements?
5. What subjects did you like most and least? Why?

General Questions

1. What qualities are you looking for in your next supervisor?
2. What supervisory style do you think you have?
3. What are your long-term career goals?
4. How does this position fit in with your long-term career goals?
5. What are you looking for in your next position that has been lacking in previous positions?

Points to Ponder

1. The various points to be kept in mind for recruitment are as below:
   a. Position description
   b. Recruitment sources
   c. Preinterview information
2. The following points have to be considered while selecting a candidate:
   a. Initial screening interview
   b. The interview process
   c. Background verification
   d. Job offer

 **Self-Assessment Exercises**

1. Write a short note on recruitment.
2. Describe in detail about the various sources of recruitment.
3. Write a short note on selection process.
4. Enumerate various characteristics of an effective interview process.
5. Write a short note on retention of pharmacy personnel.
6. Discuss in brief about various factors considered in analysing staff retention.

Channels of Distribution

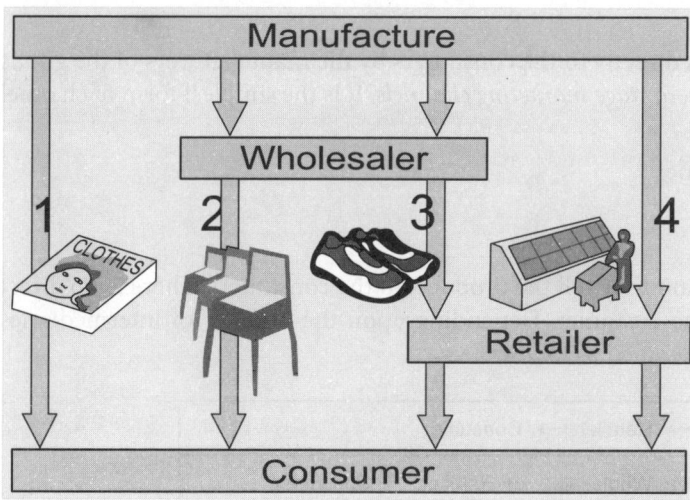

INTRODUCTION

A channel of distribution is the route taken by the goods as they move from the producer to the ultimate consumer. It is the last component of the total marketing process. The ultimate aim of every producer is to get the goods delivered to the consumers. He manufactures the goods. The customer comes to know about the product through advertising and the next step is to see that the goods are available to the consumers. The *trade channels* or *channels of distribution* signifies various trade links connecting the producer and the ultimate consumer.

It includes producers, wholesalers and retailers, and sometimes mercantile agents are also included. But channels of distribution does not include transport agencies, insurance companies, banks, warehouses and other nonmiddlemen institutions though they perform very important functions in the aid of trade but they do not play any major role in negotiating purchase and the sale of products.

ADVANTAGES OF DISTRIBUTION CHANNELS

The advantages of the channels of distribution are as follows:

1. Time utility and place utility. Consumers can get the goods at the place and at the time they require the goods.
2. Marketing costs are less.
3. Due to the financial pooling from different sources, financial burden on the producer is less.
4. Due to a large network, more promotional efforts are carried out by each category, hence more advertisement for the product.
5. Creation of more employment potential and standard of living.

The distribution channels may be grouped under two major heads:

1. Direct selling 2. Indirect selling

Direct Selling

Direct selling refers to the selling of goods directly to the consumers by the manufacturers of the goods without any intermediaries. It is called as *zero stage marketing channels*. It is the simplest form of channel of distribution.

Manufacturer ⟶ Consumer

Indirect Selling

The manufacturer sells to intermediaries and they sell the products to the consumers. There is no direct contact between the manufacturer and the customer. Depending upon the number of intermediaries present, the channels of distribution are classified as follows:

One stage	Manufacturer ⟶ Retailer ⟶ Consumer
Two stage	Manufacturer ⟶ Wholesaler ⟶ Retailer ⟶ Consumer
Three stage	Producer ⟶ Distributor ⟶ Wholesaler ⟶ Retailer ⟶ Consumer

Producer and consumer or direct sale (Zero stage marketing)

Direct selling means the selling of goods and services by the manufacturer to the consumer. The producers establish a connection with the consumers directly through door-to-door salesmen, direct mail or by its own retail outlets.

Direct Selling is gaining ground nowadays because of exorbitant distribution costs through sale intermediaries like retailers and wholesalers. This method is usually adopted to sell industrial goods of high value and also goods like perishable commodities. In this type of selling, the marketing activities are performed by the producer himself.

Producer, retailer and consumer

This is single phase distribution where the manufacturer sells the goods to retailer who in turn sells them to the consumer. This is a popular method of distribution because of the emergence of the supermarkets and the big departmental stores. The retailer procures the goods in large quantities from the manufacturer and sells them to the consumers.

Producer, wholesaler, retailer and consumer

This is called *two stage marketing* where two intermediaries are involved. This is the traditional channel of distribution for the sale of consumer goods. This channel is most suitable for markets that are widely scattered.

Producer, distributor, wholesaler, retailer and consumer

This type of distribution network is required when large number of retailers and wholesalers are part of the network. Hence, it becomes difficult for the producer to keep contact with such large sales agencies. The producer, thus, employs few distributors.

Usually the consumer goods are produced in large scale and everyone requires these goods. Therefore, a big channel of distribution is required. Where the industrial goods are costly and the requirements are few, a short channel of distribution is required.

FACTORS TO BE CONSIDERED IN THE SELECTION OF DISTRIBUTION CHANNELS

The selection of the right channels of distribution is the most powerful element in the selling of products. Even the best goods cannot be sold out, if the right channel of distribution is not selected and vice versa. While taking a decision in this matter, the organization should carefully consider the following factors:

1. Market factors
2. Product factors
3. Organization factors
4. Market intermediaries factors

Market Factors

The various considerations while selecting a market for a product are as follows:

Type of market

The manufacturer should first decide whether his product is meant for the consumer market or the industrial market. If it is for the industrial market, there is no need of a middleman because the industrial users secure goods in large quantities directly from the producer. If it is a consumer market, the retailers and wholesalers will be included in the channel of distribution.

Consumer potential

If the product is intended for very large number of people, it will become difficult for the producer to distribute the goods efficiently, whereas if the of customers are small in number, the manufacturer can sell the goods directly to customers.

Quantum of goods

Direct selling is convenient for large quantity of goods, whereas when the products are sold in smaller quantities, the retailers and the wholesalers are there to distribute the product.

Tastes and preferences of consumers

The buying behaviours of the consumer, credit facility, single stop shopping, etc., are some of the factors useful in the choice of the distribution channel.

Product Factors

The nature and the category of the products also have a good influence on the selection of a suitable channel of distribution. The important product considerations are as follows:

Value of goods

If the products manufactured are very costly like diamonds, super computers, etc., they are directly sold. For cheaper goods like toothpaste, stationary, soaps, etc., the consumption is very high. Hence, a very long channel of distribution is required.

Product category

A manufacturer producing several products of the same category like soaps, toothpaste and toothbrushes, etc., requires a small channel of distribution. They can be moved in the same channel of distribution whereas products falling in the varied category requires more number of channels of distribution.

Popular products

Popular products having a good brand identity and because of their popularity can be sold through longer channel of distribution while, products that are not standardized can be sold directly by the producer to the customer.

Nature of the product

If the product is highly technical in nature, it is usually distributed directly to the user. This happens mostly in case of industrial goods. Products of nontechnical nature like consumer goods are usually sold through a chain of outlets.

Size and weight

If the goods are heavy, then in order to minimize the physical handling of the goods and the cost factor, they are usually distributed directly to the customer.

Spoilage

If the goods are perishable items and if they are subjected physical or fashion perishability they have to be sold as early as possible directly to the consumers. Nonperishable items usually have a longer channel of distribution.

Organization Factors

The nature and the size of the manufacturer is also an important factor to be considered while deciding on the channel of distribution. Some of the important aspects to be considered in this category are as follows:

Financial capability

A strong financial company can distribute products on its own by employing its own sales force and retail outlets, whereas the financially weaker company cannot do this and has to use the services of retailers and the wholesalers for this purpose.

Control of distribution

If the channel of distribution is under the control of the manufacturer, it has to be a shorter one. By having the control it is possible to have aggressive promotion of the product.

Scale of operation

If the scale of (operation) production is small, it is not possible to sell directly. Hence, wholesalers and retailers are required to sell the products. For a big manufacturer, if he is manufacturing a wide variety of products he can sell the products directly to the customers by opening retail outlets in different parts of the country.

Market Intermediaries Factor

There should be good cooperation and assistance between the middlemen and the manufacturer. Sometimes the middleman does not want to sell the manufactures because the processing of the manufacturers will not suit them or sometimes the retailers ask for a more credit period. The manufacturer will select a channel that offers a good sale potential in the long run. Similarly the large manufacturers usually select middlemen who are financially sound and can offer long-standing credit facility to the customers.

 DIFFERENT CHANNELS OF DISTRIBUTION

As discussed above, the channels of distribution are broadly classified into two groups—direct selling and indirect selling.

Direct Selling and the Middlemen

In direct selling the manufacturer sells his products directly to the customers by employing his own salesmen or middlemen who contacts the consumer.

Direct selling is advantageous because the middle men are eliminated and hence the goods utility became cheap, moreover the incentives can be directly given to the customers. It is also possible for the manufacturer to give information regarding the products to the customer and also get a feedback directly. Nowadays direct selling is gaining wide popularity and many manufacturers are adopting this technique for selling the products.

Indirect Selling and the Middlemen

Indirect selling adopts middlemen who act as a link between the producer and the consumer. They are engaged in the marketing and help in the purchase and sale of goods and services.

The middlemen usually charge for the services they have rendered to the manufacturers and the consumers. In the absence of the middlemen the manufacturers will have to perform all the functions of selling the products themselves. Middlemen are important since they give feedbacks to the manufacturer regarding the requirements of the customers from the goods.

 TYPES OF MIDDLEMEN

Middlemen can be mainly classified into two kinds as follows:
1. Mercantile agents or agent middleman or functional middleman
2. Merchant middleman or merchants

Mercantile Agents

These are the intermediaries who perform important services for the exchange of the goods but do not handle the goods in the capacity of the owners. They assist in the buying and selling of the goods by taking part in the negotiations. They do not sell the products; hence they do not earn profits. They charge remuneration for the services undertaken in the form of commission or brokerage.

Mercantile agents are of the following types:

1. Commission agents
2. Auctioneer
3. Brokers
4. Factor or del-credire agents

Commission agents

They sell goods on behalf of the seller. They physically possess the goods, negotiate the sale of goods and make necessary arrangements for the transfer of title of the goods to the consumers. They also perform the associated function of marketing like warehousing, assortments and assembling of goods, and final disposal. A certain percentage of commission is paid to them for their services.

Auctioneers

Auctioneers are the mercantile agents to sell goods on behalf of their principals by undertaking auction of goods. They take physical possession of goods from the sellers, put for display before the prospective buyers and receive bids from the purchasers (bid means the price that the buyer is willing to pay for the goods being auctioned). The highest bidder gets the goods. The highest bid is at least equal to the minimum reserved price fixed for the product. If the highest bid happens to be lower than the minimum reserved price fixed, then the auctioneers can cancel the auction. Auctioneer gets a certain percentage for the services rendered by him.

Brokers

A broker is a mercantile agent who negotiates purchases or sells goods on behalf of the other parties. He neither takes the physical possession of goods nor change of title of goods on his name but only facilitates the exchange of goods by bringing the buyer and seller together. He gets a brokerage that is a percentage of the value of the transaction involved.

Del-credire agents or factors

A del-credire agent locates the prospective buyers and also guarantees the payment of the prices of the goods on their behalf. In case any buyer fails to pay, he pays on the behalf of the buyer. For this additional responsibility an extra commission is charged.

Merchant Middlemen or Merchants

Also known as *traders* or *dealers* in goods and services, they carry out buying and selling on their own name for profit. They take possession and become owners of the products and transfer the title of ownership to the buyer when the goods are sold. The middlemen belonging to this category are as follows:

1. Wholesaler
2. Retailer

Wholesalers

They are the merchants to buy and sell the goods in large quantities and generally deal in a narrow range of goods. They provide an important link between the manufacturer and the retailer. He possesses the title to the goods and he takes up several marketing risks in the process of distribution of goods. He purchases goods in large quantity and sells them in smaller quantities to the retailers. The wholesalers are usually located far away from the ultimate consumers. The wholesalers handling pharmaceutical products require a drug license from the drug control department of the concerned state. He sells the products to the pharmacist and physicians. A *wholesaler* is called a *stockiest* if he handles the products of a single manufacturer.

Classification of wholesalers

The wholesalers can be classified into three types namely:

1. Manufacturer wholesaler
2. Retail wholesaler
3. Wholesaler proper or pure wholesaler.

Manufacturer wholesaler. He undertakes the manufacturing of goods along with the distribution to the retailers. They may not only sell their own products to the retailers, but also make large scale purchases from other manufacturers to meet the demand of the materials. In this way their turnover is increased and the sale price and overhead expenses are reduced by eliminating the wholesalers.

Retailer wholesaler. A wholesaler combines his business of wholesale with the function of retail trade. They purchase goods in large quantities directly from the producers and sell them both to the producers, as well as, to the consumers.

Pure wholesaler. Pure wholesaler is a merchant who deals only in business relations. He neither manufactures, nor sells the goods directly to the consumers.

Sometimes they are also known as *distributors wholesaler*. He purchases goods from a number of manufacturers in large quantities and sells them to the retailers in small quantities. He has a warehousing facility and also arranges for transportation of goods to the retailers.

The wholesalers specializing only in a particular line of product are known as *single line wholesaler*.

Functions of wholesalers

The functions of wholesalers are as follows:

Assembly of goods. He places orders to various producers and collect different of types goods at one place and resells them to the retailers.

Distribution. The wholesalers distribute the goods to the retailers, who are generally widely scattered.

Storage. Wholesalers help the goods to assemble in the warehousing to supply them to the retailers whenever they order. They relieve the manufacturer and the retailers from the burden of making storage arrangement.

Transportation. He moves the goods from the place of production to his own warehouse and from there to the retailers. Usually he has his own lorries or transportation facilities for the purpose of transportation of goods.

Financing. Wholesalers provide financial assistance in the form of credit to manufacturers and the retailers.

Risk taking. Bulk buying and storage of goods involve several risks like accidental damage to goods, vagaries of nature, change of demand, etc. These risks are born by the wholesaler.

Pricing. The price fixed by the wholesaler is based on the price at which the retailer charges from its customers.

Grading and packaging. The wholesalers' grade the goods into different categories based on the quality and also pack the goods in smaller containers.

Market research. The wholesaler is close to the retailers and hence he gets information regarding the preferences and the tastes of the customer. Hence, he is in a position to advice the manufacturer regarding the product and price fixations to fit the customer needs.

Promotion. He also performs several advertising and promotional activities to increase the sale of the products. He also assists the retailers in the dispersal of goods.

Advantages of wholesale trade
The advantages of wholesale trade are as follows:

1. **Services to producers**
   a. Financial help to producers by giving advance.
   b. Assistance in marketing functions like sales promotions and advertisement.
   c. Feedback information (marketing research).
   d. Facilitates large scale production by placing advance orders of the goods.
   e. Shares the risk with the producer by bulk buying and storage.
   f. Helps in adjusting the demand and supply and hence in stabilizing the price of goods.

2. **Services to Retailers**
   a. Provision of transportation to retailers.
   b. Help in promoting the products to retailers.
   c. Retailers get discount on bulk purchasing from the wholesaler.
   d. Gives advance information to the retailers regarding the new products of the manufacturer.
   e. Provides credit facilities to the retailers.
   f. The retailers free from the risk of large stock.

3. **Services to the consumers and society**
   a. Provides latest information regarding the products.
   b. Prevents price fluctuation of the products by constantly supplying enough goods to the market.

Disadvantages of the wholesalers
Following are the disadvantages of the wholesalers:

1. The price of the product is increased due to increase in the margin of profit by wholesalers.
2. Sometimes they create artificial scarcity of goods by hoarding the goods.

Retailers

A retailer sells the goods to the customers and maintains good liaison with the wholesaler, manufacturer and the consumer. He is the middleman between the wholesaler and the actual consumer. He collects various kinds of goods from numerous sources and sells them to the consumers in small quantities. They are generally located at the popular residential areas. Retail business is organized on proprietorship or partnership basis.

Functions of retailers

Following are the functions of the retailers:

Wide variety of goods. Various items according to the needs of consumers are kept by him. He should know the potential of the goods and he should know the tastes of the consumers.

Transport. Retailers usually have their own facilities for transportation of goods from the godowns of the wholesalers.

Financing. He provides credit facility to the consumers.

Market research. He is in close contact with the customers. Hence, he knows the tastes and preferences of the customers. This information will be useful to the manufacturers.

Sales promotion. He exhibits the goods in his counters and helps in the promotion and sale of goods.

Services performed by retailers

He performs a number of services not only to the wholesalers and manufacturers but also to the actual consumers.

Services to the producer-wholesaler. The services performed by the retailers to the producer-wholesaler are as follows:

1. They are the best link between the producer and the customer. They help in the distribution of goods.
2. They take over the function of dealing with large number of people and selling goods in very small quantities, thus relieving the wholesalers from his job.
3. Without the service of the retailers, it is not possible to introduce a new product in the market.
4. They provide the latest information with regard to tastes, fashions and demand of the consumers to the wholesalers who in turn transmit the same to the producers.
5. Sometimes they make advance payments for the goods to be received, this helps in financing the wholesalers.

Services to the consumers. The services offered by the retailers to the consumers are as follows:

1. They sell goods to the consumers in the smallest possible quantities according to the needs of the customers.
2. They keep a large variety of goods and thus offer a wide choice to the customers.
3. The retailers keep personal contact with the customers, listen to their complaints and try to satisfy them. He passes these genuine complaints to the manufacturer wholesalers for rectification or substitution of goods.
4. They advice the customers regarding the suitability, use and maintenance of the products.
5. They also provide free home delivery and after sales services to regular customers.
6. The retailers often grant credit facility to the needy customers thereby helping them in times of need.
7. They allow cash discount to the consumers on the product sold.
8. They provide fresh and latest products to the consumers.
9. Since the retail shops are generally situated near the residential areas, so it is convenient for the customers to meet their daily requirements.
10. Some retailers render day and night services that are very helpful in times of emergency.

Type of retailers

Based on the size of operation, retailing activity is classified into small scale retailing and large scale retailing.

Small scale retailing includes mobile retailers and fixed shopkeepers. They are discussed below:

Mobile retailers. Mobile retailers have no fixed premises. They move from place to place for selling the goods. They are also known as *Itinerant retailers*. Hawkers, market traders and pavement-sellers come under this category.

Fixed shop retailers. Fixed shop retailers operate from fixed premises. Small scale fixed retail shops are located near the residential areas. They deal in all categories of consumer goods. Some shops also provide free home delivery and services also.

Large scale retailers. Large retail outlets have become the current practice in big towns and cities. They cater well to the fast changing needs of the urban population. These include supermarkets, shopping malls, etc. Several advantages of a large scale retailing are effective sales promotion, creative selling, increased turnover and employment of skilled people for better coordination and control. These outlets provide one stop shopping for customers and are usually centrally located. They offer the convenience of purchasing goods and products under one roof.

Small scale retailers

Street hawkers and peddlers. This concept is as old as civilization. In this type of retailing, the vendors carry all the household requirement of the customers and sell them moving from one house to another. They do not have fixed premises. Much capital is not required and majority do business based on borrowing. Since it is convenient for the customer to get the goods at his house, hawkers do good business. The quality of goods, however, is not superior.

Street traders. Street traders offer a wide assortment of items of common use. They sell their products at relatively low prices. They pick up small shops temporarily. These traders sell their goods at pavements of busy roads, near railway stations, temples, cinema halls, etc.

Market traders. This type of trading activity can be seen at weekly, fortnightly or monthly fairs. They move from place to place. During holidays, when the big shops are closed, traders put up their tents and sell goods. The goods sold by them are usually cheap and related to domestic and household items.

Street stalls. Street stalls can be seen at street crossings or near the junction of the main roads. They usually consist of a Kiosk having elevated platform and a table to keep the items. The street stalls usually sell inexpensive goods like cigarettes, matches, ball pens, toothpastes, etc.

General stores. General stores are usually set up in residential areas. They maintain all kinds of items required by the families residing in the colony for their daily use. They provide a great service to the consumers because several daily requirements are made available in an earshot distance.

A general store is usually managed by a single proprietor who establishes good rapport with the local residents of the colony. A general store may be a single line store or a multi line store. A single line store sells only items of a single category, e.g. cloth store or a medical store.

Second-hand goods stores. Second-hand goods stores deal with seconds or items once used such as books, clothes, furniture and electrical appliances. These stores collect their items during auctions and also from customers directly by striking a bargain.

Retail departmental store. A departmental store is a big store or retail organization engaged in retail trade of wide assortment of goods under one roof. The store is divided into well-defined departments for better coordination and control. Every department is related to a particular line of products. The organization is centrally controlled. Each department confines its activities to a particular line of business.

The departmental store deals in a very wide range of products. The main object of a departmental store is to satisfy the consumer needs at one place, to save him the trouble of running about to purchase everyday necessities.

Advantages. The advantages of a retail departmental store are as follows:

1. Convenience of shopping.
2. Large assortment of goods, wider choice for customers.
3. Centrally located. Easily accessible.
4. Provision of television, recreation for children, home delivery, etc.
5. Economy of large scale operations.
6. Better promotional and ad campaigns to educate the consumers.
7. Employment of competent sales persons. Increased customer satisfaction and services.
8. Due to a large purchase in bulk, better discounts can be given to the customers.

Disadvantages. The disadvantages of a retail departmental store are as follows:

1. The cost of running the business is very high.
2. High operational costs, hence goods become costlier.
3. Since the stores are centrally located, customers face traffic congestion and the stores are not easily accessible to people living in outskirts of the city.
4. Since many employees are working, it is difficult for the owner to achieve better coordination and supervision.
5. There is lack of 'personal touch' with the customers. The paid salesman may fail to give personal attention to a large number of customers of the store.

Multiple shops or chain stores. Multiple shops are the group of shops in the same branch of retail trade under a centralized management and dealing in similar lines of product. A single business firm opens a number of branch shops that are situated at different localities in the city and in different parts of the country. The main objective is providing shopping facilities to the customers near their residence. The multiple shops are centrally controlled and receive supplies from the central office and remit the sales proceeds regularly to the central office. They have uniformity of operation and each branch deals in a similar line of goods. The price of all items is fixed by the head office and the same is charged at every branch. Purchasing, pricing, and advertising are done centrally. There is only decentralization of selling. They display the goods in identical manner and sell the same type of goods. Generally, they deal only in a limited variety of products and all the goods are usually consumer goods. They generally sell goods on cash and carry basis and do not allow credit and free delivery services to the customers. When organized by manufacturers, multiple shops aim at eliminating both the sellers and the retailers. Examples of multiple shops are: Bata, Reymonds, DCM, MTC, Usha appliances, Dabur, Hamdard, etc.

Advantages of multiple shops. The advantages of multiple shops are as follows:

1. The prices are fixed and no bargaining is done.
2. Multiple shops can easily be identified because of the uniform pattern of design and decoration of the shops.
3. Generally quality goods are sold.
4. Due to lower operational costs, the prices of goods are generally lower.
5. Common advertisement is done from a centralized place that covers the entire national network.
6. In a multiple shop system, there is direct contact between the producer and the customer so the profits of the middlemen are eliminated.

7. In multiple shops, sales are made strictly on cash payment. So there is practically no loss due to bad debts.
8. The fixed price and the standard quality of the goods help in winning the confidence of the customer.
9. There is a considerable increase in sale since the majority of branches of multiple shops are located in important localities of the city for the convenience of the customer.
10. Better market research can be done because of the direct contact with the consumer.
11. Multiple shops are run under the control of the head office that shows uniform policies in regard to all important matters. This makes it easy for the head office to exercising effective control and supervision to its attached branches.
12. The shortage of supplies at one branch can easily be met by the transfer from another branch having a surplus stock.
13. Under multiple stock systems, all purchases of the branches are made by the central office that results in bulk buying thus reducing the cost of the product.
14. There is a diversification of risks. Unsold stock can be transferred to other branches to prevent loss or damage.
15. Greater flexibility in operation because it is easier to shift a store from one place to another.

Disadvantages. The disadvantages of multiple shops are as follows:

1. It cannot offer a wide variety of products to customers because the range is limited.
2. There is a lack of free home delivery service and credit facility to customers.
3. The owner of the shops cannot make personal contact with these customers. The success of the organization depends on the branch manager.
4. The head office of the multiple shops is generally located at a far away place so there is generally no effective supervision on the staff working in its branches.
5. Since the products are of standardized nature, they cannot be adjusted to suit the needs of the local market.
6. To run chain stores, heavy investments and faithful people are required to look after the business.
7. Since only the employed staff runs the shops, they may not give full attention to the customer's satisfaction and they may also be not faithful to the owner.

Mail order business. Mail order business is a type of retail trade that involves activities taking place through post. The orders are received by post and the goods are sent to the customers by post. Mail order business is also known as *selling through post* for the retailer and *shopping by post* for the consumer. The manufacturers establish contact with the customers by means of advertisements in leading newspapers, magazines and TV, radio, etc. The manufacturers send their price lists, samples, circulars, etc., giving details of the product by post. The customer places order for the supply of goods after they go through the advertisement. Generally, the goods are sent by VPP [value payable post]. The goods are delivered to the addresses on the payment of the price to the post office that remits it to the owner of goods. Sometimes, the goods are also sent by railway or transport agencies. The bills are sent to the respective places and the customers are informed accordingly. After paying the amount to the bank, the bill is released. After presenting the bill to the delivery office of the railway or transport agencies the goods are handed over to the customers.

Characteristic. The characteristics of mail order businesses are as follows:

1. There is no need of middlemen.
2. Goods are sold without any personal contact between the buyer and the seller.

3. There is no need of a large capital.
4. There is no need of keeping goods in godowns. Shops are not required because the business can be carried on without it.
5. It is purely based on advertisement.
6. The orders are placed by post only.

Mail order business has become successful because of the following factors:

1. Development of better communication facilities and better transportation facilities.
2. Large circulation of newspapers and magazines amongst people.
3. Change in the taste of the people and their preference for a wide variety and quality of goods.

This business has become successful in the developed countries like the US and the UK. But in India it is still in the infancy stage because of low poverty and literacy rate, lack of effective advertising media, lack of standard products and fraudulent practices adopted by the traders.

For mail order business to become popular or successful, the following criteria are to be fulfilled:

1. Goods should enjoy good demands by large number of customers.
2. Goods should have reorganization and should be of standard quality.
3. Goods should not require skills in handling.
4. Goods should not be perishable items and should not get destroyed during transportation. For example, books, cosmetics, medicines, sports goods, etc., are some of the good examples.

Advantages. The advantages of mail order businesses are as follows:

1. The customer need not travel long distances to procure the goods.
2. The business can be located in less expensive localities.
3. The buyer is generally given a money back guarantee.
4. It is an economical operation since the overhead expenses like rent of the showroom, salary of the salesmen, commission to the middlemen, etc., are not required.
5. There is no need of appointing middlemen.
6. There is no need for storing of goods. The same may be procured as and when the order is received.
7. The system is very useful for those customers who live in remote areas of the country. They get their requirements fulfilled while staying home.
8. There is no danger of bad debts since the price of goods is received either in advance or collected from post office and goods sent by VPP.
9. The seller gets a very wide market to sell his products.
10. Advertisement and other promotional efforts can be optimized depending upon the quantum of orders obtained.

Disadvantages. The disadvantages of mail order businesses are as follows:

1. Risk of goods getting damaged during transportation.
2. There is lack of personal contact and the buyer cannot examine the goods before its purchase.
3. The credit facilities are not available to the customer.
4. Goods sent by post are costlier because the postal expenses are met by the customer.
5. Seldom but postal delay's and strikes can cause inconvenience to the buyer.
6. The price of goods increases because a large chunk of money is spent on the advertisement, correspondence and packing of goods.

7. Fraud can be committed on innocent customer.
8. There are no after sales services to the customers.
9. This system is suitable only for educated people.
10. This system can be used for specific type of goods. This facility is not suitable for perishable items.
11. The customers who like to make enquires have to waste time and money in correspondence.
12. Inspection of goods by the customer before purchase is not possible.
13. Customer loyalty cannot be developed because there is no personal rapport between the manufacturer and the customers.

Consumer's cooperative stores. The consumers cooperative stores is owned and operated by the consumers themselves under the cooperative society's Act. The shareholders provide the capital. Membership is voluntary. The basic purpose is to eliminate middlemen and provide service oriented benefits to the members without any profit motive. The members provide capital by purchase of shares of small denominations.

Hence, even poor consumers can become members of such society. The society purchases its requirements in bulk from the wholesalers at wholesale rates, and sells them to their member's at the market rate. A part of the profit earned in the business is given to the members as bonus on purchases and they also get a dividend on their shares. Since there are no middlemen, the consumers get products of good quality at a cheaper rate.

Sometimes certain percentage of profit is utilized for benevolent purposes.

Advantages. The advantages of cooperative stores are as follows:
1. The consumers get good quality products because the chance of adulteration by retailers is not there.
2. The overall cost of the product is reduced because large quantities are directly purchased from the manufacturer; moreover the middlemen profit is eliminated.
3. The liability of the members of the cooperative stores is limited.
4. A cooperative society can be formed easily. Large number of members join it because the value of the shares is very low.
5. The government gives good patronage to the cooperative society.
6. The society is managed on democratic norms because every member has only one vote irrespective of the number of shares held by him.
7. It promotes thrift among members and increases their economic security.
8. Unnecessary expenditure on advertisements and decoration of store is not required.

Disadvantages. The disadvantages of cooperative stores are as follows:
1. All the members of the society may not be cooperative and responsible, hence the society may suffer financial losses.
2. The society has very limited resources and hence it cannot be run on large scale.
3. There is lack of ability, experience and business training on the part of the members who are running the stores.

Supermarket. It is also known as *Super Bazar* or *Self Service Store*. It has several separate units under one roof. It is a large retailing institution selling mainly food items, items of grocery and household requirements.

A supermarket is generally located in the central shopping areas. They do not employ salesmen in large numbers. Only singleton shop assistants will be present for supervision. Goods are displayed on the well-designed racks and the consumer has a wide choice in picking up goods according to his tastes. He can touch, feel and smell the items. He has to place the selected items in a trolley and then bring them to the cashier for billing. As supermarkets follow the principle of 'self choice' there is no pressure from the salesman. These markets operate strictly on cash and carry principle and do not provide any after sales service to the clientele.

Advantages. The advantages of supermarkets are as follows:

1. Due to large scale buying and selling, the operating costs are low.
2. Customer choice is the advantage. He is free to inspect physically various items leisurely and take decision. Packaging of the goods is given importance.
3. Goods are at cheaper rates because of the lack of sales force.
4. No chances of bad debts because of the cash and carry principle.
5. All items are under one roof, hence, no need for the customer to go to several shops for purchasing of his requirements.

Disadvantages. The disadvantages of supermarkets are as follows:

1. Individual persuasion by salesman is not there. Some people do not like this technique of selling.
2. Mishandling and careless attitude of customers spoil the goods.
3. Expenditure for maintenance is high and the turnover should be high to keep the overhead expenditures under check.

Points to Ponder

1. A channel of distribution is the route taken by the goods as they move from the producer to the ultimate consumer.
2. The distribution channels may be grouped under two major heads as follows:
   a. Direct selling
   b. Indirect selling
3. The selection of the right channels of distribution is the most powerful element in the selling of products. The main factors to be considerd are as follows:
   a. Market factors
   b. Product factors
   c. Organization factors
   d. Market intermediaries factors
4. The middlemen belonging to this category are as follows:
   a. Wholesaler
   b. Retailer

 **Self-Assessment Exercises**

1. Write the main features of multiple shops.
2. Give a comparative account of retail and wholesale trade.
3. Describe briefly the function of middlemen.
4. Give the salient features of retailing.
5. Give a brief account of consumer cooperative stores.
6. Distinguish between the following:
    a. Multiple shops and departmental stores.
    b. Retail and wholesale.
7. Define the concept of wholesale? Explain the general functions of it.
8. Explain by means of a chart, the channels of distribution.
9. Discuss in detail a retail departmental store? What are its advantages and disadvantages?

Salesmanship

INTRODUCTION

Selling is a vital function of business. It is a bridge for introducing new goods and services in the market. Salesmanship is the art, discipline and the profession of selling. It is the ability to influence and win over a customer. It creates interest, arouses and maintains the demands and sells the products.

Personal selling or salesmanship is the oldest and the most effective technique of selling. It helps in understanding the needs, motives and the behaviour of people. It is also useful in knowing the habits, tastes and attitudes of the customers. Such information is useful to the manufacturers in designing better products and also improving the existing ones.

Advantages

The advantages of salesmanship or personal selling are as follows:

1. It helps in locating prospective buyers.
2. It helps in the creation of a demand for new products.
3. It provides feedback about the needs, attitudes and the behaviour of the consumers.
4. It helps to remove the objections and doubts of the consumers.
5. It helps in demonstrating the product in a very effective way.
6. It can develop durable relationships with the consumers.
7. The salesman acts as a consultant to the consumers.
8. Salesmanship gets immediate buying action.

STEPS IN THE SELLING PROCESS

Following are the steps in a selling process:

1. Presale preparation
2. Prospecting
3. Approaching
4. Presentation
5. Dealing with objections
6. Closing the sale
7. Follow-up

Presale Preparation

Selecting, training and motivating the salesman is the first step in personal selling. The salesman must have a thorough knowledge of the products, customers, competitors' products and the techniques of selling.

Prospecting

The salesman must locate the potential buyers and identify their needs. They should examine the records of the past and present customers to find out the nature and attitudes of the potential buyers. Potential customers can also be spotted through observation, inquiry and by consulting dealers.

Approaching

A salesman should approach the customer to secure his attention. He should be polite and courteous while approaching the customers. A salesman at the counter should pleasantly greet the customer and make him feel at home. In case he is busy with some other customer, he should assure the customer that he would attend to him very soon. He has to be very careful in approaching the new customer as the first impression is the last impression. He should talk with confidence and be graceful in his manner.

Presentation

The object of presentation is to convince the customer that he needs this type of product or service and this particular product or service will in fact fulfil his needs. The salesman should describe the salient features and uses of the product in brief and not its technical details such as description about drug formulation, its chemical composition, its pharmacological actions and side effects, etc.

The selling points and advice should be given without any hesitation. However, arguments should be avoided at all costs. To win an argument is to lose the customer and to lose the argument is to lose the sale. The success of a salesperson depends upon the degree to which he or she is able to match his or her presentation with the attitude of the consumer.

Dealing With Objections

Certain objections may be raised by the customer after presentation, which should be welcomed. Those objections that are mostly regarding the price, quality and design are helpful in discovering the doubts of the customer. The salesman should not lose patience if a customer asks for many questions and takes time in reaching a decision. The main aim of the salesman should be to remove the customer's objections in one way or the other, so that the customer is satisfied with the product.

Closing the Sale

Once the customer has made up his mind to buy the product, the salesman should close the sale in a cordial manner. The customer should be made to feel that he has made the right choice. It is difficult to close the sale if the customer has not yet come to a decision. However, under no circumstances, the customer should be pressurized to go for a particular item. He should guide the customer in making the choice but should not impose his own views. Sometimes a minor adjustment in price, assurance of the good, after sale service, etc., helps in overcoming the hesitant buyers.

The salesman should thank the customer at the time of delivery of the goods and all social courtesy should be extended to him. He should assure the customer of a still better service in future.

Follow-up

Further follow-up is not practicable in case of retail pharmacy as customers do not visit the pharmacy as frequently as they do other shops. But representatives of the suppliers generally follow-up for stock sold in to be sold out by effective salesmanship.

FUNDAMENTALS OF SUCCESS IN SALESMANSHIP

Salesmanship is a highly skilled profession and like any other profession demands a very high degree of proficiency in its practice. The pioneers of this art have evolved a number of principles that should be followed by new entrants in this field. The important fundamentals of success in salesmanship are as under:

Knowledge of Self

The personality of the person selling goods is very important. A repulsive salesman may drive the customer away while a charmingly cheerful salesman may not only attract customers, but win them permanently for the organization. It is, therefore, very important for the salesman to analyse and ascertain the qualities that the job requires and the qualities that he himself possesses. The salesman should be conscious of his weakness and constantly make efforts to overcome them. Salesmen are not born; they are created by systematic training. The self-assessment of his own personality helps the salesman to get benefit of the strengths in his personality and avoid the display of his weakness.

Knowledge of the Product

Customers generally forget about the physical deficiencies of a salesman if impressed with his knowledge of his line and his calibre in solving their problems. Customers expect a thorough knowledge of the product from the salesman because of their own ignorance. Nowadays, a large number of new products are coming in the market and customer wants the salesman to guide him regarding its nature, design and function. Salesman has not only to guide and advise them but also has to satisfy their curiosity about the utility of the products and remove their suspicions, objections and apprehensions. To do this, it is necessary for the salesman to know the in and out of the product.

The salesman should know the following important things about his product:

1. Manufacturing details
2. Nature of the product
3. Comparative study of other similar products and their selling point
4. Distribution policies adopted by the company to sell them.

Knowledge of the Company

The knowledge of the company is essential for a salesman. The modern salesman sells not only the product but also his company, its prestige, reliability, friendliness, achievements, long-standing accessibility and experience. He should know about the distributive as well as the sales promotion policies of the company or the organization. A knowledge of all these things is essential to impart confidence in the salesman to help him reconcile his selling efforts to the requirements of the situation and to enable him to serve the company as well as the customers more efficiently.

Knowledge of the Customers

The salesman should have a thorough knowledge of his customers so that he can size up the customer quickly and correctly, to motivate him rightly and satisfactorily, and to win him permanently and positively. The salesman should understand and appreciate three important points:

1. Motivation of the buyer to buy
2. The nature and requirements of the customer
3. The dealing with different types of customers

Knowledge of the Techniques of Selling

The knowledge of techniques is essential for effective selling. There are a few important principles of selling that the salesman should learn. They are discussed as follows:

1. The salesman should see that the prospect (would be customer) is well attended to.
2. He should try to understand the requirements of his customers well.
3. He must always be prepared to help him and for this he should create the necessary confidence in him.

4. He should suggest the items to meet the customer's requirements. He must ensure that his need is suitably met.

There are few important pieces of advice that a salesman should remember in dealing with the customers:

1. Treat the customers as one would like to be treated.
2. Building of the customer's satisfaction is more important than making a sale at its cost.
3. Customer is a real boss of the salesman because the continuity of the salesman's job and the possibility of his promotion, all depends upon the customer he builds for his business.
4. Never annoy or embarrass the customers because with these methods, there is a danger of losing them.
5. Always try to be sympathetic, sincere, sensible, helpful, courteous and cooperative in dealing with customers. Salesman should always have a constructive and positive approach.
6. Always serve the customers to the best of one's abilities.
7. Sale should be the ultimate goal of a salesman. What means he adopts to achieve it will largely depend on the circumstances of each case.
8. Always be on the lookout for new customers. Plan his prospects and make them his customers by successful approach, effective sales presentation, convincing explanation and profitable close of sale.
9. Plan the sales strategy to break the customer's sales resistance successfully and allay his apprehensions, doubts and objections convincingly.

SALES PROMOTION

The main aim of any business is to earn maximum profit and this is possible only through maximum sales. Selling in the market is a tough job because of the stiff competition. It is necessary to create demand.

Even the best product cannot be sold in the market until it is brought to the notice of the prospective buyers or they are motivated to buy it.

Sales promotion is a science and technique employed to increase the sale. The maximum sales can be achieved by using various techniques of sales promotion. Sales promotion includes those marketing activities, other than personal selling advertising and publicity that stimulate consumer purchasing and dealer effectiveness such as window display, shows and expositions, demonstrations, etc.

OBJECTIVE OF SALES PROMOTION

The objectives of sales promotion are as follows:

1. To introduce new products
2. To attract new customers
3. To maintain old customers
4. To improve public image of the firm
5. To popularize a brand name of the product
6. To assist salesmen and the dealers
7. To induce customers to purchase more items
8. To reduce the unit cost of the product by increasing the large scale production
9. To increase the standard of living of the customers

10. To stimulate demand by explaining special features of the products
11. To inform the public of the availability of the new and improved products which they want to buy.

TECHNIQUES OF SALES PROMOTION

Sales promotion in a drug store includes advertising, publicity, display of goods, patient counselling and drug information service. Following are some methods that are commonly used to promote sale:

Free Samples

Many pharmaceutical firms send their medical representatives to the physicians for detailing and distribution of free samples of their manufactured goods. The technique is a very useful way of introducing new products. However, it is a very expensive method and is used only by big concerns.

Trading Stamps

Trading stamps are issued to customers through the retailers in proportion to the amount of purchase. The customer goes on collecting the stamps on his purchases. Once he has collected stamps of an adequate amount, he obtains a free product in exchange of his stamps. This technique induces customers to buy products from those retailers who offer such stamps.

Coupons

Coupon is a certificate that entitles its holder to a specified saving on the purchase of a specified product. A firm may distribute the coupons through mail, newspapers, magazines or retailers. The holders of coupons can buy the product at a discount from the retailers. The firm reimburses the retailers for the value of coupons collected by him from his customers. The retailers generally do not like this scheme because it creates financial and accounting problems for them.

Premium or Bonus Offer

It acts as an inducement to purchase products on the part of the consumers. The consumer is offered a different product along with the actual product which he intended to buy. It induces new users to purchase the product (offered as premium) that they may have never bought. The premium offered can be of three types:

1. With pack premium
2. A reusable container
3. Free-in-the mail premium

With pack premium

The free product is given along with product purchased by the customer. For example, one stainless steel teaspoon is inserted as a free gift inside the 240 ml bottles of cough syrup.

A reusable container

The product is packed in a container that has utility for the customer after it is consumed. For example, an Ayurvedic Baidyanath Chyawanprash is available in attractive container which can be reused in the kitchen.

Free-in-the mail premium

A free gift is given to the customer on sending a proof of purchase, i.e. cash memo or wrapper of the product.

Prize Contests

The contest may be held for the customers, salesmen and dealers. They are required to write a slogan or complete a sentence about the utility of the product. Attractive prizes are given for the best entries.

Fairs and Exhibitions

Fairs and exhibitions are organized to display and popularize products of the firm. For example, in various medical and pharmaceutical conferences, seminars, a scientific congress, the pharmaceutical firms and their allied industries participate in the exhibitions organized by their organizing committee. On such occasions, the firm also distributes free literature to introduce itself and its products.

Temporary Price Reduction

The offer is generally made by manufacturers to reduce the retail price of his product temporarily in order to attract consumers to buy it in preference to other brands that are already available in the market. In this way he can increase the purchases by the present users and induce the new users to use his product.

Indoor Display

Indoor display is done to remind the customers about the product whenever they visit the drug store. Indoor display includes counter cards, banners, wall signs and display bins, etc.

Public Relations

It is essential for maintaining cordial relationship between the enterprise and the public by influencing or informing the customers about it, so that they can make favourable and good opinion towards the enterprise. Nowadays, the enterprises have started setting up a separate public relations department to win the confidence of the public towards the enterprise. Sometimes health programmes can be sponsored, such as National Pharmacy Week, Immunization Programme, National Diabetic Week, Pulse Polio Programme. These programmes help to build professional image and interaction with the customers.

LIMITATIONS OF SALES PROMOTION

The limitations of sales promotion are as follows:
1. It is a short lived method, so one cannot rely on it forever.
2. It cannot remove the shortcomings of the product.
3. The methods of sale promotion are costlier that increase the cost of the finished product.

4. It may be helpful for the consumer goods but not for all types of industrial products.
5. There may be overstocking of the gift items offered by an enterprise if they are good and costly.
6. It leaves its impact only for a very short period, unless it is repeated frequently.

SALESMAN

A person who is engaged in selling goods to the customers is known as a *salesman*. It is generally said that salesman are born and not made. However, it is not true these days, because any person who wants to adopt a sales profession gets intensive coaching and training. The success of a firm mainly depends on the performance of their sales force. Therefore, it is essential to engage well-qualified trained, energetic and young people as the company's sales force.

Qualities of a Salesman

Following are the qualities a salesman must possess:

1. Personal qualities
2. Mental qualities
3. Social qualities
4. Vocational skills

Personal Qualities

The salesman must possess the following personal qualities:

1. A good salesman must have an attractive personality.
2. He must possess good health and sound physique. A salesman's job involves a great physical strain because of its touring nature. So a person with a good health can work effectively.
3. He should have a clear voice and his tone of speaking should be natural so as to impress the clients.
4. He should also be well-dressed because it adds to his charm. A pleasing and charming personality always creates a good impression on the buyers.

Mental Qualities

A good salesman must have the following mental qualities:

1. A good salesman should possess a sound memory, presence of mind, imagination, foresightedness, sound judgement and initiative.
2. He should be intelligent enough to understand the nature and the requirements of the potential buyers.
3. He must have the imagination to look at things from the view point of the customer. A salesman can win the regular and permanent customers only through good mental qualities.

Social Qualities

The social qualities that a good salesman must possess are as follows:

1. A good salesman must have a liking for people and the ability to mix with them.
2. He must not be shy or of reserved nature.
3. He should be sincere, dependable, cooperative and honest.

4. A salesman has to deal with different types of customers. Therefore he should have patience to listen to his customers and remove their objections.
5. He should always be polite and courteous while dealing with his customers. He must help the customers in selecting the right type of goods. Courtesy costs nothing but wins favour and permanent customers.

Vocational Skills

The vocational skills that a good salesman must possess are as follows:

1. A good salesman must have specialized knowledge of the selling techniques.
2. Salesmanship is a highly skilled vocation. It requires certain training and an aptitude to have a thorough knowledge of the product, customers and the competitive products already available in the market. Such knowledge is essential to handle objections of the customers and also for convincing them to buy the products. A person cannot be a good salesman unless he has the required ambition and the enthusiasm to become a successful salesman.

ADVERTISING

Advertising is an art, used to familiarize the public with the product by informing of its description, uses, it's superiority over other brands, sources of its availability and price, etc. Advertising is not merely propaganda but is a paid form of communication. The advertiser has to pay for the space or time used to communicate the message to his customers.

Objectives of Advertising

The objectives of advertising are as follows:

1. To create a demand for a new product by explaining its utility.
2. To increase its sales by attracting new customers.
3. To maintain the existing demand by fighting competition.
4. To assist the salesmen in their selling efforts.
5. To warn the public against the imitation of products of the firm.
6. To enhance goodwill of the firm.
7. To build and retaining brand loyalty or preference.

Advantages of Advertising

The advantages of advertising are as follows:

1. It helps in the introduction of new products in the market.
2. It promotes the sale of goods and services by persuading the people to buy them.
3. It helps in creating a demand and hence a regular production.
4. It enables a firm to face competition in the market for its survival.
5. It enables a firm to improve its reputation by highlighting its achievements to the public.
6. It provides information and also educates the consumers to buy better quality goods at lower prices.
7. It leads to improvement in the standard of living of the common public by stimulating their desires for better things.

8. It generates employment for artists and other persons in the line.
9. It provides revenue to newspapers, magazines, TV channels and radio.
10. It leads to the increase in production, which in turn reduces the overhead expenses. Hence it helps in bringing down the selling price of the goods.
11. It enables the manufacturer to expand his market.
12. It helps in maintaining uniformity and stability of prices.

Disadvantages of Advertising

Following are the disadvantages of advertising:

1. It multiplies the needs of the people by inducing them to buy things which they do not really need or cannot afford to buy.
2. It increases the cost of production.
3. It does not necessarily increase the demand and sale of the product. It simply shifts the demand from one seller to another.
4. It involves a huge wasteful expenditure because the majority of advertisements either escapes the attention of the people or are ignored by them.
5. Many a time, the facts are misrepresented in the advertisement.

Parts of an Advertisement

Following are the main parts of an advertisement:

1. **Heading:** The heading or the caption is used to attract the attention of the people. It may be a word, a phrase or even a question about the product or the service being advertised. It should not be very long.
2. **Theme:** The theme gives the basic idea about the product and highlights its distinctive advantages. It conveys an image of the product being advertised. For example, a D-Cold tablet contains the theme of being effective against cough and the symptoms of cold. Moov ointment contains the theme of being effective for backache.
3. **Picture:** Generally an advertising copy contains a photograph of the product being advertised. The photograph of the product is often combined with the photo of the model or the star possessing or using the product. It enables the customers to recognize or identify the product.
4. **Arguments:** Nowadays, arguments in favour of the advertised products are given in the advertisement. The purpose of giving the argument is to convince the customers about the utility of the product. For example, the advertising copy for Anacin Tablets contains the argument 'it is microfined'.
5. **Closing part:** The closing part of an advertising copy very often repeats in brief the contents of the advertisement. In some cases, the name and the address of the drug store where the product is available are given in this part.

Essential Features of Good Advertisement

The text or the body of an advertisement is known as an *advertising copy*. It contains the headline, message, advertiser's name and address, photographs, etc. The advertising copy should be carefully drafted so as to include the following essential features:

1. It should be made attractive by using pictures, headlines, attractive boarders, etc., so as to make people read, see or listen to it.

2. It should create a permanent impression on the minds of people. Repeated use of a brand name or a trade mark is very helpful.
3. It should give useful suggestions to the public. For example, the advertisement of Vicks 500 tablet suggests its use for cold and cough.
4. It should educate the people about the use of the product and its benefits. For example, in the advertisement of the baby milk powder, the instructions for preparing milk are required to be given.
5. It must contain solid arguments and proof to convince the consumers about the superior quality of the product. For example, the Anacin tablet relieves pain faster as it is microfined.
6. It should create the need for the product in the minds of the people. It should appeal to the various instincts of the people.
7. It should induce people to buy the advertised product.

Media for Advertising

The means used to transmit the message from the advertiser to the public is known as the *advertising media*. The following are some means through which advertising is done:

1. Press advertisement: For example, newspapers and magazines.
2. Literature advertisement: For example, letters, circulars, catalogues and leaflets.
3. External advertisement: For example, posters on walls and electric display.
4. Miscellaneous advertisement: For example, TV, radio, window display, cinema slides, video-cassettes, etc.

Advertisement and the Pharmaceutical Industry

Regarding advertising of pharmaceutical products, the WHO has resolved as below:

'The advertisement of pharmaceutical products should be truthful. There should not be any wrong statement regarding its contents and their percentage. It should provide full details regarding the action and uses, proprietary name as well as the generic name, dosage form, mode of administration, side effects, treatment of toxic effects, precautions and contra-indications. The above statements should be truthful, scientifically correct and proved.'

The purpose of advertising in the ethical pharmaceutical market is the same as that for any other product but there are many restrictions to it.

A customer (patient) cannot use a medicine without proper prescription of a physician. The majority of pharmaceutical products are ethical products and their direct advertisement is prohibited according to the Drugs and Magic Remedies (objectionable advertisement) Act. However, general or home remedies products, such as pain balm, inhalers, Iodex, antiseptic creams and other products which do not require a prescription for their purchase can be advertised by any of the direct methods of advertisement.

The following methods are used for advertising pharmaceutical products:

1. Direct mailing
2. Newspapers, professional magazines and journals
3. Television, radio and other audiovisual media
4. Personal contact or detailing
5. Outdoor advertisement
6. Miscellaneous methods

Direct mailing

In direct mailing, a mailing list of the registered medical practitioners, chemists and druggists is prepared. Letters, leaflets, folders and catalogues are sent to them regularly through mail to inform them of the details of the products manufactured by the firm. Mail advertising has a personal appeal because it is addressed to a particular person. It also maintains secrecy in advertising. The main drawback of this technique of advertising is that it has a limited coverage.

Newspapers, professional magazines and journals

Newspapers are indispensable means of advertising products that are produced on a mass scale. The daily newspaper has a wide circulation and reaches a very large number of people. Advertising through newspapers is relatively economical than through other media. The advertisement can be repeated as many times as it is desired. Newspaper advertising is considered useful particularly for items of mass appeal and general consumer goods.

Periodicals or magazines issued at varying time intervals also constitute a powerful medium of advertising. In the pharmaceutical industry, advertisement in professional magazine and journals, are also very useful, because it is read by professionals related to the medical and pharmacy profession. The main drawback is the restricted circulation and limited flexibility.

Television, radio and other audiovisual media

Television is the latest fast growing medium of advertising. It is a very effective medium because it appeals to both the eye and the ear. The product can be demonstrated and explained on the television. However, it is a very costly method of advertising. Radio advertising is becoming more popular these days and the advertisements are generally transmitted through commercial services of the All India Radio. Radio advertisements carry an effective appeal as they reach out to all sections of the society. People can listen to them even when they are busy with other activities. The big pharmaceutical companies generally sponsor entertaining programmes on TV and radio to popularize themselves and their products.

Personal contact or detailing

Personal contact or detailing is a process of sales promotion and advertisement by personal contacts. The pharmaceutical manufacturers engage people (sales representatives and medical representatives) for making personal contacts with sellers or prescribe and influence them in favour of their products.

This method of advertisement is very costly. However, it is preferred by the pharmaceutical manufacturing companies for the following reasons:

1. It provides an opportunity to inform the physicians and retailers about the new products of the firm.

2. It also helps to refresh the memory of the physicians regarding the old products of the firm.
3. It helps to clear any doubts a physician may have regarding a particular product of the company.
4. It helps to have a feedback from the physician regarding the products of the firm.
5. It provides the company with an opportunity to demonstrate and give a detailed explanation of its products.

Outdoor advertisement

Outdoor advertisement is becoming very popular nowadays. It means the exhibition of an advertisement at street corners, railway stations, bus stands, on moving vehicles, etc. Outdoor advertising is carried out in a number of ways to attract the attention of the passer by. Following are some methods of outdoor advertising:

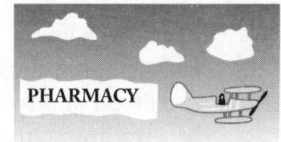

1. **Skywriting:** It is the modern method of advertising. Balloons printed with messages and illustrative pictures are flown in the sky. In the advance countries, aeroplanes are also used to display the illuminated banners with the message in the open skies during late evening.
2. **Posters or hoardings:** Posters are pasted or otherwise exposed on walls, roadsides, street corners, bus terminus, railway stations, etc. The message may be printed on paper or written on metal sheet. The message must be brief so that it can be read within a few minutes.
3. **Sandwichmen:** They carry posters containing the message to be advertised and move through different localities of the city. They are dressed in fancy attires and carry on their persons the posters. They shout slogans or beat drums to attract the attention of the public.
4. **Transit advertising:** The advertisement is done by travelling displays and car cards. Travelling displays are those advertisements that are displayed outside the moving vehicles. The message printed on them is generally read by passengers while boarding the vehicles or while getting down from them. Car cards are posters that are displayed inside railway carriage, buses, taxis, trams and other vehicles.

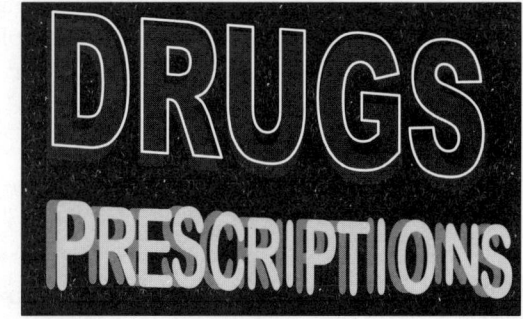

5. **Electric signs and neon signs:** These signs are generally installed on rooftops or at busy street corners or crossings in order to draw the attention of the public. These are visible only in the night. The lights of various colours and shades are used to attract the attention of passers by. This method is very costly.

Miscellaneous methods

Many pharmaceutical firms offer gift items to the physicians and retailers to pass on to selective customers. These items may be diaries, ball pens, pen holders, desk trays, key chains, paper weights and calendars. These articles are of daily use and, therefore, are a continuous reminder of the product and the firm. Generally the name and address of the advertiser is printed or inscribed on those items.

Points to Ponder

1. Following are the steps in a selling process:
   a. Presale preparation
   b. Prospecting
   c. Approaching
   d. Presentation
   e. Dealing with objections
   f. Closing the sale
   g. Follow up
2. Following are the techniques of sales promotion:
   a. Free samples
   b. Trading stamps
   c. Coupons
   d. Premium or bonus offer
   e. Prize contests
   f. Fairs and exhibitions
   g. Temporary price reduction
   h. Indoor display
   i. Public relations
3. Advertising is an art, used to familiarize the public with the product by informing of its description, uses, it's superiority over other brands, sources of availability and price, etc.
4. The following are some means through which advertising is done:
   a. Press advertisement: For example, newspapers and magazines.
   b. Literature advertisement: For example, letters, circulars, catalogues and leaflets.
   c. External advertisement: For example, posters on walls and electric display.
   d. Miscellaneous advertisement: For example, TV, radio, window display, cinema slides, video-cassettes, etc.

 **Self-Assessment Exercises**

1. Define *sales promotion*.
2. Name different techniques of sales promotion.
3. Define the term *salesmanship*.
4. Name the various steps in the selling process.
5. Explain the term *salesman*.
6. Define *personal selling*.
7. Define *advertising*.
8. Name the various methods used for advertising the pharmaceutical products.
9. Define detailing.

10. Define *canned detailing*.
11. Define, *outdoor advertisement*.
12. Name the various media of advertisement.
13. Name the different qualities of a salesman.
14. What are the objectives of sales promotions?
15. Write the advantages of salesmanship.
16. What are the personal qualities of a good salesman?
17. State the objectives of advertising.
18. Distinguish between advertising and publicity.
19. What are the various media for advertising?
20. What are the main advantages of advertising?
21. Discuss the disadvantages of advertising.
22. Write the essential features of good advertisement.
23. Write the difference between advertisement and sales promotion.
24. Give the various points of advise to medical representative
25. Write the important advises which a salesman should follow.
26. Discuss the important principle of selling
27. Give a specimen of model detailing.
28. Explain the term *sales promotion*. Discuss the various techniques of sales promotion. Write the objectives of sales promotion.
29. What various methods would you suggest for an effective sales promotion campaign for your firm's product that has recently shown some decline in sales?
30. What is personal selling? Discuss the various steps in a sales process. What are the advantages of salesmanship?
31. Define the term *advertising*. Discuss the various media for advertising. Write the advantage and disadvantages of advertising.
32. Discuss the various methods used for advertising pharmaceutical products. Mention the essential features of good advertisement.
33. Explain the term *salesmanship*. Discuss the various steps in the selling process. Write the advantages of salesmanship.
34. Explain the qualities of good salesman.
35. Define the term *advertising*. Discuss the different parts of advertisement. Write the essential features of a good advertisement.
36. Explain the term *salesmanship*. Write the fundamentals of success in salesmanship.
37. Define *detailing*. Discuss the different stages of detailing.
38. Define *detailing*. Write advantages and disadvantages of canned detailing. Write a specimen of model detailing.
39. Write short notes on:
    a. Qualities of salesman
    b. Advertising
    c. Salesmanship
    d. Detailing
    e. Essential features of a good advertisement.

Establishment of a Pharmaceutical Factory

INTRODUCTION

A prescription pharmaceutical company, as well as its close relatives, the proprietary drugs and toiletries companies is a complex organization. Under its roof a team of scientists and technicians come together representing virtually all the sciences, along with the contribution made by the management executives, lawyers, accountants, engineers, system analysts and many others, whose abilities and talents maintain the viability of this unique business enterprise. Unlike any other major industry the products of a pharmaceutical industry can intimately affect the lives, health, welfare and basic needs of the people. In order to achieve the predetermined goals of such a unique business enterprise, besides the multidisciplinary scientific background, business training, sense of accuracy and control of uniquely qualified personnel, it is mandatory to also have the knowledge of a complex health related industry.

Choice of Site

The selection of an appropriate site for a factory establishment is ascertained in terms of the area and the type of land. The size of land is dependent upon the number of units to be established and the future expansion plans. While selecting the size of the land, due consideration is also given to the concept of urban arts, i.e. ample opportunity for landscaping that is not only important for its aesthetic value but also to provide good working atmosphere to the employees of the corporate. The nature of the land at the potential site is ascertained by topographic evaluation that provides a detailed description of a limited area of land such as shallow or deep land, drainage conditions and frequency of earthquakes, if any. The land selected should have a very good drainage system for underground water, as it is of high importance for the cellar floor to be constructed. If the nature of the land does not permit ample drainage, the seepage of water into the cellar floor will lead to the growth of moths and insects, rendering the areas unsuitable for storage as required by some industries. In cases where the cellar floor is not constructed, a constant erosion of the beams and pillars takes place that results in the increased maintenance expenditure. Ideally, in any industry the beams of the building should be strong enough to bear at least two more stories during the future expansion of the project. In case the site selected is in the suburban area, consideration is also given to the transportation system available, especially the public transport system to enable at least 95% of the workers to reach comfortably round the clock, if required. The potential site should be readily approachable by land (railway and self-driven vehicles), air and/or sea for transportation of raw materials and finished goods.

The community protection forces such as the police, fire tenders and ambulances should be available at nearby place to cope up with any emergency. Sometimes consideration is also given to the bringing of labour forces from the city to the site during labour unrest. Above all, the cost of electricity, water supply and sewage disposal facilities is also accounted before the selection of a potential site.

TRENDS IN LOCATION OF PLANT

There are basically five trends followed in the plant location. They area as follows:

1. Location in suburban area or in small town
2. Location in an industrial village
3. Centralization trend in location
4. Decentralization trend in location
5. Ecological or pollution control trend

Location in Suburban Area or in Small Town

With the rapid growth of cities, the location of plant is being encouraged in the suburban areas. The suburban location offers almost all practical advantages to the conventional location. To promote the suburban industrialization, the facility for production and essential services are often rendered at lower rates along with low assessment values of land and more tax rebates. It also enables a larger land size at a lower cost with extension provisions in any direction at later stages. The suburban location enables off street loading and unloading of the consignments, eliminating the need to bring the goods deep inside the factory that is not practicable in any of the other locations.

Suburban plant location also permits the modern building design and landscaping that provides a serene atmosphere and helps in improving the public and customer relations. Suburban location has a slight disadvantage of distance as the total travel distance may increase, but it is believed that the time consumed to cover the distance once out of the city is far less in comparison to when located in the central area.

Location in an Industrial Village

With the growing competition in the states, the villages are industrialized. They are aided by the development corporations. The state development corporations provide a readymade shed, and free water and electricity supplies for a few years duration or at subsidized rates. It also gives incentives for a limited area, limited number of labourers and turnover of the industry. Sometimes buildings are constructed are per the requirements of the industrialists and are given on lease or at subsidized rent.

Such locations often suffer from a long-term labour and management problem and there is a tremendous pressure on the state exchequers as a lot of money is involved that might shatter the economy, if any such project fails. In such locations, as long as the state corporations monitor the production and sale of the goods, the industrial unit is progressive.

Centralization Trend in Location

There is a growing trend of industrial centres in areas controlled by the local government or state authorities or private agencies or a group of industrialists. These provide small plots for development. The cost of building and the labour is sometimes taken up in part by the authority or the owner of the land. Such industrial centres also provide readymade sewage, water supply, electricity lines and also the facilities of public protection force.

The biggest advantage of such a trend is that the growth of industrial development is very high and also the allied materials required for production are readily available. This trend offers special advantage to the beginner in providing a greater confidence and support and he can go into production in the shortest possible time with a higher growth rate.

Decentralization Trend in Location

Decentralization trend is an upcoming trend that means spreading out the plant in various parts or into various units. This trend is widely followed by large industrial houses or in a growing industry where the plant takes up a gigantic size. In most of such industrial houses with expansion plans, decentralization is a must as the communication gap increases and the decision taken at the top levels is not conveyed properly due to which the production suffers and it is also difficult to provide large number of skilled workers within a territory.

The plant can be decentralized in two ways:

1. Horizontal decentralization (unit method of decentralization)
2. Vertical decentralization (subsidiary method of decentralization)

In horizontal decentralization, at each unit finished goods are manufactured starting with the raw materials to the final products and each unit is self-sufficient. Each unit acts complimentary to the other. Target is met irrespective of the closure of one or more units.

In vertical decentralization, different components are manufactured in different units and then assembled in one unit or a subsidiary. One subsidiary plant acts complimentary to the main unit. It offers advantage that all the parts can be obtained from such units in quantities as and when required and the number required for the complete operation is also less. The only disadvantage is that the market has to be set up before the production and one has to wait for the production of final goods.

Ecological and Pollution Control Trends

With the growing awareness to the pollution hazards, in recent factory laws it has become mandatory to consider various ecological factors before the selection of location. To exercise such control especially in an industry producing lot of smoke, toxic and other industrial wastes, the applicability of environmental engineering is a must to be accounted before the selection of location.

Placement of Building within the Site

The placement of building could either be a single storied or a multistoried setup or sometimes a combination of both. The choice of placement is dependent upon the location and the nature of the industry. A single storey is preferred to a heavy industry and if possible in a suburban area due to larger area available. A single storied setup offers various advantages as follows:

1. It provides very high flexibility for the plant layout with ample expansion opportunities.
2. With such a setup, the landscaping problem to provide aesthetic value to the construction does not arise.
3. A line production unit is easy to assemble, i.e. the transformation of raw materials to the finished goods takes place in a series of processes that considerably reduces the labour requirement.
4. A line production unit eliminates the possibility of contamination of products as they are held in abeyance during production.
5. With single storied layout it is very easy to modify the unit without changing the route of the material layout.
6. Lower material handling is achieved that reduces the haphazard movement of the material.

A multistoried setup is desirable when the placement is in an industrial centre and where lighter goods are manufactured. Many pharmaceutical houses have multi storied placements with the heaviest section on the ground floor along with maintenance and packaging section requiring constant movement of the material. This setup is convenient for light industries and it offers the following advantages:

1. It enables maximum use of area per square feet of the land available.
2. The gravity flow of material can be achieved and the material can be made to slide down using conveyer belts and saves the part of energy required for their transportation.
3. With growing scarcities of loan incentives, a cellar floor is given instead of tax rebates, concessions and electricity supply, etc.

Besides these advantages this setup exhibits certain problems especially the control of constant and slow vibrations that cause the slow but steady damage to the building. In a multistoried setup, the height of the floor cannot be increased as is possible in case of single storied setup resulting in over installation charges of machinery and equipments on every subsequent floor. Though the incentives for the construction of cellar floor are given, it cannot be used for production or storage because of the seepage of water through the walls and thus cannot be used for employee facilities such as changing clothes or as a waiting room. However, rarely water proofing of the wall may be carried out.

PLANT FACILITIES

With the adoption of modern management techniques, unlike the yesteryears, the adequate plant facilities are a must to be provided to the workers mainly due to the strong trade unions, management associates recommendation and on humanitarian grounds. Prominently amongst these facilities are the air-conditioning and illumination facilities for the employees.

Air Conditioning

Every kind of equipment practically generates heat or moisture or fumes or dust that could affect the material machines. With the ever increasing cost of the raw materials, no chance can be taken in degradation of the materials during production or storage. The fines generated may cause health hazards for which a company has to pay heavy compensation, incidental charges and medical facilities. Therefore it is in the interest of the company to provide air-conditioning facilities not only to avert any problems but also to provide better working conditions for a better output. This can be achieved by installation of central air-conditioning unit or by the use of two or three air conditioners for a small area to provide ideal temperature and moisture conditions. Ideally the temperature is maintained from 25 to 28°C for maximum efficiency.

The dust generated by machines not only results in the wear and tear of the machine components but also provides a media for the growth of microorganisms. Generally the dust control is a part of the air conditioning system but sometimes it may otherwise be controlled by the use of vacuum cleaners.

Illuminations

Ideal illumination should be cool to the eyes not producing any strain. The illumination is not calculated by the incandescence alone but also in relation to the paint on the walls. For an efficient illumination, the colour of the walls should neither completely reflect nor absorb the light. Generally, the fluorescent lamps are widely used as the energy, consumption is low (100 W fluorescent lamp is equivalent to 300 W candle bulb). The use of coloured fluorescent tubes is not recommended, however, day cool or night cool varieties may be used.

Noise

Noise is generated due to the friction and vibration produced by the moving parts of a machine. The sound produced can be categorized as pleasant, pleasing, harsh or trouble making. The noise produced is measured in decibels. It is known that the noise generated to about 100 decibels is sufficient to cause the resonance of the ear drums that will ultimately get damaged resulting in deafness. The noise below 70 decibels is not harmful to the human ears so it is preferable to control the noise below 60 decibels.

To quite the noise producing elements, a constant lubrication and maintenance of the moving parts of the machine is necessary. The use of noise absorbers such as fait coverings baffles and false ceiling is recommended for the construction of audio graphic controlled rooms. Sometimes a slight modification in the machinery design may be suggested such as the use of shock absorbers in the fixed vibrating machines that do not impart resistance to the movement of the machine or by placing the machine in a remote area where none or less numbers of workers are working.

LAYOUT AND AREA REQUIREMENT FOR EACH DEPARTMENT

Almost every pharmaceutical industry has a separate department for the manufacturing of each dosage form products. The layout of each department can be studied under the following heads:

1. Layout of stores in an industry
2. Layout of injectable unit or sterile area
3. Layout of tableting section
4. Layout of oral liquid preparations, creams and ointments section

Layout of stores in an industry

Stores are defined or said to be a suborganization in a setup where materials required or obtained are held in abeyance till inspected, approved and stocked till it is indented by the consumer departments. A store should have a standard specification of the materials that should be of good quality. There must be a simple method of accounting the materials and there must be a regular flow of the materials. Conditions of storage should be proper and thus a properly designed store is needed.

Layout: The store room should preferably be located on the ground floor with ample space for storage of bulk drugs (Figure 19.1).

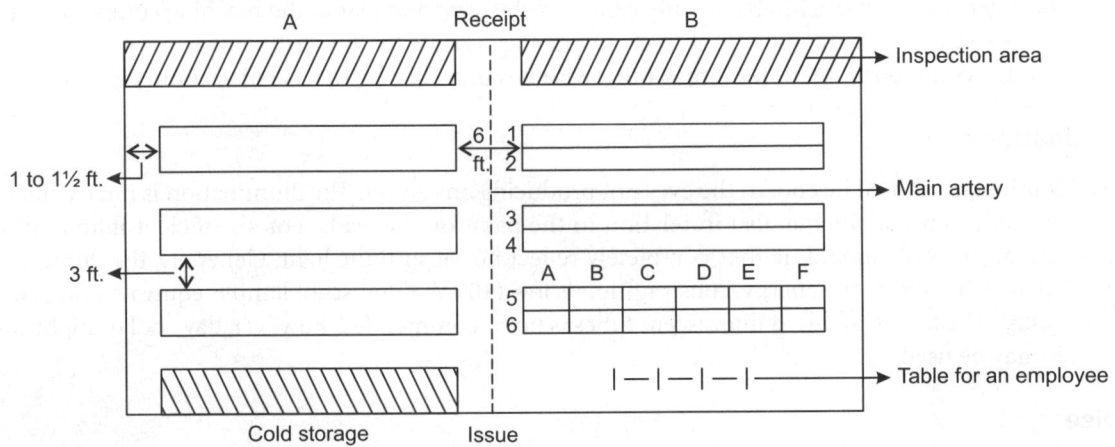

Figure 19.1. Layout of a Store Room

Adequate storage facilities should be there so that the drugs, chemicals, biologicals, etc., do not deteriorate by moisture or heat.

An ideal store should have two entrances, one for receipt entry and the other for the issue of materials. The receipt entry should be at the outer wall to facilitate the approach of large consignments. But in many cases, it is not possible to have the receipt entry at the outer wall then the store should be at the anterior near the corridor where the material can be held in abeyance. Sometimes two entrances in the opposite directions are not possible. In such cases the entries on the same end should be provided, one for entry and other for exit.

Generally racks are used for storage of materials. They are made of angle iron, having partition or racks with doors. However, these are not recommended as these occupy large space. In case of costly items two closed bins may be used. The bin should be 2½ ft. in height, 2 ft. in depth and 3 ft. in length.

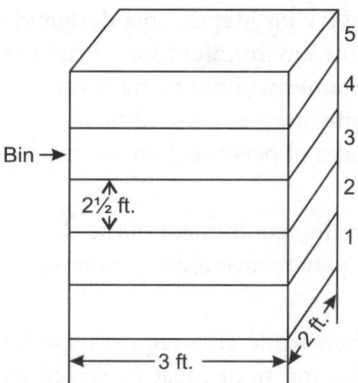

Figure 19.2. Layout of a Rack

One rack is not sufficient so other racks are placed back to back and are 3–6 ft. and the racks should be placed about 1–1½ ft. from the wall to avoid moisture or expansion during summer and also allowing for cleaning without touching the walls thus avoiding contamination (Figure 19.2). The height of the racks depends upon the height of the ceiling and should be about 2/3 the height. The number of racks depends upon the area of the room. Well-planned store should occupy 60–70% of the prime area. Since large numbers of products are to be stored in the store, a definite location code is followed in order to identify the product or the material placed in the store. For this purpose, an analysis is carried out after studying the inventory namely:

FSN—Fast moving, Slow moving, Nonmoving materials.

HML—Heavy, Medium, Light materials.

According to the above analysis, fast-moving materials are placed near the issue exit while nonmoving on the farthest end and in the individual racks, heavy items at the lower most bin while the light items on the top.

A ready record (ledger book) is maintained for immediate identification and the delivery of materials. Nowadays bin cards are used that resemble the catalogue. Each card is used for a single item which records the dates of receipt or issue, balance and credit of material. Ledgers or bin card code have four digits.

Certain other principles may also be used such as FIFO (First In First Out). Materials can be entered in the ledger or bin cards in alphabetical order but this may cause problems as the number of materials are known by different names. They may thus be categorized and stored depending upon their use or type of dosage form.

Layout of Injectable Unit or Sterile Area

The sterile product quickly become totally unacceptable if the environment in which it is processed is contaminated or if the manufacturing procedure is not properly carried out.

The production of the parenteral preparations is normally divided into five sectional areas such as the clean up area, the preparation area, the aseptic area, the quarantine area and the finishing or packaging area. All these areas should be designed and constructed for effective ease of cleaning, efficient operation, attractiveness and comfort of personnel.

The extra requirements are necessary for aseptic area designed to provide an environment wherein the preparation may be exposed to the environment for a brief period during subdivision from a bulk container to the individual dose container without being contaminated. The contamination of concern includes dust, lint and microorganisms normally found floating in the air, lying on counters and other surfaces, on clothing and body surfaces of personnel, in the exhaled breath of personnel and deposited on the floor.

Ideally a sterile room should meet the requirement of the class I clean room as defined by the federal standard 209b, which states that such an environment contains no more than 100 particles per cubic ft. of 0.5 micrometres and larger size.

In order to achieve the above, the aseptic area requires special construction features designed for maximum security. The ceiling, walls and floor must be sealed so that they cannot be contaminated. These ceiling, walls and floors are not only washed but also treated with an antiseptic wipe or spray before each use. All counters should be constructed of stainless steel and hung from the wall so that there are no legs for the dirt to accumulate. All light fixtures utility service lines, ventilation fixtures should be framed in the walls or ceiling to eliminate legs and joint location for the accumulation of dust and dirt. As much accessible, tanks containing the compounded product and the mechanical equipment should remain outside the aseptic area and the product should be fed into the area through hose lines. Mechanical equipment that must be located in the aseptic areas should be fitted as completely as possible within a stainless steel cabinet in order to seal the operating parts, and their dirt producing and accumulating tendencies from the aseptic environment. Mechanical parts that will contact the parenteral products should be demountable so that they can be sterilized.

Personnel entering the aseptic area should enter only through an airlock. They should be attired in sterile coveralls with sterile hats, masks and foot covers. Movement within the room should be minimal and the in-and-out rigidly restricted during a filling procedure. The requirements for the preparation of room and for the personnel may be somewhat relaxed if the product is to be sterilized in a sealed container.

The air in the aseptic area can be one of the greatest sources of contamination. To maintain the aseptic conditions, besides the various precautions followed, it is extremely necessary to clean the air before it is allowed to enter into the aseptic area. Clean rooms are generally classified into two categories:

1. Conventional clean room systems
2. Laminar flow clean room systems

Conventional clean room systems

The term *conventional clean room* is applied where a lower degree of cleanliness such as class 10 000 clean room is followed. It is defined as an environment containing not more than 10 000 particles per cubic ft. of 0.5 micrometres and larger size.

Conventional clean room system deals with the air handling, i.e. air conditioning whereby the dust particles, humidity and temperature is controlled. This dehumidified, cooled and filtered air is made to enter the room at a velocity of 800 ft./min. Conventional clean room standards can be attained by the use of specific number of air conditioners depending upon the total volume of the air in tons in the room (Figure 19.3).

Conventionally two air conditioners, one at the ceiling and the other at the bench level are fixed in a room. Diffusers are also employed to throw the particles towards the corner. In most of the cases the bench is placed in the central area that is comparatively cleaner as compared to the other parts of the

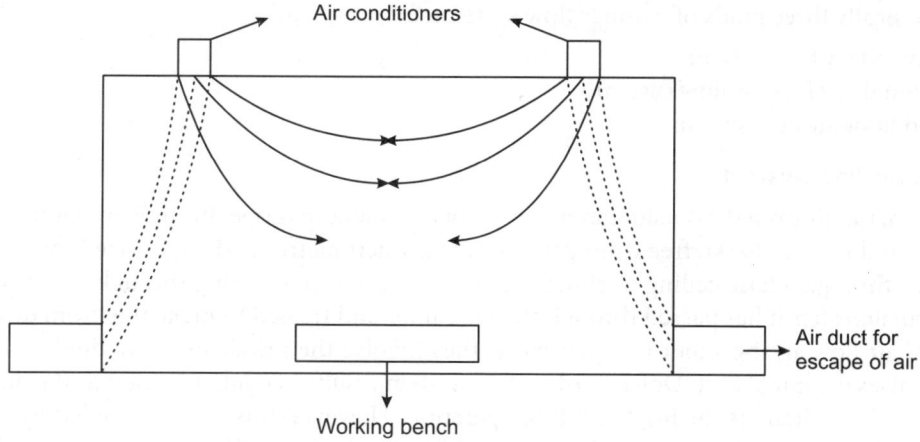

Figure 19.3. Conventional Clean Room System

room, thus leaving most of the area useless increasing both the maintenance and the production cost. In a conventional clean room there are about 16–20 air changes per hour that results in the formation of dust pockets which get disturbed easily with slight turbulence. It is very difficult to maintain a conventional clean room area and its establishment is disadvantageous for reasons such as:

1. Lot of space is wasted.
2. Temperature, humidity and dust are controlled all at one time which becomes difficult.
3. Formation of the dust pockets occur that contaminates the area. Conventional clean room system is not suitable for the aseptic processing units but instead it is used for maintaining general cleanliness in the establishment.

Laminar flow clean room system

In this system, the laminar air flow provides a total sweep of a confined area because the entire body of air moves with uniform velocity along the parallel lines, originating through HEPA filters occupying one entire side of the confined area. Therefore it bathes the entire area with a very clean air, sweeping away the contaminants. The effective air velocity is 100 ± 20 ft./min. The laminar air flow system offers various advantages over a conventional clean room system that are as follows:

1. The people working in the area do not feel the movement of the air or chill.
2. Any part of the room can be utilized without any restriction.
3. As the body of the air moves with a uniform velocity along parallel lines, the capacity to carry the dust particles is more as compared to the conventional clean room system.
4. With the velocity of air being 100 ft./min the possibility of the formation of dust is negligible as it does not permit the settling of dust particles.
5. There are as many as 100 air changes per hour per cubic feet which enables lesser dust pockets with low maintenance cost.
6. The sterile area attained is of very high order thus no chemical means of sterilization is needed.
7. Unlike the conventional airflow system, the humidity, dust and temperature are regulated as separate entities reducing the load on the filters, and if required the cooling and heating equipments may be separately employed to maintain a constant temperature.

There are basically three kinds of laminar flow systems.

1. Downward air flow system
2. Horizontal or cross air flow system
3. Wall to floor air flow system

Downward air flow system

In this system, the air from the outside, after a series of treatment (passage through prefilters, electrostatic precipitator and HEPA filters), free from particles of 0.3 micrometres and larger size is allowed to enter into the area through a false ceiling washing the entire area and re-entering through the false floor. The air is recirculated after it has passed through the false floor and treated to make free from dust particles. This type of air flow arrangement is expensive as they involve the installation of a double set of HEPA filters that raises the initial cost. Downward air flow system results in contamination as the dust particles may fall into the containers during the filling operation. However, this can be avoided by starting the work after waiting for a while to permit the particles to settle down. This arrangement is the best for aseptic processing units (Figure 19.4).

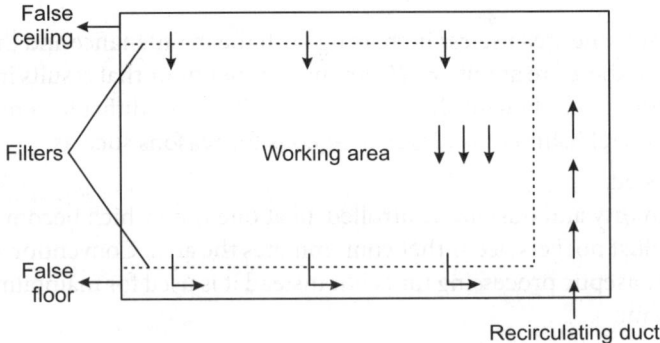

Figure 19.4. Downward Air Flow System

Horizontal or cross air flow system

In this, the air flow pattern is along the horizontal lines that may introduce contamination due to the obstruction caused by the presence of operators in the room and the entire flow of the particles is disturbed. Besides the paniculate contamination, there is apparent danger while dealing with the penicillin powder or viable microorganism (Figure 19.5).

Wall-to-floor air flow system

In this air flow system, the laminar flow is allowed to enter from the wall and made inclined towards the floor covering the working bench area which is maintained aseptic. By employing such an arrangement both aseptic and nonsterile conditions are achieved in the same area. This is preferred whenever a portable system is desired. However, the cost of installation is very high (Figure 19.6).

Based on the above air flow systems, horizontal laminar airflow work benches and the vertical laminar flow portable rooms are widely used (see Figures 19.7 and 19.8). In any of these assemblies, the air from the outside is first allowed to pass through a prefilter usually of glass wool, cotton or shredded plastic to remove larger particles. Then it is treated by passage through an electrostatic precipitator. Such a unit induces an electrical charge on the particles in the air and removes them by attraction to the oppositely

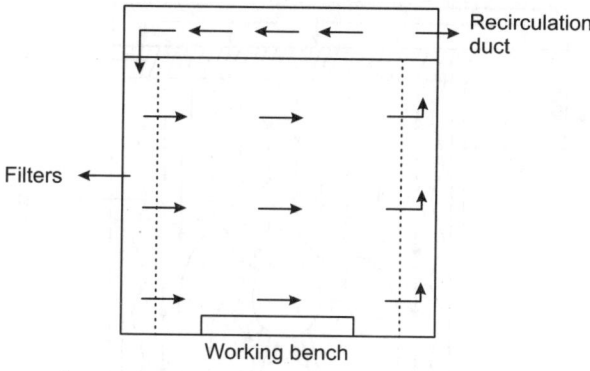

Figure 19.5. Horizontal Air Flow System

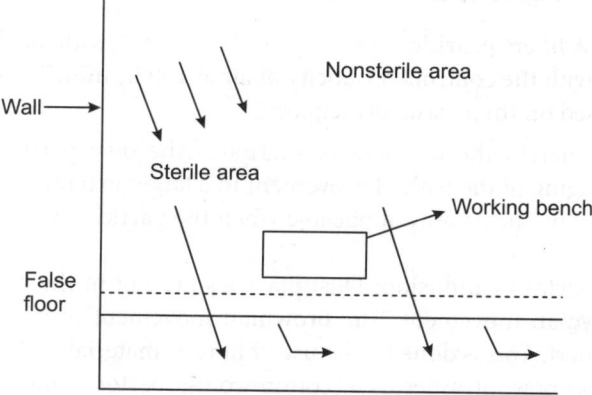

Figure 19.6. Wall to Floor Air Flow System

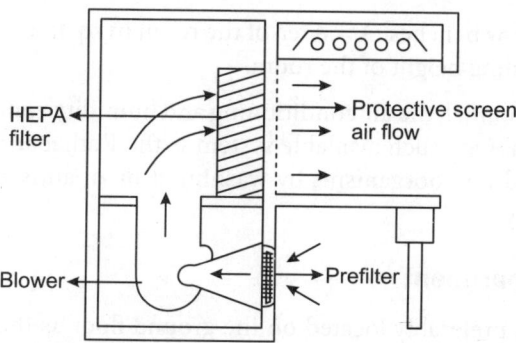

Figure 19.7. Horizontal Laminar Flow Work Bench

charged plates. The air then passes through the most efficient cleaning device, a HEPA (Higher Efficiency Paniculate Air) filter having an efficiency of at least 99.97% in removing the particles of 0.3 micrometres

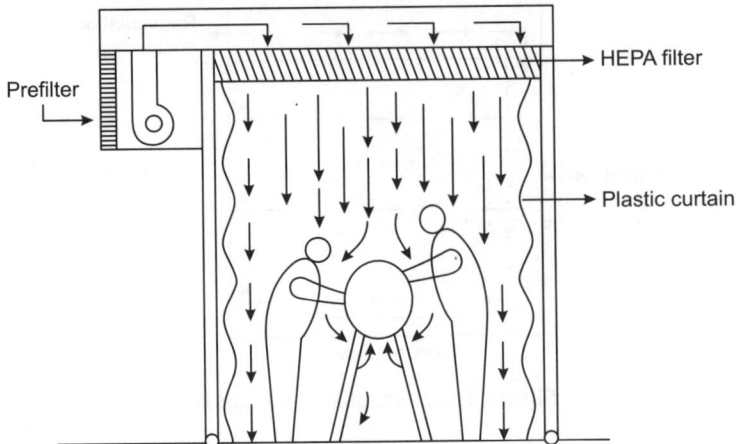

Figure 19.8. Vertical Laminar Flow Portable Room System

or larger in size. The HEPA filters provide a working area of 2 × 2 ft. with an ability of filtering about 29 billion particles per hour with the controlled velocity of air at 100 ft./min. The mechanism of working of laminar film system is based on three basic principles:

1. Inertial deposition wherein the moment of inertia of the dust particles is reduced due to the obstruction and changing of the path of movement to a larger extent.
2. Capture by interception: This is only applicable when the particles are controlled to the order of 1 micron size.
3. Capture of small particles by diffusion: Dust particles present in the colloidal mixtures are small and they show brownian movement. The brownian movement of the particles is inhibited that makes them to fall apart. This is done by the use of fibrous material such as cotton wool, glass wool or combination of cotton wool, asbestos or cotton wool-asbestos-plant fibre.

The number of laminar flow benches required for a room of a given area to give 100 recycles/hour through a HEPA filter can be determined using the formula:

N= AH/240 F

Where N = No. of Laminar flow benches. A = Area of the room in sq. ft. F = No. of 2 ft × 2 ft HEPA filters in the filter pack and H = Ceiling height of the room.

For the comfort of the personnel, the air conditioning and humidity control should be simultaneously incorporated into the system. One such available system is the Kathabar System (surface combustion) that cleans the air of dirt and microorganisms by washing it in an antiseptic solution and at the same time controlling the humidity.

Layout of Tabletting Department

The tabletting department is preferably located on the ground floor as the production involves the use of large number of heavy machinery and equipment (Figure 19.9). Tabletting department is subdivided into three sections namely:

1. Granulating section
2. Tabletting section
3. Coating section

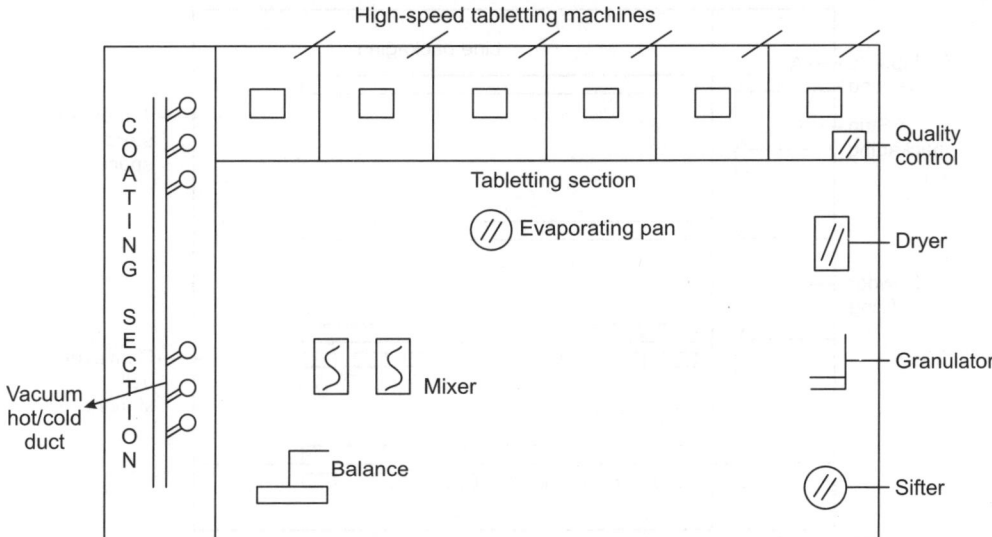

Figure 19.9. Layout of Tabletting Section

In most of the organizations, there is no provision for substores in any of these sections due to the possibility of contamination and a large area is required for adequate storage and maintenance. The material is, therefore, procured from the central store by issuing the requisition for the material required in the following morning.

In the granulating system, the mixer may be used both for granulation and mixing of material. During the granulation, trolleys with hangers are used to hold the trays containing wet granules which are then pushed into the dryer for drying. The dried granules are then sent for tabletting and if required, to the coating section.

Packaging department

For the packaging of variety of dosage forms into various containers, a packaging line is established alongside the preparing or the filling area. During the packaging, any of the preparation packed into the final containers is subjected to physical quality control inspection before it is finally packed into the cartons. In order to ascertain the number of personnel required in a packaging line up to achieve the maximum output, the time motion study is carried out depending upon the rate of production and output (Figure 19.10).

Area requirement for each department

According to the drugs and cosmetics act every department in an industrial unit should legally comply with the minimum area and equipment requirement that are established depending on the production, site of machinery and necessary working area. Schedule M possess all the relevant information in terms of minimum area and equipment requirement and is as follows:

1. For ointment, emulsions, lotions section minimum of 300 sq. ft. is required for basic installation.
2. Syrup, Elixirs and solution section requires 300 sq. ft.
3. Pills and compressed tablet area requires 300 sq. ft. each for granulating, tabletting and coating section.
4. Parenteral preparations require 600 sq. ft. in the form of cabins separated from one another for washing of containers, preparation of solutions, filling and sealing, sterilization and testing.

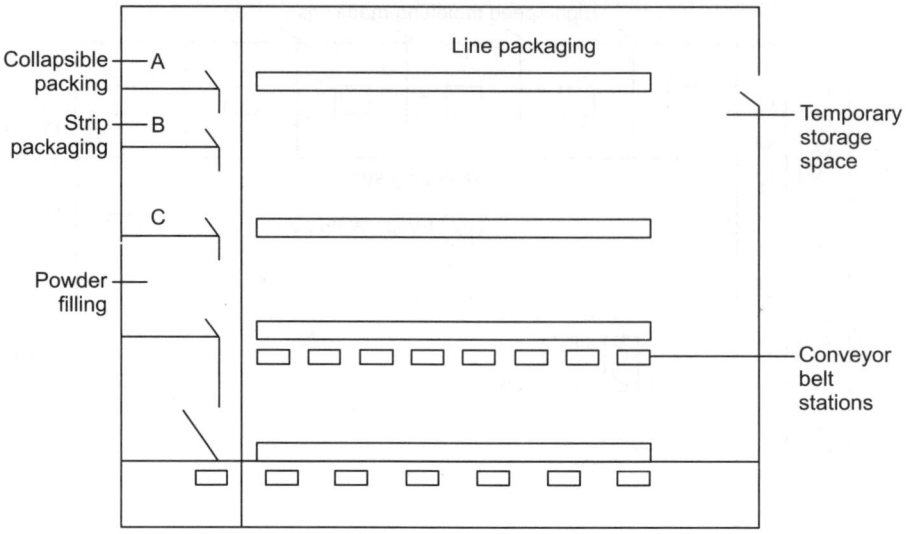

Figure 19.10. Layout of Packaging Department

5. Powders require 300 sq. ft. area.
6. Filling of hard gelatin capsules requires 200 sq. ft. area.
7. Surgical dressings and bandages require 300 sq. ft. + additional 300 sq. ft. in case of medicated surgical dressings.
8. For eye preparations 200 sq. ft. area is needed.
9. Pessaries, suppositories and bougies require 200 sq. ft. minimum area + 300 sq. ft. if granulation and compression technique is adopted.
10. Chemical repacking unit requires min. of 200 sq. ft. area.
11. Minimum of 6 sq. ft. per worker is to be added to all the areas of installation.

Points to Ponder

1. There are basically five trends followed in the plant location. They are as follows:
   a. Location in suburban area or in small town
   b. Location in an industrial village
   c. Centralization trend in location
   d. Decentralization trend in location
   e. Ecological or pollution control trend
2. The layout of different pharmaceutical departments should be categorised under the following heads:
   a. Layout of stores in an industry
   b. Layout of injectable units or sterile areas
   c. Layout of the tableting section
   d. Layout of the oral liquid preparations, creams and ointments section

 **Self-Assessment Exercises**

1. Describe various trends in the location of a plant.
2. Write short note on following:
    a. Layout of stores in an industry
    b. Layout of injectable unit or sterile area
    c. Layout of tableting section
    d. Layout of oral liquid preparations, creams and ointments section
3. What is HEPA filter?
4. Describe in detail about laminar air flow system.
5. Write a note on conventional clean room systems.
6. Give the area requirement for different departments of a pharmaceutical industry.

Pharmaceutical Export

INTRODUCTION

The pharmaceutical industry is one of the fastest growing sectors of the Indian economy and has made rapid strides over the years. From being an import dependent industry in the 1950s, the industry today, has not only achieved self-sufficiency but also started exporting drugs and pharmaceuticals to more than 150 countries of the world. The leading Indian companies have established infrastructures in over 60 plus countries like the USA, Europe, Japan, etc., who are the front leaders in the pharmaceutical world.

The Indian pharma industry has gained a global recognition for producing low cost high quality bulk drugs as well as formulations. The export turnover has reached the tune of Rs 15 000 crore by the end of year 2004–05 and is growing at a rate of 25% annually. It is predicted that in another three to four years, the export turnover will surpass the domestic turnover. The Indian dugs and pharmaceuticals are gaining wide acceptance in all countries. Indian drugs are providing a healing touch not only to our people in India but also to many others in the developed, developing and underdeveloped countries.

The Indian pharmaceutical companies are now concentrating on the export markets and are building their marketing network in these markets. Looking at the scenario, export is the biggest growth opportunity for the Indian pharma industry in the near future.

Pharma Exports—Great Time Ahead

India is one of the top ten producers of bulk drugs in the world and 60% of India's bulk drugs production is exported.

Generic exports to the developed countries have significantly picked up in the recent past. Several blockbuster patented products will lose patent protection in the coming years opening the market opportunity of USD 70–80 bn. This will provide ample opportunities to the pharma companies in the generic drug markets to capture a large market share.

The pharmaceutical companies are upgrading their manufacturing facilities and implementing good manufacturing practices. Most of the companies are obtaining international regulatory approvals like USFDA, MHRA, TGA, MCC, etc., to tap the regulated and semiregulated markets.

The companies are coming up with cost effective, truly world-class products. Global sourcing, low overhead costs, mass productions are also playing an important role in increasing the exports.

The pharmaceutical industry is witnessing the setting up of SEZs (special economic zones) that will make the exports more attractive.

Potential Markets for Exports

The growth in the pharma exports, despite the pressing generic competition in the global markets, is also due to the increased ANDA (abbreviated new drug applications) approvals in the US markets and through the contribution from relatively less regulated markets in Latin America, Australia (the growth is 20–25%) and the emerging markets in the regions of the Middle East and Africa. The export potential of these markets is significant because of lower competition and less entry barriers.

Global Pharmaceutical Sales by Region in USD Billions

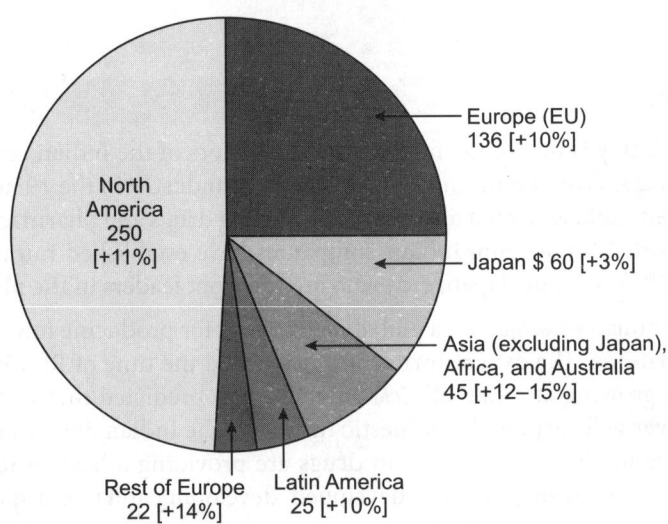

STEPWISE PROCEDURE FOR EXPORT OF PHARMACEUTICALS PRODUCTS

Before the pharmaceutical company starts actual export of their products to any country, it is very important to understand the prerequisites. They are as given below:

1. Registration of the product with the respective statutory authority.
2. Appointment of the agent or representative in that country.

Registration with the respective regulatory authorities like the USFDA (United States Food and Drugs Administration) in the US, MHRA (Medicine and Healthcare Regulatory Agency) in the UK, TGA (Therapeutic Goods Administration) in Australia and so on, is a must before exporting drugs and pharmaceuticals to these countries. Every country has its own systems and norms for the registration of pharmaceutical products. Either it is the Ministry of Health or other independent departments who take care of the registration.

Selection of the Markets for Export

It is necessary to do a proper groundwork about the markets and the countries targeted for the export of pharmaceuticals. The markets are thoroughly studied on various aspects like political stability, socioeconomic conditions, government policies, business environment, investment incentives, status of judiciary, etc.

Following are some of the parameters to be studied about the targeted markets:

1. Market potential for the products to be exported (i.e. acceptability of the present composition or strength).
2. Registration requirement, cost of registration and the period to complete the registration of each product.
3. Labeling and packaging requirements (pack size, language).
4. Local regulatory guidelines (including those related to the Intellectual Property Rights) and standards practiced.
5. Market distance (by sea or by air).
6. Marketing costs.
7. Distribution network.

Sequence of Activities in the Pharmaceutical Export

Following is the sequence of activities in pharmaceutical exports:

1. Receive orders from overseas agent
2. Communicate the orders to the factory
3. Factory selects the relevant batch and complies to the special requirements
4. Documents are prepared by the exports office (refer list below)
5. Documents are passed to the CHA (Custom House Agent)
6. CHA prepares the shipping bill and does other documentation
7. CHA books airspace or shipping space and communicates the same
8. Goods are released from the factory with relevant excise or other documentation
9. Goods are handed over to the CHA to airlift or to send by ship

List of Documents to be Passed on to the CHA (Custom House Agent)

Following is the list of documents to be passed on to the CHA:

1. Invoice
2. Packing list
3. GR form
4. Contract (if required)
5. Letter of credit
6. DEPB passbook (duty entitlement passbook)
7. Certificate of origin (if required)
8. Instruction for shipping bill

Technical Documentation

To start with the actual exports of the pharmaceuticals, there are number of prior requirements to be completed, including the most important one, i.e. preparation and submission of registration dossiers for the products to be exported to that country. The registration formats or requirements. The cost and period to complete the registration differs from one country to another.

However, the following documents or certificate(s) are required to comply with the registration requirements:

1. FDA License copy
2. Free Sale certificate
3. WHO-GMP certificate
4. Details of manufacturing facilities
5. Details of quality control systems
6. Technical details about the product mentioning the following:

   a. Pharmacology and Pharmacokinetics
   b. Manufacturing and packaging process
   c. Quality procedures mainly
   d. Method of analysis of raw material
   e. Method of analysis of finished products
   f. Stability data of at least three batches of the product
   g. Validation protocol and data of the three batches
   h. Summary of the clinical trials about the safety and efficacy of the product with published references
   i. Summary of the bio availability studies

7. Samples of sales pack with the QC test report

Export Registration Authorities in Some Countries

Country	Approving authority
Abu Dhabi	Abu Dhabi Center for Herbal Medical Care
Bangladesh	Ministry of Health and Planning
Czech and Slovak	State Institute for Drug Control
Burma/Myanmar	Myanmar Drug Committee
Eritrea	Pharmacy Department of the Ministry of Health
Ethiopia	Pharmacy Department of the Ministry of Health
Ghana	The Registrar Pharmacy Board
Kenya	Pharmacy and Poisons Board
Kuwait	Drug Controller and Registration Board
Malaysia	Drug Control Authority
Philippines	Directorate General of Pharmacy Affairs and Drug Control
South Africa	Bureau of Food and Drugs
Sri Lanka	Cosmetics Devices and Drug Authority
Sudan	BADAR Drugs and Chemicals Co. Ltd.
Singapore	Republic of Singapore, Ministry of Health
Thailand	Drug Controller Division Regulatory Authority FDA
UK	Medicine and Healthcare Regulatory Agency
USA	Food and Drug Administration (FDA)
Vietnam	Ministry of Health
Zambia	Pharmaceutical Registration Department

Points to Ponder

1. India is one of the top ten producers of bulk drugs in the world and 60% of India's bulk drugs production is exported.
2. The prerequisites for export of pharmaceuticals products are as follows:
   a. Registration of the product with the respective statutory authority
   b. Appointment of the agent or representative in that country
3. List of the documents to be passed on to the custom house agent are as follows:
   a. Invoice
   b. Packing list
   c. GR form
   d. Contract (if required)
   e. Letter of credit
   f. DEPB passbook (Duty Entitlement Passbook)
   g. Certificate of origin (if required)
   h. Instruction for shipping bill

Self-Assessment Exercises

1. Describe in detail about the procedure for export of pharmaceutical products.
2. How will you select the correct market for the export of pharmaceutical products?
3. Enumerate the sequence of activities in the pharmaceutical export.
4. Give the list of the documents to be passed on to the CHA (Custom House Agent).
5. Write a note on *technical documentation*.

CHAPTER

21

Accounting and Its Principles

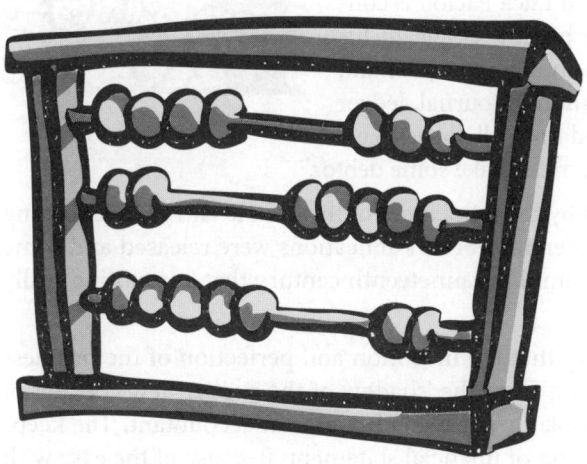

INTRODUCTION

Whenever your mother asks you to go to the nearby grocery store to buy items of daily use like match-box, candlestick, soap cake, coffee, spices, etc., you need not pay for these items immediately. When you buy these items, the storeowner immediately opens the page of a notebook with your father's name on it. He records the value of the items purchased. At the end of the month, your father goes to him. He again opens the same page, tells the total amount to be paid and records when your father makes the payment. In a similar manner, he keeps the record of other customers also. Whenever he gets the commodities from the suppliers he records it and also records the payment he makes to them. Similarly every business small or big, sole proprietor or a firm keeps a record of the business transactions. Have you ever thought why do they keep a record of business transactions? If they do not keep the record how will they know how much, when and to whom they are to make payments, or from whom how much and when they are to receive payments, or what they have earned after a particular period and so on. Recording of transactions by a businessman in proper books and in a systematic manner is known as *accounting*.

HISTORY

Evolution of accounting as per the Indian mythology is by Chitra Gupta, who is responsible for maintaining accounts in God's court. A book on *Arthashasthra* written by Kautilya, who was a minister in Chandra Gupta's kingdom twenty-three centuries ago, mentions the accounting practices in India. It describes how accounting records have to be maintained. In China and Egypt accounting was used for maintaining revenue records of the government treasury.

A book on *Arithmetica Geometrica, Proportion at Proportionality* (review of Arithmetic and Geometric proportion) by an Italian Luca Pacioli is considered as the first authentic book on double entry book keeping. In his book he used the present day popular terms of accounting debit (Dr) and credit (Cr). He also discussed the details of memorandum, journal, ledger and specialized accounting procedures. He also stated that, 'all entries have to be double entries, i.e. if you make one creditor you must make some debtor.'

The years following Pacioli's treatise were marked by the refinement of the double entry book keeping system and by the use of an accountant in the commercial world. Publications were released and some accountant associations were formed, but it was not until the nineteenth century that accounting really became a profession.

It was not until the dawn of the twentieth century that the invention and perfection of the business machines of today took the business of recordkeeping from the 'shadow of the pen'. A new concept of accounting valuation began to take form and the book keeper really became an accountant. The keeping of books was no longer restricted to the preparation of financial statement. Because of the ease with which facts could be recorded, accumulated and analysed, the accountant began to devote his time to the interpretation of booked facts and as a result, became a member of the management team.

NEED AND ROLE OF ACCOUNTING

Many consider that accounting has a role to play only in business and not in domestic life. This is not, factually, correct. In fact, we see the beginning of accounting in every wise housewife. In case, a housewife records her domestic transactions, connected with money, regularly, she can collect a lot of valuable information. Many intelligent housewives, though not literate, maintain a small dairy to record receipts on one page and all payments on the other page. Receipts are not always many, either in the form of income of the husband, her supplementary earnings, gifts from relations, etc. List of payments is relatively more on different items say milk, education, entertainment, food, and clothing and, finally,

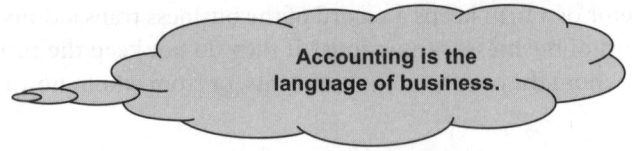

Accounting is the
language of business.

planned commitments on savings, etc. She can conveniently find, at the end of the month, how much she has spent on the different items of expenditure. This exercise helps her in planning her expenditure as income is, often, beyond her control. The family, not she alone, can learn useful lessons, when they review, where they have gone wrong in estimating or not controlling their spending. It would, equally, facilitate the family to plan and achieve their dreams, together, be it owning a home, car to drive, long-term goals of the education of children, retirement life and many more things that they wish to achieve. Yes, the need of accounting is more for business.

The main purpose of language is communication of ideas. Similar is the purpose and role of accounts for a business. A businessman has to keep a systematic record of the financial activities of his firm so that he can know the financial position. What it owns are assets and what it owes are the liabilities. It is necessary for every businessman to know where he stands in many respects:

1. What he owns?
2. What he owes?
3. Whether he has earned profit or suffered loss over a period?
4. What is his financial position? Is he better off or moving towards bankruptcy?

Only accounts give answers to these questions.

These days in many growing areas, the form of business has been the joint stock company. By law, these firms have to keep the books of accounts to meet the requirements of the Companies Act. The purpose of accounting is narrow to many. Many consider that the role of accounting is limited to maintaining books of accounts for a limited purpose like filing income-tax returns to satisfy the curiosity of the income-tax department. This is only a part of the full story.

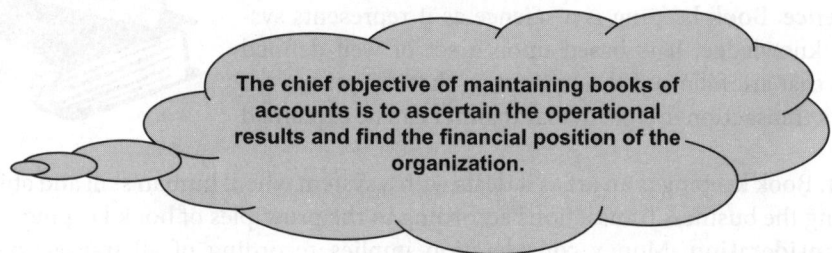

The chief objective of maintaining books of accounts is to ascertain the operational results and find the financial position of the organization.

But, the above is not the end; rather in the modern era, it is only a beginning. The role and importance of accounting in a firm depends more on the person who heads the role. Many think the role of accounting is to record transactions in the books of accounts. With the pace of computerization, the role of accounting for recording the transactions has diminished.

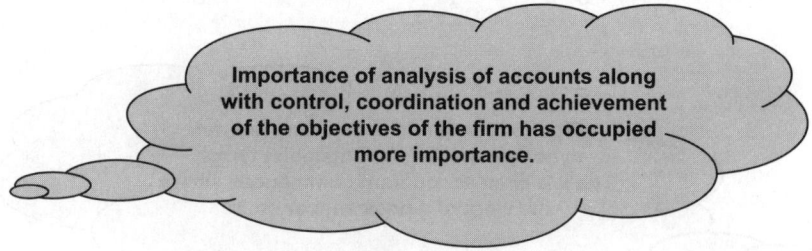

Importance of analysis of accounts along with control, coordination and achievement of the objectives of the firm has occupied more importance.

Need of accounting is not limited to business organizations. Even the nonprofitable firms like clubs, charitable institutions, hospitals and education institutions maintain books of accounts to know their state of affairs.

Nowadays, the combined role of accounting and finance has assumed more importance than the individual role of accounting. It is no surprise that the finance manager can change the fortunes of the organization, if he is, really, competent. For this reason, he is associated with every decision-making process, from recruitment of staff to the final stage, liquidation. No wonder, the organization may sink, if he fails to deliver that is expected of him. A good finance manager, normally, is an asset to the firm he works in, while he becomes a liability, if he is not practical in making the objectives of accounting and finance to tailor the needs of the business.

MEANING AND DEFINITION OF BOOK KEEPING

The art of recording business transactions in a systematic manner is termed as *book keeping*. It is the name given to a system that is concerned with recording and summarizing business transactions accurately so as to know the true state of affairs of a business.

Definition of Book Keeping

R.N. Carter in his book on *Advanced Accounting* defines book keeping as the 'Science and art of correctly recording in books of accounts all those business transactions that result in the transfer of money or money's worth'. This definition reveals the following features of book keeping:

1. **It is a science.** Book keeping is a science as it represents systematized knowledge. It is based upon a set of well-defined principles that are followed throughout so that the reason for recording a transaction in a particular manner can be explained fully.
2. **It is an art.** Book keeping is an art as it deals with a system where human skill and ability is involved in recording the business transactions according to the principles of book keeping.
3. **Money consideration.** Money consideration implies recording of all transactions that can be expressed in terms of money.

Kohler in his *Dictionary for Accountants* defined book keeping as 'the process of analysing, classifying and recording transactions in accordance with preconceived plan'. This definition brings forth the following three aspects of accounting.

1. **Analysis.** It refers to identifying various expenses incurred during a period of time.

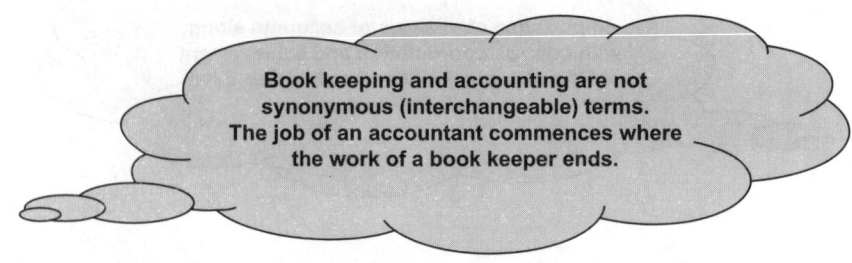

Book keeping and accounting are not synonymous (interchangeable) terms. The job of an accountant commences where the work of a book keeper ends.

2. **Classification.** It refers to the grouping of like items of expenses into a common group.
3. **Recording.** It refers to entering the transactions in the basic books and later posting them into another set of book known as *ledger*.

B.G. Vickery in his book *Principles and Practice of Book Keeping* defines book keeping as 'the art of recording pecuniary or business transactions in a regular and systematic manner'. This definition emphasizes the recording of monetary transactions of the business on a day-to-day basis and in a systematic manner, i.e. according to the set of rules and regulations of book keeping.

ACCOUNTING—SCIENCE OR ART?

Accounting is a science as accounts are prepared in accordance with certain basic principles and laws that are universally accepted. However, accounting is not a perfect science like Physics or Chemistry, where experiments can be conducted in a laboratory and specific conclusions can be drawn. Some people have reservations to treat accountancy as a science.

Accounting is a science as well as an art.

Accounting is, definitely, an art. Art is a technique that helps in achieving the desired objectives. Accounting has some definite objectives to be fulfilled. Accounting is an art because it prescribes the process through which the objectives are fulfilled. The American Institute of Certified Public Accountants also defines accounting as an art.

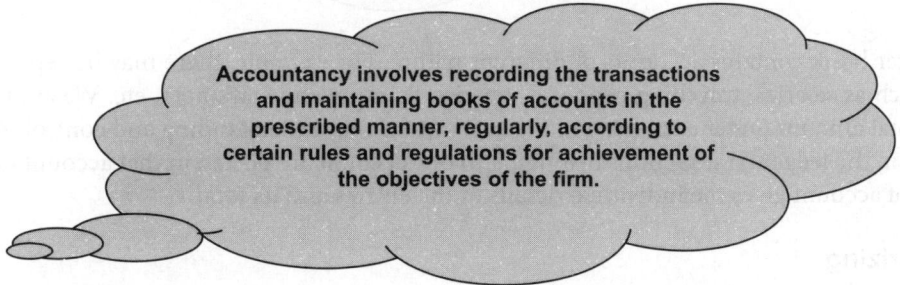

Accountancy involves recording the transactions and maintaining books of accounts in the prescribed manner, regularly, according to certain rules and regulations for achievement of the objectives of the firm.

DEFINITION AND EXPLANATION OF ACCOUNTING

The American Institute of Certified Public Accountants, which has played a noble part in the development of accounting, defines the concept as follows:

'Accounting is the art of recording, classifying and summarizing in a significant manner and in terms of money, transactions and events which are, in part, at least, of a financial character, and interpreting the results thereof'.

Once we break the definition for better understanding, we find the term accounting contains the following components:

1. Recording

Recording is the basic function of accounting. Events and transactions that are of a financial character, either fully or partly, are recorded in an orderly manner in the book of accounts. The transactions are recorded in a journal, as and when they happen or occur. Journal is further subdivided into cash journal or cash book (for recording cash transactions), purchases journal (for recording credit purchases) and sales journal (for recording credit sales). All these books are called *subsidiary books*. If subsidiary books are maintained, the transactions are not recorded in the journal and are recorded in these books, directly. Only those transactions that do not find a place in the subsidiary books are recorded in the journal. After recording all transactions in the journal, if they are, later, posted into different accounts of the ledger, the workload would be heavy. In fact, work is duplicated too. To reduce the avoidable workload, each firm maintains subsidiary books, depending upon its individual requirements.

It is not necessary to record all financial transactions, first, in the journal, if the concerned subsidiary book is maintained, before posting is made into the concerned accounts. Say, cash transactions are posted into the cash book, directly, without posting them in the journal.

2. Classifying

All similar transactions are grouped and posted in one book called the *ledger*.

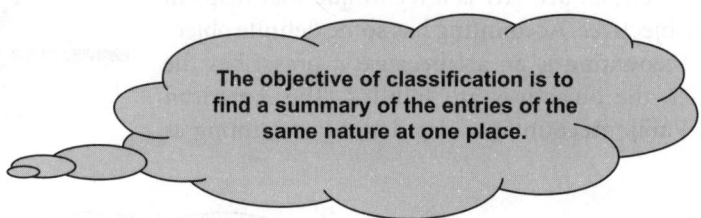

The objective of classification is to find a summary of the entries of the same nature at one place.

This ledger book contains accounts of different nature. For example, there may be separate heads of accounts such as salaries, travelling expenses, repairs, printing and stationery, etc. We are interested to know the total amount under each head of the account for our understanding and control. All accounts find a place in the ledger. Transactions belonging to one account are posted in that account in the ledger. Each head of account gives the individual details of the entries and its total.

3. Summarizing

When posting is complete in the ledger, totals are made for the debit and the credit side in each head of the account and the final balance (heavier balance), be it debit or credit, is arrived at.

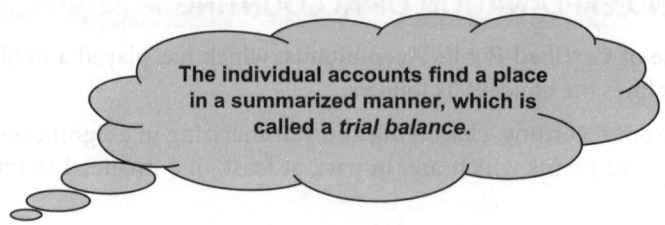

The individual accounts find a place in a summarized manner, which is called a *trial balance*.

Income statement (trading and, profit and loss account) and balance sheet are prepared from the trial balance.

4. Deals with Financial Transactions

Accounting transactions that are of financial character only, are recorded in the books of accounts. In other words, if a transaction cannot be expressed in terms of money, they are not recorded in the accounting books.

However, payments made to employees (salaries), their contribution (sales) and, ultimately, profits appear in the accounting books as they are expressed in terms of money. Again, expenses incurred on their welfare, in recognition of their efforts, be it bonus or medical aid, also appear in the books of accounts.

5. Analysis and Interprets

This is the final and an important function of accounting. A distinction is to be made between the two terms—analysis and interpretation. Analysis refers to the methodical classification of data. If unconnected data are grouped together, understanding is not possible. All assets belonging to the current assets are to be grouped together, similarly all current liabilities. If current assets and current liabilities are mixed together, data would be confusing. Interpretation means drawing conclusions from the data and explaining the conclusions in a simple language, easy to understand to plan further course of action.

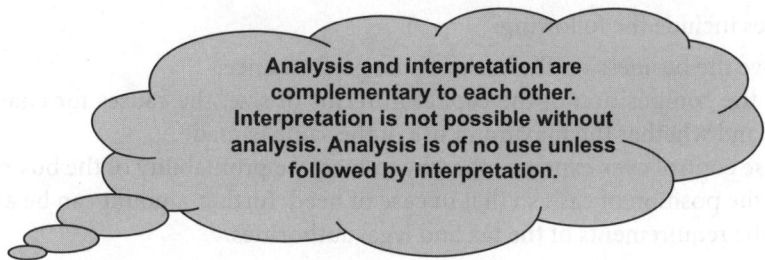

Analysis and interpretation are complementary to each other. Interpretation is not possible without analysis. Analysis is of no use unless followed by interpretation.

6. Communication

Communication is the final product of accounting. Financial statements, i.e. profit and loss account, and balance sheet are the means of communication.

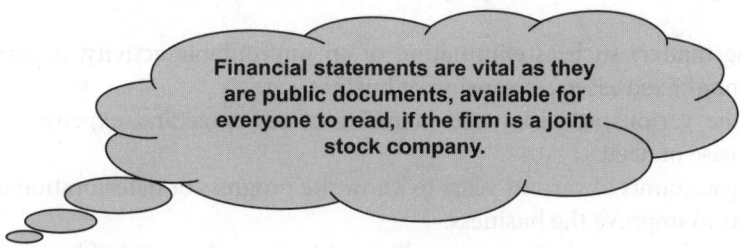

Financial statements are vital as they are public documents, available for everyone to read, if the firm is a joint stock company.

Accounting reports, normally in the form of accounting ratios, graphs, diagrams, fund flow statements are the additional information that are made available to the management for decision making.

Modern management wants the data in a simple form, easy to understand and ready to act, immediately. Even the modern management wants cooked food, just like our students!

OBJECTIVES OF BOOK KEEPING

The objectives of book keeping can be summarized under the following headings:

1. Main Objectives

The main objectives of book keeping are as follows:

a. To know the result of the business over a period of time. The result of a business may be profit or loss.
b. To know the financial position of business at a given point of time. This can be known by presenting all assets and liabilities in the form of a statement known as *balance sheet.*
c. To maintain all records for a given period to serve as permanent reference in future.
d. To know the amount that a business owes to others for having bought goods on credit basis.
e. To know the amount due to business by others on account of goods sold on credit basis.
f. To meet the provisions of various laws as in the case of joint stock companies that have to prepare accounts according to the Provisions of Companies Act 1956.

2. Other Objectives

The other objectives include the following:

a. To improve the business on the basis of past performance.
b. To know the composition of the capital in terms of size, the causes for change in the capital structure and whether the maximum use of the same is made.
c. To exercise control over expenses thereby to increase profitability of the business.
d. To know the position of cash so that in case of need, further amount can be arranged.
e. To meet the requirements of the tax and legal authorities.

ADVANTAGES OF BOOK KEEPING

Accounting information is useful to the following categories of people:

1. **To the management of a business**

a. In evaluating various alternative proposals so as to take maximum benefits from the best alternatives.
b. In deciding matters such as elimination of an unprofitable activity, department or product, replacement of fixed assets, expansion of business, etc.
c. Planning the various activities and planning of revenues and expenses, and arranging for finance in case of need.
d. Comparing accounts of various years to know the progress or deterioration of the business and take actions to improve the business.
e. Accounting information helps in providing evidence in the court of law in case of legal action taken by others.
f. Accounting information helps in assessing the income tax, sales tax and property tax of the business.

g. Accounting information constitutes one of the basis for borrowing loans from external sources.

h. It helps to detect errors and frauds that have taken place in the business.

2. **To the investors**

a. Types of property owned by the business.

b. Sources and amount of earnings made or losses incurred by the business.

c. Particulars such as stock position, debts owed, debts due, etc.

d. Whether the rate of earnings is high or low.

3. **To the employees:** It provides information to the employees so as to claim fair wages, bonuses and other welfare facilities.

4. **To the government**

a. The accounting information helps the government to extend subsidies and incentives, and other exemptions to certain types of businesses.

b. The industrial progress can be known by the government of the country. It can formulate industrial policies for further growth and development of industries.

c. It enables the government to assess the income from the industrial sector.

d. It helps in amending various laws or enacting laws governing the functioning of the business enterprises.

e. It helps the government in deciding the price control, wage fixation, excise duties, sales tax, etc.

5. **To the consumers:** Customers are not overcharged as the selling price is fixed on the total expenses incurred by adding a reasonable rate of profit.

6. **To the prospective investors:** It helps the prospective investors in choosing the right type of investment depending upon the profit earning capacity of the business enterprises and the profit earned during the past few years.

7. **To the creditors and suppliers:** Creditors can decide the solvency position of the business through the accounting information. Similarly, suppliers can also decide whether goods can be sold in future on a credit basis.

OBJECTIVES OF ACCOUNTING

The following are the objectives of financial accounting:

1. To Keep Systematic Records

Accounting is done to keep a systematic record of all the financial transactions. If they are not recorded, the transactions have to be remembered. It is not practically possible to remember and it is an unnecessary strain to the human brain.

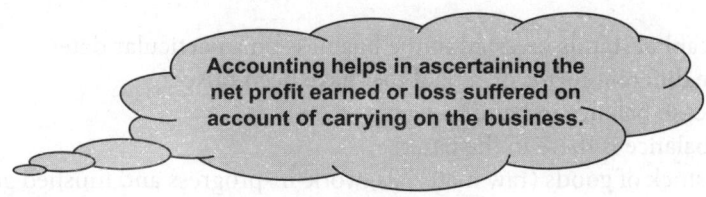

Accounting helps in ascertaining the net profit earned or loss suffered on account of carrying on the business.

2. To Ascertain the Results of Operations, That Is, Profit or Loss

Business is conducted for making profits. Every business is interested to know the operational results of the efforts made.

For the purpose, a statement called the *income statement* or the *profit and loss account* is prepared. In this account, the revenues resulting from the transactions of the period and the consequent expenses incurred are recorded. A comparison of the two shows whether there has been a profit or loss. If the revenue exceeds expenses, there is profit. On the other hand, if expenses exceed income, there is loss. It is necessary to know, periodically, to take corrective steps, in time. Accounting helps to provide the information about the operational results of the firm. In the absence of information, how can action be initiated at all?

The profit and loss statement is useful for the management, lenders, investors, the proprietor or the partners or the shareholders, tax authorities and workers, etc. For example, from its study, one can decide upon the possible courses of action such as increasing the scale of production, introducing a new product, a revision in the selling price or the advertising policy, etc. Lenders can know, from a study of it, how their amounts have been utilized. Investors may decide on its basis whether or not they should keep their money invested in the firm. Shareholders can evaluate the efficiency, success, etc., of the management.

3. To Ascertain the Financial Position of the Business

For a businessman, it is not sufficient to ascertain the profit or loss only. It is also necessary to know the financial health of the firm. For this purpose, a statement listing assets, liabilities and the owner's capital is prepared. Such a statement is called the *balance sheet*. Some people call it the *position statement*.

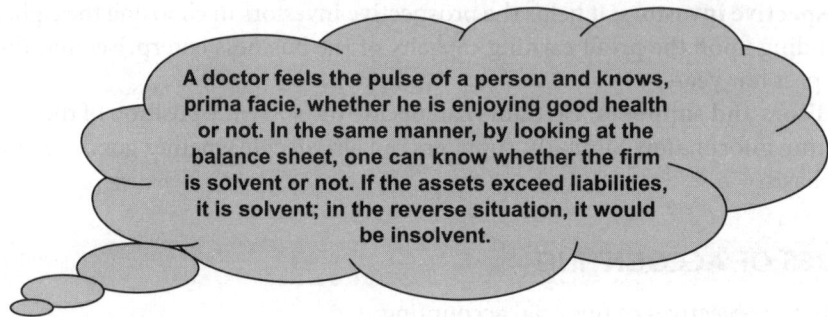

A doctor feels the pulse of a person and knows, prima facie, whether he is enjoying good health or not. In the same manner, by looking at the balance sheet, one can know whether the firm is solvent or not. If the assets exceed liabilities, it is solvent; in the reverse situation, it would be insolvent.

The balance sheet serves like a barometer for ascertaining the financial health of a business.

4. To Provide Control and Protect Business Assets

Accounting helps in knowing the information and exercising control over the properties of the business and their proper utilization. Accounting provides information to the manager or the proprietor regarding the following:

a. How much capital stands invested in the business on a particular date?
b. What are the different forms of capital that have been raised?
c. What is the cash balance in hand?
d. How much balance is there in the bank?
e. What is the stock of goods (raw materials, work-in-progress and finished goods) on hand?

    f.   How much money is receivable from the customers?

    g.   How much money is owed to the creditors?

    h.   How much money stands invested in the fixed assets?

The answers to the questions enable the firm to see that money is not kept idle or under utilized.

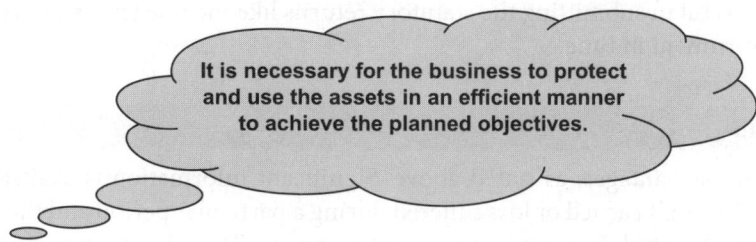

It is necessary for the business to protect and use the assets in an efficient manner to achieve the planned objectives.

It should be noted that the objectives stated above are those of financial accounting alone. The other branches of accounting—cost accounting and management accounting—have their own objectives that are of assistance to the management in the functions of planning, control and making decisions.

5. To Provide Information to the Tax Authorities

Almost everyone who has income, above the prescribed limit, is liable to pay tax, be it income tax or sales tax. Tax authorities require regular, accurate and prompt returns, otherwise there may be penalties. Financial accounting enables the firm to send the required returns, in time. In case, the tax authorities levy more tax, the business firm would be in a position to reduce the unnecessary tax liability, by showing the supporting accounting records.

6. To Facilitate Rational Decision Making

The management can delegate any function, but not decision making. Production, sales, purchase, finance, even research and development can be delegated.

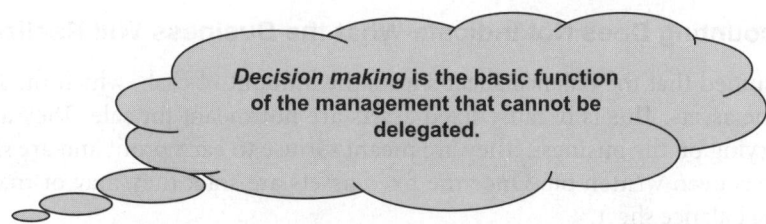

Decision making is the basic function of the management that cannot be delegated.

In the absence of accounts, there is no information about the past. In the absence of information, there is no basis for taking any decision and planning for the future.

ADVANTAGES OF ACCOUNTING

The following are the advantages of book keeping and accounting:

1.   A firm can know the exact profit or loss made by it in a particular period.

2.   The reasons leading to the profit or loss can also be ascertained.

3.   The financial position of the business concern can be assessed.

4. The firm can know the amount due by debtors and the amount due to the creditors.
5. The efficiency or performance of the department or section can be ascertained.
6. The approximate cost of production of goods manufactured can be known.
7. Based on the financial results, it can decide on the products to be manufactured, the activities to be continued and what activities to be dropped.
9. Accounting is useful in submitting the statutory returns like income tax, sales tax, commercial tax, etc., to the government in time.

LIMITATIONS

Accounting has many advantages, as stated above. Significant information is available from financial accounting such as the profit earned or loss suffered during a particular period and the financial position at the end of a specified period. But, it has some limitations too. These limitations must be kept in mind when the information provided by financial accounting is used. Some of the limitations arise from the fundamental principles, concepts and assumptions.

The limitations are as follows:

1. Profit Shown in Financial Accounting Is Not Fully Exact

Most of the transactions are recorded on the actual basis such as the sale or purchase or receipt and payment of cash. Some estimates have also to be made for ascertaining the profit or loss. The estimates may relate to useful life of an asset likely bad debts and the probable market price of the stock of goods.

In the absence of actual information, certain estimates have to be necessarily made in respect of the expenditures incurred for which bills have not, yet, been received, before the closure of the books of accounts, etc.

People are bound to have different opinions in respect of such things and the estimates, naturally, differ from one person to another. This may also lead to a different figure of profit or loss being shown by different people. Thus, the profit figure cannot be treated as exact.

2. Financial Accounting Does Not Indicate What the Business Will Realize, if Sold

It is not to be presumed that the balance sheet shows the amount of cash, which the firm may realize, by the sale of all the assets. This is because fixed assets are not meant for sale. They are purchased for the purpose of carrying on the business. They are meant for use to earn profit and are shown at cost less depreciation that has been written off. Once the fixed assets are sold, they may or may not realize the values shown in the balance sheet.

3. Financial Accounting Does Not Tell the Whole Story

It is known that in the books of accounts, only such transactions and events are recorded that can be expressed in terms of money. There are, however, many other important factors, which, though not recorded in the books of account, may make or mar the firm such as relationship with the workers, popularity of the goods produced, quality and calibre of the management, integrity, farsightedness, etc. They are invisible, in value, and play a significant role in the success or failure of the company. Unless such factors are kept in mind, it would be very difficult to assess the future of the firm.

4. Accounting Statements May Be Drawn up Differently

Due to the different methods being employed say for valuing the closing stock; it is possible to arrive at different figures of profits that give different financial pictures. There are different methods for providing depreciation, which is treated as expenditure in arriving at the profits of the company.

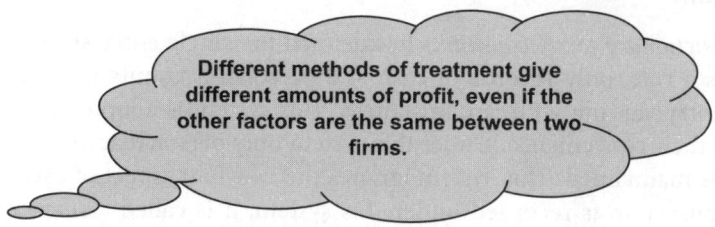

Different methods of treatment give different amounts of profit, even if the other factors are the same between two firms.

If one firm adopts the straight line method while the other adopts written down method for providing depreciation, the operational results of both the firms would be different, even though other factors are the same. Also, in spite of the various principles, there have been attempts in the past to show a false financial position. This is chiefly done by deliberately entering wrong figures so as to either inflate profits or to deflate them. One should therefore, always apply some checks to establish whether or not the financial statements can be taken to be reasonably correct. It is better to get them audited. Audited accounts present a reliable picture.

5. All Assets Are Not Shown in the Financial Statements

Human resources are an important factor for the success of the concern. Devotion, sincerity and integrity of the employees are very valuable for any firm.

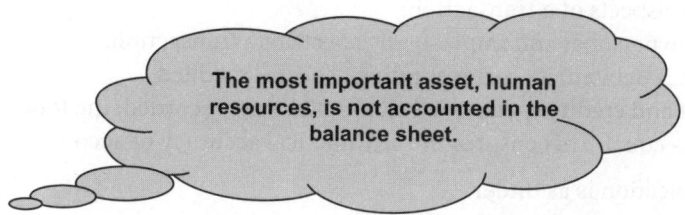

The most important asset, human resources, is not accounted in the balance sheet.

6. Manipulation

Accounting results are based on the information supplied to it. If the management is biased, it may feed manipulated information to prove its point of view. Accountants can show the results of business, as desired by the owners of the business. This may be done by omitting certain amounts, under estimating or over estimating the value of the assets. For example, if machinery is debited to the purchases accounts, profits of the business will be reduced. Accountants, at the instance of the management, may manipulate accounts.

7. Impact of Inflation

Due to inflation, many of the figures appearing in the financial statements are out of date.

SYSTEM OF BOOK KEEPING

Book keeping can be prepared and maintained under two systems. They are known as 1. single entry system; and 2. double entry system.

Single Entry System

Kohler in his book *Dictionary for Accountants* has defined the single entry system as a system of book keeping in which, as a rule, only records of cash and personal accounts are maintained. It is always incomplete double entry varying with circumstances. This system is adopted by small business enterprises for the sake of their convenience. Under this system only personal accounts of debtors and creditors, and cash book is maintained. This system ignores the two-fold aspect of each transaction. As only one aspect of the transaction is recorded under this system, it is called a *single entry system*. So this system is considered as an incomplete and unsatisfactory accounting system. Accurate information of the operations of the business is also lacking under this system.

Double Entry System

The double entry system of accounting is based upon the exchange value of money or money's worth. As such we find two aspects in every business transaction—the receiving aspect and the giving aspect. Under this system, every transaction is recorded twice, one on the debit side, i.e. the receiving, and the other on the credit side, i.e. the giving aspect. For example, when a businessman buys goods worth Rs 10 000, he exchanges money for the goods. Similarly, when he hires the services of a manager, he gives the money for having derived the service. Thus every transaction has two aspects—one receiving of benefit and another giving the benefit, and both these aspects are recorded under this system of book keeping. The features of a double entry system can be summarized under the following points:

1. It records the two aspects of a transaction.
2. It records both the personal and impersonal aspects of a transaction.
3. While one aspect is debited, its corresponding aspect is credited.
4. Because the debit and credit aspects of all transactions are recorded, the total of the debit and credit columns is always equal. This ensures the arithmetical accuracy of accounts.

Another type of classification is as under:

1. **Cash system:** It is used where only cash transactions take place and the object of concern is not to make profit.

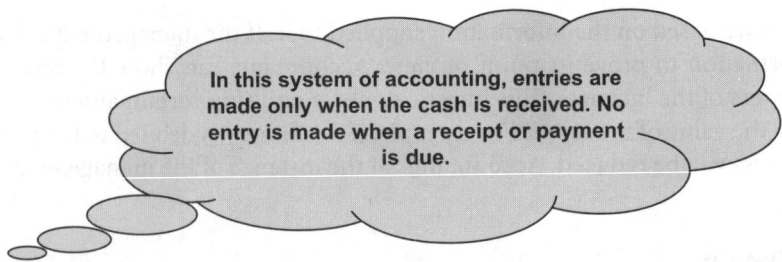

In this system of accounting, entries are made only when the cash is received. No entry is made when a receipt or payment is due.

In case of club, library, educational institute, religious trust, etc., the objective of the concern is not to make profits. Only a cash book is kept under this system.

Some professionals like doctors, lawyers and chartered accountants follow this system of accounting. It is interesting to know why these professionals follow it. With these professionals, there is no certainty of receipt. Once treatment is received and if the fee is not collected immediately, how many patients would remember the doctor (till the next ailment) to pay the fee, later? Even before the actual receipt, if the books of accounts show the fee amount as income, tax has to be paid on the income not received. If the fee is not received at all, tax would be paid on the income, not earned! One more point. Bad debts would be more, if the fee is not collected, immediately, after rendering the services. In these professions, it is better to recognize income only on actual cash receipt.

2. **Mercantile system of accounting:** In this system of accounting, the accounting entries are made when the payment or receipt is merely due. It is not necessary that the actual receipt or payment has to take place. For instance, when a service is received and the actual payment is not made, and books of accounts are to be closed for the yearend, the payment due is recognized and recorded for the services received. To illustrate, repairs have been made for machinery. The bill for the repairs is received, but not paid. Books of accounts are to be closed as the year has come to an end. The payment due for the services received is recorded, before the books are closed. In other words, repairs though not paid, are recognized as expense and a liability is created. Even if the bill is not received, repairs are estimated and the relative amount is provided as expense. Similarly, when a sale is made and the sale proceeds are not received, the amount due on the sale is recorded as an asset and the income is recognized. The idea is to record all the transactions as if they are completed in all aspects. The objective is to ascertain the correct profit position of the firm.

ADVANTAGES OF A DOUBLE ENTRY SYSTEM OF BOOK KEEPING

The advantages of a double entry system of book keeping are as follows:

1. It records all the transactions considering both the aspects of the transactions. Hence, it gives the complete information about the business.
2. By recording both the debit and credit aspects it ensures the mathematical accuracy or correct preparation of accounts.
3. It enables to prevent misappropriation and frauds involved in recording the transactions.
4. By recording all types of transactions it reveals the correct result of the business in a year.
5. By recording all assets, liabilities and capital it reveals the true financial position of the business.
6. The accounting system satisfies the external parties including the government, tax authorities, etc.

DISADVANTAGES

The disadvantages of the double entry system of book keeping are as follows:

1. It involves the maintenance of many books and ledgers that are very expensive.
2. It involves more of clerical labour.

DIFFERENCES BETWEEN BOOK KEEPING AND ACCOUNTING

Very often the terms book keeping and accounting are used interchangeably. However, these two concepts are not identical. They differ from each other in the following aspects:

	Book keeping	Accounting
1.	In book keeping, the financial transactions are recorded in a set of books.	In accounting the errors are detected and they are rectified through adjustments.
2.	It is the first stage of maintaining accounts and as such it cannot give any conclusions about the performance of a business.	It is second stage that gives useful information to draw conclusions about the performance of a business.
3.	Book keeping does not show the result and the financial position of the business.	Accounting shows the results and the financial position of the business.
4.	Book keeping is undertaken by clerks, who have less responsibility.	The accounting is undertaken by accountants, who have more responsibility.
5.	It is concerned with posting the entries in the ledgers.	It is concerned with checking whether posting is accurately done.
6.	It is concerned with the totalling of journal and ledgers and to find out the balances in all the accounts.	It is concerned with preparation of a trial balance with the help of balances of the ledger accounts.
7.	Book keeping does not require special knowledge and ability.	Accounting requires special knowledge and ability.

BRANCHES OF ACCOUNTING

There are three branches of accounting. They are as follows:

1. Financial Accounting

Financial accounting refers to a branch of accounting that deals with the financial transactions of a business. It is mainly concerned with the preparation of two important statements as follows:

    a.   Income statement or profit and loss account
    b.   Positional statement or balance sheet.

This information serves the needs of all those who are not directly associated with the management of business. Thus, financial accounts are concerned with external reporting as it provides information to external authorities. In this book the entire study relates to financial accounting. However, financial accounting suffers from certain limitations. These limitations are as follows:

    a.   It provides only past data.
    b.   It reveals only the overall results of the business.
    c.   It is static in nature.
    d.   There is a possibility of manipulation of financial account.
    e.   It fails to exercise control over resources of the business.
    f.   It fails to provide adequate data for managerial decision making.
    g.   It fails to provide adequate data for price fixation.
    h.   It does not use any technique to reduce the expenses that are responsible for the decrease in profit.

To overcome these disadvantages the other branches of accounting were evolved.

2. Cost Accounting

Kohler in his *Dictionary for Accountants* defines cost accounting as that 'branch of accounting dealing with the classification, recording, allocation, summarization and reporting of amount and prospective costs'. An analysis of this definition reveals the following aspects of cost accounting:

a. Classification, which refers to the grouping of like items of costs into a common group.
b. Recording, which refers to the posting of cost transactions into various ledgers maintained under the cost accounting system.
c. Allocation, which refers to the allotment of costs to various products or departments.
d. Summarization, which refers to the condensing of cost information for quick interpretation and for taking prompt action to improve the inefficiencies.
e. Reporting, this refers to furnishing of cost data on a regular basis so as to meet the requirements of the management.

3. Management Accounting

The terminology published by the Institute of Cost and Management Accounting, London, defined management accounting as 'the application of professional knowledge and skill in the preparation and presentation of accounting information in such a way as to assist management in the formulation of policies and in the planning and control of the operation of the undertaking. It is a branch of accounting that furnishes useful data in carrying out the various management functions such as planning, decision making and controlling the activities of a business enterprise'.

TERMINOLOGY OFTEN USED—SOME BASIC TERMS

The following terms are often used. For proper understanding, they are explained in an easy language.

1. Capital

Capital is the amount, initially, invested while commencing the business. Capital need not be in the form of cash, alone. Capital can be introduced in the form of goods or any type of assets. Even after the commencement of business, additional capital can be introduced. Additional capital is, normally, introduced for the purpose of expansion. Profit in the business is added to the capital. Loss made in the business is reduced from the capital. So, if the business is profitable, capital would be on the increase, year after year. However, drawings may be made in the course of business. If the concern is sustaining continuous losses, the capital would be on the decrease, year after year.

The term capital is defined as the excess of assets over liabilities. Suppose, assets are Rs 1 00 000 and liabilities are Rs 40 000, the capital is Rs 60 000 (Rs 1 00 000 – Rs 40 000).

$$\text{Capital} = \text{Assets} - \text{Liabilities}$$

Assuming, the firm has made a profit of Rs 20 000. After profits, the balance in the capital account is Rs 80 000 (Rs 60 000 + Rs 20 000).

2. Drawings

Drawings is the amount withdrawn from the business by the proprietor or the partner in a partnership firm. Drawings can be, again, cash or goods. Drawings are reduced from the capital amount. Drawings reduces the balance in the capital account.

3. Turnover

The total amount of sales during a particular period is called *turnover*. The turnover can be cash sales or credit sales or both.

4. Discount

The allowance or concession granted to a retailer by the wholesaler or dealer is called *discount*. It is of two types a. trade discount, and b. cash discount.

Trade discount

Trade discount is allowed by a dealer to the retailer or buyer to induce him to buy more from him. Normally, the retailer is in the habit of buying say 50 or 100 pieces at the most, at one time. If the normal price of goods is Rs 100, the dealer may offer the retailer or buyer 10% if he buys say 200 pieces, at one time. Here, the trade discount is offered to him to lure him to buy more, at one time. The buyer may be tempted to buy more to take advantage of the trade discount, though such huge quantity he may not require, at one time, generally.

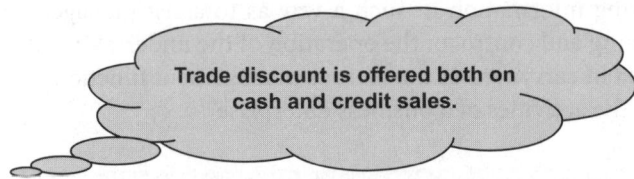

Trade discount is offered both on cash and credit sales.

Invoice shows the list price or retail price. Where trade discount is allowed, the same is also shown in the invoice. Trade discount is allowed as a fixed percent on the list price.

Net Price = List Price – Trade Discount

It is important to note that the net price is entered as sale value by the seller in the accounts. Equally, the net price is entered as purchase amount by the buyer in the accounts.

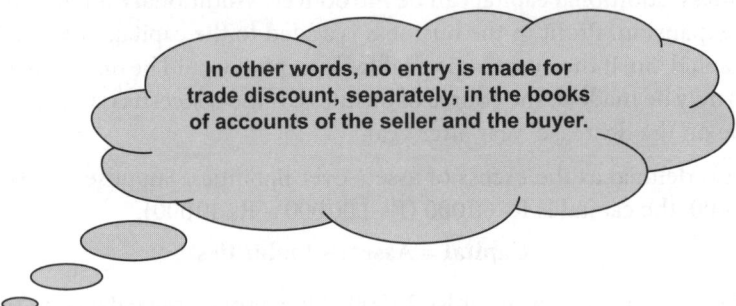

In other words, no entry is made for trade discount, separately, in the books of accounts of the seller and the buyer.

It has to be mentioned in the narration about the trade discount given on the list price.

Cash discount

Cash discount is allowed by the seller to encourage the customer to make early payment, before the credit period expires. Suppose, a dealer has made a credit sale, offering one month period of credit, the buyer has all the right to make the payment on the last date of the credit period allowed. So, the buyer can make the payment on the 30th day from the date of purchase. To induce the buyer to pay before the expiry of the credit period, the seller may offer him 1% cash discount, if the payment is made within 15 days from the date of sale. So, here, the buyer can enjoy a cash discount by paying the seller on the 15th day from the date of sale. If goods sold are worth Rs 500, the buyer can pay only Rs 495, after enjoying the cash discount of Rs 5.

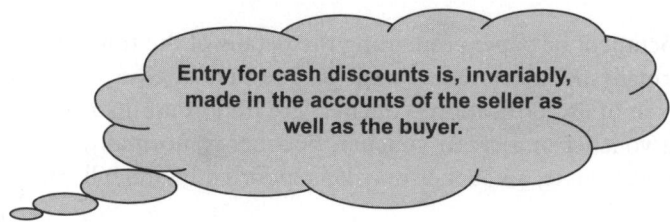

Entry for cash discounts is, invariably, made in the accounts of the seller as well as the buyer.

To the seller, it is discount allowed, while the same is discount received for the buyer. Cash discount comes into picture as and when the credit sales are made. There is no cash discount on cash purchases. Many students, it is observed during teaching, wrongly think that cash discount is allowed on cash sales. This is not the case.

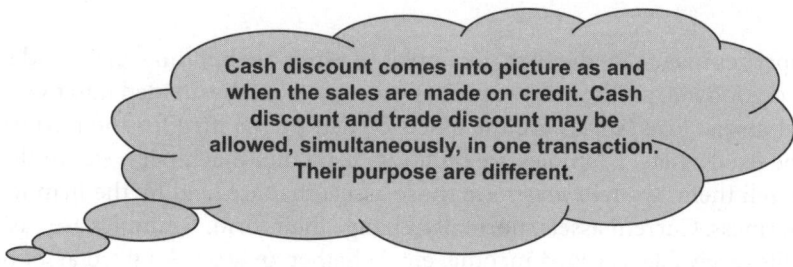

Cash discount comes into picture as and when the sales are made on credit. Cash discount and trade discount may be allowed, simultaneously, in one transaction. Their purpose are different.

5. Debtor or Book Debt

The person to whom the goods or services are sold on credit is called *debtor*. The amount due from the debtor is called *book debt*. Another name is *accounts receivable*.

6. Creditor

The person, from whom the goods or services are purchased on credit, is called the *creditor* till the payment due to him is made.

7. Bad Debts

The amount that cannot be recovered from a debtor is called a *bad debt*. Bad debts result in the reduction of profits of the firm. Bad debts are charged to the profit and loss account. In other words, bad debts are treated as an expenditure, as the amount due to be received would no longer be received.

8. Transaction

Transaction refers to the exchange of goods and services, big or small like purchase of machinery or pencil. The exchange of the dealing has to be expressed in terms of money. Transaction can be either for cash or on credit. If the payment is made immediate to the transaction, it is a *cash transaction*. If the payment is postponed or deferred for a future date, it is called a *credit transaction*.

9. Voucher

Voucher is a written document or paper containing the details of the transaction. The person who prepares the voucher, normally the accountant, signs it. The person who verifies or checks the transaction also signs it, in token of its verification. Vouchers are important instruments for future references. Voucher can be a debit voucher or a credit voucher. Voucher is, normally, accompanied by supporting documents as proof. For example, a voucher may be supported by the bill. Here, bill is the evidence of payment.

10. Equity

All claims against the assets of the firm are called as *equity*. The claim of the outsiders is called *creditor's equity* or *liabilities*. The claim of the proprietor is called *owner's equity* or *capital*.

11. Assets

Assets are the properties owned by the firm. Examples of assets are building, plant and machinery, debtors, bills receivable, goodwill, preliminary expenses, etc. Assets can be divided into two categories—fixed assets and current assets. *Fixed assets* are the assets owned by the firm for the purpose of conducting business, using the fixed assets. Examples are building, plant and machinery, etc. In the normal course, the firm does not sell them. *Current assets* are those assets that are held by the firm for the purpose of carrying on the business. Current assets, normally, change their form. Examples are cash, bank, finished goods, debtors, bills receivable, accrued income, etc. Whether an asset is a fixed asset or a current asset depends on the nature of the business that is carried on. Normally, a car is a fixed asset, say, to a wholesale cloth merchant. For a second hand car dealer, cars are meant for sale. So, they are current assets to him. It is necessary to know whether the asset is meant for sale or used for conducting the business. If the asset is meant for sale, it is a current asset. If the same asset is used in business to earn profits to that business, the same asset is a fixed asset.

12. Liabilities

Liabilities are the amounts that are payable. Advances or loans received have to be repaid. Till the date of repayment, they are liabilities. Goods or services when bought on credit are shown as creditors, which are also liabilities.

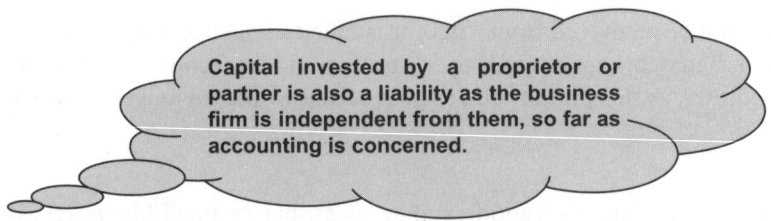

Capital invested by a proprietor or partner is also a liability as the business firm is independent from them, so far as accounting is concerned.

This is the reason why the capital is shown on the liability side in the balance sheet. Capital, loan, outstanding expenses and bills payable are some of the examples of liabilities.

13. Debit

The entry made on the debit side of the account is called *debit*. The abridged form is 'Dr'.

14. Credit

The entry made on the credit side of the account is called *credit*. The abridged form is 'Cr'.

15. Entry

The record made in the books of accounts in respect of a transaction or an event is called an *entry*.

16. Books of Account

The registers or books maintained by any business firm or institution for recording the business transactions are called *books of account*.

NEED OF ACCOUNTING PRINCIPLES

In the olden days, the common form of businesses had been sole proprietors or partnership firms. It was sufficient to have understood the accounting records. Their financial statements were personal and confidential and were not shared as public documents. In the case of joint stock companies, the financial statements are public documents. In modern days, joint stock companies, be it a private limited or a public limited, has become the normal form of business.

There are several parties interested in their financial statements ranging from shareholders, creditors, employees and the government to potential investors. If every business follows its own accounting practices, the final accounts may not be understandable to all such parties in a similar and uniform manner. Unless the accounting transactions are recorded according to certain definite principles, it becomes difficult to maintain uniformity of understanding. Hence, a definite need has been felt to follow uniform accounting principles from the stage of recording the transactions to the stage of preparing the financial statements.

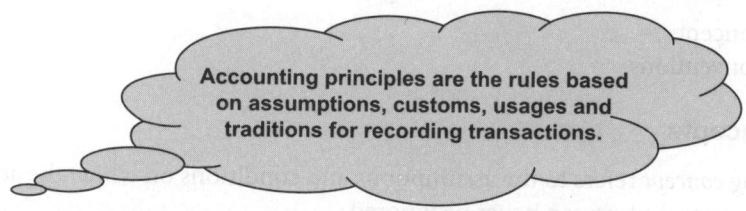

Accounting principles are the rules based on assumptions, customs, usages and traditions for recording transactions.

GENERALLY ACCEPTED ACCOUNTING PRINCIPLES

Transactions are recorded in accounts, following certain fundamentals, concepts and conventions, which are called as *Generally Accepted Accounting Principles*.

The chief objective behind the accounting principles is that the accounting statements should be both reliable and informative. This objective can be achieved when there is a certain common agreement and compliance about the accounting principles.

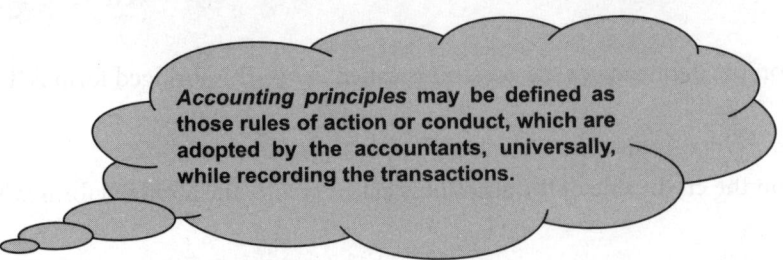

Accounting principles may be defined as those rules of action or conduct, which are adopted by the accountants, universally, while recording the transactions.

Every profession has developed its own jargon and vocabulary. Like all other professions, accounting has also developed its own concepts and conventions. These concepts and conventions have been evolved after centuries of experimentation and their use have, now, become accepted principles.

These principles are known as generally accepted accounting principles. Generally Accepted Accounting Principles (GAAP) may be defined as those rules of action or conduct that are derived from experience and practice, and when they prove useful, they are accepted as principles of accounting.

They are, however, not rigid. They are subject to change. They have evolved in order to deal with practical problems experienced by a preparer and a user rather than to reflect some theoretical ideal.

However, it should be mentioned, at the outset, that an application of many concepts does involve subjective judgment about the selection of methods available for choice, on the part of a person who is preparing the accounts. Depreciation can be provided on fixed assets, either on the basis of straight line method or written down method. Both the methods are recognized. If different methods are applied on the same financial data, it shows different financial results. This means that two different persons using the same source data could produce two entirely different sets of financial statements, with different operational results and financial position. There is no difference of opinion whether depreciation on fixed assets is to be provided or not. Here, the subjective judgment relates to the selection of method of depreciation and not providing for depreciation on the fixed assets.

According to the American Institute of Certified Public Accountants (AICPA), the principles that have substantial authoritative support become a part of the generally accepted accounting principles.

Accounting principles are divided into two categories:

1. Accounting concepts
2. Accounting conventions

Accounting Concepts

The term *accounting concept* refers to the assumptions and conditions on which the accounting is based. Basic assumptions of accounting can never be ignored.

The different accounting concepts are discussed under the following heads:

1. Separate entity concept

According to this concept, business is considered as a separate entity, distinct from the person who owns it. This concept is also known as *business entity concept*. In other words, business is treated as a unit or entity apart from its owner, creditors and others. It may appear strange that a person can sell goods for himself. However, it would make sense once it is understood that the private affairs of the proprietor are to be made separate from the business. Let us take a practical example in our daily life. If the daughters of the proprietor take away the garments they like from their father's boutique shop and these transactions

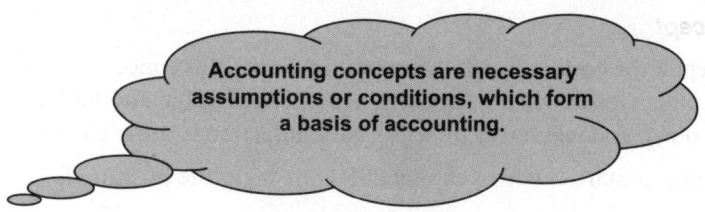

are not recorded with the reasoning that the business and proprietor are not different, what is the consequence? The year end accounts show shortage of stock as they are not recorded, at all. The manager of the shop may be made accountable for the shortages shown. Business may show reduced profits or even loss due to the fancy habits of the daughters of the proprietor. Remember, the proprietor has more than one daughter and their habits are fancier too! For this reason, capital invested by proprietor or partner of a business is shown as capital, under the liability side. Consumption of garments is treated as personal withdrawal and those transactions may be recorded, at best, at their cost price. In the absence of such treatment, profit would be low and thus, the financial position is distorted.

This concept has now been extended for various divisions of a firm in order to ascertain the results of each division, separately.

2. Money measurement concept

Accounting records only those transactions that can be expressed, in terms of money, though quantitative records are kept, additionally. If the events or transactions cannot be expressed in monetary value, however important they are, they are not recorded in accounts. Services of the finance manager and the chief executive officer are very valuable and due to their significant contribution, the firm might have turned from its earlier loss to become a profit-making firm. Their presence in the firm is valuable and their exit may be a serious bolt to its continued success. Though they are assets to the firm, in the real sense, but monetary measurement is not possible so the accounting books do not exhibit them. Qualities like workforce skill, morale, market leadership, brand recognition, quality of management, etc., cannot be quantified in monetary terms and so are not accounted for in the books of accounts.

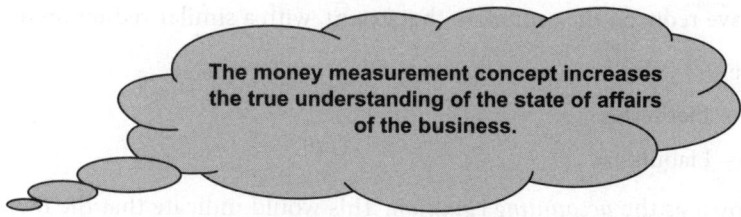

For example, if a business has a cash balance of Rs 20 000, plot of land 5000 square meters, two air-conditioners, 1000 kg of raw materials, 20 machines and 50 chairs and tables and so on, there is an absence of the money measurement concept. These different types of assets cannot be added to give useful information. One cannot assess the worth of the firm. But, if the same are expressed in terms of money in accounts—Rs 20 000 cash balance, Rs 2 lakh of plot, Rs 40 000 of air-conditioners, Rs 2 52 000 of raw materials, Rs 4 60 000 of machines and Rs 2 35 000 of furniture (chairs and tables)—it is possible to add them and use them for any comparison and for understanding the financial position of the firm. When the value of the assets is expressed in terms of money, precise information is available with intelligible financial picture. It is then more useful for any other purpose.

3. Dual aspect concept

The dual aspect concept is the basic concept of accounting. As per this concept, for every debit, there is a corresponding credit. In other words, when a transaction is recorded, debit amount has to be equal to the credit amount. This is also known as *double entry principle*. No transaction is complete without the double aspect.

When a new business is started with a capital of Rs one lakh, the position is expressed as under:

Capital (equities) = Cash (assets)

100 000 = 1 00 000

Equities are of two types. They are the owner's equity and the outsider's equity. Owner's equity (or capital) is the claim of the owners against the assets of the business. Outsider's equity (or liabilities) is the claim of the outsiders such as creditors, loan providers and debenture holders against the assets of the company.

Someone, either the owner or he outsider, has a claim against the assets of the business. So, the total value of the assets is equal to the total value of the capital and the liabilities.

Equities = Assets

Capital + Liabilities = Assets

In the above situation, if an outsider (creditor) has supplied machinery for Rs 50 000 on credit, the situation would appear as follows:

Capital Rs 1 00 000 + Creditors Rs 50 000 = Cash Rs 1 00 000 + Machinery Rs 50 000

If the business has acquired an asset, the source could be any one of the following:

1. New asset is in place of an asset given up; or
2. Liability has been created for its acquisition; or
3. There has been profit to purchase; or
4. The proprietor has contributed more capital to finance.

Similarly, if there is an increase in liability, there must have been an increase in the assets. Alternatively, loss would have reduced the capital, to that extent, with a similar reduction in assets.

Thus, at any time

Assets = Capital + Liabilities

Capital = Assets − Liabilities

The above is known as the *accounting equation*. This would indicate that the owner's share is always equal to the left out assets, after paying the outsiders.

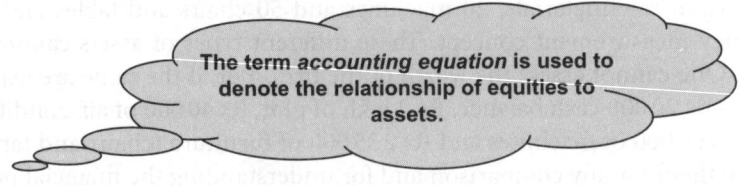

The term *accounting equation* is used to denote the relationship of equities to assets.

The above concept establishes the arithmetical accuracy of the accounts and enables the detection of errors in accounting and provides a strict watch on the activities of the employees.

4. Going concern concept

The underlying idea of this concept is that the business would continue for a fairly long period to come. The accounting transactions are recorded from this point of view. On account of this concept, the accountant does not take into account the market value of the fixed asset (forced value of asset, as if business would be liquidated) for preparing the balance sheet. Depreciation is charged on the original cost of the fixed assets on the basis of the expected lives, considering that the business would continue, in future, at least for a reasonable period, at least sufficient to the life of the assets. At the time of preparing the final accounts, we take into consideration the outstanding expenses and the prepaid expenses on the presumption that the business will continue in future too.

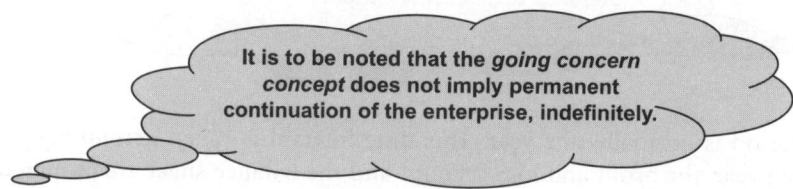

It is to be noted that the *going concern concept* does not imply permanent continuation of the enterprise, indefinitely.

It rather presumes that the enterprise will continue in operation long enough such that the cost of the fixed assets would be charged over the usual lives of the assets. Moreover, the concept applies to the business, as a whole. Even if a branch or a division of the business were closed, the ability of the business to continue would not be affected.

5. Cost concept

Cost concept is closely related to the going concern concept. Cost is the basis for all accounting in respect of fixed assets. If a plot of land is purchased at Rs 1 00 000, it has to be shown at that amount, even though the subsequent market price becomes Rs 1 50 000. In other words, the subsequent changes in the market prices are ignored. Even if the price falls to Rs 80 000, the fall is equally ignored in respect of fixed assets.

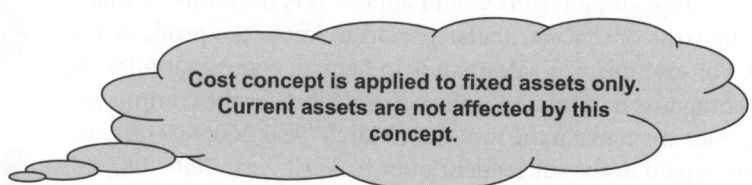

Cost concept is applied to fixed assets only. Current assets are not affected by this concept.

It does not mean that the fixed assets are valued at the historic cost, the original price at which they are acquired, for all the years. At the time of purchase, they are recorded at the original cost and later depreciation is charged, based on the original cost. For presentation in the balance sheet, depreciation is deducted from the original cost and the net value is shown on the assets side.

Thus, the fixed asset depreciates during the economic life of the asset and, finally, is sold as scrap.

However, cost concept is largely becoming irrelevant due to the continued inflationary tendencies. This is the growing reason for inflation accounting.

6. Accounting period concept

According to the going concern concept, every business would exist for a longer duration. That longer duration is divided into appropriate segments or periods for studying the results shown by the business for each period.

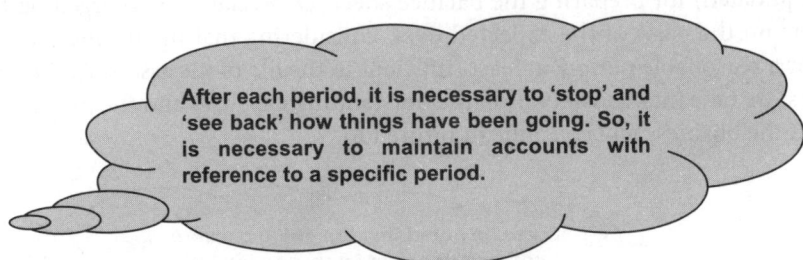

After each period, it is necessary to 'stop' and 'see back' how things have been going. So, it is necessary to maintain accounts with reference to a specific period.

The specific period is normally one year. This time interval is called *accounting period*. At the end of each accounting year, the profit and loss account and the balance sheet are prepared. Profit and loss accounts show the financial results, while the balance sheet shows the financial position. When making comparisons, the accounting period should be similar. In other words, the results of one year cannot be compared with the results of another period where the period has been only six months. Suitable adjustments are to be made before comparison of results of different periods for proper evaluation and conclusion.

7. Matching concept—periodic matching of costs and revenues concept

This concept is also known as *matching concept*. The main motto of every business is to make maximum profits, at the earliest. Hence, everyone tries to find the cost and revenue during a particular accounting period and compare the financial results with the preceding year to find out whether the business is progressing or going down. Unless the costs are associated properly with the revenues of the corresponding period, misleading results would appear. It is necessary to match the revenues with the costs of that particular period to know the profit or loss during that period. For example, if a salesman is to be paid commission for the sales made, for the comparison of sales, it is immaterial whether the commission is paid or not. If the sales are made in the month of March (year 2006–07) and the commission, in cash, is paid in the subsequent month, April (year 2007–08), it is necessary to make provisions for the commission in the year 2006–07 for proper comparison of the net profits.

Excess of accomplishments over efforts is called *profits*. On account of this concept, adjustments for prepaid expenses, outstanding expenses, accrued income and unearned income have to be made, while preparing the accounts, at the end of the year, for proper comparison of profits of different years.

Matching concept requires suitable adjustment for deferred expenditure. What is meant by deferred expenditure? *Deferred expenditure* is that amount of expenditure that has been incurred but not charged to profit and loss account and postponed for charging against a future period.

The argument is that the benefit of the expenditure would last over the future period. Deferred expenditure is amortized on the basis of this matching concept. Relying on this concept, the deferred expenditure would be charged against the future incomes of the business. The classical example is the research and development expenditure. Benefit of the R&D expenditure would last for a considerable period. So, it is appropriate to charge the expenditure over the future period, spread in instalments. The underlying idea is that the benefit of income should bear the share of expenditure as future income is the consequence of the expenditure incurred, in the past. So, the expenditure is matched to the income period.

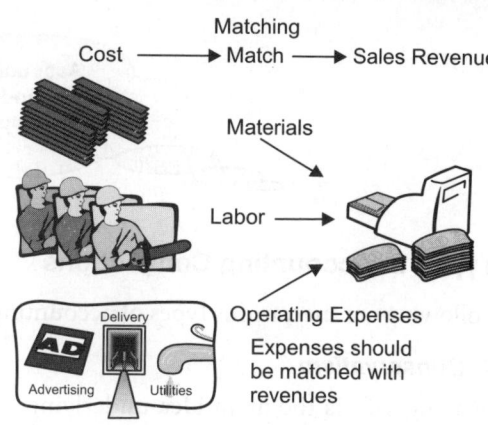

8. Realization concept

According to this concept, profit is recognized as and when realized. Now, the important issue is, what is the actual point of sale and when is profit deemed to have been accrued?

To make the point clear, let us take a small example. Radhi & Co. a boutique shop owner has placed an order with Dheera & Co. for the supply of readymade garments. On receiving the order, Dheera & Co. has purchased the required cloth, engaged labour and started manufacturing too.

As per the terms of the agreement, Dheera & Co. has received the advance too from Radhi & Co. before the execution of the order. Now, the issue is what is the actual time of sale? Is it at the time of receiving the order, time of receiving the advance, placing the order for the supply of cloth or engaging the labour? The actual time of sale is when the goods are delivered by Dheera & Co. to Radhi & Co. Till such time, no profit can be recognized.

However, there are two exceptions to the above rule as given below:

1. In case of a hire purchase sale, the ownership of goods passes from the seller to the buyer only when the last instalment is paid. This is from the legal view point. However, sales are presumed to have been made to the extent of the instalment received and the instalment outstanding (i.e. instalment is due, but not received). In other words, profit is recognized by the seller on the instalments received and due, without waiting for the receipt of the last instalment. The later is the accounting viewpoint for recognition of profits. The reason is simple. Otherwise, there would be no profit, till the last instalment period.
2. In case of contract accounts, the contractor may be liable to pay only when the whole work is completed as per the terms of the contract. However, profit is recognized on the completed work, certified by the proper agency, year after year, for the purpose of accounting.

ACCOUNTING CONVENTIONS

By accounting conventions, we mean the usages and customs of accounting. Customs or usage is a practice, which is in vogue, since long. We mostly use these conventions in preparing the final accounts, as they are useful for better understanding.

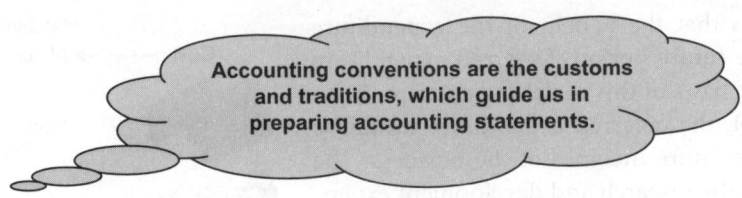

Accounting conventions are the customs and traditions, which guide us in preparing accounting statements.

Types of Accounting Conventions

Following are the various types of accounting conventions:

1. Conservatism

Conservatism

'Playing safe' is the main idea underlying this convention. In the initial stages of accounting, not actual profits, but, even anticipated profits were recorded. But, the anticipated profits did not materialize, thus the confidence in accounting was shaken.

In consequence, accounting has started to follow the rule 'anticipate no profit and provide for all possible losses'. For example, the closing stock is valued at cost price or market price, whichever is lower. The effect of the above is that in case the market price comes down, then the 'anticipated loss' is to be provided for. But, if the market price goes up, then the 'anticipated profits' is to be ignored. When the

When in doubt, choose the solution that will be least likely to overstate assets and income.

lower of the two is taken into account for valuation of the closing stock, no anticipated profit is booked, but all possible loss is taken care of.

This concept emphasizes that profits should never be overstated or anticipated. Basically, the concept says that whenever there are two equally acceptable methods, the one, which is more conservative, will be accepted. When a judgment is based on general estimates, if there is a dilemma as to which is correct, the most conservative estimate will be accepted. When there is a probability of getting profit or loss, profit will be ignored, but loss will be taken into account.

If an optimistic view of profits is taken, then dividends may be paid out of profits that have not been earned. Critics point out that conservation to an excess degree results in the creation of secret reserve. Even prudence does not justify the creation of secret reserves. Creation of secret reserves is not allowed. If allowed, it provides an opportunity to the management to cover their inefficiencies from the secret reserves so created. So, the creation of secret reserves is also quite contrary to the doctrine of disclosure. Conservatism concept needs to be applied with more caution so that operational results are not distorted. This concept, principally, applies to the current assets.

2. Consistency

Consistency is a fundamental assumption of accounting. It is presumed, unless otherwise stated that accounting practices are unchanged, year after year. If the accounting practices are changed, the fact is to be mentioned and its impact is to be quantified.

If the closing stock is valued at cost or market price, whichever is lower, the same principle is to be applied, every year. Similarly, if the fixed assets are depreciated according to the diminishing balance

method, the same method is to be consistently followed. Following diminishing balance method for one year and straight line method for the next year would distort the results. It does not mean ignoring change for betterment. The important point is that departure for better techniques are allowed, but the effect of change has to be arrived at and specified. Otherwise, comparison would give misleading results. So, if the valuation of the closing stock is changed from the earlier stated one (cost or market price, whichever is lower) to the valuation based on the market price alone, then in the year of change, the change has to be stated and, equally, the impact of change, in terms of profits, is to be quantified in notes to accounts.

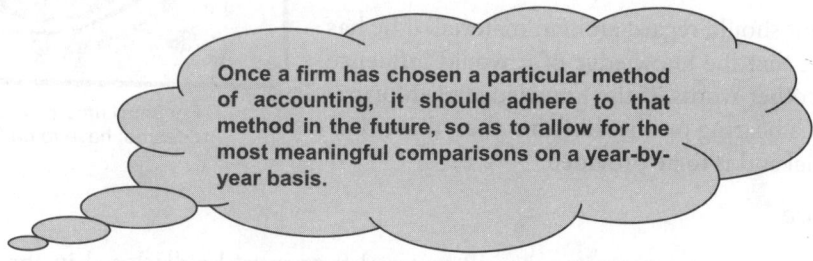

Once a firm has chosen a particular method of accounting, it should adhere to that method in the future, so as to allow for the most meaningful comparisons on a year-by-year basis.

However, consistency does not mean inflexibility. But when there are compelling reasons for a change, that change should be reported. If adoption of a change results in inflating or deflating the profit figures and financial position, compared to the previous year, a suitable note about the impact of change on operational results and financial position has to be given in the notes to the accounts of the financial statements.

3. Materiality

Materiality refers to the relative importance of an item or event. This convention emphasizes that all material facts should be recorded in accounting. The accountant should attach importance to material

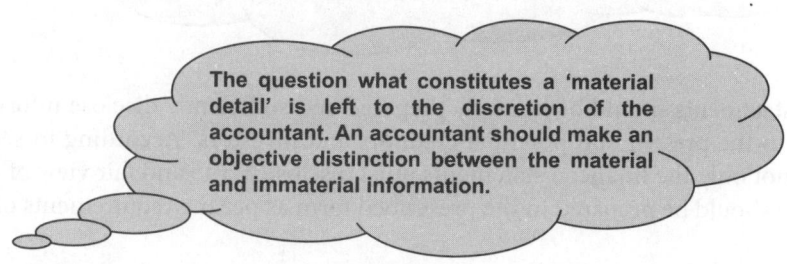

The question what constitutes a 'material detail' is left to the discretion of the accountant. An accountant should make an objective distinction between the material and immaterial information.

details and ignore insignificant details. While sending a statement of account to the debtor, the exact amount receivable from the concerned debtor is to be shown. However, when the summary of debtors is presented to the top management, the individual debtors are rounded to the nearest thousand. Here, the management is not interested to know the minute details to the last rupee. The Companies Act permits preparation of financial statements to the nearest rupee.

Similarly, even the income tax payable is rounded to the nearest rupee.

Materiality is defined in the International Accounting Standards Board's *Framework for the Preparation and Presentation of Financial Statements* in the following terms:

'Information is material, if its omission or misstatement could influence the economic decision taken on the basis of the financial statements. Materiality depends on the size of the item or error judged in the particular circumstances of its omission or misstatement. Thus, materiality provides a threshold or cut-off point rather than being a primary qualitative characteristic which information must have, if it is to be useful'.

Those who make accounting decisions continually confront the need to make judgments regarding materiality. Is this item large enough for users of the information to be influenced by it?

The accountant should regard an item material, if he has reason to believe that the knowledge of it would influence the decision. In other words, if the knowledge of information would have a bearing on the decision, then that information is material and is to be provided.

Materiality

For small amounts, GAAP does not have to be followed.

4. Full disclosure

The convention of *disclosure* means that all material facts must be disclosed in the financial statements. For example, in case of sundry debtors not only the total amount of sundry debtors should be disclosed, but also the amount of good and secured debtors, the amount of good, but unsecured debtors and amount of doubtful debts should be stated. Full disclosure does not mean disclosure of each and every piece of information.

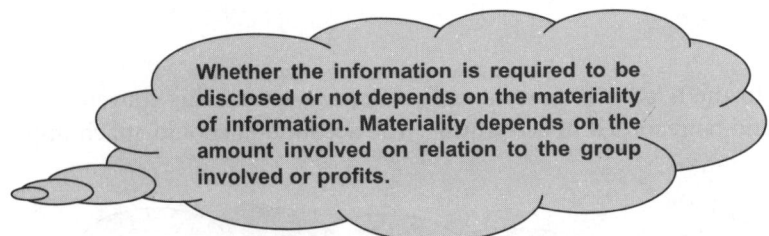

Whether the information is required to be disclosed or not depends on the materiality of information. Materiality depends on the amount involved on relation to the group involved or profits.

The financial statements should be honestly prepared and sufficiently disclose information that is of material interest to the present and potential creditors and investors. According to section 211 of the Companies Act, not only the financial statements must disclose a true and fair view of the affairs of the company, but also should be prepared in the prescribed form as per the requirements of the Act.

Full disclosure

- ✓ Financial Statements
- ✓ Balance Sheet
- ✓ Income Statement
- ✓ Retained Earnings Statement
- ✓ Ca\sh Flow Statement

Circumstances and events that make a difference to financial statement user's should be disclosed.

Appending notes to accounts and providing information in the notes is a sufficient disclosure of information. The notes to accounts are provided below the balance sheet. Generally, information relating to contingent liabilities, market value of investments and other information required to be disclosed is mentioned in notes and providing information in this manner is considered sufficient compliance of law.

THE ACCOUNTING CYCLE

In the process of preparing accounts of any organization, five important steps are involved. These steps are as follows:

1. Recording in the Memorandum Book or Waste Book

First of all, the various transactions are recorded in a book which is known as *memorandum book* or *waste book*. This book serves as a statistical book to know the number of transactions recorded in a crude form. This type of book is maintained by small traders such as petty shopkeepers.

2. Recording in the Journal

From the memorandum book the transactions are recorded into another book known as *journal*. In this book the transactions are recorded more systematically by following the principles of double entry system of book keeping. This facilitates chronological recording of all transactions without ignoring any transaction.

3. Recording in the Ledger

The third step involved in accounting system is to post all the entries from the journal into another book known as *ledger*. This book shows the balance in each account for a given period and facilitates in further processing of accounts.

4. Preparation of Trial Balance

All the balances that are shown by the various accounts in the ledger are then transferred to a statement known as *trial balance*. The preparation of a trial balance also ensures the arithmetical accuracy of the accounts prepared in various ledgers.

5. Preparation of Final Accounts

The last step involved in the preparation of accounts is to prepare the final accounts. The final accounts consist of the trading and profit and loss account, and a balance sheet. The trading account reveals the gross profit or gross loss of the business, whereas the profit and loss account reveals the net profit or net loss of the business. The balance sheet discloses the financial position of the business.

After the accounting period for which the accounting record is closed, again journal, ledger, trial balance and final accounts are prepared. Thus, the cyclic movement of the transactions through the books of accounting is a continuous process. It goes on for the whole period of business in yearly cycle. This cyclic movement is briefly called the *accounting cycle*.

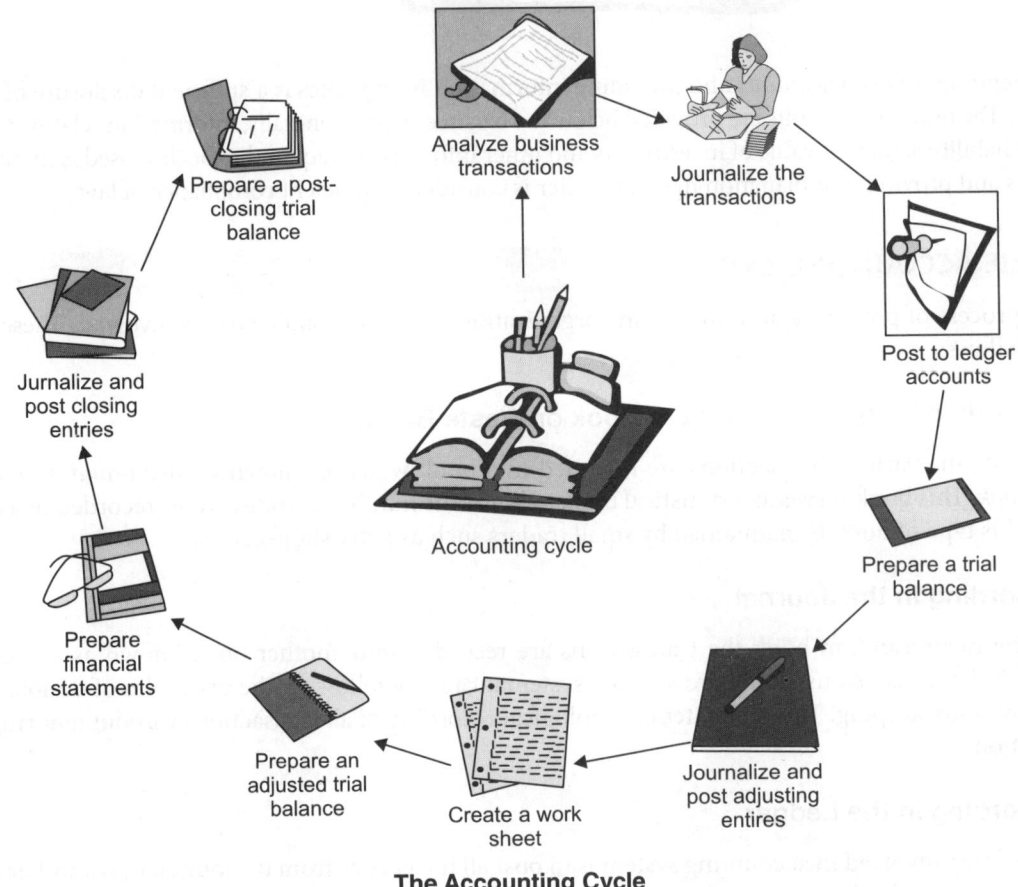

The Accounting Cycle

TYPES OF ACCOUNTS

For the purpose of recording business transactions, accounts are classified into three categories:

1. Personal Accounts

They are the accounts of persons with whom the business deals. They can be divided into three categories as follows:

a. Natural personal accounts

They are people who are created by God. For example, Suresh's account, Apeksha's Account and Kuhu's Account, etc.

b. Artificial personal accounts

These are artificial persons, i.e. any limited company, bank, insurance company, partnership firm, government body, cooperative society or a club.

c. Representative personal accounts

These accounts represent a certain person or a group of persons. For example, if rent is due to the landlord, the amount is credited to an outstanding rent account, not to the landlord account. Similarly, if the salary is due (amount not paid) to the employees and, in the meanwhile, books of accounts are closed, the amount due would be credited to the outstanding salaries account. Only one account is opened for all the employees, the 'outstanding salaries account'. If the individual employee accounts are to be opened, there would be many, resulting in unnecessary workload, as the purpose of the account is temporary to show a liability till the amount is paid. It is immaterial to whom the amount is payable as the nature of the account shows the total amount due to the employees for services rendered. The amount represents salary payable. All such accounts are termed as *representative personal accounts*.

The rule is:

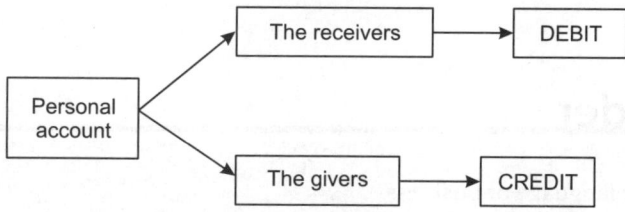

2. Real Accounts

Real accounts relate to the business property and such things that can be touched. Real accounts are further divided into two categories:

a. Tangible real accounts

Examples of such accounts are cash account, furniture account, building, stock account, etc. It is important to note that the bank account is a personal account, not the real account. Many think cash and bank represent property and the purpose of holding is the same so they think bank account is also a real account. Balance lying in the Bank of India is to be distinguished from the balance in Andhra Bank. Bank balance is related to the institution where it is kept.

b. Intangible real accounts

These accounts represent such things that cannot be touched, though they can be measured in terms of money. Examples are goodwill, patents and trademarks, etc.

The rule is:

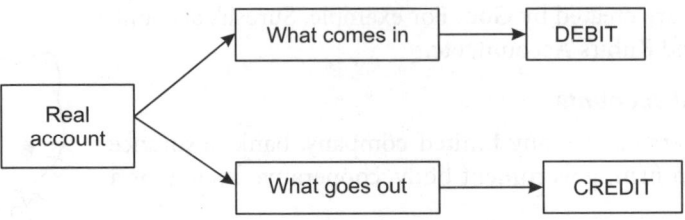

3. Nominal Accounts

Nominal accounts include all expenses, losses, incomes and gains. Examples of such accounts are rent, rates, lighting, insurance, salaries and dividends, etc.

The rule is

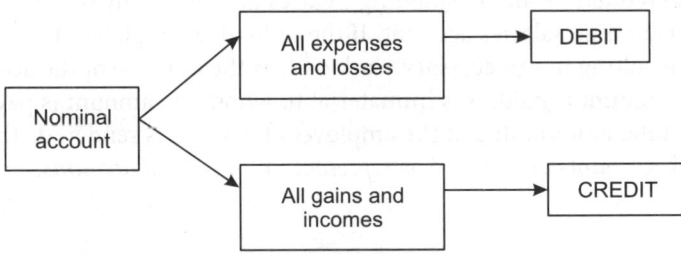

Points to Ponder

1. Accounting is the language of business.
2. Accounting is the art of recording, classifying and summarizing in a significant manner and in terms of money, transactions and events which are, in part, at least, of a financial character, and interpreting the results thereof.
3. Book keeping can be prepared and maintained under two systems.
   a. Single entry system; and
   b. double entry system.
4. There are three branches of accounting
   a. Financial accounting
   b. Cost accounting
   c. Management accounting
5. Accounting principles are divided into two categories:
   a. Accounting concepts
   b. Accounting conventions
6. Accounts are classified into three categories
   a. Personal accounts
   b. Real accounts
   c. Nominal accounts

Self-Assessment Exercises

1. Define the term *accounting*.
2. List the main objectives of accounting.
3. What information do the external and internal users need?
4. Name the various branches of accounting.
5. What is the basic accounting equation?
6. Name the various accounting concepts that are generally used.
7. What is GAAP?
8. What does the term *accounting concept* mean?
9. Define the term *accounting convention*.
10. What is the entity concept?
11. What is the matching concept? Why should a business firm follow this principle?
12. Enumerate the various accounting conventions.
13. What is the limitation of money measurement concept?
14. What are the various basis used for determining the period during which revenue is realized?
15. Define *accounting*. What are the main objectives of accounting?
16. What is meant by 'Accounting'? Describe the different branches of accounting.
17. Distinguish between:
    a. Financial accounting and management accounting
    b. Financial accounting and cost accounting
    c. Internal users and external users
18. Define the term *accounting concept*. How does it differ from *accounting convention*? Explain the entity concept and dual aspect concept.
19. Write short notes on:
    a. Matching concept
    b. Money measurement concept
    c. Cost concept
    d. Revenue realization concept
    e. Accounting period concept
20. Define the term *accounting convention*. Explain the following conventions:
    a. Materiality
    b. Conservation
    c. Consistency
21. Define personal account, real account and nominal account.
22. Explain the different types of accounts with examples.
23. Explain the rules of debit and credit.
24. Explain the meaning of an account. What are the different types of accounts? Explain each type of account with suitable examples.

The Journal

Chapter Overview

❖ Introduction
❖ Steps in journalizing
❖ Tips for journalizing
❖ Opening journal entry
❖ Compound journal entry

INTRODUCTION

The journal is a tabular record where business transactions are analysed in terms of debits and credits, and recorded in a chronological order prior to being transferred to the ledger accounts. Because the transactions are initially recorded in the journal, it is also referred to as the *book of original entry* or the *book of prime entry*.

> A journal is called a *book of original entry*
> (prime entry) because all business transactions
> are first recorded in the journal.

An entry made in the journal is called a *journal entry*. In every business, the accountant enters the business transactions datewise in a chronological order on the debit and the credit sides, along with the narration according to the principles of double entry. The process of recording transactions in the journal is called *journalizing*.

To record transactions, the first step is to record in a journal. The performa of journal is as under:

Year Date	Particulars	LF	Amount (Dr)	Amount (Cr)
	(Narration)			

Thus, a journal contains five columns as discussed below:

1. Date: The year, month and the date of transactions are written in the date column. The year is recorded at the top of the date column of each journal page. The month is written in the first line of the date column. Neither the month nor the year is repeated on the page unless the month or the year changes. The date of each transaction is recorded in the journal.

2. Particulars: The title of the account to be debited is listed at the left of the particulars column and traditionally recorded first. The abbreviation 'Dr' is written after the name of the account debited. The title of the account to be credited is listed on the line below the account debited and is indented, i.e. placed about an inch to the right of the date column.
The abbreviation 'To' is to be written before the name of the account credited.

The narration is written below the credited account. The narration should be as brief as possible and consistent with the disclosure of all the information necessary to understand the transaction being recorded. Thereafter, a line is drawn that signifies that the transaction is complete.

3. Ledger Folio or LF: LF stands for ledger folio. Every entry in the journal is to be posted in the ledger. After posting in the ledger, the folio number of the ledger is mentioned in the journal. Similarly, in the ledger, the folio of the journal is mentioned for cross-referencing to facilitate easy identification and verification.

4. Amount (Dr): This column shows the amount that is to be debited to the account shown against.

5. Amount (Cr): This column shows the amount that is to be credited to the account shown against.

The totals of the debit and credit columns are to be made on every page to confirm the correctness of the arithmetical accuracy as per the principle 'for every debit, there has to be a corresponding credit'. If the total of the debit and credit do not agree, it is an indication that the amounts have not been entered correctly in the journal. Adequate care is needed as the subsequent accounting work is dependent upon the correctness of the entries made in the journal.

STEPS IN JOURNALIZING

In order to journalize the transactions the following steps are to be adopted:

Step 1	:	Analysis of the transaction to identify whether the given transaction is cash or a credit transaction.
Step 2	:	Ascertaining the accounts involved in the transaction are worth recording.
Step 3	:	Ascertaining the nature of the accounts to which the accounts identified through step 2 belong, i.e. personal, real or nominal.
Step 4	:	Ascertaining which account is to be debited and which account is to be credited.
Step 5	:	Recording the transaction in a journal in the form of an entry.

TIPS FOR JOURNALIZING

Following are the tips for journalizing:

1. Clarity of Fundamentals

To pass the correct journal entries, we must ascertain answers to the following questions:
1. Which accounts would be affected by the transaction?
2. What is the nature (real, personal or nominal) of those affected accounts?
3. Which account will be debited or credited and why?

2. Open Purchase or Sales Account, Instead of Goods Account

Goods are purchased as well as sold. If we debit and credit the goods account, how do we know the amount of purchases and sales, separately? A consolidated goods account does not give the totals of the purchases and sales, separately. For this reason, the goods account is not opened, but the purchases and sales accounts (of goods) are to be opened, separately, to know the amount of purchases and sales. Similar is the case with the purchase returns and sales returns. Accounts are to be, separately, maintained to get the totals and details.

3. Which Account Is Relevant for Passing the Journal Entry?

Often, which account is to be debited or credited is a dilemma for the students. Some of the situations are explained below:

Treatment of cash or credit transactions
1. Sold goods for Rs 1000 cash.
2. Sold goods to Kina for Rs 1000 cash.
3. Sold goods for Rs 1000.
4. Sold goods for Rs1000 on credit to Kina.

In transactions, 1 and 2, the goods are sold for cash. It is immaterial to whom the goods are sold, when it is for cash. It is a cash transaction. The transactions are cash sales, and the sale proceeds have already been received in cash. Students do not have a problem in debiting the cash account but they often face the problem in identifying the account for crediting. Which account is to be credited, whether the sales or Kina's account? If Kina's account is credited, we have to pay the amount to her as she stands as our creditor in our accounting books. Kina is not to be paid any amount. So, there is no need, at all, to credit her account. Therefore, the sales account is to be credited.

In the transaction 3, it is not clear whether the goods have been sold for cash or credit. Needless to say, it is a cash sale. The reason is that if it was a credit sale, the party's name would have been given for recording recovery to debit her account. In transaction 4, no such confusion exists as it is a credit sale. So, in this case, Kina's account is to be debited and the sales account is to be credited. It is only when a credit sale is made that the question of recovering the amount comes up. Similar is the case with purchases. When a cash purchase is made, it is immaterial for us to know the person from whom the purchase has been made. But, when a credit purchase is made, the name of the party is required to credit the party's account. If the transaction does not mention, whether it is for cash or credit purchase and the party's name is not given, the transaction is treated as a cash purchase.

4. Treatment of Payment or Expenses

When a payment is made to a person, check whether the payment is made to him for any services, already, rendered. In such a case, the amount is to be debited to the concerned expense account. If the amount has been paid, in advance, the amount would be recovered, later, in case, the assured service is not received. So, the person to whom the payment is made is to be debited.

Let us explain.
1. Salary paid to Aadi Rs 1000
2. Payment made to Meet Rs 2000 as advance for repairs

In the first case, we debit the salary account, not Aadi's account. For the services rendered by Aadi, the payment is made and so Aadi does not repay the amount, later. So, Aadi's account is not to be debited, but the salary account.

In the second case, Meet has not rendered any service at the time of payment. So, the repairs account is not to be debited, but Meet's account is to be debited. If Meet does not undertake repairs, as agreed, we have to recover the amount from him. Till such time, he stands as a debtor in our accounting books. Once Meet repairs and submits the bill for Rs 2000, then the following entry is passed:

Repairs account .... Dr	2000	
To Meet		
(Being repairs incurred as per bill number ....dated .... submitted by Meet)		2000

5. Treatment of Income or Receipt

When any amount is received, check whether the amount received is for the services rendered. If the amount is for the services rendered to that extent, credit the amount to the service account, say the commission account. If the amount is received, without providing any service, the amount is to be credited to the party who has paid the amount as the amount is refundable or adjustable, depending on the extent of services rendered. Let us explain:
1. Commission received from Pankaj Ltd. Rs 1000
2. Advance for commission received from Nikhil Rs 5000

In the first case, commission has been received and the situation indicates that the services have been, already, provided. So, credit the commission account.

In the second case, services have not yet been provided, but the advance has been received. If we do not provide services, we have to refund the advance amount. If services provided are not to the extent of the advance, even the balance is to be refunded. So, here, we credit Nikhil's account with Rs 5000 for the advance received. If we render commission services for Rs 4000 and submit the bill, then we debit Nikhil's account and credit the commission account with Rs 4000. Nikhil's account now shows a credit balance of Rs 1000, indicating the balance amount payable to him.

6. Treatment of Trade Discount

When a seller gives a deduction on the list price, it is known as *trade discount*. Normally, a trade discount is given to encourage higher quantum of purchases. Suppose, the list price is Rs 1000 and a trade discount of 10% is offered, then the Net amount = List price –Trade discount, Rs 900 would be paid.

Suppose, goods are sold on credit to Rajvi for Rs 10 000 with a trade discount of 10%, sale is recorded with the net price, in the books of the seller:

Rajvi account ....Dr	9000	
To sales account		9000
(Being goods sold to Rajvi, on credit, after allowing a trade discount of 10% as per the invoice no. ... dated ....)		

7. Treatment of Cash Discount (Full Settlement)

To make prompt payment, a cash discount is normally allowed. At times, some reduction in the form of discount is allowed to receive the full and final settlement. To the person who allows the discount, it is expenditure. Discount is an income to the person getting it.

For example, Radhi has to pay Rs 10 000 to Dheera. The amount is pending for a long period. To encourage Radhi to make the full payment in one go, Dheera offers her Rs 500 as cash discount and Radhi makes the payment by cheque to take advantage of the discount. In the books of Radhi, the journal entry will be shown as under:

Dheera account .... Dr	10 000	
To discount received account		500
To bank account		9500
(Being cheque issued to Dheera, after deducting cash discount)		

8. Treatment of Personal Expenses of the Owner

Sometimes, the proprietor or a partner withdraws cash from the business for his personal use that is known as *drawings*. Some of the articles dealt in the business may also be consumed that is to be recorded as drawings, in kind. If the transaction is not recorded, there would be a shortage in stock and at the same time, profits would not be correct to the extent of the drawings made.

When daughters of a pharmacy store owner take some medicines, they are to be recorded. They would be treated as sales, but at cost price as goods are sold to the owner.

For example, Sardar & Co. runs a pharmacy store and her daughters Megha and Kinara takes medicines for their use worth Rs 2000. The normal profit is 20% on sales. The transaction is to be recorded as under:

Drawings account .... Dr	1600	
To sales account		1600
(Being the withdrawal of goods at cost price)		

Illustration: 1

Journalize the following transactions in the book of Shri Manyak, a chemist, who started business from 1 June 2009.

June 2009		Rs
1	Started business with cash	10 000
2	Buys medicines for cash	5000
3	Sold medicines to Megha	3000

June 2009		Rs
5	Sold medicines for cash	4000
6	Received cash from Megha	2500
13	Purchased furniture from Nikhil	2400
18	Paid for shop rent	500
20	Purchased medicines from Bhavik	3500
30	Cash paid to Bhavik	1000
30	Received commission	500

Solutions and notes:

1. All the transactions are to be analysed first, before journalizing them.
2. The terms *purchases* and *sales* are used for purchases of medicines and sales of medicines respectively.

ANALYSIS OF TRANSACITON

Date	Nature of transaction	Two accounts involved	Types of accounts	How each aspect is affected	Rule of entry	Accounts to be debited or credited	
2009	Step I	Step II	Step III	Step IV	Step V	Debit	Credit
June 1	Cash received from Mayank the proprietor as capital	Cash	Real	Cash comes in	Debit what comes in	Cash a/c	–
		Capital	Personal	Mayank is giver	Credit the giver	–	Capital a/c
June 2	Cash purchases of medicines	Goods	Real	Goods comes in	Debit what comes in	Goods a/c or purchases	–
		Cash	Real	Cash goes out	Credit what goes out	–	Cash a/c
June 3	Credit sale of medicines to Megha	Megha	Personal	Megha is receiver	Debit the receiver	Megha a/c	–
		Goods	Real	Goods goes out	Credit what goes out	–	Goods a/c or (sales)
June 5	Cash received for sale of	Cash	Real	Cash comes in	Debit what comes in	Cash a/c	–
		Goods	Real	Goods goes out	Credit what goes out	–	Goods a/c (sales)
June 6	Received cash from Megha on account	Cash	Real	Cash comes in	Debit what comes in	Cash a/c	–
		Megha	Personal	Megha is giver	Credit the giver	–	Megha
June 13	Credit purchase of furniture from Nikhil	Real	Furniture	Debit what comes in	Furniture comes in	Furniture a/c	
		Nikhil	Personal	Nikhil is giver	Credit the giver	–	Nikhil a/c
June 18	Cash paid for expenses rent	Rent	Nominal	Rent is expense	Debit the expense	Rent a/c	–
		Cash	Real	Cash goes out	Credit what goes out	–	Cash a/c
June 20	Credit purchase of medicines	Goods	Real	Good comes in	Debit what comes in	Goods a/c (purchases)	–

Date	Nature of transaction	Two accounts involved	Types of accounts	How each aspect is affected	Rule of entry	Accounts to be debited or credited	
	Medicines from Bhavik	Bhavik	Personal	Bhavik is giver	Credit the giver	–	Bhavik a/c
June 30	Cash paid to Bhavik on account	Bhavik	Personal	Bhavik is receiver	Debit the receiver	Bhavik	–
		Cash	Real	Cash goes out	Credit what goes out	–	Cash a/c
June 30	Cash received for commission	Cash	Real	Cash comes in	Debit what comes in	Cash a/c	–
		Commission	Nominal	Commission	Credit all income	–	Commission a/c

JOURNAL OF SHRI MAYANK

Date	Particulars	LF	Amount	Amount
2009				
June 1	Cash a/c	Dr	10000	
	To Mayank's capital a/c (Being cash invested to start business)			10000
June 2	Purchase a/c	Dr	5000	
	To cash a/c (Being cash purchases of medicines as per cash memo number)			5000
June 3	Megha	Dr	3000	
	To sales a/c (Being sale of medicine on credit)			3000
June 5	Cash a/c	Dr	4000	
	To sales a/c (Being cash sales of medicines)			
June 6	Cash a/c	Dr	2500	
	To Megha (Being cash received on account)			2500
June 13	Furniture a/c	Dr	2400	
	To Nikhil (Being furniture bought on credit)			2400
June 18	Rent a/c	Dr	500	
	To cash a/c (Being shop rent paid)			500
June 20	Purchase	Dr	3500	
	To Bhavik (Being medicines purchased on credit)			3500
June 30	Bhavik	Dr	1000	
	To cash a/c (Being cash paid on account)			1000
June 30	Cash a/c	Dr	500	
	To commission a/c (Being commission received)			500
	Grand Total		32400	32400

OPENING JOURNAL ENTRY

After the working of the firm in the previous year, a firm will start new books of accounts to the current year. The entries to start new books are known as *opening entries*. The method is to debit the opening balances of assets and to credit the opening balances of liabilities, including capital. If the amount of capital in the beginning is not known, it can be calculated by the formula:

Assets – Liabilities = Capital

Illustration: 2

A trader in pharmaceutical goods finds his state of affairs on 1 January 2009 as under:

Cash account Rs 5000; Sundry debtors Rs 2350; Building Rs 2500, Stock of medicines Rs 3750; Furniture Rs 850; His creditor amount to Rs 2100.

Date	Particulars	LF	Dr	Cr
2009				
Jan 1	Cash a/c Dr		5000	
	S. Debtors a/c Dr		2350	
	Building a/c Dr		2500	
	Stock a/c Dr		3750	
	Furniture a/c Dr		800	
	To creditors a/c			2100
	To capital a/c			12300
	(Balance brought forward from the previous year)			

Illustration: 3

Jitendra Yadav's statement of affairs on 1 July 2009 is as under:

Cash Rs 6000; Stock-in-trade Rs 3700; Debtors: Hari Rs 2000, Gajera Rs 9000; Amount due to Vijay Rs 500, Rumit Rs 1500.

His transactions for the month of July are given as under:

July 2009		Rs
1	Sold goods to Raju	2000
5	Sold goods to Pinal	1375
7	Bought goods from Krishna Medical Stores	4000
19	Purchased goods from Hiren for cash	2710
27	Cash sales	2000
29	Paid cash to Krishna Medical Stores	3000
30	Received from Raju	1500
	Received from Pinal	375
	Paid rent for the month	100
31	Purchased goods from Rumit	
	Trade discount 10%	1000
	Paid to Gajera Rs 475 in full settlement of his account	
	Paid salary	150

JOURNAL OF JITENDRA YADAV

Date	Particulars	LF	Debit (Rs)	Credit (Rs)
2009				
July 1	Cash a/c Dr		6000	
	Stock a/c Dr		3700	
	Hari Dr		2000	
	Gajera Dr		9000	
	To Gajera			500
	To Rumit			1500
	To capital a/c			18700
	(Being opening entry)			
July 1	Raju Dr		2000	
	To sales a/c			2000
	(Being goods sold on credit)			
July 5	Pinal Dr		1375	
	To sales a/c			1375
	(Being goods sold on credit)			
July 7	Purchases a/c Dr		4000	
	To Krishna Medical Stores			4000
	(Being goods purchased on credit)			
July 19	Purchases a/c Dr		2710	
	To cash a/c			2710
	(Being cash purchases)			
July 27	Cash a/c Dr		2000	
	To sales a/c			2000
	(Being cash sales)			
July 29	Krishna Medical Stores Dr		30000	
	To cash a/c			3000
	(Being cash paid on account)			
July 30	Cash a/c Dr		1875	
	To Raju			1500
	To Pinal			375
	(Being cash received on account)			
July 31	Rent a/c Dr		100	
	To cash a/c			100
	(Being rent paid)			
July 31	Purchases a/c Dr		900	
	To Rumit			900
	(Being goods purchased on credit)			
July 31	Gajera Dr		500	
	To cash a/c			475
	To discount a/c			25
	(Being cash paid and discount received)			
July 31	Salaries a/c Dr		150	
	To cash a/c			150
	(Being salary paid)			
	Grand total	Rs	39310	39310

COMPOUND JOURNAL ENTRY

When two or more transactions of a similar nature are to be debited or credited, one entry for the same is to be recorded instead of separate entries, provided that the transaction is for the same day. Similar transaction means, the transaction where one common account is either to be debited or credited. The usual entry is made for discount allowed as well as discount received.

Illustration: 4

Journalize the following transactions

2009	
Jan 1	Started business with Rs 15 000 paid into bank Rs 5000
Jan 3	Bought furniture for Rs 900
Jan 4	Purchased good from Ankit & Co. for Rs 4000 for cash
Jan 5	Sold goods for Rs 1700
Jan 7	Paid telephone rent for the year Rs 400
Jan 8	Purchased goods for Rs 1000 from Lal & Co.
Jan 10	Paid Rs 100 for advertisement by cheque
Jan 11	Bought one typewriter for Rs 750 from Universal Typewriting Co. on credit
Jan 12	Sold goods to Goti & Co. for Rs 2900
Jan 13	Withdrawn Rs 350 from the bank for private use
Jan 16	Sold goods to Jalaram & Co. for Rs 650 for cash
Jan 25	Received cash from Goti & Co .Rs 2850 discount allowed Rs 50
Jan 26	Paid to the bank Rs 2500
Jan 31	Issued cheque for Rs 300 in favour of the landlord for rent of January
Jan 31	Paid salaries to staff Rs 600
Jan 31	Issued cheque for Rs 950 in favour of Lal & Co. in full settlement of their account

JOURNAL

Date	Particulars	LF	Debit (Rs)	Credit (Rs)
2009				
Jan 1	Cash a/c Dr		10 000	
	Bank a/c Dr		5000	
	To capital a/c			15 000
	(Being business started with cash Rs 10 000 and with bank Rs 5000)			
Jan 3	Furniture a/c Dr		900	
	To cash a/c			900
	(Being furniture purchased for cash)			
Jan 4	Purchase a/c Dr		4000	
	To cash a/c			4000
	(Being medicines purchased for cash)			

Date	Particulars	LF	Debit (Rs)	Credit (Rs)
Jan 5	Cash a/c Dr		1700	
	To sales a/c (Being cash sales)			1700
Jan 7	Telephone rent a/c Dr		400	
	To cash a/c (Being telephone rent paid)			400
Jan 8	Purchases a/c Dr		1000	
	To Lal & Co. (Being goods purchased on credit from Lal & Co.)			1000
Jan 10	Advertisement a/c Dr		100	
	To bank a/c (Being advertisement expenses paid by cheque)			100
Jan 11	Typewriter a/c Dr		750	
	To Universal Typewriter Co. (Being typewriter purchased on credit)			750
Jan 12	Goti & Co. Dr		2900	
	To sales a/c (Being goods sold to Goti & Co. on credit)			2900
Jan 14	Drawing a/c Dr		350	
	To bank a/c (Being withdrawn from bank for private use)			350
Jan 16	Cash a/c Dr		650	
	To sales a/c (Being goods sold for cash)			650
Jan 25	Cash a/c Dr		2850	
	Discount a/c Dr		50	
	To Goti & Co. (Being cash received and discount allowed)			2900
Jan 26	Bank a/c Dr		2500	
	To cash a/c (Being cash deposited with the bank)			2500
Jan 31	Rent a/c Dr		300	
	To bank a/c (Being rent paid to landlord by cheque)			300
Jan 31	Salaries a/c Dr		600	
	To cash a/c (Being salary paid to staff in cash)			600
Jan 31	Goti & Co. Dr		1000	
	To bank a/c To discount a/c (Being amount paid by cheque and discount)			950 50
	Grand total		35 050	35 050

Points to Ponder

1. A journal is called a book of original entry (prime entry) because all business transactions are first recorded in the journal.
2. A journal contains five columns
   a. Date
   b. Particulars
   c. Ledger Folio or LF
   d. Amount (Dr)
   6. Amount (Cr)
3. The entries to start new books are known as opening entries.

Self-Assessment Exercises

1. What is general journal?
2. What is special journal?
3. Name the various types of special journal.
4. What is the purpose of providing LF in the journal
5. What are books of original entry? Why is a journal subdivided? Give a specimen of general journal with four imaginary entries.
6. What is a special journal? Give a specimen of such a journal showing at least five entries.

EXERCISE 1

Enter the following transactions in the journal of M/s Bhavik Medical Hall for the month of July 2009.

2009			Rs
July	1	Mr Bhavik Kumar started his business with a capital	100 000
	1	Bought furniture for cash from Modern Furniture	5000
	2	Purchase good for cash	25 000
	3	Purchase goods from Sunil on credit	30 000
	5	Sold goods to Hetal on credit	8000
	6	Goods sold	5600
	8	Cash sales to Jinal Solanki	6300
	9	Goods sold for cash	4700
	11	Cash paid to Ram Lal	5200
	13	Paid trade expenses	25
	14	Paid advertisement expenses	400
	15	Received interest from Khodidas	150

2009			Rs
	18	Deposited cash into bank	1000
	21	Paid rent	450
	23	Paid insurance premium	650
	24	Withdrawal of cash for personal expenses by the owner	2000
	26	Paid to meet miscellaneous expenses	250
	29	Investment of cash in business by Bhavik Kumar	30000
	31	Paid salary to staff	2400

EXERCISE 2

Mr Rajat Patel, a retail pharmacist, has the following assets and liabilities on 1 April 2004.

Assets: Cash Rs 9000; Stock in trade Rs 50000; Furniture Rs 4500; Due from Rambhai Rs 5000, Due from Bhuptani Rs 4000.

Liabilities: Amount due to Hariharan Rs 2000 and Sukhvinder Rs 1600; Loan from bank Rs 5000.

Following transactions took place during the month of April 2004.

2004			Rs
April	1	Sold goods to Vishal	4000
	3	Sold goods to Mukeshbhai	1340
	9	Bought goods for cash from Vaibhav Medical Hall	7000
	14	Purchase goods from Dharmesh on credit	2190
	19	Cash sales	4320
	20	Paid cash to Royal Chemist	6400
	29	Received from Vishal	4000
		Received from Mukeshbhai	1340
		Paid money to Dharmesh	2190
	30	Paid rent for the month	2100
		Purchased goods from Hariharan with trade discount 10%	6000
		Paid to Hariharan in full settlement of his account	4000
		Paid salary to staff	10000

EXERCISE 3

Enter the following entries in the journal of M/s Dipti Pharmaceuticals for the month of March 2006.

2006			Rs
March	1	Mrs Dipti started her business with a capital in cash	200000
		Paid in the bank	5000
	2	Bought raw materials for cash from M/s Dholakia & Co.	40000
	3	Cash sales to Dinesh	70000
	6	Paid salary to staff	20000
	7	Purchase goods from Sitaram & Co. for cash	4000

2006				Rs
	8	Paid telephone rent		1200
	10	Purchase goods from M/s Tanna traders		1000
	11	Paid cheque for advertisement		1500
	12	Sold goods to M/s Chand & Co. on credit		2900
	14	Withdrawal of money from bank for private use		1300
	18	Paid in to bank		3200
	23	Received cash from Patel & Co.		4200
		Discount allowed		140
	27	Paid in to bank		7600
	31	Issued cheque in favour of landlord for rent		2500
		Issued cheque in favour of Patel & Co.		4600
		Sold goods to Sharma & Co. on credit		2600

Cash Book

INTRODUCTION

On your birthday you received a gift of cash from your parents, grand parents and some of your relatives. In the meantime, you got back some money that you had lent to your friend as loan. You spent this money in buying books and clothes. You went to see movies with your friends and purchased some toys for your niece. As per habit, you noted down all receipts and payments in your notebook. At the end of the month, you calculated the balance of cash in hand and tallied it with the actual cash balance with you. You may maintain a separate book to record these items of receipts and payments. This book is known as *cash book*.

Cash book is a book in which all transactions relating to cash receipts and cash payments are recorded. It starts with the cash or bank balance at the beginning of a period. Generally, it is made on a monthly basis. This is a very popular book and is maintained by all organizations—big or small, profit or not-for-profit. It serves the purpose of both a journal, as well as, the ledger (cash) account. It is also called the *book of original entry*. When a cash book is maintained, the transactions of cash are not recorded in the journal and no separate account for cash or bank is required in the ledger.

OBJECTIVES OF CASH BOOK

The cash book serves three important purposes. They are as follows:

1. To know the total cash received and the total cash paid during a given period of time
2. To know the cash balance for a given period of time
3. To know whether the cash balance on hand and at the bank are correct

TYPES OF CASH BOOKS

Following are the four types of cash books:

1. Single-column cash book or simple cash book
2. Two-columnar cash book
3. Three-columnar cash book
4. Petty cash book

Single-Column Cash Book

A cash book that contains only one column of amount is called a *single-column* or a *simple cash book*. A cash account is divided into two sections by a central vertical line. The debit entries are made on the left-hand side and the credit entries are made on the right-hand side. The abbreviation 'Dr' and 'Cr' are written at the top-left and right-hand corner respectively. The word 'To' is written before debit entries and word 'By' is written before credit entries. The format of a single-column cash book is given below.

Dr								Cr
Date	Particulars	LF	Amount	Date	Particulars	LF	Amount

Columnwise explanation is as follows:

Date: In the date column, the year, month and date of transactions are recorded in a chronological order.

Particulars: In the particulars column, the name of the account in respect of which cash has been received or payment has been made is written. The account pertaining to the receipts of cash is recorded on the debit side and those pertaining to cash payments on the credit side.

Ledger Folio: The ledger folio column records the page number of the ledger book on which the relevant account is prepared.

Amount: The amount column records the amount received on the debit side and the cash paid on its credit side.

Illustration: 1

Prepare a simple cash book from the following transactions.

2005		Rs
May 1	Cash in hand	10 000
May 2	Purchased machinery	4000
May 2	Purchased furniture	1000
May 2	Purchased building	4000
May 6	Purchased goods for cash	1000
May 15	Goods sold for cash	1800
May 23	Paid salaries	300
May 23	Paid wages	200
May 23	Paid to Harish	500
May 27	Received form Ashok Kumar	1000

CASH BOOK

Dr								Cr
Date	Particulars	LF	Amount (Rs)	Date	Particulars	LF	Amount (Rs)	
2006				2006				
May 1	To balance c/d		10 000	May 2	By machinery a/c		4000	
May 15	To sales a/c		1800	May 2	By furniture a/c		1000	
May 27	To Ashok Kumar		1000	May 2	By building a/c		4000	
				May 6	By purchases a/c		1000	
				May 23	By salaries a/c		300	
				May 23	By wages a/c		200	
				May 23	By Harish		500	
				May 31	By balance c/d		1800	
			12 800				12 800	
June 1	To balance c/d		1800					

Two-Columnar Cash Book

There is a great importance of discount in cash transactions. If a businessman receives or allows cash discount, then the two-columnar cash book is needed to record it. In this type of cash book, the following two columns are provided on each side of the cash book:

1. The first column is for discount, which is a nominal account
2. The second column is for cash, which is a real account

The payment of cash discount is posted in the discount column on the debit side and the receipt of cash discount is shown on the credit side of the discount column in the cash book. The discount columns on each side are totalled without balancing.

The cash columns are recorded in the same way as in the simple cash book. The balance of the cash columns is ascertained in the same manner as the balancing of simple cash book.

The format of a two-columnar cash book is given below.

Dr									Cr
Date	Particulars	LF	Discount	Cash	Date	Particulars	LF	Discount	Cash

Illustration: 2

Enter the following transactions (cash and discount columns).

2001		Rs
July 1	Cash in hand	2000
July 5	Paid to Gohil	300
	Discount allowed by him	10
July 8	Cash purchases	400
July 10	Received from B.K. Gadhvi and Sons	980
	Discount allowed	20
July 16	Cash sales	900
July 21	Paid to Chavda & Sons	395
	Discount allowed by them	5
July 26	Paid wages	50
July 31	Paid to Narayan & Bros in full settlement of their account which shows a credit balance of Rs 420	395

CASH BOOK

Dr									Cr
Date	Particulars	LF	Discount (Rs)	Cash (Rs)	Date	Particulars	LF	Discount (Rs)	Cash (Rs)
2001					2001				
July 1	To balance b/d			2000	July 5	By Gohil		10	300
July 10	To B.K. Gadhvi and Sons		20	980	July 8	By purchases a/c			400
July 16	To sales a/c			900	July 21	By Chavda & Sons		5	395
					July 26	By wages			50
					July 31	By Narayan & Bros		25	395
					July 31	By balance c/d			2340
			20	3880				40	3880
Aug 1	By balance b/d			2340					

Three-Columnar Cash Book

The three-columnar cash book is a popular form of cash book. In this type of cash book, the following three columns are provided on each side:

1. The first column is for discount, which is a nominal account
2. The second column is for cash, which is a real account
3. The third column is for bank, which is a personal account

The following procedure is adopted while posting a transaction in the three-columnar cash book:

1. When the amount is received in cash, it is recorded on the debit side in the cash column and the discount allowed to the party, concerned in this connection, is recorded in the discount column of the debit side.
2. All cash payments are to be recorded on the credit side in the cash column and the discount received from the party, concerned in this respect, shall be recorded on the credit side of discount column.
3. When cash is received and then sent to the bank for deposit, then the bank account is debited on the debit side, and the cash account is credited on the credit side. Similarly, when cash is withdrawn from the bank, for office use, the cash account is debited, on the debit side and the bank account is credited on the credit side. Such entries are called *contra entries* and the letter 'C' is recorded in the ledger folio column.
4. When a cheque is received from the customer, it should be entered in the bank column straightaway because cheques will have to be sent to the bank. In case the cheque is received but the same has been sent to the bank for deposit on a later date, then it is presumed that it is kept in the cash box and treated as cash.
5. When a cheque is endorsed to a person, then the entry will be just like a cash payment.
6. When a crossed cheque is received, it is recorded on the debit side in the bank column, but when a bearer or other cheque is received, it is recorded on the debit side in the cash column.
7. When a bank charges commission or a collection charge for service rendered with due intimation, the customer should enter this item on the credit side of the cash column. If these changes are made by the bank without any intimation then these items should be recorded on the credit side in the bank column.

The format of a three-columnar cash book is given below.

Dr											Cr
Date	Particulars	LF	Discount	Cash	Bank	Date	Particulars	LF	Discount	Cash	Bank

Illustration: 3

Enter the following transactions in three-columnar cash book.

2009	
April 1	Balance of cash in hand Rs 4000 and in the bank Rs 10 000
April 2	Received cash from Manhar Rs 1000 and allowed him discount Rs 30
April 3	Paid into the bank Rs 2000
April 4	Paid to Dinesh & Co. by cheque Rs 320 in full settlement of their account for Rs 350
April 5	Received from cash sale, cash Rs 275 and cheque Rs 225
April 6	Paid for cash purchases by cheque Rs 645
April 7	Paid by cheque to Radhika & Co. Rs 725 in full settlement of Rs 800
April 8	Drew for office use Rs 900 and Rs 100 for personal use
April 11	Paid cash for advertisement Rs 45
April 15	Drew cheque of Rs 500 for personal use
April 19	Paid salaries to staff by cheque Rs 1250
April 20	Paid life insurance premium Rs 300
April 23	Paid rent Rs 400
April 26	Purchased, by cheque, office furniture worth Rs 375
April 30	Received a cheque of Rs 580 from Mayur & Co. in full settlement of their account for Rs 620

CASH BOOK

Dr											Cr
Date	Particulars	LF	Discount (Rs)	Cash (Rs)	Bank (Rs)	Date	Particulars	LF	Discount (Rs)	Cash (Rs)	Bank (Rs)
2009						2009					
April 1	To balance b/d			4000	10000	April 3	By bank a/c	C		2000	
April 2	To Manhar		30	1000		April 4	By Dinesh & Co.		30		320
						April 6	By purchases a/c				645
April 3	To cash a/c	C			2000	April 7	By Radhika & Co.		75		725
April 5	To sales a/c			275	225	April 8	By cash a/c	C			900
						April 8	By drawings a/c				100
April 8	To bank a/c	C		900		April 11	By advertisement a/c			45	
						April 15	By drawings a/c				500
April 30	To Mayur & Co.		40		580	April 19	By salaries a/c				1250
						April 20	By drawings a/c			300	
						April 23	By rent a/c			400	
						April 26	By furniture a/c				375
						April 30	By balance c/d			3430	7990
			70	6175	12805				105	6175	12805
May 1	To balance			3420	7990						

Petty Cash Book

A petty cash book is used to record all cash payments of smaller denominations. The examples of such payments are printing and stationery, postage and telegrams, carriage and cartage, travelling expenses, etc. All transactions of this type if recorded in the cash book amounts to overloading it. To reduce the burden of the chief cashier, a petty cashier is appointed and he is given a small amount of cash say Rs 200 or Rs 500 which is quite sufficient to meet the expenses of the above nature for a given period of time, say, a month. The petty cashier incurs the petty expenses and makes the entry in the petty cash book. The payment of such expenses is supported by vouchers or receipts at the end of the period like in a month. The petty cashier submits the accounts to the chief cashier. After examining the accounts of the petty cashier, the chief cashier will again pay him the actual amount spent by him. Thus, it will be seen that the petty cashier will have the same amount of cash balance that he had on the first day of the previous month.

Types of Petty Cash Book

Petty cash book can be maintained under two types:

1. Simple petty cash book
2. Analytical petty cash book with imprest system

Simple petty cash book

A simple petty cash book resembles a simple cash book discussed earlier with one difference. Instead of providing separate columns for date and particulars on both the debit and the credit sides, a single column is provided for the date and particulars. In other words, this type of petty cash book will not have two sides and, therefore, it does not resemble an account. However, a column is provided on the extreme left of the page to record the amount of petty expenses received by the petty cashier from the chief cashier. One distinct feature of this book is that all expenses are recorded in the particulars column. This book is closed at the end of a given period to know the balance. The balance is then carried forward to the next month and the transactions for that month are subsequently recorded.

The format of simple petty cash book is given below.

Dr						Cr
Amount (received)	Cash book folio	Date	Particulars	Voucher no.	LF	Amount (paid)

Analytical petty cash book with imprest system

The analytical petty cash book with imprest system is a modified type of a simple petty cash book. It consists of two sides, as in the case of any other type of cash book, i.e. the debit and the credit sides. The debit side is used to record the imprest or the petty cash received by the petty cashier from the chief cashier at the beginning of the month. The credit side is used to record various petty expenses. These petty expenses are analysed into various columns to indicate the nature of the petty expenses. Hence, this type of petty cash book is also known as *analytical petty cash book*. In other words, a separate column is provided for each item of petty expenses. So this type of petty cash book is also known as the *columnar petty cash book*. Whenever any petty expense is incurred, it is first recorded in the total payment column. Subsequently they are recorded under the relevant expense column. These facilities the total amount of petty expenses of different types incurred every month by adding the relevant columns. It also facilities the posting of the periodical total of each column to the ledger instead of posting individual expenses. It is also possible to know the total petty expenses of all types incurred for a given period of time. This system is also known as *imprest system* of petty cash book. Under this system, the chief cashier hands over a certain amount of cash to the petty cashier for a specific period, say, a month. At the end of the month, the petty cashier will submit the account to the chief cashier, who will in turn hand over the exact amount spent by the petty cashier in the preceding month. Thus, the petty cashier will have the same balance of cash as he had in the previous month to start with. This balance of amount that remains the same throughout the commencement of every month is known as *imprest amount* and the type of cash book using this principle is called as *imprest system* of cash book.

The format of analytical petty cash book is given below.

Dr												Cr
Date	Particulars	Total amount	Date	Particulars	Voucher no.	Total amount	Conveyance	Stationary	Postage and telegrams	Cartage	Miscel-laneous	Remarks

Advantages of Petty Cash Book

Following are the advantages of a petty cash book:
1. It saves labour as all petty expenses are neither recorded in the cash book nor in the ledger.
2. It saves the head cashier a lot of time as the petty expenses are recorded in the petty cash book.
3. It is very simple to record all the petty expenses in various columns of petty cash book.
4. There are less chances of fraud as it is essential to keep the vouchers of all petty expenses.

Illustration: 4

Record the following transactions in analytical petty cash book.

2005		Rs
Aug 1	Amount received from the head cashier	50.00
Aug 2	Purchased stationary	5.00
Aug 5	Postage	10.50
Aug 7	Printing charges	5.00
Aug 10	Paid tonga charges	1.00
	Coolie charges	1.50
Aug 15	Sent a telegram to thin and fat	1.20
Aug 25	Postage	2.10
Aug 26	Printing charges	8.50
Aug 28	Purchased (Twine), *sutle, sua*, etc.	1.00
Aug 29	Paid cartage	0.50
Aug 30	Stationary purchased	1.20
Aug 31	Paid for rickshaw charges	0.50

ANALYTICAL PETTY CASH BOOK

Receipt	Date	C.B. folio	Particular	Voucher number	Payments	Postage and telegram	Stationary	Printing	Coolies	Twine Expenses	Sundries
Rs					Rs	Rs	Rs	Rs	Rs	Rs	Rs
	Aug										
50.00	1		To cash								
"	2		By stationary		5.00	–	5.00	–	–	–	–
"	5		By postage		10.50	10.50	–	–	–	–	–
"	7		By printing charges		5.00	–	–	5.00	–	–	–
"	10		By tonga charges		1.00	–	–	–	1.00	–	–
"	10		By coolie charges		1.50	–	–	–	1.50	–	–
"	15		By telegram		1.20	1.20	–	–	–	–	–
"	25		By postage		2.10	2.10	–	–	–	–	–
"	26		By printing charges		8.50	–	–	8.50	–	–	–
"	28		By twine expenses		1.00	–	–	–	–	1.00	–
"	29		By cartage		050	–	–	–	0.50	–	–
"	30		By stationary		1.20	–	1.20	–	–	–	–
"	31		By rickshaw charges		0.50	–	–	–	0.50	–	–
"			By balance b/d		12.00						
50					50.00	13.80	6.20	13.50	3.50	1.00	–
12.00	Sep 1		To balance b/d								
38.00			To cash								

OTHER DAY BOOKS

In big firms, there are large numbers of transactions of a similar type. In order to maintain a proper record of all such transactions, the firm maintains special journals for this purpose known as *day books*. The following day books are commonly used:

1. Purchases journal
2. Sales journal
3. Purchases return journal
4. Sales return journal
5. Bill receivable book
6. Bill payable book
7. Journal proper

Purchases Journal

The purchases journal is also called the *invoice book* and is used for recording the purchase of goods on credit. The cash purchases are not recorded in it instead they are recorded in the cash book. Other purchases such as purchase of office equipment, furniture, building (i.e. assets) are recorded in a general journal if purchased on credit, or in a cash book if purchased for cash.

The entries in the purchases journal are recorded from the invoices or bills received from the suppliers of the goods. The trade discount and other details are not recorded in the purchases journal.

The transactions that are properly recorded in the purchases journal are then posted to the ledger. The posting to the individual supplier account may be done daily on the credit side of their accounts. The monthly total of the purchases book is posted to the debit side of purchases account in the ledger.

The format of the purchases journal is given below.

Date	Invoice no.	Name of the supplier	LF	Amount

Sales Journal

The sales journal is also called a *day book* and is used for recording the sale of goods on credit. The cash sales are recorded in the cash book. If an asset is sold on credit, it is recorded in the general journal. The entries into the sales journal are recorded from the sales invoices or bills issued by the firm to the customers.

The transactions recorded in the sales journal are then posted to the ledger. The posting to the individual customer accounts may be made daily on the debit side of their accounts. The monthly total of the sales journal is posted to the credit side of the sales account.

The format of the sales journal is given below.

Date	Invoice no.	Name of the customer	LF	Amount

Purchases Returns Journal

The purchases returns journal is used for recording transactions relating to return of goods purchased on credit. When the goods purchased are returned to the supplier for any reason, a debit note is prepared in duplicate. The original one is sent to the supplier for making necessary entries in his books and the duplicate copy is kept for official record. A debit note contains the name of the party to whom the goods have been returned, details of the goods returned and reason for returning the goods. Each debit note is numbered serially and dated.

The individual amounts are posted immediately by making a debit entry in the party's account. The monthly total of the purchases returns journal is credited to the purchases return accounts.

The format of the purchases returns journal is given below.

Date	Debit note no.	Name of the supplier	LF	Amount

Sales Return Journal

The sales return journal is used for recording transactions relating to the return of goods that were sold by the firm to the customers on credit. On receipt of goods from the customer, a credit note is prepared in duplicate. The credit note contains details relating to the name of the customer, details of the goods received back and the amount. Each credit note is serially numbered and dated.

The individual amounts are posted immediately by making an entry on the credit side of the party's account and the monthly total of the sales returns journal is debited to sales returns account.

The format of the sales returns journal is given below.

Date	Credit note no.	Name of the customer	LF	Amount

Bill Receivable Book

Sometimes the seller sells the goods on credit for the amount to be paid by the buyer; the seller draws a bill, sending it to the buyer for his acceptance. The purchaser signs the bill. This means that he accepts the liability of repaying the amount after a stipulated period. After the buyer (debtor) signs the bill, it comes back to the seller. This bill is the bills receivable for the seller. All transactions relating to the bills receivable are entered in this book. At the end of an accounting period, the amount remaining in the bill receivable book will be taken to the debit side of the trial balance and also to the asset side of the balance.

Bill Payable Book

Sometimes the buyers buy goods on credit. The seller draws a bill that is duly accepted by the buyer and sends it to the seller (creditor). This bill is the bills payable to the buyer. He has to pay the amount after a stipulated period. The bill will be in the possession of the seller. But the buyer has to pay the amount. When the amount is paid, the bills payable comes back to the acceptor (i.e. buyer or debtor). All transactions relating to the bills accepted for having purchased goods on credit will be entered in this book. The balance remaining in this book is the credit balance that is taken to the liabilities side of the balance sheet.

Journal Proper

For a small business concern, journal proper is the only book of original entry. The use of journal proper is much restricted. Only those transactions that cannot be entered in any other subsidiary books are recorded in this book. The following types of transactions are entered in the journal proper:

1. Opening entries
2. Closing entries
3. Adjusting entries
4. Transfer entries
5. Rectifying entries
6. Credit purchases and credit sales of things that are not meant for selling at a profit
7. Entries regarding dishonour of bills
8. Goods taken by the proprietor for his personal use
9. Loss of goods by theft, smuggling, fire, etc.

Points to Ponder

1. Cash book is a book in which all transactions relating to cash receipts and cash payments are recorded.
2. There are the four types of cash books
    a. Single-column cash book or simple cash book
    b. Two-columnar cash book
    c. Three-columnar cash book
    d. Petty cash book
3. Petty cash book can be maintained under two types
    a. Simple petty cash book
    b. Analytical petty cash book with imprest system
4. The various other day books commonly used are
    a. Purchases journal
    b. Sales journal
    c. Purchases return journal
    d. Sales return journal
    e. Bill receivable book
    f. Bill payable book
    g. Journal proper

 **Self-Assessment Exercises**

1. Explain the meaning of cash book.
2. What do you understand by a petty cash book?
3. What is a contra entry? How is it distinguished in the cash book from other entries?
4. Explain the meaning and the utility of cash book. What are different types of cash books? Describe each type of cash book.

5. What is a petty cash book? How will you maintain the petty cash book? Explain it by giving a format of a petty cash book.

EXERCISE 1

Prepare a simple cash book from the following transactions of Bhavesh Modi of M/s Modi Medical Stores.

2004	-	Rs
Jan 1	Bhavesh Modi started business with cash	80 000
Jan 4	Purchased goods for cash	4000
Jan 5	Sold goods for cash	4350
Jan 6	Bought furniture for cash	2700
Jan 8	Paid interest to Ajay	600
Jan 12	Received commission	200
Jan 18	Purchased goods from Mohanlal and paid cash	2100
Jan 22	Paid for petty expenses	425
Jan 24	Withdrew cash for personal use	4000
Jan 25	Goods sold to Prakash for cash	1800
Jan 30	Paid for trade expenses	450
Jan 31	Received cash from Rohit	2300
Jan 31	Paid salaries	4450
Jan 31	Received rent from Hemant	1500

EXERCISE 2

Enter the following transactions in two-columnar cash book of Vaibhav Medical & Surgical Stores.

2006		Rs
June 1	Started business with cash	50 000
June 2	Purchased goods for cash	25 000
June 5	Received cash from Amrut	32 000
June 7	Paid cash to Lakhan Singh	2900
	Discount allowed	200
June 10	Paid wages	3200
June 12	Received from Harmeet	2100
	Discount allowed	50
June 15	Paid into bank	6000
June 17	Cash sales	2500
June 20	Purchased stationary for cash	250
June 24	Paid to Jay	3900
	Discount allowed	100
June 26	Received from Harmeet	1 900
	Discount allowed	100
June 30	Paid salaries	2000

EXERCISE 3

Prepare a three-columnar cash book from the following transactions.

2003			Rs
April	1	Cash in hand	4800
		Cash at bank	3000
	3	Paid into bank	4500
	6	Purchased goods for cheque	1300
	7	Bought furniture for cash	6400
	9	Received cash from Sunil	1890
		Discount allowed	200
	10	Drew from bank for office use	4000
	13	Received cash from Rajababu	1600
		Discount allowed	100
	16	Cash sales	4000
	24	Paid to Ranjit	3900
		Discount allowed	200
	26	Withdrew from bank for personal use	5000
	28	Paid trade expenses	450
	30	Paid rent in cash	500
	30	Paid into bank	4500

EXERCISE 4

Record the following transactions in petty cash book.

2005			Rs
June	1	Paid to petty cashier	2000
	2	Taxi fare for manager	450
	3	Wages to casual workers	300
	4	Stationery	90
		Bus fare	80
	5	Postage stamps purchased	40
	5	Telegram	160
	5	Repairs to furniture	80
	6	Taxi fare to salesmen	190
	6	Telegram	20
	7	Paid for postage	80
	7	Stationery	120
	8	Refreshment to customers	200
	9	Cartage to goods purchased	140

Ledger

INTRODUCTION

We have already discussed the meaning of accounting. Accounting involves recording, classifying and summarizing the financial transactions. The recording is done in the journal. The classification of the recorded transactions is done in the ledger.

Ledger is the book that contains, in a summarized and classified form, a permanent record of all the transactions of a business. A ledger is a collection of all the accounts debited or credited in the general journal and various special journals. A ledger may be in the form of a bound register or cards or separate punched sheets maintained in a loose leaf binder. A ledger is divided into separate sections called *accounts*; each occupies a page or two or even more pages. The pages of a ledger are called *folios* and are numbered. It is easy to find any account in the ledger by going through the alphabetical index provided on the front page.

NEED FOR LEDGER

The journal records all the transactions in a chronological order as they occur. As the journal contains numerous transactions it is not possible to ascertain the net effect of the transactions on each individual asset, liability, the owners' equity, revenue and expense account. For example, there may be 100 or more transactions affecting the cash spread throughout the journal. So to ascertain the net change in cash, all these effects are to be brought together in the cash account. This is accomplished through a ledger. The focus of the ledger is on the individual accounts of the business. In this manner, we can show for each account the cumulative effect of all the transactions that affect that account.

A ledger account is divided into two sections by a central vertical line. All the debit entries are made on the left hand side and the credit entries are made on the right hand side. The abbreviation 'Dr' and 'Cr' are placed at the top left and right hand corner respectively. The word 'To' is written before the debit entries and the word 'By' is written before the credit entries. In practice, each side of the account has four columns to record the following details of each transaction:

1. The date on which a transaction is recorded
2. Particulars relating to a transaction
3. Page number of the book of original entry
4. The amount involved in the transaction.

The format of the ledger account is given below:

Dr							Cr
Date	Particulars	JF	Amount	Date	Particulars	JF	Amount

ADVANTAGES OF LEDGER

The importance of a ledger is evident from the following advantages:

1. **Knowledge of accounts:** The information about each account is known immediately, which is not possible from the journal.
2. **Details of income and expenditure:** Separate accounts are opened for each head of income and expenditure. So, the information is available about the expense and income, accountwise.
3. **Test of accuracy:** A trial balance is prepared, taking the summary of all accounts opened in the ledger and the arithmetical accuracy is tested.
4. **Knowledge of assets and liabilities:** As separate accounts are opened for each asset and liability, the position of each asset and liability is immediately known.
5. **Evidence in business disputes:** The ledger is proof enough to be used as sufficient evidence in courts for business disputes.

DIFFERENCE BETWEEN A JOURNAL AND A LEDGER

The journal and a ledger are the most important books of double entry system of accounting. Following are the important differences:

S. no.	Journal	Ledger
1	Is the book of prime entry	Is the book of final entry
2	As soon as the transaction originates, it is recorded in the journal	Transactions are posted in the ledger after the same have been recorded in the journal
3	Transactions are recorded in order of occurrence, i.e. strictly in the order of dates	Transactions are classified according to the nature and are grouped in the concerned accounts
4	Narration (brief description) is written for each entry	Narration is not required
5	Ledger folio is written	Folio of the journal or subjournal is written
6	Relevant information cannot be ascertained readily e.g. cash in hand cannot be found out easily	Since transactions of a particular nature are grouped at one place, therefore, relevant information can be ascertained
7	Final accounts cannot be prepared directly from the journal	Ledger is the basis of preparing the final accounts
8	Accuracy of the books cannot be tested	Accuracy of the books is tested by means of the list of balances
9	The debit and credit amounts of a transaction are recorded in adjacent columns	The debit and credit amounts of a transaction are recorded in two different sides of two different accounts
10	The journal has two columns, one for debit amount and the other for credit amount	The ledger has two sides, the left side is the debit side and the right side is the credit side
11	Journal is not balanced	Every account in the ledger is balanced at the appropriate time
12	With the computerization of accounting, a journal may not be used for routine transactions like, receipts, purchases, sales, etc.	The ledger cannot be avoided. However, it may be a loose leaf ledger or a computerized ledger. But a ledger is a must

POSTING OF LEDGER FROM JOURNAL

The following steps are involved in posting entries from the journal to the ledger:

1. After going through the index of the ledger, locate the account to be debited or credited as entered in the journal.
2. If an account is to be debited, enter the date of transaction in the date column on the debit side.
3. In the particulars column, write the name of the account that has been debited in the journal. For example, Mr Shyam pays Rs 1 00 000 in cash as his capital, the cash is debited and Shyam's capital is credited in the journal. While posting this transaction to the ledger, in the cash account on the debit side in the particulars column, 'Shyam's capital' will be entered indicating that cash was received by way of Shyam's capital. In the Shyam's capital account, in the ledger on the credit side in the particulars column, the word 'cash' will be recorded, indicating that Mr Shyam gave cash to the firm as capital. This procedure is followed while transferring all entries from the journal to the ledger.
4. Enter the page number of the journal in the folio column and write the page number of the ledger on which a particular account appears in the journal.
5. Enter the relevant amount in the relevant amount column.

   Note:
1. The same procedure is adopted for entering credit entries from the journal to the ledger.
2. An account is opened only once in the ledger and all entries that are related to a particular account are posted in it.

POSTING OF LEDGER FROM CASH BOOK

The following rules are applied while posting a transaction from the cash book to the ledger:

1. The left side of the cash book shows receipts made in cash or through the bank. So all the accounts appearing on the debit side of the cash book are credited because cash or cheque has been received in respect of them.

2. The right side of the cash book shows all the payments made in cash or through the bank. All the account names appearing on the credit side of the cash book are debited as cash or cheque has been paid in respect of them.

3. In case the bank column is maintained in the cash book, the bank account is not opened in the ledger. The bank column itself services the purpose of the bank account. All entries that are marked 'C' (i.e. contra entries) are ignored while posting from the cash book to the ledger.

4. Posting from the petty cash book is made at the end of the month when the totals of various amount columns of are taken. The total amount is posted as sundries indicating that all petty amounts for the month have been put together to the debit side of the concerned ledger accounts. The ledger folio number is written under every total expense amount to indicate that the entry has been posted in the ledger. In the folio column of the ledger account, the page number of the petty cash book is written for cross or future reference purposes.

BALANCING OF ACCOUNTS

When posting is complete in each account, balancing is to be done. To do balancing, first total the heavier side of the account and put the same total on the other side and arrive at the balance. Such balance is called *balance c/d*.

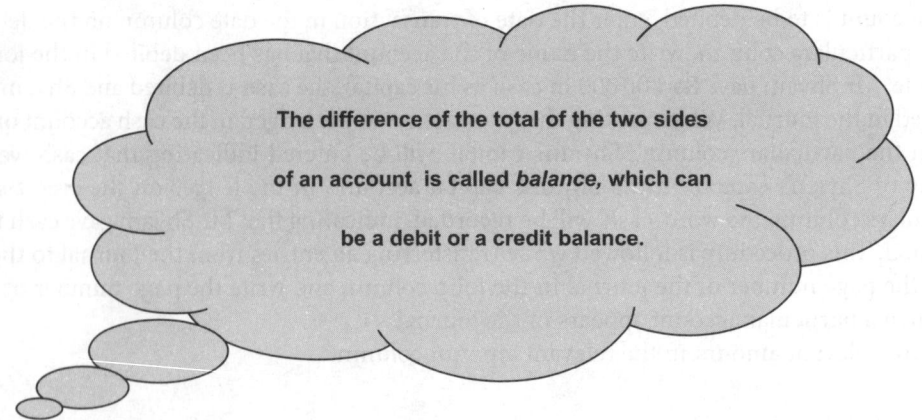

The difference of the total of the two sides of an account is called *balance*, which can be a debit or a credit balance.

Balance in the account has to be brought down. Such balance is called *balance b/d*. The balance that is brought down appears in the trial balance. If the brought down balance is debit, the amount appears under the debit column in the trial balance. Similarly, if the balance brought down is credit, the balance appears under the credit column in the trial balance. Both debits and credits should be equal in the trial balance. If both the debits and credits are equal, it is an indication that there is arithmetical accuracy. In other words, while recording the transactions in the book of accounts, for every debit a corresponding credit has been made. However, it does not give the guarantee that the accounts are debited and credited, correctly. There is a possibility that one account may be wrongly debited or credited, instead of the correct account. In such a situation, the trial balance may agree but the accounts appearing in the trial balance may not show the correct picture. In such an event, a rectification of entries has to be made, as and when the errors are found. Balance b/d is the closing balance of the account for the year concerned. The same amount would become the opening balance for the next year.

Illustration: 1

Journalize the following transactions. Post them into a ledger.

July 2009		Rs
1	Ram commenced business with cash	12000
2	Deposited into bank	9000
3	Purchased goods for cash	500
4	Bought furniture for office use	1400
10	Drew from bank for office use	1000
13	Goods sold to Salman	600
15	Bought goods of Raheman	410
18	Paid trade expenses	100
19	Received cash from Salman Allowed him discount	590 10
25	Paid wages	50
28	Paid Raheman in full settlement	400
30	Paid rent	100
31	Interest on capital	100

JOURNAL

Date	Particulars	LF	Debit (Rs)	Credit (Rs)
2009				
July 1	Cash a/c Dr		12000	
	To Ram's capital a/c (Being business commenced with Rs 12000 cash as capital)			12000
July 2	Bank a/c Dr		9000	
	To cash a/c (Being cash deposited into bank)			9000
July 3	Purchases a/c Dr		500	
	To cash a/c (Being goods purchased for cash)			500
July 4	Furniture a/c Dr		1400	
	To cash a/c (Being office furniture purchased)			1400
July 10	Cash a/c Dr		1000	
	To bank a/c (Being cash withdrawn for office use)			1000

Date	Particulars	LF	Debit (Rs)	Credit (Rs)
July 13	Salman a/c	Dr	600	
	To sales a/c (Being goods sold on credit)			600
July 15	Purchases a/c	Dr	410	
	To Raheman (Being goods purchased on credit)			410
July 18	Trade expenses a/c	Dr	100	
	To cash a/c (Being trade expenses paid)			100
July 19	Cash a/c	Dr	590	
	Discount a/c	Dr	10	
	To Salman (Being cash received and allowed discount)			600
July 25	Wages a/c	Dr	50	
	To cash a/c (Being payment of wages)			50
July 28	Raheman a/c	Dr	410	
	To cash a/c To discount a/c (Being cash paid and discount received)			400 10
July 30	Rent a/c	Dr	100	
	To cash a/c (Being rent paid)			100
July 31	Interest on capital a/c	Dr	100	
	To Ram's capital a/c (Being interest on capital credited)			100
Total Rs			26270	26270

LEDGER
CASH ACCOUNT

Dr								Cr
Date	Particulars	LF	Amount (Rs)	Date	Particulars	LF	Amount (Rs)	
2009				2009				
July 1	To Ram's capital		12000	July 2	By bank a/c		9000	
July 10	To bank a/c		1000	July 3	By purchases a/c		500	
				July 4	By furniture a/c		1400	
July 19	To Salman a/c		590	July 18	By trade expenses		100	
				July 25	By wages a/c		50	
				July 28	By Raheman a/c		400	
				July 30	By rent a/c		100	
				July 31	By balance c/d		2010	
			13590				13590	
Aug 1	To balance b/d		2040					

RAM'S CAPITAL ACCOUNT

Dr							Cr
Date	Particulars	LF	Amount (Rs)	Date	Particulars	LF	Amount (Rs)
2009				2009			
July 31	To balance c/d		12100	July 1	By cash a/c		12000
				July 31	By interest on capital a/c		100
			12100				12100
				Aug 1	To balance b/d		12100

BANK ACCOUNT

Dr							Cr
Date	Particulars	LF	Amount (Rs)	Date	Particulars	LF°	Amount (Rs)
2009				2009			
July 2	To cash a/c		9000	July 10	By cash a/c		1000
				July 31	By balance b/d		8000
			9000				9000
Aug 1	To balance b/d		8000				

PURCHASES ACCOUNT

Dr							Cr
Date	Particulars	LF	Amount (Rs)	Date	Particulars	LF	Amount (Rs)
2009				2009			
July 3	To cash a/c		500	July 31	By balance b/d		910
July 15	To Raheman a/c		410				
			910				910
Aug 1	To balance b/d		910				

SALES ACCOUNT

Dr							Cr
Date	Particulars	LF	Amount (Rs)	Date	Particulars	LF	Amount (Rs)
2009				2009			
July 31	To balance c/d		600	July 13	By Salman		600
			600				600
				Aug 1	To balance c/d		600

FURNITURE ACCOUNT

Dr							Cr
Date	Particulars	LF	Amount (Rs)	Date	Particulars	LF	Amount (Rs)
2009				2009			
July 4	To cash a/c		1400	July 31	By balance c/d		1400
			1400				1400
Aug 1	To balance b/d		1400				

SALMAN'S ACCOUNT

Dr								Cr
Date	Particulars	LF	Amount (Rs)	Date	Particulars	LF	Amount (Rs)	
2009				2009				
July 13	To sales a/c		600	July 19	By cash a/c		590	
					By discount a/c		10	
			600				600	

RAHEMAN'S ACCOUNT

Dr								Cr
Date	Particulars	LF	Amount (Rs)	Date	Particulars	LF	Amount (Rs)	
2009				2009				
July 18	To cash a/c		400	July 31	By purchases a/c		410	
	To discount a/c		10					
			410				410	

TRADE EXPENSES ACCOUNT

Dr								Cr
Date	Particulars	LF	Amount (Rs)	Date	Particulars	LF	Amount (Rs)	
2009				2009				
July 18	To cash a/c		100	July 31	By balance c/d		100	
			100				100	

DISCOUNT ACCOUNT

Dr								Cr
Date	Particulars	LF	Amount (Rs)	Date	Particulars	LF	Amount (Rs)	
2009				2009				
July 19	To Salman		10	July 28	By Raheman		10	
			10				10	

WAGES ACCOUNT

Dr								Cr
Date	Particulars	LF	Amount (Rs)	Date	Particulars	LF	Amount (Rs)	
2009				2009				
July 25	To cash a/c		50	July 31	By balance c/d		50	
			50				50	
Aug 1	To balance b/d		50					

RENT ACCOUNT

Dr				Cr			
Date	Particulars	LF	Amount (Rs)	Date	Particulars	LF	Amount (Rs)
2009				2009			
July 30	To cash a/c		100	July 31	By balance c/d		100
			100				100
Aug 1	To balance b/d		100				

INTEREST ON CAPITAL ACCOUNT

Dr				Cr			
Date	Particulars	LF	Amount (Rs)	Date	Particulars	LF	Amount (Rs)
2009				2009			
July 31	To cash a/c		100	July 31	By balance c/d		100
			100				100
Aug. 1	To balance b/d		100				

Points to Ponder

1. Ledger is the book that contains, in a summarized and classified form, a permanent record of all the transactions of a business.
2. Ledger is a book of final entry while journal is a book of original entry.
3. When posting is complete in each account, balancing is to be done.

 Self-Assessment Exercises

1. What is the purpose of a ledger?
2. Define ledger.
3. Explain the meaning and purpose of the ledger folio.
4. What is the difference between a journal and a ledger?
5. How is balancing of an account done?
6. What is the purpose of providing LF in the journal and JF in the ledger account?
7. Explain the meaning of *posting*.
8. Explain the meaning and the utility of a ledger. How will you make a posting from a journal and a cash book to a ledger?

EXERCISE 1

Journalize the following transactions. Post them into a ledger.

2006		Rs
March 1	Commenced business with cash	1000
March 3	Bought goods from Shah & Co.	150
March 5	Paid to Shah & Co. on account	50
March 9	Bought goods from Vikram & Sons	100
March 12	Purchased goods from Limbani Bros.	75
March 14	Purchased goods from Manthan Bros.	125
March 17	Purchased stationary from Pushpadeep Stores	50
March 21	Purchased furniture for cash	100
March 24	Paid Vasava & Sons	140
March 26	Sold goods to Manthan Bros.	150
March 28	Paid for cash purchases	400
March 30	Paid wages	135
March 31	Paid rent	125

EXERCISE 2

Journalize the following transactions. Post them into a ledger.

2002		Rs
May 1	Bought goods of Somani	18000
May 3	Sold to Bhavin	20000
May 4	Bought of Rakesh	24000
May 6	Sold to Piyush	10000
May 8	Paid to Somani by cheque	30000
May 18	Received cheque from Bhavin	40000
May 18	Allowed him discount	1000
May 19	Sold goods to Naresh	16000
May 20	Paid rent by cheque	3000
May 21	Sold to Rakesh	20000
May 30	Paid salaries in cash	6000

Trial Balance

INTRODUCTION

In the earlier chapters, you have learnt about the basic principles of accounting that for every debit there will be an equal credit. It implies that if the sum of all the debits equals the sum of all credits, it is presumed that the posting to the ledger in terms of the debit and credit amounts is accurate. The trial balance is a tool for verifying the correctness of the debit and credit amounts. It is an arithmetical check under the double entry system that verifies that both aspects of every transaction have been recorded accurately. This chapter explains the meaning and the process of preparation of the trial balance, and the types of errors and their rectification.

MEANING OF TRIAL BALANCE

A trial balance is a statement showing the balances or the total of debits and credits, of all the accounts in the ledger, with a view to verify the arithmetical accuracy of posting into the ledger accounts. Trial balance is an important statement in the accounting process that shows the final position of all the accounts and helps in preparing the final statements. The task of preparing the statements is simplified because the accountant can take the account balances from the trial balance instead of looking them up in the ledger.

Table 25.1 shows an example of the format of a trial balance.

Table 25.1. Trial Balance of … as on 31 March 2009

Particulars	LF	Balance amount	
		Debit	Credit
Total			

It is normally prepared at the end of an accounting year. However, an organization may prepare a trial balance at the end of any chosen period that may be monthly, quarterly, half-yearly or annually depending upon its requirement.

In order to prepare a trial balance the following steps are taken:

1. Ascertain the balances of each account in the ledger.
2. List each account and place its balance in the debit or credit column, as the case may be. (If an account has zero balance, it may be included in the trial balance with zero in the column for its normal balance.)
3. Compute the total of the debit balances column.
4. Compute the total of the credit balances column.
5. Verify that the sum of the debit balances equals the sum of the credit balances. If they do not tally, it indicates that there are some errors. So one must check the correctness of the balances of all accounts. It may be noted that all assets expenses and receivables account shall have debit balances whereas all liabilities, revenues and payables accounts shall have credit balances.

Account title	LF	Debit amount (Rs)	Credit amount (Rs)
Capital			√
Land and buildings		√	
Plant and machinery		√	
Equipment		√	
Furniture and fixtures		√	
Cash in hand		√	
Cash at bank		√	
Debtors		√	
Bills receivable		√	
Stock of raw materials		√	
Work in progress		√	
Stock of finished goods		√	
Prepaid insurance		√	
Purchases		√	
Carriage inwards		√	

Account title	LF	Debit amount (Rs)	Credit amount (Rs)
Carriage outwards		√	
Sales			√
Sales returns		√	
Purchases return			√
Interest paid		√	
Commission / Discount received			√
Salaries		√	
Long-term loan			√
Bills payable			√
Creditors			√
Outstanding salaries			√
Outstanding interest earned		√	
Advances from customers			√
Drawings		√	
Reserve fund			√
Provision for doubtful debts			√
Total		xxx	xxx

OBJECTIVES OF PREPARING THE TRIAL BALANCE

The trial balance is prepared to fulfil the following objectives:

1. To ascertain the arithmetical accuracy of the ledger accounts

As stated earlier, the purpose of preparing a trial balance is to ascertain whether all the debits and credits are properly recorded in the ledger or not and that all accounts have been correctly balanced. As a summary of the ledger, it is a list of the accounts and their balances. When the totals of all the debit balances and credit balances in the trial balance are equal, it is assumed that the posting and balancing of accounts is arithmetically correct. However, the tallying of the trial balance is not a conclusive proof of the accuracy of the accounts. It only ensures that all debits and the corresponding credits have been properly recorded in the ledger.

2. To help in locating errors

When a trial balance does not tally (that is, the totals of the debit and the credit columns are not equal), we know that at least one error has occurred. The error (or errors) may have occurred at one of the following stages in the accounting process:

    a. totalling of subsidiary books,

    b. posting of journal entries in the ledger,

    c. calculating account balances,

    d. carrying account balances to the trial balance, and

    e. totalling the trial balance columns.

It may be noted that the accounting accuracy is not ensured even if the totals of debit and credit balances are equal because some errors do not affect the equality of debits and credits. For example, the bookkeeper may debit a correct amount in the wrong account while making the journal entry or in posting a journal entry to the ledger. This error would cause two accounts to have incorrect balances but the trial balance would tally. Another error is to record an equal debit and credit of an incorrect amount. This error would give the two accounts incorrect balances but would not create unequal debits and credits. As a result, the fact that the trial balance has tallied does not imply that all entries in the books of original record (journal, cash book, etc.) have been recorded and posted correctly. However, equal totals do suggest that several types of errors probably have not occurred.

3. To help in the preparation of the financial statements

Trial balance is considered as the connecting link between accounting records and the preparation of financial statements. For preparing a financial statement, one need not refer to the ledger. In fact, the availability of a tallied trial balance is the first step in the preparation of the financial statements. All revenue and expense accounts appearing in the trial balance are transferred to the trading and profit and loss account, and all liabilities, capital and assets accounts are transferred to the balance sheet.

PREPARATION OF TRIAL BALANCE

A trial balance can be prepared in the following three ways:
1. Totals method
2. Balances method
3. Totals-cum-balances method

Totals Method

Under the totals method, the total of each side in the ledger (debit and credit) is ascertained separately and shown in the trial balance in the respective columns. The total of the debit column of trial balance should agree with the total of the credit column in the trial balance because the accounts are based on a double entry system. However, this method is not widely practiced, as it does not help in assuming the accuracy of balances of various accounts and preparation of the financial statements.

Balances Method

Balances method is the most widely used method in practice. Under this method the trial balance is prepared by showing the balances of all ledger accounts and then totalling up the debit and credit columns of the trial balance to assure their correctness. The account balances are used because the balance summarizes the net effect of all transactions relating to an account and helps in preparing the financial statements. It may be noted that in a trial balance, normally in place of balances in individual accounts of the debtors, a figure of sundry debtors is shown, and in place of the individual accounts of creditors, a figure of sundry creditors is shown.

Totals-cum-balances Method

Totals-cum-balances method is a combination of the totals method and the balances method. Under this method, four columns for amount are prepared—two columns for writing the debit and credit totals of various accounts, and two columns for writing the debit and credit balances of these accounts. However, this method is also not practiced because it is time consuming and hardly serves any additional or special purpose.

Let us now learn how the trial balance will be prepared using each of these methods with the help of the following example:

Illustration 1

Mr Rawat's ledger shows the following accounts for his business. Help him in preparing the trial balance using: 1. Totals method, 2. Balances method, 3. Totals-cum-balances method.

Rahul's Capital Account

Dr							Cr
Date	Particulars	JF	Amount (Rs)	Date	Particulars	JF	Amount (Rs)
31 Dec 2005	Balance c/d		60000	01 Jan 2005	Balance b/d		40000
					Cash		20000
			60000				60000
				01 Jan 2006	Balance b/d		60000

Rohan's Account

Dr							Cr
Date	Particulars	JF	Amount (Rs)	Date	Particulars	JF	Amount (Rs)
31 Dec 2005	Cash		40000	01 Jan 2005			
	Balance c/d		20000		Balance b/d		10000
					Cash		20000
			60000				60000
				01Jan 2006	Balance b/d		60000

Machinery Account

Dr							Cr
Date	Particulars	JF	Amount (Rs)	Date	Particulars	JF	Amount (Rs)
31 Dec 2005	Balance c/d		20000	31 Dec 2005	Depreciation		3000
					Balance b/d		17000
			20000				20000
01 Jan 2006	Balance b/d		17000				

Rahul's Account

Dr							Cr
Date	Particulars	JF	Amount (Rs)	Date	Particulars	JF	Amount (Rs)
01 Jan 2005	Balance c/d		15000	31 Dec 2005	Cash		55000
	Sales		60000		Balance b/d		20000
			75000				75000
01 Jan 2006	Balance b/d		20000				

Purchases Account

Dr							Cr
Date	Particulars	JF	Amount (Rs)	Date	Particulars	JF	Amount (Rs)
2005							
	Rohan		50 000				
	Cash		12 000				
			62 000				

The trial balance under the three methods is illustrated below:

Trial balance as on 31 March 2005
(Using Totals Method)

Account title	LF	Debit total (Rs)	Credit total (Rs)
Rawat's capital			60 000
Rohan		40 000	60 000
Machinery		20 000	3 000
Rahul		75 000	55 000
Sales			70 000
Cash		1 00 000	57 000
Wages		5 000	
Depreciation		3 000	
Purchases		62 000	
Total		3 05 000	3 05 000

Trial balance as on 31 March 2005
(Using Balances Method)

Account title	LF	Debit total (Rs)	Credit total (Rs)
Rawat's capital			60 000
Rohan's capital			20 000
Machinery		17 000	
Rahul		20 000	
Sales			70 000
Cash		43 000	
Wages		5 000	
Depreciation		3 000	
Purchases		62 000	
Total		1 50 000	1 50 000

Trial balance as on 31 March 2005
(Using totals-cum-balances method)

Account title	LF	Debit total (Rs)	Credit total (Rs)	Debit balance (Rs)	Credit balance (Rs)
Rawat's capital			60 000		60 000
Rohan		40 000	60 000		20 000
Machinery		20 000	3000	17 000	
Rahul		75 000	55 000	20 000	
Sales			70 000		70 000
Cash		1 00 000	57 000	43 000	
Wages		5000		5000	
Depreciation		3000		3000	
Purchases		62 000		62 000	
Total		3 05 000	3 05 000	1 50 000	1 50 000

Illustration: 2

From the following balances extracted from the books of a trader, prepare a trial balance as on 31 March 2006.

Accounts	Balances (Rs)		Balances (Rs)
Cash in hand	4200	Salaries	12 000
Cash at bank	16 800	Advertisement	2400
Bills receivable	18 000	Insurance	1600
Bills payable	16 000	Furniture	7500
Sundry debtors	24 600	Stock	18 600
Sundry creditors	32 400	Office rent	2000
Capital	50 000	Drawings	18 000
Carriage inward	2700	Purchases	75 000
Sales	1 05 000		
Salaries	12 000		
Advertisement	2400		

Trial Balance as on 31 March 2006.

Name of the account	Balances (Rs)	Balances (Rs)
Cash	4200	
Bank	16 800	
Bills receivable	18 000	
Bills payable		16 000
Sundry debtors	24 600	
Sundry creditors		32 400
Capital		50 000
Drawings	18 000	
Sales		1 05 000

Name of the account	Balances (Rs)	Balances (Rs)
Purchases	75 000	
Carriage inward	2700	
Salaries	12 000	
Advertisement	2400	
Insurance	1600	
Furniture	7500	
Rent	2000	
Stock	18 600	
Total	2 03 400	2 03 400

SIGNIFICANCE OF AGREEMENT OF TRIAL BALANCE

It is important for an accountant that the trial balance should tally. Normally a tallied trial balance means that both the debit and the credit entries have been made correctly for each transaction. However, as stated earlier, the agreement of the trial balance is not an absolute proof of accuracy of the accounting records. A tallied trial balance only proves, to a certain extent, that the posting to the ledger is arithmetically correct. But it does not guarantee that the entry itself is correct. There can be errors, which affect the equality of the debits and credits, and there can be errors, which do not affect the equality of the debits and credits. Some common errors include the following:

1. Error in totalling of the debit and credit balances in the trial balance.
2. Error in totalling of the subsidiary books.
3. Error in posting of the total of subsidiary books.
4. Error in showing the account balances in the wrong column of the trial balance, or the wrong amount.
5. Omission in showing an account balance in the trial balance.
6. Error in the calculation of a ledger account balance.
7. Error while posting a journal entry: a journal entry may not have been posted properly to the ledger, i.e. posting made either with the wrong amount or on the wrong side of the account or in the wrong account.
8. Error in recording a transaction in the journal: making a reverse entry, i.e. the account to be debited is credited and the amount to be credited is debited, or an entry with wrong amount.
9. Error in recording a transaction in the subsidiary book with the wrong name or the wrong amount.

ACCOUNTING ERRORS

The main purpose of preparing the trial balance is to test the arithmetical accuracy of the account books. However, it must be kept in mind that tallying of the trial balance does not mean that no errors have been committed in the accounting records. We may remember that the following types of errors are not reflected in the trial balance:

1. Errors of commission
2. Errors of omission

3. Errors of principle
4. Compensating errors

ACCOUNTING ERRORS

Errors of Commission

These are the errors that are committed due to the wrong posting of transactions, wrong totalling or balancing of the accounts, wrong casting of the subsidiary books or wrong recording of the amount in the books of original entry, etc. For example: Raj Hans Traders paid Rs 25 000 to Preetpal Traders (a supplier of goods). This transaction was correctly recorded in the cashbook. But while posting to the ledger, Preetpal's account was debited with Rs 2500 only. This constitutes an error of commission. Such an error by definition is of clerical nature and most of the errors of commission affect in the trial balance.

Errors of Omission

The errors of omission may be committed at the time of recording the transaction in the books of original entry or while posting to the ledger. These can be of two types:
   a. Error of complete omission
   b. Error of partial omission

When a transaction is completely omitted from recording in the books of original record, it is an error of complete omission. For example, the credit sales to Mohan, Rs 10 000, is not entered in the sales book. When the recording of transaction is partly omitted from the books, it is an error of partial omission. If in the above example, the credit sales had been duly recorded in the sales book but the posting from the sales book to Mohan's account had not been made, it would have been an error of partial omission.

Errors of Principle

Accounting entries are recorded as per the generally accepted accounting principles. If any of these principles are violated or ignored, the errors resulting from such violation are known as *errors of principle*. An error of principle may occur due to the incorrect classification of expenditure or receipt between the capital and the revenue. This is very important because it will have an impact on the financial statements. It may lead to under or over stating of income or assets or liabilities, etc. For example, the amount spent on additions to the buildings should be treated as capital expenditure and must be debited to the asset account. Instead, if this amount is debited to the maintenance and repairs account, it has been treated as a revenue expense. This is an error of principle. Similarly, if a credit purchase of machinery is recorded in the purchases book instead of journal proper or the rent paid to the landlord is recorded in the cash book as payment to the landlord, these errors are errors of principle. These errors do not affect the trial balance.

Compensating Errors

When two or more errors are committed in such a way that the net effect of these errors on the debits and credits of accounts is nil, such errors are called *compensating errors*. Such errors do not affect the tallying of the trial balance.

For example, if the purchases book has been overcast by Rs 10 000 resulting in excess debit of Rs 10 000 in the purchases account and sales returns book is undercast by Rs 10 000 resulting in short debit to the sales returns account, it is a case of two errors compensating each other's effect. One plus is set off by the other minus, the net effect of these two errors is nil and so they do not affect the agreement of the trial balance.

SEARCHING OF ERRORS

If the trial balance does not tally, it is a clear indication that at least one error has occurred. The error (or errors) needs to be located and corrected before preparing the financial statements. If the trial balance does not tally, the accountant should take the following steps to detect and locate the errors:

1. Recast the totals of the debit and credit columns of the trial balance.
2. Compare the account head or the title and the amount appearing in the trial balance with that of the ledger to detect any difference in the amount or omission of an account.
3. Compare the trial balance of the current year with that of the previous year to check additions and deletions of any accounts, and also verify whether there is a large difference in the amount, which is neither expected nor explained.
4. Redo and check the correctness of the balances of individual accounts in the ledger.
5. Recheck the correctness of the posting in the accounts from the books of original entry.
6. If the difference between the debit and credit columns is divisible by 2, there is a possibility that an amount equal to one-half of the difference may have been posted to the wrong side of another ledger account. For example, if the total of the debit column of the trial balance exceeds by Rs 1500, it is quite possible that a credit item of Rs 750 may have been wrongly posted in the ledger as a debit item. To locate such errors, the accountant should scan all the debit entries of an amount of Rs 750.
7. The difference may also indicate a complete omission of a posting. For example, the difference of Rs 1500 given above may be due to the omissions of a posting of that amount on the credit side. Thus, the accountant should verify all the credit items with an amount of Rs 1500.
8. If the difference is a multiple of 9 or divisible by 9, the mistake could be due to the transposition of figures. For example, if a debit amount of Rs 459 is posted as Rs 954, the debit total in the trial balance will exceed the credit side by Rs 495 (i.e. 954 − 459 = 495). This difference is divisible by 9. A mistake due to wrong placement of the decimal point may also be checked by this method. Thus, a difference in the trial balance divisible by 9 helps in checking the errors for a transposed mistake.

RECTIFICATION OF ERRORS

From the point of view of rectification, the errors may be classified into the following two categories:

1. Errors which do not affect the trial balance.
2. Errors which affect the trial balance.

This distinction is relevant because the errors which do not affect the trial balance usually takes place in two accounts in such a manner that it can be easily rectified through a journal entry whereas the errors which affect the trial balance usually affect one account and a journal entry is not possible for rectification unless a suspense account has been opened.

Rectification of Errors That Do Not Affect the Trial Balance

These errors are committed in two or more accounts. Such errors are also known as *two sided errors*. They can be rectified by recording a journal entry giving the correct debit and credit to the concerned accounts. Examples of such errors are: complete omission to record an entry in the books of original entry; wrong recording of transactions in the book of accounts; complete omission of posting to the wrong account on the correct side; and errors of principle.

The rectification process essentially involves:

    a.   Cancelling the effect of the wrong debit or credit by reversing it; and
    b.   Restoring the effect of the correct debit or credit.

For this purpose, we need to analyse the error in terms of its effect on the accounts involved that may be:

    a.   Short debit or credit in an account; and/or
    b.   Excess debit or credit in an account.

Therefore, the rectification entry can be done by:

    a.   Debiting the account with short debit or with excess credit,
    b.   Crediting the account with excess debit or with short credit.

The procedure for rectification for such errors is explained with the help of following examples:

1.   Credit sales to Mohan Rs 10 000 were not recorded in the sales book. This is an error of complete omission. The effect of such an error is that Mohan's account has not been debited and the sales account has not been credited. Accordingly, recording the usual entry for credit sales will rectify the error.

Mohan's a/c	Dr	10 000	
To sales a/c			10 000

2.   Credit sales to Mohan Rs 10 000 were recorded as Rs 1000 in the sales book. This is an error of commission. The effect of wrong recording is shown below:

Mohan's a/c	Dr	1000	
To sales a/c			1000

The correct effect should have been:

Mohan's a/c	Dr	10 000 ·	
To sales a/c			10 000

Now that Mohan's account has to be given an additional debit of Rs 9000 and the sales account has to be credited with an additional amount of Rs 9000, the rectification entry will be:

Mohan's a/c	Dr	9000	
To sales a/c			9000

3.   Credit sales to Mohan Rs 10 000 were recorded as Rs 12 000. This is an error of commission. The effect of wrong entry is shown below:

| Mohan's a/c | Dr | 12 000 | |
| To sales a/c | | | 12 000 |

The correct effect should have been:

| Mohan's a/c | Dr | 10 000 | |
| To sales a/c | | | 10 000 |

You can see that there is an excess debit of Rs 2000 in Mohan's account and an excess credit of Rs 2000 in the sales account. The rectification entry will be recorded as follows:

| Sales's a/c | Dr | 2000 | |
| To Mohan's a/c | | | 2000 |

4. Credit sales to Mohan Rs 10 000 was correctly recorded in the sales book but was posted to Ram's account. This is an error of commission. The effect of the wrong posting is shown below:

| Ram's a/c | Dr | 10 000 | |
| To sales a/c | | | 10 000 |

The correct effect should have been:

| Mohan's a/c | Dr | 10 000 | |
| To sales a/c | | | 10 000 |

Notice that there is no error in the sales account. But Ram's account has been debited with Rs 10 000 instead of Mohan's account. Hence, the rectification entry will be:

| Mohan's a/c | Dr | 10 000 | |
| To Ram's a/c | | | 10 000 |

5. The rent paid of Rs 2000 was wrongly shown as payment to the landlord in the cash book. The effect of the wrong posting has been:

| Landlord's a/c | Dr | 2000 | |
| To cash a/c | | | 2000 |

The correct effect should have been:

| Rent a/c | Dr | 2000 | |
| To cash a/c | | | 2000 |

The landlord's account has been wrongly debited instead of the rent account. Hence, the rectification entry will be:

| Rent a/c | Dr | 2000 | |
| To Landlord's a/c | | | 2000 |

Rectification of Errors Affecting the Trial Balance

The errors that affect only one account can be rectified by giving an explanatory note in the account affected or by recording a journal entry with the help of the suspense account. The suspense account is explained later in this chapter. Examples of such errors are: error of casting; error of carrying forward; error of balancing; error of posting to the correct account but with the wrong amount; error of posting to the correct account but on the wrong side; posting to the wrong side with the wrong amount; omitting to show an account in the trial balance. An error in the books of original entry, if discovered before it is posted to the ledger, may be corrected by crossing out the wrong amount by a single line and writing the correct amount above the crossed amount and initialling it. An error in an amount posted to the correct ledger account may also be corrected in a similar way, or by making an additional posting for the difference in amount and giving an explanatory note in the particulars column. But errors should never be corrected by erasing or overwriting since it reduces the authenticity of accounting records and gives an impression that something is being concealed. A better way, therefore, is by noting the correction on the appropriate side for neutralizing the effect of the error. Take for example a case where Shyam's account was credited short by Rs 190. This will be rectified by an additional entry for Rs 190 on the credit side of his account as follows:

Shyam's Account

Dr							Cr
Date	Particulars	JF	Amount	Date	Particulars	JF	Amount
					Difference in amount posted short on.....		190

Take another example, the purchases book was undercast by Rs 1000. The effect of this entry is on the purchases account (debit side) where the total of the purchases book is posted.

Purchases Account

Dr							Cr
Date	Particulars	JF	Amount	Date	Particulars	JF	Amount
	Undercasting purchases book for the month of....		1000				

SUSPENSE ACCOUNT

When the trial balance does not tally in spite of the best efforts, the difference is put to a newly opened account known as *suspense account*. Thus, the trial balance is made to tally in order to avoid the delay in the preparation of final accounts. If the debit side of the trial balance exceeds the credit side, the difference is put on the credit side of the trial balance. In this case, the suspense account will show a credit balance. If the credit side of the trial balance exceeds the debit side, the difference is put on the debit side of the trial balance. In this case, the suspense account will show a debit balance. The suspense account is an imaginary account used as a temporary measure only for the purpose of reconciling a trial balance. When the errors affecting the suspense account are located, the rectification entries are passed with the help of the suspense account. Thus, when all errors are located and rectified, the suspense account will automatically stand closed, i.e. it will not show any balance. But if the suspense account still shows a balance, it will indicate that certain errors are still to be discovered and rectified. In such cases, if the suspense account shows a debit balance, it is taken to the balance sheet on the assets side and on the contrary, if it shows a credit balance it is taken to the balance sheet on the liabilities side.

The following points should be noted while passing rectification entries with the help of suspense account:

1. Suspense account is used to rectify only those errors which affect the trial balance.
2. If the account that is to be rectified is debited in the rectifying entry, the suspense account will be credited to complete the double entry.
3. If the account which is to be rectified is credited in the rectifying entry, the suspense account will be credited to complete the double entry.

RECTIFICATION OF ERRORS IN THE NEXT ACCOUNTING YEAR

If some errors committed during an accounting year are not located and rectified before the finalization of financial statements, the suspense account cannot be closed and its balance will be carried forward to the next accounting period. When the errors committed in one accounting year are located and

---

Guiding Principles of Rectification of Errors

1. If error is committed in books of original entry then assume that all postings are done accordingly.
2. If error is at the posting stage then assume that recording in the subsidiary books have been correctly done.
3. If error is in posting to a wrong account (without mentioning side and amount of posting) then assume that the posting has been done on the right side and with the right amount.
4. If posting is done to a correct account but with the wrong amount (without mentioning side of posting) then assume that the posting has been done on the correct side.
5. If error is posting to a wrong account on the wrong side (without mentioning the amount of posting) then assume that posting has been done with the amount as per the original recording of the transaction.
6. If error is of posting to a wrong account with the wrong amount (without mentioning the side of posting) then assume that posting has been done on the right side.
7. If posting is done to a correct account but on the wrong side (without mentioning the amount of posting), then assume that the posting has been done with correct amount as per the original recording.
8. Any error in posting of individual transactions in subsidiary books relates to an individual account only, the sales account, purchase account, sales return account or purchases return account are not involved.
9. If a transaction is recorded in the cash book, then the error in posting relates to the other affected account, not to cash account or bank account.
10. If a transaction is recorded through journal proper, then the phrase 'transaction was not posted' indicates error in both the accounts involved, unless stated otherwise.
11. Error in casting of subsidiary books will affect only that account where the total of the particular book is posted leaving the individual personal accounts unaffected.

rectified in the next accounting year, the profit and loss adjustment account is debited or credited in place of accounts of expenses or losses and incomes or gains in order to avoid the impact on the income statement of the next accounting period. You will learn about this aspect at an advanced stage of your studies in accounting.

Points to Ponder

1. Trial balance shows the final position of all the accounts and helps in preparing the final statements.
2. A trial balance can be prepared in the following three ways
   a. Totals method
   b. Balances method
   c. Totals-cum-balances method
3. Following types of errors are not reflected in the trial balance
   a. Errors of commission
   b. Errors of omission
   c. Errors of principle
   d. Compensating errors
4. From the point of view of rectification, the errors may be classified into the following two categories:
   a. Errors which do not affect the trial balance.
   b. Errors which affect the trial balance.

Self-Assessment Exercises

1. What is a *trial balance*? Write the main objectives of a trial balance.
2. Explain the meaning of a *trial balance*. What are the different methods of preparing a trial balance?
3. Discuss the various errors disclosed by a trial balance with suitable examples.
4. Explain the meaning and purpose of a trial balance.
5. If a trial balance tallies, can it be concluded that there are no errors? Comment on it.
6. Describe the method of preparing a trial balance.
7. Explain an error of commission with a suitable example.
8. Discuss an error of omission with a suitable example.
9. Explain the error of principle with a suitable example.
10. Describe a compensating error with a suitable example.
11. Discuss the errors which do not affect a trial balance.
12. What are the causes of accounting error?
13. Discuss the errors which do not affect the trial balance.

14. Define the term *suspense account*.
15. Write the importance of suspense account.

EXERCISE 1

Prepare a trial balance of M/s Multiplying Enterprise as on 31 December 2006.

Accounts	Balances (Rs)	Accounts	Balances (Rs)
Cash in hand	2500	Debtors	18200
Cash at bank	14500	Creditors	16600
Capital	70000	Opening stock	8700
Drawing	9000	Wages	6700
Purchases	60000	Rent	5000
Sales	82000	Salary	8400
Machine	35000	Bills payable	11400
Furniture	12000		

EXERCISE 2

Prepare a trial balance as on 31 March 2006 from the following balances of Sabana.

Dr Accounts	Balances (Rs)	Cr Balances (Rs)
Cash in hand	3100	
Bank overdraft		18250
Opening stock	24600	
Purchases	59800	
Sales		72350
Sabana's capital		50000
Drawings	12000	
Carriage inward	1600	
Rent	2400	
Commission		2100
Interest	780	
Furniture	5220	
Creditors		13600
Debtors	27800	
Building	20000	
Suspense		1000
	157300	157300

EXERCISE 3

There was a difference of Rs 725 in a trial balance. It has been transferred to the credit side of suspense account. Later on the following errors were discovered. Pass the rectifying entries and prepare a suspense account.

1. An amount of Rs 375 has been posted in the debit side of commission account instead of Rs 275.
2. Goods of Rs 200 purchased from Sohan Lal have been posted to his account as Rs 250.
3. Total of sales return book was overcast by Rs 475.
4. A credit amount of Rs 50 was posted as Rs 150 to the debit side of a personal account.
5. Goods of Rs 300 were sold to Mahesh, but it was recorded in the purchase book.

Financial Statements

INTRODUCTION

After the preparation of the trial balance, the management of a business enterprise proceeds to get the financial statements prepared. The purpose of preparing financial statements is to enable the management to have a periodical review of the progress made by the enterprise to deal with the following:

1. The present status of the investments in the business.
2. The results achieved during the period under review.

The term *financial statements* means the two statements prepared at the end of the accounting period of the enterprise, e.g. the balance sheet (statement of the present financial position) and the profit and loss account (income statement). The two statements together are called the *final accounts* in traditional accounting language.

Advantages of Financial Statements

The accounting information given in the financial statements is made by the following:

1. **Management:** The management can review the up-to-date progress made by the enterprise and can then decide about the necessary course of action to be taken in the future.
2. **Creditors:** The creditors can decide about extending, maintaining or restricting the flow of their credit to the business.
3. **Shareholders:** On the basis of the financial statements, the shareholders are in a position to judge the future prospects of their investments and thus decide either to sell or continue with the ownership of their shares in the firm.
4. **Employee unions:** The employee groups or unions can find the present financial condition of the firm from the financial statements and are thus able to decide whether the firm is in a position to pay higher wages, bonus, etc.

Limitations of Financial Statements

Following are the limitations of the financial statements:

1. The profit shown in the profit and loss account and the financial position revealed by the balance sheet cannot be exactly true since these statements are only interim reports. The exact financial position of the business can be known only when the business is either liquidated or sold.
2. The balance sheet is affected by various factors such as fixed assets, going concern concept and conventions like conservatism and consistency. As such, the balance sheet does not reveal the exact financial position of the concern as is claimed by it.
3. Many items in the financial statements are influenced by personal judgments. Hence, the quality of statements therein depends on the competence and the integrity of those who prepare it.
4. Financial statements record and reveal only those facts that can be expressed in terms of money. Other important information like the working conditions of the employees, administrative setup, sales policies of the company, quality of products introduced by the company, etc., find no mention in a balance sheet.

PROFIT AND LOSS ACCOUNT

The profit and loss account reveals the net profit earned or the net loss suffered by a firm in course of its business operations during the accounting period. It is prepared at the end of the financial year of the business.

The main purpose of the profit and loss account is to ascertain the net profit or the net loss from business operations. The net income of the current year can be compared with that of the previous years and the deviations in income of different periods may be analysed to ascertain the factors responsible for such deviations. Such an analysis is helpful in controlling expenses incurred in running the business enterprise and in the sale of goods and thus eliminating wastage.

Preparation of the Profit and Loss Account

On determining the gross profit or gross loss from the trading account, the gross profit is recorded on the credit side of the profit and loss account and the gross loss is recorded on the debit side of the profit and loss account.

After this, the other incomes or gains such as rent received, interest received, commission earned, discount received, etc., are credited. The expenses or losses such as salaries, rents, advertisement expenses, business expenses, printing, stationery, etc., are recorded on the debit side. The grand total on both the debit and the credit sides are obtained. If the grand total on the credit side is more than that on the debit side, it shows a net profit. If the grand total on the debit side is more than that on the credit side, it shows a net loss. The net profit or a net loss, as the case may be, is taken to the capital account of the proprietor. While the net profit is added to the capital account, net loss is deducted therefrom.

Illustration: 1

Prepare the trading, profit and loss account of S.C. Malhotra of Imperial Medical Store for the year ended 31 December 2006 from the following particulars.

	Rs	Rs
Opening stock	10000	
Rent and rates	300	
Trade expenses	600	
Returns inward	600	
Sales		84000
Purchases	50000	
Purchases returns		300
Carriage inwards	200	
Wages	500	
Discount	40	
Discount received		50
Commission	20	
Salaries	2000	
Legal expenses	50	
Audit fees	70	
Bank charge	50	
Sales tax	60	
Interest on drawings		100
Interest on investment		200
Repairs and renewals	260	

Closing stock Rs 5000.

TRADING PROFIT AND LOSS ACCOUNT
For the year ending 31 December 2006

Detail		Rs	Detail		Rs
To opening stock		10 000	By sales	84 000	
			Less returns	600	85 400
To purchase	50 000		By closing stock		5000
Less returns	300	49 700			
To wages		500			
To carriage inwards		200			
To gross profit c/d		30 000			
		90 400			90 400
To salaries		2000	By gross profit b/d		30 000
To discount		40	By discount		50
To commission		20	By interest on drawings		200
By legal expenses		50	By interest on investment		100
To audit fees		70			
To bank charges		50			
To sales tax		60			
To repairs and renewals		260			
To rent and rates		300			
To trade expenses		600			
To net profit transferred to capital a/c		26 900			
		30 350			30 350

Points Worth Noting in the Profit and Loss Account

Various types of items are included in a profit and loss account. A detailed description of some of these items is given below for better understanding of how a profit and loss account is prepared.

1. **Salaries:** Salaries paid to the employees are debited to the profit and loss account. The item 'salaries and wages' is treated as salaries and is debited to the profit and loss account. However, the items 'wages and salaries' is treated as wages and is debited to the trading account.
2. **Rent:** The amount of rent paid is shown on the debit side of the profit and loss account. However, in case of rent received, it is an item of income and as such it will appear on the credit side of the profit and loss account.
3. **Discount:** Discount is of two types:
   a. trade discount, and
   b. cash discount.
   The trade discount is given on bulk purchases and bulk sales. It is deducted from the amount of purchases and sales before they are recorded in the books. Hence, no further treatment is given to the trade discount.
   A cash discount is given to the creditors or customers in order to encourage prompt payment of dues. When the discount is received from creditors, it is considered as income and is shown on the credit side of the profit and loss account. When the discount is allowed to customers, it is regarded as an expense and hence, it is debited to the profit and loss account.

4. **Commission:** To increase sales, agents are appointed on commission basis. The commission so paid is an indirect expense and is debited to the profit and loss account. The commission paid on the purchase of goods is debited to the trading account.

5. **Printing and stationery:** Printing and stationery includes all expenses relating to printing bills, invoices, registers, files, letterheads, hand bills, office stationery, etc. It is an indirect expense and is debited to the profit and loss account.

6. **Advertisement:** To boost the sales of products, suitable publicity is necessary. It is an essential expenditure for any business. Hence, it is debited to the profit and loss account since it is an indirect expense.

7. **Carriage outwards or freight outwards:** These expenses are incurred by way of transportation charges in respect of goods sold. It is treated as an indirect expense and is debited to the profit and loss account.

8. **Bad debts:** An irrecoverable debt is known as a *bad debt*. This is a loss item for business and hence appears on the debit side of the profit and loss account.

9. **Repairs:** Repairs to plant, machinery, building, etc., are indirect expenses and are, therefore, debited to the profit and loss account.

10. **Drawings:** Drawing represents the money or goods withdrawn by the proprietor from business for his personal use. This is debited to the capital account, e.g. premium paid on his life insurance policy is treated as 'drawings' and is deducted from the capital account. It is not to be taken to the profit and loss account.

11. **Income tax:** In case of a trader, income tax paid is treated as a personal expense and is, therefore, deducted from the capital account. However, in case of companies or partnership firms the income tax is debited to the profit and loss account.

12. **Loss or gain on assets sold:** Sometimes a business enterprise may sell its fixed assets such as furniture, machinery, building, etc., in course of its business operations and thus may incur a loss or make a profit on its sale. The loss on the sale of a fixed asset is treated as a revenue loss and is debited to the profit and loss account. The profit made on sale of a fixed asset is treated as a revenue gain and is credited to the profit and loss account.

13. **Loss by fire, theft, etc.:** Loss due to theft, etc., is considered as an abnormal loss and is debited to the profit and loss account.

BALANCE SHEET

The balance sheet is a statement of accounts prepared for the purpose of ascertaining the exact financial position of the business on the last date of the financial year under review. It is called balance sheet because it is prepared on a sheet of a ledger folio. While the assets are recorded on the credit side, the liabilities are shown on the debit side of the balance sheet.

Uses of a Balance Sheet

Following are the uses of a balance sheet:

1. It provides information as to the total amount of money involved in running the business enterprise.
2. It shows the financial state of the business firm as on a particular date.
3. It gives information regarding the nature and cost of the assets of the firm.
4. The information regarding the nature and cost of the firm liabilities is available from a balance sheet.

Preparation of a Balance Sheet

In a balance sheet are given the names of all those accounts that have balances, i.e. accounts of assets, liabilities and owner's equity. While the accounts of capital and liabilities shown on the left-hand side are known as *liabilities*; assets and other debit balances are given on the right-hand side and are called *assets*. Items generally included in a balance sheet are as under:

1. **Current assets:** *Current assets* are those that are either in the form of cash or can be easily converted into cash within a year, e.g. cash at bank, bills, stock, prepared expenses, debtors, short-term securities, etc.

2. **Fixed assets:** Assets held on a long-term basis in the business such as land, machinery, building, furniture, etc., are called *fixed assets*.

3. **Current liabilities:** Liabilities expected to be cleared within a year are called *current liabilities*. These are usually paid out of current assets. Salaries, wages, commission, bank overdraft, rent, taxes, payment to creditors, bills payable, etc., are all current liabilities.

4. **Long-term liabilities:** Those liabilities that mature for payment after a period of one year or more and do not require sale of any assets for their payment are known as *long-term liabilities*, e.g. loans that are repayable after a period of more than one year, mortgages on estate holdings of the business, etc.

5. **Investments:** *Investments* represent funds invested in government securities, shares of companies, etc. These are shown at cost price in the balance sheet. If on the date of preparation of the balance sheet, the market price of an investment is lower than its cost price, this fact is brought in the balance sheet by appending a suitable note.

6. **Capital:** *Capital* is the excess of the firm's assets over its liabilities. It represents the amount originally invested by the proprietor or partners and is increased by profit and decreased by losses and drawings.

7. **Drawings:** *Drawings* are the sums of money or goods withdrawn by the proprietor from the business for his personal use. Drawings by the proprietor have the effect of reducing the balance in the capital account. Therefore, the drawing account is closed by transferring its balance to his capital account.

Grouping and Reordering of Assets and Liabilities

The items included in a balance sheet need to be properly grouped and presented in a particular order. The term grouping means putting together items of a similar nature under a common head. The assets and liabilities are then shown in a particular order that can be done in one of the following two methods:

1. Order of liquidity
2. Order of permanence

Order of liquidity

Order of liquidity means the order in which the assets and the liabilities can be converted into cash. For example, the most liquid asset, e.g. cash in hand is shown first and the least liquid asset, e.g. goodwill is shown at the end. Similarly the liabilities of a business are arranged in order of urgency of their repayment. For example, the ones that are most urgent as regards repayment, e.g. short-term creditors are shown first and the least urgent, e.g. long-term creditors are shown at the end.

Order of permanence

Order of permanence is exactly the reverse of the first method stated above. According to this method, the permanent assets and liabilities are shown first, followed by current assets and liabilities. The business enterprises that are run by a sole proprietor or by a group of partners generally follow the first method to marshal their balance sheets, whereas joint stock companies prepare their balance sheets in order of permanence.

BALANCE SHEET

Liabilities	Rs	Assets	Rs
Current liabilities		Liquid assets	
Bills payable		Cash in hand	
Sundry creditors		Cash at bank	
Bank overdraft		Floating assets	
Long-term liabilities		Sundry debtors	
Loan from bank		Investments	
Debentures		Bills receivable	
		Stock in trade	
		Prepaid expenses	
Fixed liabilities		Fixed assets	
		Machinery	
		Building	
		Furniture and fixtures	
Capital		Fictitious assets	
		Advertisement	
		Miscellaneous expenses	
		Profit loss a/c	
		Intangible assets	
		Goodwill	
		Patents	
		Copyright	
Total		Total	

Note. For contingent liability, if any.

Illustration: 2

From the following trial balance, draft the balance sheet of Nidhi Medical Hall as on 31 December 2002.

Particulars	Balance Dr (Rs)	Balance Cr (Rs)
Land and building	80 000	
Plant and machinery	42 000	
Furniture	10 000	
Motor vehicle	14 000	
Stock on 31.12.02	48 000	
Debtors and creditors	8000	25 000
Cash in hand	2000	
Bank overdraft		60 000
Drawings and capital	10 000	90 000
Investments	6000	
Net profit		45 000
	2 20 000	2 20 000

Solution:

Balance sheet of M/s Nidhi Medical Hall as on 31 December 2002

Dr				Cr
Liabilities	**Amount (Rs)**		**Assets**	**Amount (Rs)**
Bank overdraft	60 000		Cash in hand	2000
Creditors	25 000		Investments	6000
Capital	90 000		Debtors	80 000
Add net profit	45 000		Closing stock	48 000
	1 35 000		Furniture	10 000
			Motor vehicle	14 000
			Plant and machinery	42 000
Less drawing	10 000	1 25 000	Land and building	80 000
		2 10 000		2 10 000

Difference between Trial Balance and Balance Sheet

	Trial balance	Balance sheet
1	It is prepared to check the arithmetical accuracy of posting of transactions to the ledger.	It is prepared to know the financial position of the business enterprise on a given date.
2	A trial balance can be prepared at any time. It may be prepared at the end of a month or a quarter.	A balance sheet is generally prepared at the end of the accounting period.
3	It shows 'debit balances' and 'credit balances'.	It shows the 'liabilities' and 'assets'.
4	All types of accounts find their place in a trial balance.	In balance sheet accounts of assets, liabilities, capital and those accounts that are in force on the date of the balance sheet are presented.
5	Generally, the opening stock appears in a trial balance and not the closing stock.	Only the closing stock appears on the assets side of the balance sheet.
6	It is not possible to have information about the net profit or net loss.	The information about the net profit earned or the net loss incurred is provided in a balance sheet.
7	It can be prepared without making any adjustments regarding prepared expenses, incomes received in advance, etc.	It cannot be prepared without making adjustments regarding prepared expenses, outstanding expenses, income received in advance, making provision for possible losses, etc.
8	It is not essential to prepare a trial balance.	It is essential to prepare a balance sheet at the end of the accounting period.
9	Trial balance is not recognized by the court.	Balance sheet is recognized by the court.

Difference between Profit and Loss Account, and Balance Sheet

	Profit and loss account	Balance sheet
1	In profit and loss account the nominal accounts are shown.	In a balance sheet the personal accounts and the real accounts are shown.
2	The aim of the profit and loss account is to provide information regarding net profit or net loss.	The aim of the balance sheet is to know the financial position of the business.
3	It is a ledger account giving information about debits and credits.	It is only statement of assets and liabilities.
4	It is an account, so the words 'To' and 'By' are used.	It is a statement and the words 'To' and 'By' are not used.
5	The balance of the profit and loss account indicates profit or loss.	The total on both sides of a balance sheet is always the same.
6	The account shows profit or loss made by the business as on a fixed date.	It shows the financial position of the business enterprise on a fixed date.

ANALYSIS OF FINANCIAL STATEMENTS

Financial analysis is a process of evaluating the relationship between the component parts of financial statements to obtain a better understanding of the financial position and performance of a firm. The steps involved in financial analysis are as follows:

1. Select the information relevant to the purpose of analysis from the financial statements.
2. Arrange the information in a way so as to highlight significant relationships.
3. Interpret the relationships and draw relevant conclusions from them.

Financial analysis is useful to different groups in the society. However, the purpose of analysis varies from one group to another. For example, the management of a firm is interested in the overall performance of the firm, the shareholders and investors are interested in the earning per share, the debenture holders want to know the capital structure and the earning position of the company, whereas the banks and other short-term creditors are interested in the composition of current assets and current liabilities of the firm.

METHODS OF FINANCIAL ANALYSIS

Financial analysis can be made by the following methods:

Comparative Financial Statements

Comparative financial statements contain figures of two or more consecutive years, which give a comparative view of the financial performance of a firm. A comparative profit and loss account gives expenses and revenues of two consecutive years. Similarly a comparative balance sheet contains the amounts of assets and liabilities at two different points of time, e.g. on 31.3.09 and 31.3.10. Such statement reflects the nature and trend of changes in the financial performance of the company. Under the Companies Act 1956, the companies are required to give figures for the current year as well as the previous year in their profit and loss accounts and balance sheets.

Common Size Financial Statements

In the common size financial statements, the figures are converted into percentages to some common base. For example, in the profit and loss account, the sale figure is assumed to be 100 and all figures are expressed as a percentage of sales. Similarly, in the balance sheet, the total of assets or liabilities is taken as 100 and all other figures are expressed as percentages of this total.

Funds Flow Analysis

Funds flow analysis reveals the changes in the working capital position of an enterprise. It indicates the sources from where the working capital was obtained and the purpose for which it was used.

Ratio Analysis

Ratio analysis is the most popular method of financial analysis. Moreover, it is simple and more informative. The term ratio refers to the numerical relationship between two items. A ratio by itself does not reveal much but its comparison with a similar ratio of the past or of a similar firm is very useful in judging the performance and the financial position of the enterprise. A financial analyst can use various types of ratios for different purposes. The various accounting ratios are:

1. Liquidity ratios
2. Solvency ratios
3. Activity ratios
4. Profitability ratios
5. Miscellaneous ratios

Liquidity Ratios

Liquidity ratios constitute ratio analysis of the short-term financial position, are used to measure the ability of the firm to meet its current obligations. The following two ratios come under the head:

1. Current ratios
2. Quick ratios

Current ratios (CR): CR is also called the *working capital ratio* and is the most widely used of all analytical devices based on the balance sheet. It matches the current assets of the firm to its current liabilities.

$$\text{Current ratio} = \frac{\text{Current assets}}{\text{Current liabilities}}$$

Generally a current ratio of 2 is considered satisfactory. A current ratio of two means for every one rupee of current liabilities, two rupees of current assets are available to pay them. A satisfactory current ratio enables a firm to meet its short-term obligations and thereby ensures smooth operation of business.

Quick ratios: Quick ratio is also called *acid test ratio*. It is used to measure the ability of the firm to convert its current assets quickly into cash in order to meet its current liabilities.

$$\text{Quick ratio} = \frac{\text{Quick assets}}{\text{Quick liabilities}}$$

Quick assets means current assets that can be converted into cash immediately or on a short notice without decrease in the value. Quick assets include cash and bank balances, securities and debtors. Quick ratio is more useful than the current ratio as it provides a more rigorous test of the firm's liquidity. Generally, a quick ratio of 1 is considered satisfactory.

Solvency Ratios

Solvency ratio is also known as *leverage ratio*. Solvency means the liabilities as an when they mature for payment. It also indicates the financial risk to long-term creditors. It measures the relationship between the owner's funds and the creditor's funds. The greater the proportion of the owner's funds, the higher is the solvency of the firm. Solvency is measured by following two ratios:

1. Debt equity ratio (D/E Ratio)
2. Debt to total capital

Debt equity ratio (D/E ratio): D/E is used to measure the relative claims of the creditors and the owners.

$$\text{Debt equity ratio} = \frac{\text{Long-term debt}}{\text{Share holders equity}}$$

where, Shareholder equity = Equity share capital + Surplus + Preference share capital.

Debt equity ratio is an important tool of financial analysis for evaluating the financial structure of a company. A high debt equity ratio means the shareholder stake in the company is low. A low debt equity ratio indicates a higher stake for shareholders. The appropriate debt equity ratio will depend upon the nature of the company's earnings.

Activity Ratios

Activity ratio is also known as *efficiency ratios*. These are intended to measure the efficiency with which the firm manages and utilize its assets. An activity ratio is a test of the relationship between sales and the various assets of a firm. Some of the important turnover ratios are as follows:

1. Inventory turnover ratio (ITR)
2. Capital turnover ratio

Inventory turnover ratio: Inventory turnover ratio is also known as *stock turnover ratio*. It is used to measure the firm inventory management. The ITR can be calculated by anyone using the following two formulae:

$$\text{Inventory turnover ratio} = \frac{\text{Cost of good sold}}{\text{Average inventory}}$$

$$\text{Inventory turnover ratio} = \frac{\text{Net sales}}{\text{Average inventory}}$$

A high inventory turnover ratio indicates under investment in the inventory and involves risk of the firm becoming 'out of stock'.

Similarly, a very low inventory turnover may indicate over investment in inventory that results in higher costs. Thus, a firm should have a proper inventory turnover.

Capital turnover ratio: This ratio measures the relationship between the sales and the capital employed in the business, i.e.

$$\text{Capital turnover ratio} = \frac{\text{Sales}}{\text{Capital employed}}$$

Profitability Ratios

Profitability ratios are designed to highlight the end results of business activities. So these ratios are useful to measure the operating efficiency of the company. The various ratios that are covered under these are as follows:

1. Gross profit ratio
2. Net profit ratio
3. Return on investment

Gross profit ratio: Gross profit means sales minus the cost of goods sold.

$$\text{Gross profit ratio} = \frac{\text{Gross profit}}{\text{Net sales}} \times 100$$

Gross profit depends upon the selling price, sales volume and cost. A high gross profit is a sign of good management and indicates that the cost of sales is relatively low. It may also indicate that the selling price of goods has increased without a corresponding increase in the cost of goods sold. The other possibility is that the cost of goods sold might have declined without a corresponding decline in the selling price of the goods. A low gross profit ratio is due to an increase in the cost of goods sold or decline in the selling price due to the inferior quality of the product or lack of demand, etc.

Net profit ratio: The ratio is also known as *net profit margin*. It measures the relationship between the net profit and the net sales.

$$\text{Net profit ratio} = \frac{\text{Net profit}}{\text{Total sales}} \times 100$$

where, net profit means gross profit minus operating expenses. Net profit ratio is helpful in determining the efficiency with which the operations of the firm are being managed.

Return on investment (ROI): The overall profitability of an enterprise can be measured by relating its net profit to its investment. There are three different concepts of investments that are given below:

$$\text{(i) Return on assets} = \frac{\text{Net profit after taxes}}{\text{Total assets}} \times 100$$

$$\text{(ii) Return on capital employed} = \frac{\text{Net profit after taxes}}{\text{Capital employed}} \times 100$$

Capital employed means the long-term funds supplied by the creditors and shareholders of the company.

$$\text{(ii) Return on share holders equity} = \frac{\text{Net profit after taxes}}{\text{Equity share capital}} \times 100 + \frac{\text{Preference}}{\text{share capital}} + \frac{\text{Retained}}{\text{earning}}$$

The return on investment is a useful measure for judging the overall efficiency of an enterprise. It indicates as to what degree the long-term funds of the business have been properly utilized.

Miscellaneous Ratios

The following are some of the ratios that are not covered under the main categories:

Earning per share: It is used to measure the amount of earning against each share.

$$\text{Earning per share} = \frac{\text{Net profit after taxes}}{\text{Total number of share}} \times 100$$

Dividend per share: It is used to measure the amount of dividend paid against each share.

$$\text{Dividend per share} = \frac{\text{Total amount paid to share holder}}{\text{Outstanding number of shares}}$$

Dividend payout ratio: The ratio is utilized to evaluate the shareholder's return.

$$\text{Dividend payout ratio} = \frac{\text{Dividend per share}}{\text{Earning per share}}$$

Dividend yield ratio: It is utilized to evaluate the shareholder's return in relation to the market value of share.

$$\text{Dividend yield ratio} = \frac{\text{Dividend per share}}{\text{Market value of share}}$$

Earning yield ratio: The ratio is also used to find out the return given to the shareholder in lieu of the market value of the share.

$$\text{Earning yield ratio} = \frac{\text{Market value of share}}{\text{Earning per share}}$$

Interest coverage ratio: It is also known as *debt service ratio* and is very useful to test the debt servicing capacity of the firm.

$$\text{Interest coverage ratio} = \frac{\text{Net profit before deduction of interest and taxes}}{\text{Fixed interest charges}}$$

Advantages of Ratio Analysis

The advantages of ratio analysis are as follows:

1. It helps in easier and better understanding of the profit and loss account and balance sheet.
2. The accounting ratios of one firm can be compared with those of the others to judge the relative financial position of different firms. This helps the management to detect the weaknesses and strengths of the firm.
3. Ratio analysis enables the firm to judge whether its financial position is improving or deteriorating over the years.
4. It helps in future planning.

Disadvantages of Ratio Analysis

Following are the disadvantages of ratio analysis:

1. The ratios are based on the information contained in the financial statements. The ratios become unreliable if the data given in the financial statement is not accurate and up-to-date.
2. Due to the changes of price level from one period to another, the assets acquired at different periods are shown in balance sheet at different prices. As such, the accounting ratios based on those figures cannot be compared.
3. Ratios are useful indicators only when they are compared with similar ratios of other firms. It is difficult to compare the firms because they may have different accounting periods or different composition of assets.
4. Ratios are only a postmortem of what has happened. They do not reveal the future events.
5. Ratio reflects only the financial aspect of business.

Points to Ponder

1. The term 'financial statements' means the two statements prepared at the end of the accounting period of the enterprise, e.g. the balance sheet (statement of the present financial position) and the profit and loss account (income statement).
2. The profit and loss account reveals the net profit earned or the net loss suffered by a firm in course of its business operations during the accounting period.
3. The balance sheet is a statement of accounts prepared for the purpose of ascertaining the exact financial position of the business on the last date of the financial year under review.
4. Financial analysis can be made by the following methods:
    a. Comparative financial statements
    b. Common size financial statements
    c. Funds flow analysis
    d. Ratio analysis
5. The various accounting ratios are as follows:
    a. Liquidity ratios
    b. Solvency ratios
    c. Activity ratios
    d. Profitability ratios
    e. Miscellaneous ratios

 **Self-Assessment Exercises**

1. Define *financial statements*.
2. Explain the term *profit and loss account*.
3. What do you know about balance sheet?
4. Define the term *financial analysis*.
5. Explain the term *ratio analysis*.
6. Explain the meaning of *solvency ratio*.
7. Define *current ratio*.
8. What do you know about *inventory turnover ratio*?
9. What are financial statements? What information do they provide?
10. What are the advantages of financial statements?
11. Mention the various limitations of financial statements.
12. What is a profit and loss account? Why is it prepared?
13. What are the methods of grouping and reordering of assets and liabilities for the purpose of preparing balance sheet?
14. Discuss the various steps that are involved in financial analysis.
15. What are the advantages of financial analysis?

16. Mention the points of distinction between a trial balance and a balance sheet.
17. Differentiate between the profit and loss account, and the balance sheet.
18. What are financial statements? Discuss the advantages and limitations of financial statements.
19. Explain the term *profit and loss account*. How is it prepared? Discuss five items that are included while preparing a profit and loss account.
20. What is a balance sheet? What are its characteristics? What is the need for preparing a balance sheet?
21. What is a balance sheet? Detail the various items that are included in a balance sheet.
22. What do you know about financial analysis? Discuss the various methods of making a financial analysis.
23. What do you understand by grouping and reordering (Marshalling) of assets and liabilities? Explain the ways in which a balance sheet may be marshalled.
24. Differentiate between the following pairs:
    a. Trial balance and balance sheet
    b. Profit and loss account, and balance sheet
25. What do you know about *ratio analysis*? Mention the advantages and disadvantages of ratio analysis.
26. Explain the following terms:
    a. Ratio analysis
    b. Liquidity ratio
    c. Current ratio
    d. Solvency ratio
    e. Inventory turnover ratio
    f. Gross profit ratio
    g. Net profit ratio

EXERCISE 1

From the following balance extracted from the books of Ramesh Medical Stores, prepare a trading and profit and loss account for the year ended 31 March 2008 and a balance sheet as on that date.

	Rs		Rs
Cash in hand	10000	Sales	92400
Drawings	2400	Returns outward	2600
Returns inwards	1600	Capital	60000
Carriage and import duty	2460	Loan from New Bank	15400
Purchases	76000	Discount (Cr)	2500
Rent	1200	Bills payable	4200
Power	1800	Creditors	22500
Interest	1540	Sales tax collected	3500
Audit fees	1400	Sales tax paid	4000
Legal charges	200	Insurance	200
Buildings	20000	Commission (Dr)	800
Debtors	17500	Incidental expenses	2000
Bills receivable	5600	Horses and vehicles	3800
Loan (Dr)	4200	Travelling expenses	800

	Rs		Rs
Furniture	4400	Goodwill	15000
Machinery	9000		
Cycle shed	2000		
Wages	12000		
Salaries	4000		

Adjustments:
(1) Closing stock Rs 40350.
(2) Outstanding expenses: wages Rs 1000; salaries Rs 400.
(3) Depreciation furniture @ 5%, machinery @ 10%
(4) Allow 5%interest on capital.
(5) Prepaid insurance Rs 70.

EXERCISE 2

Trial balance of Arun, a pharmacist on 31 March 2004 was as follows:

	Dr (Rs)	Cr (Rs)
Capital		225000
Freehold land at cost	25000	
Furniture at cost	7500	
Building at cost	65000	
Salaries	12000	
Purchases	485000	
Sales		450000
S. debtors	45000	
S. creditors		30000
Rent received		6000
Rates and taxes	3000	
Repairs	2700	
Miscellaneous expenses	7200	
Travelling expenses	8750	
Cash in hand and at bank	49850	
	711000	711000

You are required to prepare a trading and profit and loss account for the year, and a balance sheet as on that date after taking into the under noted adjustments:
(1) Stock on 31 March 2004 was Rs 140000.
(2) Bad debts Rs 500 to be written off.
(3) Provision for doubtful debts to be made at Rs 2500.
(4) Depreciation of building at 5% and on furniture at 10% to be provided.

Bank Reconciliation Statements

INTRODUCTION

Nowadays, all business organizations conduct their daily transactions with a bank account. Only a small amount of cash is kept in the office for immediate requirements and the remaining is deposited with the bank that helps in avoiding the risk of theft, misappropriation or fraud of money. The payments are also made by cheque. The bank account provides a convenient place for the cash resources of the business. Money deposited in the bank is safe. The bank account enables the business concern to settle its debts by means of cheques. This avoids the difficulty of counting cash.

When a business organization opens an account with the bank, the bank supplies a book called the *pass book*. The pass book is a bound or loose book supplied by the bank to the depositor. This book is a copy of the depositors account in the bank's ledger. Amounts paid to and withdrawn from the bank by the depositor are entered datewise from the ledger in this book by the banker. The depositor is allowed to keep this book with him but is required to send it to the bank at frequent intervals for necessary entries into it. On its return from the bank, the depositor checks the entries therein with those in the bank columns of the cash book to ascertain their accuracy.

The businessman records all the transactions relating to his bank account in the cash book. All deposits are shown in the bank column on the debit side of the cash book and all withdrawals on the credit side. The bank also maintains a separate account in its ledger for every customer. It credits the customers account with all deposits made by him and debits it with all withdrawals.

Thus what is shown on the debit side of the cash book appears on the credit side of the passbook (i.e. the customer's account in the bank's ledger) and vice versa.

NEED FOR RECONCILIATION

Normally, entries in the pass book would tally with those in the cash book, and their balances should also be the same. But, in actual practice, they would generally differ. This may be because of some mistakes committed either by the business concern or by the bank in recording the transactions. But the main reason why, on a particular date, the balance shown in the pass book differs from the balance shown in the cash book is that many transactions are not recorded on the same date in both these books. That is, there is always some time lag between the date of recording the transaction in the cash book and the date on which it is recorded in the pass book. So, on a particular date, the balances in these two books are bound to differ.

Hence, a mechanism is required to locate the difference between the two balances and to cross check the two balances. Such a mechanism is called *bank reconciliation statement*. Bank reconciliation statement is a statement prepared mainly to reconcile the difference between the bank balance shown by the pass book and the bank cash book (ledger).

ESSENTIAL FEATURES OF BANK RECONCILIATION STATEMENTS

The essential features of bank reconciliation statements are as follows:

1. It is prepared for reconciling the difference between the cash book balance and the pass book balance.
2. It is prepared on a particular date.
3. It is prepared by the customer and not, by the banker.

OBJECTIVES of BANK RECONCILIATION STATEMENTS

The objectives of bank reconciliation statements are as follows:

1. To detect any errors that might have been committed either in the cash book or in the pass book.
2. To ascertain the bank balance that should be shown in the balance sheet at the end of the period.

ADVANTAGES of BANK RECONCILIATION STATEMENTS

The advantages of bank reconciliation statements are as follows:

1. Errors in the cash book and the pass book can be known and corrected.
2. Misappropriation (by the bank staff and the depositor) of cash or cheques deposited can be checked.

3. Delay in the collection of cheques and also the nonpayment of cheques issued can be brought to light.

REASONS FOR DISAGREEMENT IN THE PASS BOOK AND THE CASH BOOK BALANCE

The following are the reasons for the disagreement in the pass book and the cash book balance:

1. Cheques deposited in the bank for collection: When firms receive cheques from its customers (debtors), they are immediately recorded in the debit side of the cash book. This increases the bank balance as per the cash book. However, the bank credits the customer account only when the amounts in the cheques are actually realized. The clearing of cheques generally takes few days especially in case of outstation cheques or when the cheques are paid-in at a bank branch other than the one at which the account of the firm is maintained. This leads to a cause of difference between the bank balance shown by the cash book and the balance shown by the bank passbook.

2. Cheques issued but not presented for payment: When cheques are issued by the firm to suppliers or creditors of the firm, these are immediately entered on the credit side of the cash book. However, the receiving party may not present the cheque to the bank for payment immediately. The bank will debit the firm's account only when these cheques are actually paid by the bank. Hence, there is a time lag between the issue of a cheque and its presentation to the bank that may cause the difference between the two balances.

3. Interest allowed by the bank: Bankers credit the customer accounts with interest on current accounts. This will be entered in the pass book but a corresponding entry will not be found in the cash book for some time. The customers will make the entry only after seeing the pass book.

4. Interest on overdrafts and other bank charges: The bank may debit the customers account with interest on overdraft or for bank charges. These items will not be entered in the cash book immediately.

5. Dishonour of cheques and bills deposited for collection: The cheques or bills may be deposited by the customer into the bank for collection. These may be dishonoured by the party liable to make payment. The customer might have debited his bank account as soon as he deposited these instruments. He comes to know the fact of dishonour only when the bank informs him. On getting this information a credit entry is passed in the cash book. Until then the cash balance will disagree with the pass book balance.

6. Collection of interest, dividend, etc., by the bank: When the bank collects interest and dividend on behalf of the customer, then these are immediately credited to the customers account. But the firm will know about these transactions and record the same in the cash book only when it receives a bank statement. Till then the balances as per the cash book and the passbook will differ.

7. Direct payment by the bank on behalf of the customer: Sometimes the customers give standing instructions to the bank to make some payment regularly on stated days to the third parties. For example, telephone bills, insurance premium, rent, taxes, etc., are directly paid by the bank on behalf of the customer and debited to the account. As a result, the balance as per the bank passbook would be less than the one shown in the cash book.

8. Error in the pass book. The ledger clerks at the bank may commit mistakes in posting accounts of the customers. In such cases, there will be wrong entries in the pass book that will naturally not correspond with the entries in the cash book.

9. Error in the cash book. Similarly, mistakes might occur in the maintenance of the cash book. This would also result in differences between the balances of the cash book and the pass book.

10. Mistakes and frauds. Mistakes are unintentional whereas frauds are intentional. Any fraud committed either by the bank officials or the accountants of the customers would also result in discrepancies between the balance of the cash book and the pass book. One object of preparing the bank reconciliation statement is to detect such frauds or forgeries, if any, in the transaction of the bank account. For example, if a cheque is forged and the amount is withdrawn from the bank, this can easily be detected while preparing the bank reconciliation statement. In this case, there will be a debit entry (reduced balance) in the pass book without having any relevance to business transactions and no entry will be found in the cash book. Therefore, the cash book balance will be more than the pass book balance. This will provide a clue to the fraud and further investigation must be made to find the person who has drawn the amount from the bank wrongfully.

IMPORTANCE OF THE BANK RECONCILIATION STATEMENT

The bank reconciliation statement is essential to tally the bank balance shown by the cash book with the balance shown by the bank pass book. If there is any difference, it is important to identify the reasons for the difference. This is possible only by preparing a bank reconciliation statement. This statement ensures that the bank balance shown by the cash book is reconciled with that of the bank pass book. In the absence of the bank reconciliation statement, the customer cannot be sure of the correctness of the bank balance depicted by the cash book. Hence, periodic preparation of the bank reconciliation statement is essential.

STEPS INVOLVED IN PREPARING THE BANK RECONCILIATION STATEMENT

The following steps are involved in preparing the bank reconciliation statement:

1. The date on which the reconciliation statement is to be prepared should be selected. Usually the last date of the month is chosen for the purpose.
2. The balance as shown by any one book (i.e. either the cash book or the pass book) should be taken as the base. It is the starting point. This balance is to be compared with the other balance.
3. The items that cause the difference should be ascertained.
4. The effect of causes that lead to the difference is to be analysed.
5. The causes that have resulted from an increase in the balance are to be deducted from the bank balance.

The starting balance is thus adjusted and the balance as per the other book is arrived at. The following proforma is suggested:

Bank Reconciliation Statement as on _____

Particulars	Rs	Rs
Debit balance as per cash book or bank OD as per pass book		XXX
Add:		
1. Cheques issued but not presented for payment	XXX	
2. Cheques received and entered in the cash book but not sent to bank for collection	XXX	
3. Direct payments by customers into the bank a/c	XXX	

Particulars	Rs	Rs
4. Amount collected by the bank as interest, dividend, etc., entered only in the pass book	XXX	
5. Cheques not entered in the cash book deposited into the bank	XXX	
6. Wrong credit made in the pass book	XXX	
7. Wrong credit made in the cash book	XXX	
8. Cheques issued but dishonoured	XXX	
		XXX
Less:		
1. Cheques deposited but not credited in the pass book	XXX	
2. Cheques entered in the cash book but not deposited with the bank	XXX	
3. Bank charges interest, etc., debited in the pass book but not entered in the cash book	XXX	
4. Cheques, bill dishonoured not entered in cash book	XXX	
5. Payment made by bank under standing orders not entered in the cash book	XXX	
6. Cheques discounted but dishonoured	XXX	
7. Wrong debit in the cash book	XXX	
8. Wrong debit in the pass book	XXX	XXX
Balance as per pass book or cash book		XXX

Illustration: 1

On 31 March 2005, the cash book of Jigar showed a bank overdraft of Rs 7640. On the same date Jigar received the bank statement. On perusal of the statement, Jigar ascertained the following information:

1.Cheques deposited but not credited by the bank	10000
2.Interest on securities collected by the bank but not recorded in the cash book	1280
3.Dividend collected by the bank directly, but not recorded in the cash book	1000
4.Cheques issued but not presented for payment	37400
5.Bank charges not recorded in the cash book	340

From the above information, you are required to prepare a bank reconciliation statement to ascertain the balance as per the bank statement.

Bank Reconciliation Statement as on 31-3-2005

Particulars		Rs	Rs
	Overdraft as per cash book		7640
Add:	Cheques deposited but not credited by the bank	10000	
	Bank charges not recorded in the cash book	340	
			10340
			17980
Less:	Interest on securities collected by the bank but not recorded in the cash book	1280	
	Dividends collected by the bank but not recorded in the cash book	1000	
	Cheques issued but not presented for payment	37400	
			39680
	Credit balance as per the bank statement		21700

Illustration: 2

The cash book of a firm showed an overdraft of Rs 30 000 on 31 March 1999. A comparison of the entries in the cash book and the pass book revealed the following:

1. On 22 March 1999 cheques totalling Rs 6000 were sent to the bankers for collection. Out of these, a cheque for Rs 1000 was wrongly recorded on the credit side of the cash book and the cheques amounting to Rs 300 could not be collected by the bank before 1 April 1999.
2. A cheque for Rs 4000 was issued to a supplier on 28 March 1999. The cheque was presented to the bank on 4 April 1999.
3. There were debits of Rs 2600 in the pass book for interest on overdraft and the bank charges but the same had not been recorded in the cash book.
4. A cheque for Rs 1000 was issued to a creditor on 27 March 1990 but by mistake the same was not recorded in the cash book. The cheque was, however, duly encashed by 31 March 1999.
5. As per the standing instructions, the banker collected a dividend of Rs 500 on behalf of the firm and credited the same to its account by 31 March 1999. The fact was however, intimated to the firm on 3 April 1999.

You are required to prepare a bank reconciliation statement as on 31 March 1999.

Bank Reconciliation Statement as on 31-3-1999

Particulars		Rs	Rs
	Bank overdraft as per cash book		30 000
Add:	Cheques deposited but not collected	300	
	Interest on overdraft and bank charges not recorded in cash book	2600	
	Cheques issued to creditors but not recorded in the cash book	1000	
			3900
			33 900
Less:	Cheques wrongly recorded on the credit side of the cash book (1000 x 2)	2000	
	Cheques issued but not presented for payment	4000	
	Dividend collected by bank but not yet recorded in cash book	500	
			6500
	Bank overdraft as per the pass book		27 400

Points to Ponder

1. A mechanism is required to locate the difference between the two balances and to cross check the two balances. Such a mechanism is called bank reconciliation statement.
2. Reasons for the disagreement in the pass book and the cash book balance are
   a. Cheques deposited in the bank for collection
   b. Cheques issued but not presented for payment
   c. Interest allowed by the bank
   d. Interest on overdraft s and other bank charges
   e. Dishonour of cheques and bills deposited for collection
   f. Collection of interest, dividend, etc., by the bank
   g. Direct payment by the bank on behalf of the customer
   h. Error in the pass book
   i. Error in the cash book
   j. Mistakes and frauds

  Self-Assessment Exercises

1. Define the term *bank reconciliation statement*.
2. What is the importance of the bank reconciliation statement?
3. Name the factors that are responsible for the difference between the bank balance shown by the cash book and the bank pass book.
4. Why is a bank reconciliation statement prepared? Explain.
5. How is a bank reconciliation statement prepared? Submit a proforma example of the same.
6. What are the causes of the difference in the cash book and the pass book balances? How would you reconcile them?
7. Write the importance of bank reconciliation statement. Submit a proforma example of the same.

EXERCISE 1

Prepare a bank reconciliation statement and find out the balance as per pass book on 31-12-1999.

1. Cash book balance as on 31-12-1999 Rs 1 75 000.
2. Cheques amounting to Rs 80 000 issued on 28-12-1999 were presented for payment on 5-1-2000.
3. A cheque for Rs 60 000 deposited on 25-12-1999 was returned dishonored on 10-1-2000.
4. Interest on investment Rs 4000 was collected and credited by bank but no entry is there in the cash book.
5. Bank charges debited in the pass book only Rs 60.

EXERCISE 2

Prepare bank reconciliation statement as on 30-6-1980 from the following particulars.

1. Overdraft balance as per the cash book as on 30-6-80 Rs 3595.
2. Interest on overdraft was entered in the pass book only Rs 80.
3. Cheques issued but not cashed before 30-6-80 Rs 635.
4. Cheques paid into bank but not cleared Rs 1105.
5. Interest on investments collected by the bank but not entered in cash book Rs 250.

Bills of Exchange

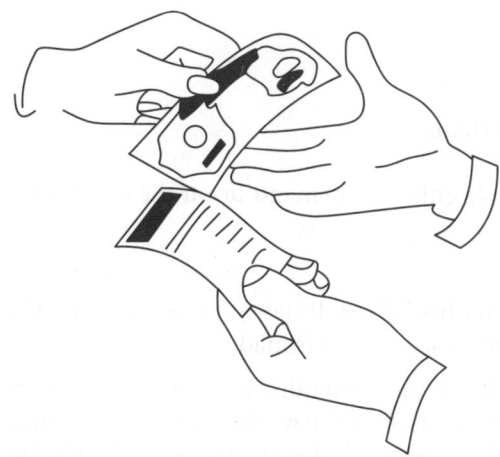

INTRODUCTION

In the modern era, a large number of business transactions are made on credit basis. In case of credit sale of goods, the purchaser usually promises to make payment after a certain period. In such a case, the seller would like to get a written undertaking from the buyer to get the payment after a fixed period. The seller prepares a document in which he puts in writing all the terms and conditions relating to the sale of goods such as the amount required to be paid; date of payment; place of payment. The buyer puts his signature on the document and it is known as *bill of exchange*.

As such, the bills of exchange are instruments of credit that facilitates the credit sale of goods. In India, these are known as *hundis* that are written in Indian languages and have been in use from the time immemorial. In Western countries, the name used for such instruments are *bill of exchange* and *promissory notes*. The same names are used nowadays in our country. All such instruments are governed by Indian Negotiable Instrument Act, 1981.

According to this Act, a bill of exchange is defined as an instrument in writing, an unconditional order signed by the maker directly to pay a certain sum of money only to or to the order of a certain person or to the bearer of the instrument.

Meaning of the Bill of Exchange

According to the Indian Negotiable Instrument Act 1881, a bill of exchange is defined as an instrument in writing containing an unconditional order, signed by the maker, directing a certain person to pay a certain sum of money only to, or to the order of a certain person or to the bearer of the instrument.

Characteristics of the Bill of Exchange

Following are the characteristics of the bill of exchange:

1. A bill of exchange must be in writing.
2. It is an order to make payment.
3. The order to make payment is unconditional.
4. The maker of the bill of exchange must sign it.
5. The payment to be made must be certain.
6. The date on which the payment is made must also be certain.
7. The bill of exchange must be payable to a certain person.
8. The amount mentioned in the bill of exchange is payable either on demand or on the expiry of a fixed period of time.
9. It must be stamped as per the requirement of law.

A bill of exchange is generally drawn by the creditor upon his debtor. It has to be accepted by the drawee (debtor) or someone on his behalf. It is just a draft till its acceptance is made.

For example, Amit sold goods to Rohit on credit for Rs 10 000 for three months. To ensure the payment on the due date, Amit draws a bill of exchange upon Rohit for Rs 10 000 payable after three months. Before it is accepted by Rohit it will be called a *draft*. It will become a bill of exchange only when Rohit writes the word 'accepted' on it and append his signature thereto communicate his acceptance.

Advantages of Bill of Exchange

The advantages of the bill of exchange are as follows:

1. It is a written evidence of debt.
2. It is a proof of all conditions of the loan.
3. It is a valid document in the eyes of the law.
4. It helps in purchasing goods on credit.
5. It helps in the fulfilment of financial need mutually by writing an accommodation bill.
6. It helps in planning cash operation. The seller knows the time when he would receive the money and as such can plan his cash operations accordingly.
9. It helps in saving of currency because with the introduction of the bill of exchanger, there is less need of currency.
10. It can be discounted through the bank in case of need before the date of its payment.

Types of Bills of Exchange

There are two types of bills of exchange:

1. **Trade bills:** The bill is written in lieu of business deeds. If the payment of the bill is not done on the due date the same can be received with the help of the court.
2. **Accommodation bills**: In order to oblige friends, often bills are drawn, accepted and endorsed by businessmen without any consideration. By accepting such a bill the acceptor is able to lend his name, and the other party (drawer) taking advantage of the reputation of the acceptor gets it discounted with his banker. After meeting his aim with this temporary finance, he (drawer) sends back money to the acceptor thus making it possible for him to meet the bill on the due date. Since such bills are accepted without consideration, therefore, there is no liability of the acceptor to the drawer. The third party takes such a bill for value; therefore, the acceptor is liable to the third party. In case payment is not made to such bills, the court cannot come to the rescue of the payee.

Parties of the Bill of Exchange

There are three parties of bill of exchange. They are as follows:

1. **Drawer:** *Drawer* is a person who writes the bill of exchange draws the money. The bill of exchange is signed by the drawer of the bill.
2. **Drawee or Acceptor:** *Drawee* is a person on whom the order is made. He is the purchaser or the debtor on whom the bill is drawn and who is liable to pay the amount mentioned in the bill. He accepts to pay the amount by writing the word 'accepted' on the bill and signs it.
3. **Payee:** *Payee* is the person who will collect the money on due date. The drawer will be the payee of the bill, if he retains the bill till the date of maturity and receives the payment. The bank may also be the payee of the bill, if the bill is discounted from the bank. In case the bill is endorsed by the drawer to a third party (endorsee), then he will be the payee of the bill. As such the drawer himself, or the bank or the endorsee may be the payee of the bill.

Date of Maturity and Days of Grace

The date on which the payment of the bill becomes due is called the *due date* or the *date of maturity*. While calculating the due date of the bill, it is compulsory to add three days to the period of the bill. These three days are called the *days of grace*. For example, if a bill is drawn on 1 June 2009 and is payable two months after the due date, its maturity will be on 4 August 2009.

The following points are very significant for calculating the date of maturity:

1. If a bill falls due in months where there are no 29th, 30th or 31st dates, the maturity date will be the last date of the month.
2. Bill drawn on 30th May or 31st May for one month will become due on 3rd July.
3. In case the due date of bill falls on a holiday, the due date will be one day earlier. For example, if a bill falls due on 26th January, its due date will be 25th January.
4. In case the due date (including the days of grace) has been declared as emergency holiday the due date will be one day later.

Specimen of the Bill of Exchange

For example, on 1 January 2009, Kanti Lal of Bardoli, sells goods of value Rs 20 000 to Naresh Kumar of Madhi on credit, the payment of which is to be made after three months. Kanti Lal draws a bill on

Naresh Kumar who accepts it and returns to Kanti Lal. In such a bill Kanti Lal will be called as *drawer* and Naresh Kumar will be called the *acceptor* of the bill.

SPECIMENS OF BILL OF EXCHANGE

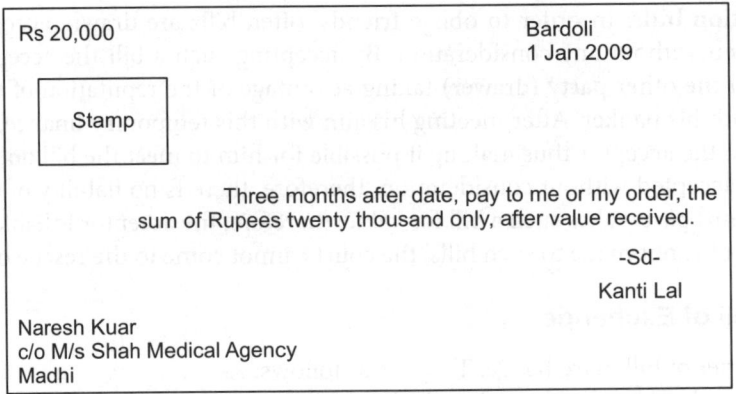

Rs 20,000

Bardoli
1 Jan 2009

Stamp

Three months after date, pay to me or my order, the sum of Rupees twenty thousand only, after value received.

-Sd-
Kanti Lal

Naresh Kuar
c/o M/s Shah Medical Agency
Madhi

Accounting Treatment

For the purpose of accounting, bills are divided into two categories:

1. Bills receivable (B/R)
2. Bills payable (B/P).

The person who is entitled to receive money draws the bill and gets it accepted from the person who is liable to pay. As such, the same bill is a bill receivable (B/R) from the point of view of the drawer and bill payable (B/P) from the point of view of the acceptor. In the words the same bill is an asset (B/R) for drawer and a liability (B/P) for the acceptor.

Different Uses of the Bills Receivable

A party that holds a bill receivable can use it in either of the following ways:

1. **Retaining of bill by the drawer till the date of maturity:** In such a case, the drawer will receive the payment of the bill on the date of maturity.
2. **Discounting of the bill from the bank:** If the holder of a B/R money, he can discount the bill from the bank before the date of its maturity or borrowing from the bank on the security of the bill. The bank deducts a certain amount of discount from the face value of the bill and pays the balance to the person discounting the bill. The discount deducted by the bank is actually the amount of interest charged by the bank for lending the money. The amount of discount depends upon the rate of interest and the remaining period of the bill.
3. **Endorsement of a bill:** *Endorsement* means the transfer of a bill of exchange from one person to another. The holder of a bill receivable can endorse the bill to another person by putting his signature at the back of the bill. The person endorsing the bill is known as *endorser* and the person to whom the bill is endorsed is called *endorsee*. An endorsee may again endorse the bill over to some other person and the process may continue to any extent. The person holding the bill at the date of its maturity will be entitled to get its payment.

4. **Sending of a bill to the bank for collection:** Sometimes, instead of discounting the bill, it is sent to the bank with the instructions to keep the bill, till maturity and collect its amount from the acceptor on that date. In such a case, the bank will not credit the customer's account until the amount of the bill is actually realized by it.

When the bills are sent for collection, the sender of the bills opens a new account in its books as 'Bills for collection account'. This is a personal account and is debited, when the bills are sent for collection and is credited when the intimation of the actual realization is received from the bank.

Other Accounting Aspects of Bills of Exchange

The other accounting aspects of the bills of exchange are as follows:

1. **Retiring a bill under rebate:** When the drawee makes the payment of the bill before its due date, it is called *retiring the bill*. In such a case, the holder of the bill usually allows him discount, technically called *rebate*. Such rebate is calculated at a specific rate per annum for the period, the payment is being made too early. The rebate is a gain to the party making the payment and an expense to the party that received the payment.

2. **Dishonour of a bill:** When the acceptor of the bill refuses to pay the amount of the bill on the date of maturity, it is called *dishonour of the bill*. In case of dishonour, the holder of the bill can recover the amount of the bill from any of the endorsers or the drawer. For this purpose, the holder of the bill must serve a notice of dishonour to the drawer and each prior endorser whom he seeks to make liable for payment. Such notice must be served immediately after the dishonour or within a reasonable time. If this is not done, the holder of the bill will lose his right to recover the amount from the party to whom such notice is not served.

3. **Noting charges:** To establish the fact that the bill was properly presented and dishonoured, the bill is usually handed over to a person called *notary public* appointed by the court. The notary public again presents the dishonoured bill to the acceptor for payment and if the acceptor still refuses to make the payment, the notary public notes down the fact of the dishonour of the bill itself. Such act of the notary public is called *noting*. The notary public charges a small fee for the services rendered which is called *noting charges*. Such charges are paid to the notary public first by the holder of the bill, but are ultimately recovered from the acceptor, because he is the person responsible for the dishonour.

4. **Renewal of bill:** Sometimes, the acceptor of a bill finds himself unable to meet the bill on the due date. In such case, he may request the holder of the bill to cancel the original bill and draw a new bill in place of the old one. If the holder agrees, a new bill will be drawn either for the full amount of the bill or for the balance amount in case of partial payment by the acceptor. In such a case, the drawer normally charges interest for the period of the new bill. The interest may be paid in cash or as is more common, may be added in the amount of the new bill.

5. **Dishonour of bill discounted from the bank:** In such a case, the noting charges will be paid by the bank. The bank will recover the noting charges from the person who discounted the bill from the bank and ultimately noting charges will be borne by the acceptor.

6. **Dishonour of bill endorsed to a third party:** In such cases, noting charges must be paid by the endorsee. The endorsee will recover the noting charges from the endorser and ultimately these will have to be borne by the acceptor.

7. **Insolvency of the acceptor:** When the acceptor of a bill becomes insolvent, it implies that he will not be in a position to meet his acceptance on the due date. As such, the bill accepted by him is

treated as dishonoured and hence, the entries will be passed on the same lines as in the case of ordinary dishonour.

Usually, some partial payment is received from the insolvent in the form of a number of paisa in the rupee, say forty paisa in the rupee, of the amount due from him. The total amount due from him is ascertained by preparing the insolvent's personal account.

The amount received from the insolvent's estate is known as *dividend* and the amount unpaid is treated as 'bad debit' in the books of the drawer. The unpaid amount is treated as 'deficiency' in the books of the insolvent.

PROMISSORY NOTE

In business dealings, a sometimes oral promise to pay is given. However, oral promises may or may not be kept. Therefore, promise is taken in writing to create a proof of debt. The purchaser of goods or debtor himself writes a note, signs it and gives it to the seller of goods. It is called a *promissory note*.

According to Indian Negotiable Instrument Act, 'Promissory note is an instrument in writing containing an unconditional undertaking signed by the maker to pay a certain sum of money only to or to the order of a certain person or to the bearer of the instrument'.

SPECIMENS OF PROMISSORY NOTE
Single Promissory Note

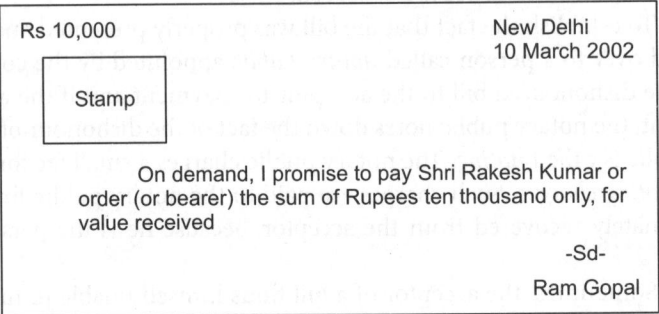

Rs 10,000   New Delhi
                                         10 March 2002

Stamp

On demand, I promise to pay Shri Rakesh Kumar or order (or bearer) the sum of Rupees ten thousand only, for value received

-Sd-
Ram Gopal

Joint Promissory Note

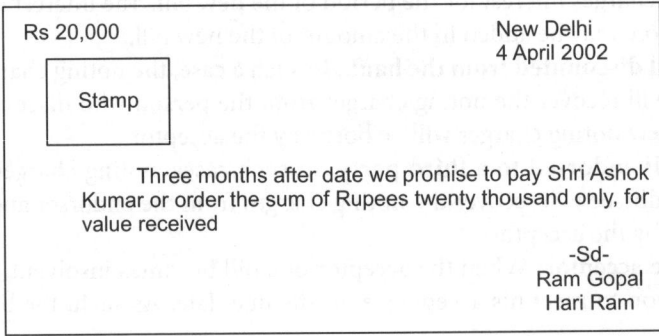

Rs 20,000   New Delhi
                                         4 April 2002

Stamp

Three months after date we promise to pay Shri Ashok Kumar or order the sum of Rupees twenty thousand only, for value received

-Sd-
Ram Gopal
Hari Ram

Characteristics of promissory note

Following are the characteristics of a promissory note:

1. It must be in writing.
2. It must contain an unconditional undertaking to pay.
3. It must be signed by the maker.
4. It must be properly stamped.
5. The amount to be paid must be specified.
6. The date and place of payment should be mentioned.
7. The promise should be to pay money only.
8. It clearly indicates the name of the party to whom the money is to be paid.
9. The promissory note cannot be made payable to the bearer.

Advantages of promissory note

The advantages of a promissory note are as follows:

1. It is the easiest method to take money on loan and to return it afterwards.
2. Promissory note itself is a proof of loan.
3. There is no need of acceptance on it.
4. The responsibility of the maker is both as an individual or combined. That is why the payee gets more security in it.

Parties to a promissory note

There are two parties to a promissory note:

1. **Maker:** He writes a promissory note and signs it.
2. **Payee:** He is entitled to get the payment.

There is no acceptor in the case of promissory note because the maker himself is liable to pay the amount.

Comparison between the bill of exchange and the promissory note

Bill of exchange	Promissory note
There may be three parties to it—the drawer, the acceptor and the payee.	There are only two parties to it—the maker and the payee.
It is drawn by the creditor.	It is drawn by the debitor.
It is an order to make payment.	It is a promise to make payment.
It needs the acceptance by the drawee.	It does not need acceptance.
The liability of the drawer is secondary. He will be liable only if the acceptor does not pay.	The liability of the drawer (maker) is primary.
Drawer can be the payee of the bill.	Maker cannot be the payee of it.
It is better to get it noted in case of dishonour.	Noting is not necessary in case of promissory note.
Only the copy is prepared in case of local bills and three copies are prepared in case of foreign bills.	Only one copy is prepared whether it is local or foreign.
There is no need of fixing the stamps on the bill payable 'on demand' but otherwise stamps would be necessary	Stamps are required to be fixed.

HUNDI

A *hundi* is a negotiable instrument written in a vernacular (local) language in accordance with the local customs. It is not governed by the Indian Negotiable Instrument Act, but by customs and practices. It is a credit instrument generally used in our local and regional markets. The word 'hundi' is a Sanskrit word 'hundi' which means 'to collect'. They are quite popular among the Indian merchants from very olden days.

Types of Hundies

Following are the different types of hundies:

1. **Darshini hundi:** A *darshini hundi* is one payable at sight. It is similar to a demand bill.
2. **Muddati hundi:** A hundi payble after a specified period of time from the date of the hundi is called *muddati hundi*. It is the equivalent of a time bill.
3. **Shahjog hundi:** 'Shah' means a respectable person well known in a place. The amount on the bill is paid to a Shah or on endorsement by Shah. If there is any fraud or if the hundi is stolen or forged, the drawee can recover the loss from the Shah. It is similar to a crossed cheque. It does not require acceptance or endorsement.
4. **Namjog hundi:** A hundi payable to the party named in the hundi.
5. **Firmonjog hundi:** A hundi payable to order.
6. **Dhanijog hundi:** A hundi payable to the owner or bearer.
7. **Zikri chit:** It is a letter written by the drawer or any other party and given to the holder of hundi.
8. **Jokhami hundi:** Seller or consignor of goods calls upon the buyer or consignee to pay the value of the goods to the holder of the hundi.
9. **Jawabee hundi:** It is a hundi through which money is remitted from one place to another with the help of a bank.

Advantages of hundies

Following are the advantages of hundies:

1. It is a good proof of indebtedness.
2. It has got all the qualities of a bill of exchange.
3. It enjoys all the legal privileges of negotiable instrument.
4. By writing a hundi, the purchaser is bound to pay a specific amount after a specific period.
5. The time of payment of hundi is fixed.
6. Hundi can be discounted if he needs the amount earlier.

Disadvantages of hundies

The disadvantages of hundies are as follows:

1. It is written in local language only.
2. It is not useful for external trade.
3. It is not a negotiable instrument.

Points to Ponder

1. Bill of exchange is defined as an instrument in writing, an unconditional order signed by the maker directly to pay a certain sum of money only to or to the order of a certain person or to the bearer of the instrument.
2. There are two types of bills of exchange
   a. Trade bills
   b. Accommodation bills
3. Promissory note is an instrument in writing containing an unconditional undertaking signed by the maker to pay a certain sum of money only to or to the order of a certain person or to the bearer of the instrument.
4. The word 'hundi' is a Sanskrit word 'hundi' which means 'to collect'.

Self-Assessment Exercises

1. Define *bill of exchange*.
2. Explain the meaning of promissory note.
3. Define the term *hundi*.
4. What do you understand by *accommodation bill*?
5. Explain the meaning of days of grace.
6. Define the term *noting of a bill*.
7. What is the meaning of renewal of a bill?
8. Define discounting of a bill.
9. What is retiring of a bill?
10. Name the parties of the bill of exchange.
11. Explain the parties of the promissory note.
12. Explain the advantages of a bill of exchange.
13. What is the difference between a *bill of exchange* and a *promissory note*?
14. Write the characteristics of the bill of exchange.
15. Explain the various parties of the bill of exchange.
16. Prepare a specimen of the bill of exchange.
17. Why do most businessmen prefer making payment by bill of exchange?
18. Explain the meaning of *noting of a bill*.
19. Describe in brief about retiring of a bill under rebate.
20. Write the advantages of a promissory note.
21. Write the essential features of promissory note.
22. Prepare a specimen of a promissory note.
23. What is a *bill of exchange*? Explain the advantages of making payment by bill of exchange. How does it differ from a promissory note?

24. What do you know about the bill of exchange? Write its main characteristics. How does it differ from a promissory note?
25. Why do the majority of businessmen prefer making payment by bill of exchange? Prepare a specimen of the bill of exchange.
26. Explain the meaning of a promissory note. Write its characteristics and advantages.

Treatment of Cheques

INTRODUCTION

A cheque is generally used for withdrawing money from a savings account with the bank. The saving bank accounts are permitted to be operated by cheques provided a certain minimum balance is maintained.

A cheque has been defined as 'an instrument in writing, containing an unconditional order signed by the maker, directing a special banker to pay on demand, a certain sum of money to a certain person or to the order of a person or to the bearer of the cheque'.

Every bank has its own printed cheque book that contains blank cheque forms with counterfoils. The cheque books and the counterfoils are serially numbered. These numbers are entered into the cheque book register of the bank and also on the ledger folio of the customer's account at the time of opening the account as well as subsequently, whenever a fresh cheque book is issued. When a new cheque book is required, the customer has to fill and sign the requisition slip given with the cheque book.

Cheque books are printed on special security paper that is sensitive to chemicals. If chemicals are put on such paper to erase the original writing, it can easily be detected.

Recently in some big cities, where the clearing of cheques is computerized, special types of cheque forms are issued by the banks that are known as MICR (Mechanized Ink Character Recognition) cheques. There is no counterfoil with such cheques. Instead a separate sheet is given in the cheque book for keeping the records of cheques issued by the account holder.

ADVANTAGES OF A CHEQUE

The payments by cheque have the following advantages:

1. It is very convenient to carry cheques from one place to another.
2. It is the safest method of money transactions.
3. The payment can be made exactly to a paisa.
4. The counterfoil of the cheque serves the purpose of a receipt for future reference.
5. The account of the money transaction is kept by the bank, so it can be used as evidence if needed.
6. It helps to economize the use of money.
7. Money can be easily sent to different parts of the country as well as to foreign countries.

The specimen of a cheque is given below:

kotak®
Kotak Mahindra Bank   **CBS**

Date _____

Pay _____ या धारक को or Bearer

Rupees रुपये _____ अदा करें | **Rs.** |

A/c No. _____   Kotak Nova Savings Account

Kotak Mahindra Bank Ltd.
Payable At-par at all branch locations of Kotak Mahindra Bank Ltd.
Pitru Chaya, Station Road,
Bardoli - 394 601.
IFSC :KKBK0000817   **Signature**

⑈000003⑈ 394485051⑆ 998900⑈ 31

PARTIES TO A CHEQUE

A cheque deals with three parties that are as follows:

1. **Drawer:** The person who draws a cheque.
2. **Drawee:** The bank or the banker on whom the cheque is drawn.
3. **Payee:** The person named in the cheque to whom the money is to be paid. Sometimes, the drawer makes the cheque in his own favour by writing the word 'Self' in place of writing any name. In such a condition, he is both a drawer and a payee. In case the payee is a fictitious person, the cheque may be treated as payable to its bearer.

REQUISITES OF A CHEQUE

The following are the main requisites of a cheque:

1. The cheque is an instrument in writing. The writing may be typed or in ink. Bankers generally do not accept cheques written in pencil in order to avoid any unauthorized alterations.
2. A cheque should be unconditional. If any condition is attached for the payment of amount, then the cheque becomes invalid.
3. A cheque is an order to the drawee (the banker) to pay the amount.
4. A cheque must be signed by the drawer in the manner in which the drawer has signed the specimen signature.
5. The bank on whom the cheque is drawn must be specified. If it is drawn on a person, who is not a banker, then it cannot be called a *cheque*.
6. The drawer should direct the drawee (the banker) to pay a fixed amount that must tally both in words and figures. It should be written as Rs 1000 only.
7. The order written in the cheque should be for the payment of money only. No other thing can be mentioned in its place.
8. The payment must be ordered to be made to a person named therein or to his order or to the bearer of the instrument.

DRAWING A CHEQUE

A cheque can be drawn by a person on the bank where he has an account. Before drawing a cheque, the drawer must ascertain that he has sufficient balance in his account in the bank to cover the amount of money written in the cheque. The cheque would be dishonoured by the bank, if his balance is less than the amount he has written in the cheque. It is an offence to issue cheque that gets dishonoured because the amount in the account is less than the amount issued.

While drawing a cheque, the drawer must be careful in respect to the following points:

1. **Date:** A cheque is honoured by the bank, if it is presented within a reasonable time after its date of issue. It is very important that the correct date is put at a proper place on the cheque. If the date is not mentioned in the cheque, the banker can put down the correct date, but generally it is returned back to the drawer as incomplete cheque. A cheque, that bears a date earlier than the date of issue, is known as *antedated cheque*. Such a cheque remains valid for payment only when it is presented before the bank. After six months it will be returned by the bank as 'stale cheque'. The stale cheque can be used when the date is renewed by the drawer. A cheque that bears a date later than the date of its issue is known as *postdated cheque*. Such a cheque can be cashed only on the due date or after it.
2. **Name of the payee:** While drawing a cheque, the drawer should dearly specify to whom the payment of the cheque should be made. If the drawer of cheque draws the cheque for himself, the word 'Self' should be written after the words 'Pay to ....'
3. **Order or bearer:** After the name of the drawer, the order or the bearer is written. The payment of order cheque is done to the drawer or to the order of the person named therein. While writing a cheque, one of the two should be mentioned. The order cheque is safer from the payment point of view.
4. **Amount:** The amount should be written very carefully, both in words and figures. The amount in words and figures must tally; otherwise, the cheque will be dishonoured. No space should be left

before or after the amount written in the cheque. The amount written in figures and words must be suffixed with the word 'only'.

5. **Signature of the drawer:** A cheque must be signed by the drawer. The drawer's signature should be complete, genuine and put preferably in ink. The signature must tally with the specimen signature given by him to the bank at the time of opening the account. In case of any doubt or suspicion about the signature, the banker may return the cheque as dishonoured.

6. **Alterations:** Any kind of alteration in the cheque can be done only by the drawer. The alterations may be related to the date, the amount, the name of the payee or the nature of the payment. Each alteration may be confirmed by the drawer's signature. The bank does not honour a cheque that has an alteration without the drawer's signature.

7. **Counterfoil:** The counterfoil of the cheque must be filled by the drawer for future reference.

TYPES OF CHEQUES

There are three types of cheques as follows:

1. **Bearer cheque:** The cheque that can be encashed by anybody, who presents it to the bank for payment, is called a *bearer cheque*. The word bearer is suffixed after the name of the payee. Bearer cheques can be transferred from one person to another without any endorsement.

2. **Order cheque:** The cheque that is payable to the payee or his order only. In such cheques, the word 'order' is suffixed after the name of the payee. A cheque is treated as the order cheque, in case the word 'order' is not written and only the name of the payee (without the suffix word 'bearer' after it) is written in the cheque. An order cheque can be transferred only after endorsement. The payment through order cheque is safe, because the person, who presents the cheque at the counter, has to prove his identity before the payment is made to him.

The payment of the bearer cheques and the order cheques are made at the counter of the bank. Hence, they are called *open cheques*. Open cheques are not safe because anyone who finds it can get the payment over the counter of the bank.

DISTINCTION BETWEEN A BEARER CHEQUE AND AN ORDER CHEQUE

	Bearer cheque	Order cheque
1	The words 'or bearer' is suffixed after the payee's name.	The words 'or order' are fixed after the payees name.
2	It can be encashed by anybody.	It can be encashed by only the payee or whom the payee orders.
3	The drawee bank is not responsible if the payment is made to a wrong person.	The drawee bank is responsible if the payment is made to a wrong person.
4	The signature of the receiver of payment works as a receipt.	The signature of the payee works as an endorsement only.
5	The ownership is transferred by delivery alone.	The ownership is transferred only after proper endorsement.
6	It is not safe.	It is quite safe.
7	It can be easily changed into an order cheque by striking off the word 'bearer'.	It cannot be changed into a bearer cheque by striking off the word 'order'.

3. **Crossed cheque:** The cheque that cannot be cashed at the counter of the bank is called *crossed cheque*. The payee cannot get the payment in cash. He can get the amount transferred to his account or after endorsing to the account of someone else. A cheque is crossed by drawing two parallel transverse lines on its face. Word like '& Co.', 'A/c payee only' or 'not negotiable' may also be written in between these lines. This is called *general crossing of cheque*.

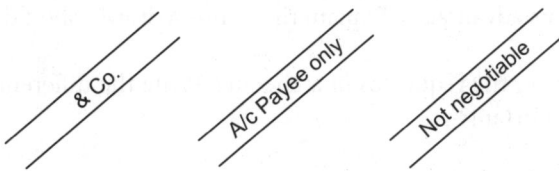

Sometimes special crossing of a cheque is done by writing the name of a particular bank to whom the payment of the cheque is to be made, on its face, either with or without the words 'Not negotiable'. The importance of this type of crossing is that a name of a particular bank is mentioned. The drawee bank will make the payment only to the mentioned bank in whose name the cheque is crossed for giving credit to the customer. Special crossing is still a safer method of making payments.

The main aim of crossing a cheque is to prevent the drawee bank and the receiver of the cheque from any kind of loss. An open cheque may be lost or stolen or the endorsement of the payee of the cheque may be forged. Under these conditions, the cheque may get into the hands of a wrong person, who may present it at the bank's counter and may receive the payment. Open cheques are always a risk. To avoid such risks, the system of crossing has been introduced.

ENDORSEMENT OF A CHEQUE

When a cheque is transferred by a payee to someone else, it has to be endorsed by the payee by putting a signature at the back of the cheque. The act of signing is known as *endorsement*. The payee is known as the *endorser*, while the person in whose favour the cheque is endorsed is called *endorsee*. The endorsement is required when the cheque is payable to the order. In the case of bearer cheques, there is no need of any endorsement.

Points to Ponder

1. A cheque is an instrument in writing, containing an unconditional order signed by the maker, directing a special banker to pay on demand, a certain sum of money to a certain person or to the order of a person or to the bearer of the cheque.
2. There are three types of cheques
   a. Bearer cheque
   b. Order cheque
   c. Crossed cheque

Self-Assessment Exercises

1. Define a cheque. Write its advantages. Explain the points a drawer should keep in mind while drawing a cheque.
2. Define a cheque. What are the requisites of a cheque? Write the different types of cheques. Why is crossing of a cheque important?
3. What is a cheque?
4. What is meant by clearing a cheque?
5. Define the term *endorsement of cheque*.
6. Explain the term *bearer cheque*.
7. Name the parties to a cheque.
8. Explain the term *order cheque*.
9. Differentiate between a bearer cheque and an order cheque.
10. Differentiate between a general crossing and special crossing.
11. Why is crossing of a cheque important?
12. Write the advantages of a cheque.

Economics

INTRODUCTION

Economics is a social science concerned with the employment of limited resources of the society, having alternative uses to produce goods and services. The word 'economics' is derived from two Greek words *oikos* (household) and *nemein* (management). Hence, economics means the management of the household in relation to the wants and means of satisfying these wants. A household has innumerable needs and wants but there are limited means to satisfy them. These scarce and limited means are called *wealth*.

Wealth Definition—Adam Smith (Classical Definition of Economics)

The classical economist, Adam Smith defined economics as the science of wealth. Here wealth is in terms of material things. But the definition does not say anything about services. Adam Smith in his treatise, 'Wealth of Nations' lays more stress on the ways and means of increasing wealth.

The above definition has a serious drawback. It gives the impression that wealth is the most important part in economics. It lays more emphasis on material (physical) goods. But services are also required for satisfying human wants and needs. Moreover this definition teaches nothing but selfishness.

The Neoclassical Definition of Wealth—Alfred Marshall

According to Dr Marshall, 'Economics is a study of mankind in the ordinary business of life'. It examines that part of the individual and social action that is most closely connected with the attainment and use of material requisites of wellbeing. Basically, business is an economic activity. Economic activities are those activities that are concerned with the acquiring and using of wealth.

Alfred Marshall rectified the defect in wealth definition proposed by Adam Smith. He gave more importance to human welfare than wealth. In his famous book captioned *Principles of Economics*, he defined economics as a study of the actions of man in a normal business life setting. This definition lays importance on man's activities and enquires how he gets and uses the income. He defined economics as a social science since it is related to the social aspects of man.

Some important inferences can be drawn from Marshall's definition of economics. They are as follows:

1. Economics is concerned with a man's ordinary business of life. It is related to his wealth getting and wealth using activities.
2. Economics is a social science. It is a study of men and how they live, and how they think in the ordinary business of life. So economics is a study of man not in isolation but as a member of a society or a social group.
3. It is related to those economic activities that promote material welfare.
4. Marshall has given a new dimension to economics. He lifted economics to the realms of a science and divested it from all political influences.

Criticism of the theory proposed by Alfred Marshall

Alfred Marshall's theory is criticized due to the following:

1. Welfare is subjective. It changes according to time, place and person and it cannot be measured exactly. Economics hence cannot be tied up with welfare.
2. According to the definition, economics deals with people living in a society but it does not throw light on all other aspects that may also have an economic perspective.
3. The word 'welfare' cannot be used along with material. There are some goods that do not promote human welfare but still they are studied in economics because they are scarce in relation to demand. So they have some price and they are economic goods. For example, liquor and cigarettes, etc., are economic goods but they do not promote welfare of the society.
4. All the goods and services that command a price and enter into the circle of exchange are economic aspects whether they are material or nonmaterial, e.g. teachers, lawyers and actors, etc., have their economic aspects because they are scarce and possess value. Hence Marshall's definition is incomplete.

Robbin's Scarcity Definition

According to Lord Robbin, 'Economics is a science that studies human behaviour as a relationship between ends and scarce means which have alternative uses'. Thus according to him, economics is a study of the 'means and ends'. Economics basically deals with how society uses their scarce resources to meet their needs and desires.

Lord Robbin's, who with the publication of his *Nature and Significance of Economic Science* in 1932, formulated his own conception of economics. In the words of Robbin 'Economics is the science which studies human behaviour as a relationship between ends and scarce means which have alternative uses'. This definition is based on the following postulates that are governed by human behaviour:

1. **Unlimited wants:** Human wants are unlimited. We cannot satisfy all our wants. If one want is satisfied another one arises. If human wants are limited, there is no economic problem. Multiplicity of wants is the main characteristic feature of the definition.

2. **Limited means:** Human wants are unlimited, but the means to satisfy the wants are limited. The economic problem arises because of unlimited wants and limited means.

3. **Means have alternative uses:** The limited means are capable of having alternative uses. For example, coal can be used in factories, railways and for generation of electricity, etc. At a time, the use of a scarce resource for one end prevents its use for any other purpose.

4. **Problem of choice:** All wants cannot be satisfied. Some wants have to be left unsatisfied. Which wants are to be satisfied and which ones to be given up is then the dilemma. More urgent wants will be satisfied and less urgent wants will be postponed.

Finally the definition distinguishes economics from technical, political, historical and other related aspects.

Thus economics is essentially a valuation process that is concerned with multiple ends and scarce means being put to alternative uses in order of their importance.

Criticism of Robbin's definition of economics

Robbin's definition of economics does not offer any solution to the problems of underdeveloped countries. The problems of underdeveloped countries are concerned with the utilization of unused resources.

Robbin has made economics a positive science. But economics is also a normative science. Robbin's definition of economics is sometimes very narrow and sometimes too wide. It is too narrow since it does not include the organizational defects that lead to idling of resources.

Economics will be an incomplete body of knowledge without the study of welfare, which Lord Robbin has neglected in his definition.

Samuelson's Costs and Benefits Definition of Economics

According to Samuelson (Nobel-laureate economist), 'Economics is the study of how people and society end up choosing, with or without the use of money to employ scarce productive resources that could have alternative uses to produce various commodities, over time and distribute them for consumption now, or in the future, among various persons and groups in the society'. It analyses costs and benefits of improving patterns of resource allocation.

A comprehensive definition of economics can be deduced from the above observations as follows:

Economics is a science that helps in achieving maximum satisfaction of wants and increasing the welfare as well as economic growth and studying those economic activities that are concerned with the efficient consumption, production, exchange and distribution of scarce means having alternative uses.

Micro economics and macro economics are the two approaches to the subject of economics. Micro economics is the study of economic actions of the individuals and small group of individuals and it is the study of individual economic units. Macro economics is the study of the economy as a whole.

There are three main branches of economics as explained below:

1. **Descriptive economics:** It is the systematic and scientific study of relevant facts of an economic activity such as foreign trade, industry, etc.
2. **Theory of economics:** This branch of economics explains the functioning of an economic system and it explains how the prices of products and services are determined.
3. **Applied economics:** This is a very important branch of economics that helps us in ascertaining the causes and the significance of economic events. Hence it causes an economic analysis of a situation. The economic theories are tested to find out how far they can be beneficially applied in formulating the economic policies.

DIFFERENT TYPES OF ECONOMIC ACTIVITIES

People are engaged in different kinds of economic activities to earn money. These economic activities are called *occupations*. The occupations that are generally adopted by humans are classified into the following three groups:

1. **Business:** *Business* means the economic activity that is primarily done with the purpose of earning profit. It involves the production of goods and services on a regular basis and carries an element of risk and uncertainty. Trading, banking, insurance and manufacturing are business activities.
2. **Profession:** *Profession* means an occupation that involves rendering of personal services of a specialized nature based on professional education, training and knowledge. For example, physician, pharmacist, lawyer, accountant, etc. The professionals generally charge professional fees from their clients for the services provided to them.
3. **Employment:** *Employment* means personal services rendered by a person to an organization under a contract of employment or service. An employee is required to perform the duties that are assigned to him by his employer. In lieu of that he receives wages or salary, allowances and other benefits of his services. Employment may be in a government department or undertaking or in a private organization.

NATURE AND SCOPE OF BUSINESS ECONOMICS

Business economics is also called *managerial economics*. Business economics deals with the use of economic models to analyse business situations. The prime function of a business management executive is decision making and future planning. *Decision making* is the process of choosing one action from two or more alternatives available. Future planning means establishing plans for the future. These plans relate to the future program of action by the business unit. The problem of choice arises because of the limited means and the firm has to make the most profitable use of these resources.

A business manager's task is made difficult by the uncertainty that surrounds business decision making. Nobody can predict accurately the future course of the business conditions. At the most, a business executive can make an intelligent guess of the likely conditions in the future. He prepares the best possible plans for the future depending on the past experience and future outlook. The business manager has to continuously take decisions about his output and sales in order to adjust to the uncertainty of the future as it unfolds to him.

LIMITATIONS OF ECONOMICS

Following are the limitations of economics:

1. Economics encompasses only those human activities that are related to wealth. It is not a comprehensive study of all human activities.
2. Economics measures everything in terms of money. There are some areas that cannot be assessed in terms of money like emotions, hopes and aspirations of the human beings.
3. Economics studies the activities of the members of the society and only real time activities. It cannot be applied to hypothetical situations.

DEMAND AND THE LAW OF DEMAND

Demand means desire. It is the quantity of commodity that the consumer is able and willing to buy at each possible price during a given period of time. A mere desire cannot become a demand. A desire that is backed up by an ability to buy and the willingness to pay the price is called *demand*. There are three elements of demand for a commodity that are as follows:

1. Desire for a commodity
2. Money to fulfil that desire
3. Readiness to part with the money.

When we speak of demand we must also state the price. Unless we state the price, the term demand has no meaning. A demand always has a price. Thus, the quantity of a commodity purchased at a given price, at a given time, in a given market is called *demand*.

Demand Schedule

Demand schedule is that schedule that expresses the relation between different quantities of commodity demanded at different prices. According to Samuelson, the table relating price and quantity demanded is called *demand schedule*.

Demand schedule is of two types as follows:

1. Individual demand schedule
2. Market demand schedule

Individual Demand Schedule

Individual demand schedule is defined as the quantities of a given commodity purchased by the consumer at all possible prices at a given moment, other things remaining equal. Table 30.1 indicates the individual demand schedule. It indicates the different quantities of Digene antacid syrup brought by a consumer at different prices at a given time.

Table 30.1. Individual Demand Schedule

Price (Rs)	Quantity demanded
10	8
20	7
30	6
40	5

Table 30.1 indicates that as the price of antacid syrup goes on increasing, the quantity demanded goes on falling.

Market Demand Schedule

In every market there are several consumers of a commodity (antacid syrup). Market demand schedule is one that shows the total demand of all consumers in the market at different prices of the commodity. So market demand schedule is defined as the quantities of a given commodity that all consumers will buy at all possible prices at a given moment of time.

Table 30.2 shows that when the price of a commodity (antacid syrup) falls, the market demand for the same increases.

Table 30.2. Market Demand Schedule

Price of antacid syrup (Rs)	A's demand	B's demand	Market demand
10	8	5	8 + 5= 13
20	7	4	7 + 4 = 11
30	6	3	6 + 3 = 9
40	5	2	5 + 2 = 7

Demand Curve

Demand curve is a graphical representation of the demand schedule expressing the relationship between the different quantities demanded at different possible prices of a commodity. The demand curve represents the maximum quantities per unit of time that consumers will purchase at various prices.

Demand curve is of two types as follows:

1. Individual demand curve
2. Market demand curve

Individual demand curve

The Individual demand curve is one that represents the different quantities of the commodity demanded by a consumer at different prices. The individual demand curve is represented in Figure 30.1. In this diagram, the demand of the commodity is shown on the X axis and price on the Y axis. DD is demand curve. Every point on the demand curve expresses the relationship between the price and the demand. When the price is Rs 40, the demand is for 5 units. When the price is Rs 10, the demand is for 8 units. Thus the slope of the demand curve indicates that at a higher price the demand is less and at lower price the demand is more.

Market demand curve

The market demand curve represents the total of the quantities of a commodity demanded by all the consumers in the market at different prices. It is the horizontal summation of the individual demand curves. The market demand curve is shown in Figure 30.2. The quantity is shown on the X axis and price on the Y axis—in Figure 30.2 (i), (ii) and (iii). In Figure 30.2 (i) demand curve of 'A', in Figure 30.2 (ii) demand curve of 'B', in Figure 30.2 (iii) the market demand curve has been shown. By adding the different points on the individual demand curves, the market demand curve DD is produced which is shown in Figure 30.2 (iii). The slope of this demand curve is also negative indicating an increase in the relationship between the price of the commodity and the quantity demanded.

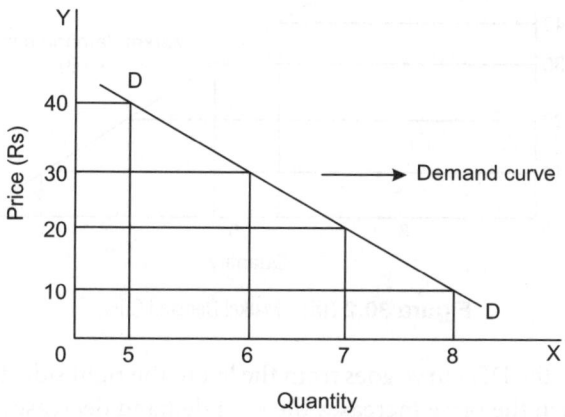

Figure 30.1. Individual Demand Curve

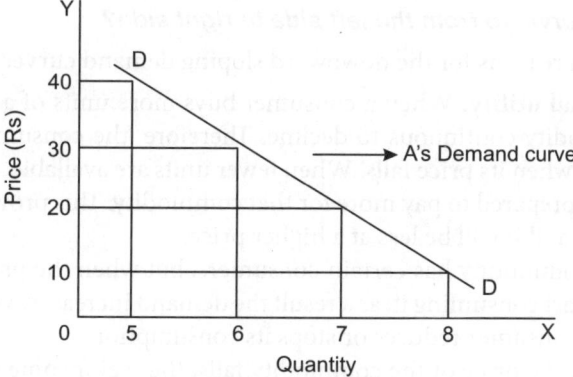

Figure 30.2 (i). A's Demand Curve

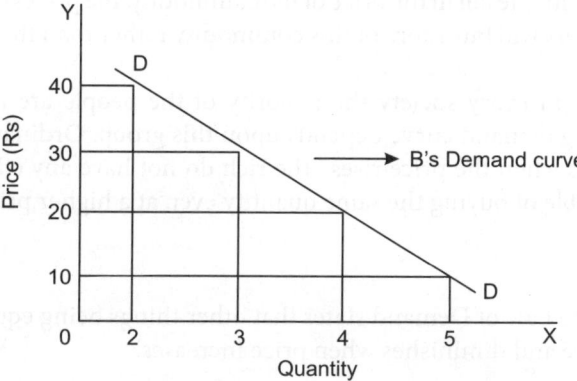

Figure 30.2 (ii). B's Demand Curve

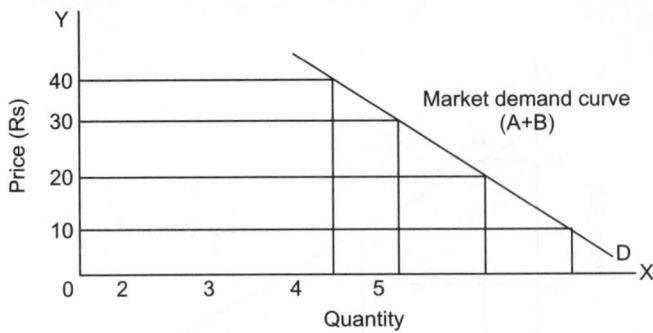

Figure 30.2 (iii). Market Demand Curve

In the above Figure 30.1, the DD curve goes from the left to the right side downwards in a straight line or in the curved form. When the price increases the total demand decreases. When the price decreases the total quantity demand increases. Hence, the relationship between the price and quantity demand is negative.

Why does the demand curve go from the left side to right side?

The following are the main reasons for the downward sloping demand curve:

1. **Diminishing marginal utility:** When a consumer buys more units of a commodity, the marginal utility of that commodity continuous to decline. Therefore, the consumer will buy more units of that commodity only when its price falls. When fewer units are available, the utility will be high and the consumer will be prepared to pay more for that commodity. This proves that the demand will be more at a lower price and it will be less at a higher price.

2. **New buyers:** Every commodity has certain consumers, but when the price of the commodity falls the new consumers start consuming it, as a result the demand increases. With the increase in price of that commodity, the consumer reduces or stops its consumption.

3. **Income effect:** When the price of the commodity falls, the real income of the consumers increase because he has to spend less in order to buy the same quantity. On the contrary with the rise in the price of the commodity, the real income of the consumer falls. This is called the *income effect*.

4. **Substitution effect:** With the fall in the price of the commodity, the prices of its substitutes remaining the same, the consumers will buy more of this commodity rather than the substitutes, as a result the demand increases.

5. **Low-income groups:** In every society the majority of the people are in the low income group. The downward sloping demand curve depends upon this group. Ordinary people buy more when the price falls and less when the price rises. The rich do not have any effect on the demand curve because they are capable of buying the same quantity even at a higher price.

Law of Demand

According to Marshall, 'The Law of Demand states that other things being equal the amount demanded increases with a fall in price and diminishes when price increases'.

Assumptions of the law of demand

The main assumptions of the law of demand are as follows:

1. Tastes and preferences of the consumers remain constant

2. There is no change in the income of the consumer
3. Prices of the related goods do not change
4. The wealth of the consumers does not change
5. Consumers do not expect any change in the price of the commodity in the near future.

Exceptions to the law of demand

In certain cases, the demand curve slopes up from the left to right, i.e. it has a positive slope. Under certain circumstances the consumers buy more when the price of commodity rises and less when the price falls (Figure. 30.3).

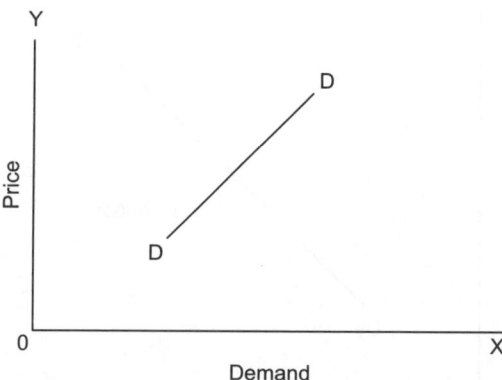

Figure 30.3. Demand Curve (Exceptional Cases)

The circumstances under which the demand curve has a positive slope are:

1. **War:** If a shortage is feared in anticipation of war, people may start buying for piling up stocks, for boarding even when the price rises.
2. **Depression:** During depression, the prices of commodities are very low and the demand for them is also less. This is because of the lack of purchasing power with the consumers.
3. **Giffen paradox:** Sir Robert Giffen in the midnineteenth century observed that the low paid workers in Britain purchased more bread when its price increased by decreasing the purchase of meat. The increase in demand for bread when the price increased is an exception to the law of demand.
4. **Conspicuous consumption or demonstration effect:** If consumers are affected by the principle of conspicuous consumption or demonstration effect they will like to buy more of these commodities, e.g. gold and diamonds. Some people buy such goods only if their prices are high.
5. **Speculation effect:** When the prices are expected to rise in the future, people buy more, e.g. shares. If they expect a fall in price, the demand for those shares fall.
6. **Income demand:** Income demand indicates the relationship between the income and the quantity of the commodity demanded. It relates to the various quantities of a commodity bought by a consumer at various levels of income in a given period of time, other things being equal. So with the help of the income demand we can say whether a commodity is superior or inferior.

Classification of goods with reference to demand

With the help of demand, the goods can be classified into five important types. They are as follows:

1. Normal goods or superior goods
2. Inferior goods

3. Giffen goods
4. Complementary goods
5. Substitutes goods

1. Normal goods or superior goods: A normal good is that good whose income effect is positive and the price effect is negative. A positive income effect means that the demand increases due to an increase in income and falls due to a fall in income. Negative price effect means that a fall in price results in the extension of demand and the rise in price results in the contraction of demand. The income demand curve for superior goods has a positive slope. The law of demand applies in case of normal goods (Figure 30.4).

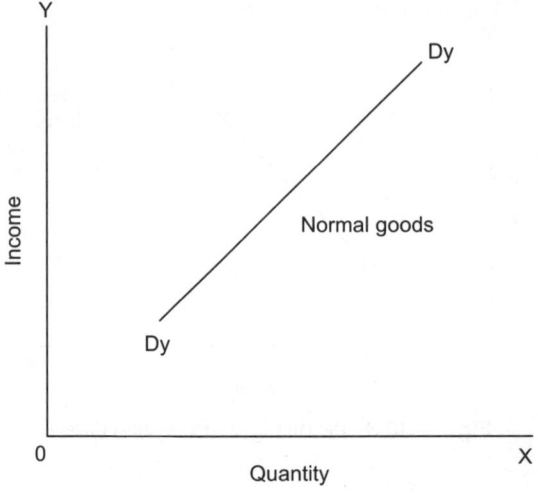

Figure 30.4. Demand Curve for Normal Goods

2. Inferior goods: An inferior good is that good whose income effect is negative. It means that an increase in consumer's income results in the decrease in demand for that commodity and a decrease in the consumer's income results in an increase in demand for that commodity. The main difference between normal goods and inferior goods is that the income effect of normal goods is positive while that of inferior goods is negative. Law of demand does not apply in this case (Figure 30.5).

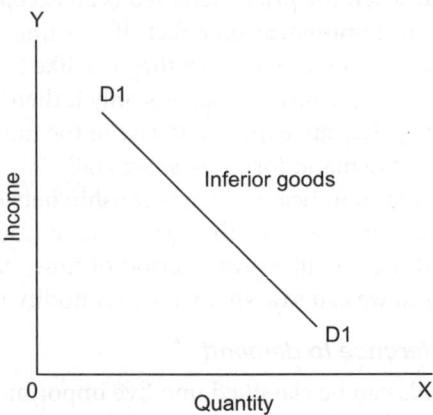

Figure 30.5. Demand Curve for Inferior Goods

3. Giffen goods: Giffen goods are those inferior goods whose income effect is negative but the price effect is positive. In other words, the demand for these goods rises due to an increase in price and falls due to a decrease in price. Giffen goods are exception to the law of demand.

4. Cross demand: Generally the demand for a commodity changes when its price changes. We also find that the demand for a commodity changes when the prices of other related goods change. This is called *cross demand.*

There are two versions in it
   a. substitutes goods and
   b. complementary goods.

5. Complementary goods: In the case of complementary goods, with the increase in the price of one commodity the quantity demanded of another commodity falls. These are those related goods that jointly satisfy a particular want. Pen and ink are complementary goods. Similarly sugar and syrup are complementary goods. If the price of a pen increases, the quantity demand for ink falls. The demand curve for these goods slopes downwards from left to right (Figure 30.6).

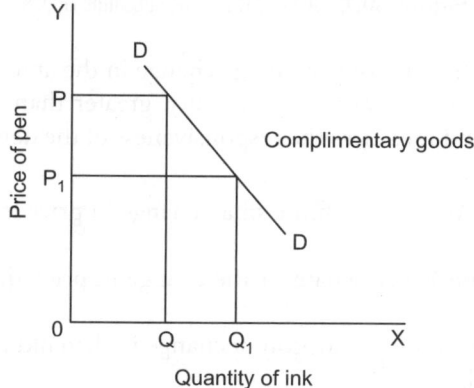

Figure 30.6. Demand Curve for Complementary Goods

6. Substitutes goods: In the case of these goods, other things remaining the same, the rise in the price of a commodity may increase the demand for the other commodity. These are those goods that can be used in place of each other. In other words substitutes are those goods where the demand of one is positively related with the price of the other. For example, coffee and tea are substitutes. If the price of coffee rises, the demand for tea increases as it becomes relatively cheaper. Therefore, the demand curve for substitutes goes upwards from left to right (Figure 30.7).

Price Elasticity of Demand

When the price changes, demand changes. But it seldom happens that the price change leads to uniform changes in demand. Sometimes the demand varies much, at other times little, even when there is a small change in price. The credit goes to Marshal who offered a solution by formulating the concept of price elasticity of demand.

'The elasticity of demand in a market is great or small according as amount demanded increases much or little for a given fall in price and diminishes much or little for a given rise in price'.

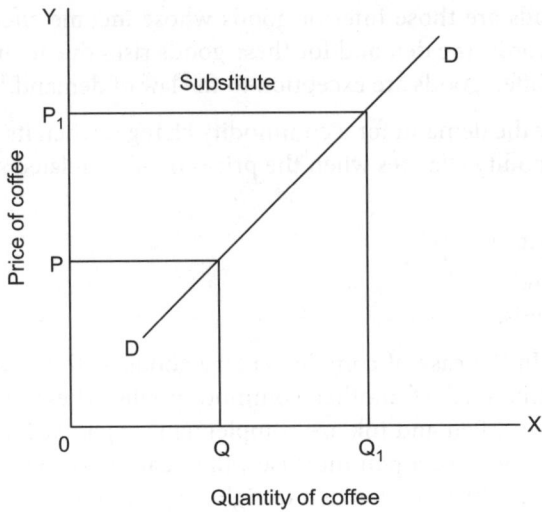

Figure 30.7. Demand Curve for Substitute Goods

Price elasticity of demand is the ratio of percentage change in the amount demanded to a percentage change in price. Price elasticity of demand may be unity, greater than unity, less than unity, zero or infinite. Price elasticity of demand measures the responsiveness of the demand to change in price. There are various types in it as follows:

1. **Perfectly elastic demand:** When an infinite small change in price leads to an infinite large change in the amount demanded.
2. **Perfectly inelastic demand:** When whatever the change in price there is absolutely no change in demand.
3. **Relatively elastic demand:** If the proportion of change in demand is more than the proportionate of change in the price level.
4. **Relatively inelastic demand:** If the proportionate change in demand is less than the proportionate change in price.
5. **Unitary elasticity of demand:** If the proportionate change in demand is equal to the proportionate change in price level.

Income Elasticity of Demand

The concept of income elasticity of demand expresses the responsiveness of a consumer demand for any commodity to the change in his income. *Income elasticity of demand* may be defined as the ratio of the percentage change in the quantity demanded of a good to the percentage change in income.

The income elasticity of demand is positive for all superior goods because the consumer demand for goods changes in the direction of the change in his income. However, it is negative in case of inferior goods.

Importance of price elasticity of demand

The concept of price elasticity of demand is of great practical importance in the formulation and understanding of a number of economic policies and problems. Some of the important applications are as follows:

1. **Monopoly price determination:** A monopolist while fixing the price for his product takes into consideration its elasticity of demand. If the demand for his product is elastic, he will profit more.
2. **Determination of price under discriminating monopoly:** Under monopoly discrimination, the problem of pricing the same commodity in two different markets also depends on the price elasticity of the demand in each market.
3. **Determination of prices of public utilities:** When the demand for public services is inelastic, a high price is charged, e.g. electricity.
4. **Determination of wages:** Price elasticity of demand is important in the determination of wages of a particular type of labour. If the demand for labour is elastic, there is no use in increasing the wages.
5. **Important to the finance minister:** Based on the elasticity of demand of a product, the finance minister imposes taxes on the products.
6. **International trade:** The concept of elasticity of demand has got great practical importance in analysing some of the complex problems of international trade such as exports, imports and balance of payments, etc.

SUPPLY AND LAW OF SUPPLY

The concept of supply occupies an important place in the economic theory. Supply of a commodity influences the price as does the demand. The supply of goods is the quantity offered for sale in a given market at a given time at various prices. It is also defined as the quantity of commodity offered for sale at a given price in a given market at a given time.

The following are the factors that differentiate the supply of a commodity:

1. Supply depends upon the aim of the industry.
2. Technical progress is useful in lowering the cost of production.
3. Substitution prices: A fall in the price of a substitute commodity and its fall in production may also cause the supply of the commodity to increase.
4. Change in cost of production: A change in the cost of production may affect the position of supply. A rise in the cost will decrease supply.

Generally the terms supply and stock are considered synonymous. But in economics they have different meanings. The amount of a commodity that a seller is willing to supply at a given price is known as *supply*. A quantity that a seller can place in the market for sale when demanded is termed as *stock*.

Types of Supply

There are two types of supply as given below:

1. **Individual supply:** It refers to the supply of a commodity by an individual firm in the market.
2. **Market supply:** It refers to the supply of a commodity by all the firms in the market producing or selling that particular commodity.

Supply Schedule

Supply schedule is a systematic and a tabular presentation of the various quantities of a commodity offered for sale at different possible prices. It has two versions as discussed below:

1. Individual supply schedule
2. Market supply schedule.

Individual supply schedule

It expresses the different quantum of goods supplied by a company at different prices.

Market supply schedule

It refers to the supply schedule of all the firms in the market producing, supplying and selling a particular good. The sum total of the firms producing a particular commodity is called *industry*. Thus, the market supply schedule refers to the supply schedule of the industry as a whole.

Law of Supply

The law of supply states that, other things remaining constant, there is positive relationship between the price of a commodity and its quantity supplied. Thus more is supplied at a higher price and less at a lower price, and higher the price, greater the quantity supplied.

Assumptions of the law of supply

Following are the assumptions of the law of supply:

1. There is no change in the prices of the factors of production.
2. There is no change in the technique of production.
3. There is no change in the goal of the firm.
4. There is no change in the prices of related goods.
5. Producers do not expect change in the price of commodity in the near future.

Exceptions to the law of supply

The following are the exceptions to the law of supply:

1. The law of supply does not apply rigorously to agricultural products whose supply is governed by natural factors. For example, if due to natural calamities the production of wheat is very less, then its supply will not increase in spite of high prices.
2. Supply of goods having social distinction will remain limited even if their prices may rise high.
3. The seller may be willing to sell more units of perishable goods although their prices may be falling.

Elasticity of supply

The elasticity of supply of a commodity measures the responsiveness of the quantity supplied to a change in price. It measures the degree to which the price is effective in calling forth or holding back the quantity. Price elasticity of supply is the percentage change in the supply of a commodity per unit of time resulting from a given percentage change in price.

There are five types of elasticity of supply as follows:

1. **Perfectly elastic supply:** A slight change in the price is attended by an infinite change in supply.
2. **Perfectly inelastic supply:** A perfectly inelastic supply is one in which the supply is completely nonresponsive to the change in price.
3. **Relatively elastic supply:** A relatively elastic supply is the one in which a given change in price produces more than a proportionate change in the quantity of supply.

4. **Relatively inelastic supply:** Relatively inelastic supply is the one in which a given change in price is attended by a less than proportionate change in the quantity supplied.

5. **Unitary elastic supply:** Unitary elastic supply is the one in which the supply equals the proportionate change in price.

Factors affecting the supply of commodity

The following factors affect the supply of commodity:

1. **The commodity price:** There is a direct relationship between the price and its quantity supplied. If the price is less, the quantity supplied is also less.

2. **Prices of related goods:** Related goods may be substitutes or goods of joint supply. If the price of substitutes increases, its supply should accordingly increase.

3. **Price of all other goods:** The supply of a good depends upon the prices of all other goods. An increase in the prices of other goods makes them more profitable for the firms. They will increase their supply. On the other hand, the supply of the goods, the price of which has not changed, will become relatively less profitable. The supply of such goods may decrease.

4. **Number of firms:** If there are more number of firms then, the market supply increases. Similarly a decrease in the number of firms will decrease the supply of a commodity in the market.

5. **Change in technology:** Introduction of new technology leads to an improvement in the techniques of production that leads to a decrease in the cost of production. Hence, profits tend to increase inducing an increase in supply.

Points to Ponder

1. The word 'economics' is derived from two Greek words oikos (household) and nemein (management).

2. A desire that is backed up by an ability to buy and the willingness to pay the price is called demand.

3. Demand schedule is of two types
   a. Individual demand schedule
   b. Market demand schedule

4. Demand curve is a graphical representation of the demand schedule expressing the relationship between the different quantities demanded at different possible prices of a commodity.

5. Demand curve is of two types
   a. Individual demand curve
   b. Market demand curve

6. The Law of Demand states that other things being equal the amount demanded increases with a fall in price and diminishes when price increases.

7. Income elasticity of demand is the ratio of the percentage change in the quantity demanded of a good to the percentage change in income.

Self-Assessment Exercises

1. Define the term *economics*. What are the main branches of economics?
2. Explain the term *demand*. How are goods classified with reference to demand?
3. What is a demand curve? Why does the demand curve slope downwards?
4. What is meant by demand? Mention the factors which influence the demand for a commodity.
5. Define supply. Discuss the law of supply.
6. What is meant by supply? Give the various factors that affect the supply of commodity.
7. Explain the law of supply with the help of a supply schedule and supply curve.
8. Explain the different types of goods with reference to demand.

Trade

INTRODUCTION

The word trade means buying, selling and exchange of goods. Trade may be described as the nucleus of a commercial activity. The trade is generally classified into the following two broad categories:

1. Internal trade
2. External trade

Internal Trade

Internal trade is also called *home trade* and consists of the sale and exchange of goods within the boundaries of a country. The payment involved in business transactions are made in the nation's own currency directly or through the banking system. The movement of goods is through the internal transport system owned by the state governments, the central government or by private agencies. The internal trade is carried on the following basis:

1. Wholesale trade
2. Retail trade

Wholesale trade

Wholesale trade involves the sale of goods in comparatively large quantities to those traders who are in direct contact with the consumers that is the retailers. The wholesaler serves as a link between the producer or the manufacturer of goods and the retail traders. In pharmaceutical trade, the wholesalers are classified into four categories:

1. Super distributors or super stockiest
2. Stockiest
3. Wholesale dealers or substockiest
4. Clearing and forwarding agents

Retail trade

In retail trade, the retailer supplies the requirements of the consumers in small quantities as per their needs. As such, he serves as a link between the wholesaler and the actual consumers.

In pharmaceutical trade, the chemist or the druggist plays the role of a retailer. Thus, a retail chemist is an outlet for providing drugs or healthcare services to the patient. A retailer dispenses the prescription of the medical practitioner and sells the medicines to the patient.

External Trade

External trade is also called *foreign trade* or *international trade*. External trade means the exchange of goods and services between citizens, business firms or the government of different countries. When goods are sold by one country to another, the payments are required to be made in the currency of the country concerned. The movement of goods is through the international transport system. Foreign trade is conducted mostly on wholesale basis and is subdivided into:

1. Import trade
2. Export trade
3. Entreport trade

Import trade

When a trader of one country purchases the goods from the trader of other countries, it is called *import trade.*

Export trade

When a trader of one country sells goods to the trader of other countries, this trade is called *export trade.*

Entreport trade

When a trader purchases goods from one country and sells the same goods to another country, it is called *entreport* trade. It is also called *re-export trade.* Re-export trade is carried on by countries that have ports conveniently situated to serve as distributing centres for neighbouring countries which import large quantities of such goods. London and Singapore have a considerable amount of re-export trade.

Many pharmaceutical companies are marketing their products to overseas countries. While exporting pharmaceutical products to other countries, amongst other things, the following conditions must be satisfied:

1. International standards for formulation are maintained.
2. International standards for packaging are also maintained.
3. The export items must be cleared by the Food and Drug Authority (FDA) of the country concerned.
4. Clinical data of the pharmaceutical product is provided.

Advantages

Foreign trade has the following advantages:

1. **Foreign exchange:** A country is able to earn valuable foreign exchange by exporting its goods to other countries. With the help of the foreign exchange, it can purchase goods of its needs from other countries.
2. **Division of labour:** International trade has forced the countries to minimize the cost of production of its goods. This is done by specializing in few products. It has resulted in the division of labour and specialization. The quality goods are available in the international market at a very reasonable rate.
3. **Benefits to consumers:** Consumers of various countries are also benefited from international trade. A variety of goods of better quality are available to them at reasonable prices. It leads to an increase in their standard of living.
4. **Increase in government income:** The government imposes import and export duties on the imports and the exports. By this way the government is able to earn a lot of revenue from the international trade.
5. **Help in natural calamities:** Natural calamities like earthquakes, floods, drought, etc., are overcome by importing the required necessities from other countries.
6. **Cultural development:** People of different countries come in contact with each other through international trade. They learn about each other's cultural heritage.
7. **Encouragement to industrialization:** Industrial development of a country largely depends upon the international trade, because it creates demand.
8. **International cooperation:** International trade improves international cooperation. Countries get better quality goods from others and also supply goods to them. It creates dependence on each other improving mutual confidence and faith.
9. **Export of excess production:** Every country tries to manufacture those products that it specializes in. The excess production of these products is exported to other countries and the goods that are needed are imported. So with the help of foreign trade, a country can consume such goods that it cannot produce.
10. **More profit:** The traders can earn more profit in foreign trade as compared to inland trade. Moreover, a trader gets a choice to sell his products wherever the prices are higher.
11. **Availability of all types of goods:** All types of goods can be made easily available from other countries that are not available in a country.
12. **Other advantages:** Foreign trade has other advantages like improvement in the standard of living, exchange of political views, improvement in the production system and elimination of monopolies.

Disadvantages

Foreign trade has the following disadvantages:

1. **Mutual dependence:** The dependence on other countries in trade sometimes creates serious problems.
2. **Exploitation:** All the countries are dependent on each other in international trade. There is no country in the world that can meet all its requirements on its own. This dependence leads to the exploitation of developing countries by the developed countries.
3. **Foreign competition:** The countries producing similar types of goods have to compete with each other in the international market. Developing countries face these problems as they are unable to compete with other developed countries.
4. **Shortage of goods in a country:** To earn more profits, sometimes the traders prefer to sell the goods to other countries than in their own country. This results in the shortage of goods within the country.
5. **Bad effects on the economy:** One country affects the economy of the other country through international trade.
6. **Fear of dumping:** The developed countries start selling their products at very low prices, thus as a result, the industries in the underdeveloped countries close down. After that they start charging higher prices.
7. **Incentive to colonization:** International trade encourages colonization. The developed countries always try to grab and rule the underdeveloped countries and foreign trade is a tool for doing that.
8. **Loss to foreign trade in war time:** During war time foreign trade becomes very difficult.
9. **Effect on culture:** There are so many goods that are not in accordance with a country's culture and traditions. The import of these goods affects the culture and civilization.

GENERAL AGREEMENT ON TRADE AND TARIFFS (GATT)

GATT is an organization of countries that are concerned with the regulation and promotion of world trade. GATT was established in 1948. The main headquarter is at Geneva. It is a result of the effort on the part of twenty-three countries to work together to reduce the tariffs that were considered to be excessive. The member countries would meet in Geneva and negotiate multilaterally on matters of trade policy. It was also to act as a forum for the settlement of disputes between nations.

Objectives of GATT

There seem to have been three basic objectives behind the establishment of GATT. They are as discussed below:

1. It was to provide a framework for the conduct of trade relations.
2. It was to provide a framework for the progressive elimination of trade barriers.
3. It was to provide a set of rules that would inhibit countries from taking unilateral action.

Principles of GATT

Following are the principles of GATT:

1. Nondiscrimination

The basic principle of GATT was that of nondiscrimination. This principle is contained in what has been known as the Most Favoured Nation (MFN) clause.

This means that a country agrees not to give better treatment to any single nation than it gives to all the contracting parties of GATT. If any country gives preferential tariff treatment to any country then that concession must be extended immediately to all other countries, so that all contracting parties benefit to the same extent.

2. Reciprocity

The reciprocity obligation requires that a country receiving a concession from another should offer an 'equivalent concession' in return.

3. Transparency

The GATT forbade the use of direct control on trade, particularly quantitative restrictions, except under special circumstances such as a balance of payments crisis.

4. The MFN clause and discrimination against countries

In the face of it, the MFN clause seems fair enough but in reality it also involves a hidden discrimination among different countries.

Exceptions to the GATT

Following are the exceptions to the GATT:
1. GATT members were allowed to apply for quantitative import restrictions in order to deal with severe balance of payments problem.
2. Another major exception to the MFN principle is that the member countries can establish free trade areas and custom unions. The most common regional grouping has been the free trade areas.
3. Tariff preferences for specific groups of countries are another exception to the MFN principle. The GATT did not object to various preferential arrangements between developed countries and their present territories.
4. Dumping: Dumping of goods takes place when a country sells its goods to another country at less than the cost of production and transport. GATT allowed this discriminatory action. Unfortunately, charges of dumping are difficult to disprove, so this provision in the GATT rules has often been misused.

President Kennedy of the US took the initiative to start a dialogue on further reduction of tariff with the major trading nations of the world. The Kennedy round tariff reductions by developing countries have been estimated at about 36–39% and affected 75% of the world trade. Agricultural products were generally excluded from the Kennedy round of agreements.

Another round talks was at Japan during 1973-79 and is known as the Tokyo round. Once again the concessions were concentrated in manufactured goods and agricultural commodities being treated differently. Moreover, textiles and clothing, leather, footwear and travel goods received lower tariff cuts and often none at all. In 1989 the 'Geneva accord' was signed, However the United States and the European community failed to reach any agreement on agricultural policy.

The Dunkel draft was the final act to be ratified by member nations of the GATT and was tabled at the end of 1991. Dunkel was the secretary general of GATT. This set of rules for the WTO was not immediately acceptable to the different blocks in world trade. Agriculture continued to be the main bone of contention between the US and the European community. Another point of disagreement among the contracting parties was the export of textiles. But some countries did not agree with the Dunkel draft particularly about textiles.

Yet another issue before the member nations pressed by the United States was that of services insurance, transport, engineering, etc. It was one of the new issues of the Uruguay round.

After extensive discussions and compromises on various issues the Dunkel draft was accepted by the USA, the European community and Japan. Other member nations were asked to ratify the draft as it is at an early date, and the 132 member nations ratified the draft one after the other. The WTO was a reality on 1 January 1995.

WORLD TRADE ORGANIZATION (WTO)

The WTO began its operations in January 1995 and was created to replace the GATT. WTO is a chartered trade organization, not just a secretariat as GATT. However, the WTO continues the work of GATT to limit harmful trade practices. WTO covers services including TRIPS and it has more compelling dispute settlement functions. By 2001 there were 142 members in it.

Structure of WTO

The ministerial conference (MC) is at the top of the structural organization of the WTO. It is the supreme governing body that takes ultimate decisions on all matters. It is constituted by the representatives of all the member countries (minister of trade).

The general council is the real engine of the WTO that acts on behalf of the ministerial conference. It also acts as the dispute settlement body and as the trade policy review body.

Further there are three committees as follows:

1. The Committee on Trade and Development (CTD),
2. The Committee on Balance of Payments Restrictions (CBOPR) and
3. The Committee on Finance, Budget and Administration (CFBA).

The WTO is conducted by the secretariat that is headed by the Director General (DG) appointed by the MC for the tenure of four years.

Objectives of the WTO

The purpose and objectives of the WTO are spelled out in the preamble to the agreement. They are discussed below:

1. To ensure the reduction of tariffs and other barriers to the trade.
2. To eliminate discriminatory treatment in international trade relations.
3. To facilitate higher standards of living, full employment, a growing volume of real income and effective demand, an increase in production and trade in goods and services of the member nations.
4. To make a positive effect that ensures the developing countries, especially the least developed, to secure a level of share in the growth of international trade that reflects the needs of their economic development.
5. To facilitate the optimal use of the world's resources for sustainable growth.
6. To promote an integrated, more viable and durable trading system incorporating all the resolutions of the Uruguay round multilateral trade negotiations.

Functions of the WTO

Following are the functions of the WTO:

1. To lay down a substantive code of conduct aiming at reducing trade barriers including tariffs and eliminating discrimination in international trade relations.
2. To provide the institutional framework for the administration of the substantive code, norms governing the conduct of member countries in the global trade.
3. To provide an integrated structure of the administration, thus to facilitate the implementation, administration and fulfilment of the objectives of the WTO agreement and other multilateral trade agreements.
4. To ensure the implementation of the substantive code.
5. To act as a forum for the negotiation of further trade liberalization.
6. To cooperate with the IMF and WB and its associates for establishing trade policymaking.
7. To settle the trade-related disputes.

EXPORT AND IMPORT PROCEDURES

Export

Export is selling of goods and merchandize to other countries crossing the geographical frontiers of the country. The foreign trade requires the services of export and import agents. A good example of export is India selling goods to the USA and England. Export earns a lot of foreign exchange for a country and helps in tilting the balance of payments.

Export Procedure

The export of goods to other countries involves several recognized procedures and systematic steps. The important procedures are given below:

1. Receipt of indent

Receipt of order from the foreign importer is called the *indent*. There are two types of indents

    a.   open indent and
    b.   closed indent.

    Open indent consists of the written request for goods required. But the closed indent consists of not only the written order for goods but also related instructions regarding the goods like the type of packing, mode of transport, insurance, etc.

2. Receipt of license for export

For exporting goods outside India, a license is required. The license for export is issued by the controller of exports. The prescribed format is available for this purpose. The person who intends to export has to fulfil all the conditions by filling the application for the purpose.

3. Procurement of goods

The goods required for the export are purchased by the exporter in the local market. The specifications listed in the indent, sent by the importer, have to be kept in mind by the exporter while procuring the merchandize.

4. Packing and labelling

The contents are packed according to the specifications issued in the indent letter. If no specifications are given, then the goods are packed according to the exporter's norms. After packing the goods, the labelling should be properly done so that the goods are recognized by the importer.

5. Appointment of forwarding agents

A forwarding agent is appointed for the shipment of the goods and other ancillary services. Forwarding agents collect the goods from the railways and other transport services and they help in arranging for the shipment, payment of export duty, insurance, loading and fulfilling other formalities of the shipment.

6. Dispatch of goods

Forwarding agents do the delivery of goods by showing the letter from the exporter already sent earlier. The arrangements are then made for the shipment of goods.

7. Foreign customs permit

The forwarding agent has to get the written permission for export from the government. This is called *customs permit*. For this, he has to fill the requisite application providing particulars like quantity of goods, nature of goods and their value, etc. Generally the permission for exports is given except for the goods that are banned for export by the government.

8. Shipping order

Once the permit by the customs is received, necessary arrangements for sending the goods by ships or freight, etc., have to be decided with the shipping company. The shipping order prepared is usually of two types

1. ready order and
2. forward order.

Ready order is given for the goods to be transported immediately and the name of the ship is specified. In the forward order, the goods are transported at a later date. The name of the ship is not mentioned in the forward order. The goods are sent after receiving the shipping orders.

9. Export duty and shipment bill

The forwarding agent fills the shipping bill or the customs house *challan* in triplicate. The detail of the goods, name of the ship, name of the exporter and his address, etc., is specified in it. The customs authorities keep one copy of the shipping bill and return two copies after receiving the customs duty. The shipping bill is of three types:

1. Duty free
2. Dutiable
3. Coastal

Duty free is applicable to goods on which the duty is not payable whereas dutiable is used for goods on which the duty is payable. Coastal is used for goods that are sent from one port to another port within the country.

10. Dock dues or challan

For sending the goods to the port, permission has to be taken from the dock authorities. For obtaining the permission, a dock *challan* is filled in duplicate and presented to the dock authorities along with the copies of the shipping order, shipping bill and the dock charges. One copy of the dock *challan* is returned to the forwarding agent. The dock authorities make necessary arrangements for loading the goods on to the ship.

11. Loading the goods

Dock officials usually load the goods onto the ship. Inspection by the customs officials is done at the time of loading of the goods and their approval is specified on the shipping bill.

12. Mate's receipt

Once the goods are loaded on to the ship, the captain of the ship gives an acknowledgment receipt to the forwarding agent. This is called the *mate's receipt*. It is of two types—clean and foul.

If the packing of the goods is satisfactory, the captain gives a clean receipt and if it not satisfactory or defective, he gives a foul receipt.

13. Bill of lading

The forwarding agent gets the bill of lading by showing the mate's receipt. A revenue stamp is affixed on every copy of the bill of lading. It is a proof that the freight has been paid.

14. Marine insurance

Marine insurance is done to cover the goods against sea perils (dangers) for an amount 10–15% higher than the value of the goods. Insurance should be done from the same company as specified in the indent.

15. Forwarding agents advice

The forwarding agent will send an account of expenses occurred adding his commission and along with the copies of the bill of lading, insurance policy bill, dock *challan*, etc., to the exporter.

16. Preparation of export invoice

Based on the specifications of the indent, the exporter will prepare the export invoice, the consular invoice and the certificate of origin (the place from where the goods originated) and sends it to the importer.

17. Payment

Payment depends upon the terms and conditions between the exporter and the importer. Usually bank drafts, bill of exchange and sometimes documents against acceptance bill and documents against the payment bill are utilized.

18. Advice to importer

When once the whole process is completed and the ship sails, the exporter will inform in advance regarding the dispatch to the importer. The information is sent to the importer so he may get the necessary documents related to the shipment ready.

Import

When a country purchases goods from other countries and brings the merchandize into the country crossing the geographical borders of the country, it is called an *import*. Usually, the goods and the services that are deficient and falling short are usually brought from the outside. In India, we import electronic goods, software accessories and other sunrise products.

Import Procedure

The following are the steps in the process of import:

1. Obtaining import license

The Ministry of Commerce usually issues the import license. The importer has to get an import license by applying in a prescribed application to the controller of imports, Government of India.

2. Foreign exchange

Since the goods are purchased in another country, the payment has to be made in the currency of the country of the origin of goods. In such cases, the permission has to be obtained from the Reserve Bank of India to get the necessary foreign exchange.

3. Placing the indent

The importer prepares the detailed specifications of the items to be imported and hands it over to any import agent. The importer can send the indent directly to the export agent of that country, if it is known to the importer.

4. Dispatch of goods by export agent

On receiving the indent, the export agent will purchase the required goods from the producers or the wholesalers, packs them as per the specifications, get them insured and sends them to the importer. He also sends all the documents of the title of the goods to the importer.

5. Obtaining shipment documents

The export agent also sends the shipment documents like the bill of lading along with other documents. On the receipt of these documents, the importer starts the process of getting the goods cleared from the port.

6. Appointment of clearing agent

The importer appoints a clearing agent at the port to get possession of his goods. He endorses all his documents in favour of the clearing agent.

7. Endorsement of delivery

After getting the documents, the clearing agent visits the office of the shipping company for the endorsement of delivery on the bill of lading or a delivery order in his favour. If any balance freight is due, it is paid off and the delivery of goods is received by the clearing agent.

8. Payment of the import duty

The clearing agent visits the customs office to get three forms known as the *bill of entry*. These forms are in three different colours—black, blue and sky blue. The black form is used for the goods on which the octroi is payable; the blue form is for the goods to be sold or used within the country; and the sky blue for the goods meant for re-export. On receiving this form, the customs authorities inspect the goods and charge the customs duty. One copy of the form is kept by the customs department while the other two copies are handed over to the agent.

9. Dock dues

The goods can be taken out from the dock only after paying the dock dues. After paying the customs duty the agent pays the dock dues by filling the necessary forms in duplicate.

10. Taking delivery of goods

Before taking the delivery of goods, the condition of the goods is checked by the agent. If the goods are not in a good condition, he prepares a report to fix the responsibility for the damage. Demurrage (fine) has to be paid if the goods are not cleared from the dock within a specified period.

11. Keeping goods in warehouse

If due to any reason, the importer is unable to pay the customs charges the goods are kept in the 'bonded warehouse'. A special entry bill is filled for this purpose. The customs authorities give a receipt called the *dock warrant* to the importer. The importer can take the delivery of goods only after the payment of the import duty.

12. Dispatch of goods by clearing agent

After getting the delivery of goods from the dock, the clearing agent sends it to the importer by rail. He gets the railway receipt (R/R) from the railway authorities and sends it to the importer, so that the importer can get the delivery of goods from the railways.

13. Receipt of documents

The agent sends the documents like R/R, vouchers of expenses and his commission bill to the importer by post.

14. Taking the delivery

The importer gets the delivery of goods from the railways or the transporter company by showing the relevant documents. The goods are transferred to the godowns of the importer.

Points to Ponder

1. Generally there are two broad categories of trade
    a. Internal trade
    b. External trade
2. The internal trade is carried on the following basis:
    a. Wholesale trade
    b. Retail trade
3. External trade is also called foreign trade or international trade. Foreign trade is conducted mostly on wholesale basis and is subdivided into:
    a. Import trade
    b. Export trade
    c. Entreport trade
4. General Agreement on Trade and Tariffs is an organization of countries that are concerned with the regulation and promotion of world trade. GATT was established in 1948.
5. The WTO began its operations in January 1995 and was created to replace the GATT.

 **Self-Assessment Exercises**

1. Define the term *trade*.
2. Name the different types of trade.
3. Define the term *import*.
4. Explain the term *export*.
5. What do you mean by *internal trade*?
6. Define the term *external trade*.
7. What are the advantages of external trade?
8. Write the disadvantages of foreign trade.
9. Discuss the classification of trade.
10. Name the agents that are involved in foreign trade.
11. What are the conditions required to be fulfilled to conduct international trade in pharmaceutical formulations?
12. Write in brief the procedure to be followed to import the goods.
13. Give in brief the procedure that is required to be followed to export the goods.
14. Write the advantages and the disadvantages of the foreign trade.

Insurance

INTRODUCTION

Insurance is a means of shifting and dividing business risk of various types. In the event of death, the assured amount is paid to the legal heirs of the deceased. The loss due to fire is compensated by the insurance company. In marine insurance, the loss of goods and freight in voyage is compensated by the insurance company. Insurance helps the businessman in carrying on the business activities with confidence and a peace of mind.

Insurance is a form of contract or agreement under which one party agrees, in return of a consideration, to pay an agreed amount of money to another party to make good for a loss, damage, injury of something of value where the insured has pecuniary interest as a result of some, uncertain event.

Insurance is a device by which loss due to some uncertain event is spread over a large number of people who voluntarily join against such an event. The agency which is helpful in this arrangement is known as the *insurance company* or *insurer*. The person who gets his life or property insured is known as *insured* or *assured*. The contract in writing is known as *policy*. The consideration to make good the loss is known as *premium*.

 ## PRINCIPLES OF INSURANCE

The following are some of the basic principles of insurance:

1. Utmost good faith

Insurance contracts are based on the principle of utmost good faith. It is a condition of every insurance contract that both the parties should display the utmost good faith towards each other in regard to the contract. Each party must reveal to the other party all information influencing the contract. Misrepresentation or failure to reveal material information gives the aggrieved party the right to regard the contract as void.

An insured is required to disclose all material facts, at the time of making the proposal, and continue to do so till the completion of the contract. If this is not done the insured has no obligation against that contract.

2. Insurable interest

The insured must have some interest in the subject matter of the insurance. Without it the contract will be a gamble and will become null and void. A person is said to have an insurable interest when he gains from the property insured and would suffer a loss if the person or the property is destroyed. If a person goes for insurance without insurable interest in the insured commodity, the contract will be null and void. For example, a person, who gets his motorcar insured against accident, has an insurable interest in it because he is the owner of that car and is using it for his benefit. In life insurance, the insurable interest must exist at the time of making the contract. In fire insurance, the insurable interest must be present both at the time of making the contract and at the time of loss of the subject matter.

3. Indemnity

All insurance contracts, other than life insurance, are contracts of indemnity (security against loss or compensation). In case of fire and marine insurance, the insurer will compensate for the actual loss caused to him by damage or destruction of the property. The insured is not allowed to make any profit on the happening of an event. For example, a building is insured for Rs 50 000 and a portion of it is burnt down. The actual loss amounts to Rs 20 000 to restore the building in its original state. So in this case, the insurance company pays Rs 20 000 only. Suppose a building whose value is Rs 50 000 is insured for Rs 1 00 000. In this case, the insurance company is liable to pay Rs 50 000 only, if the building is completely destroyed. If this principle did not apply, insurance will be a gamble. Under this principle, the insurance company pays the amount insured or the actual loss whichever is less.

4. Doctrine of subrogation

The principle of subrogation (substituting of one person for another) applies to all insurance contracts, which are contracts of indemnity, such as fire and marine insurance. According to this principle, the insurance company after making compensation acquires all his right against the third party with regard to the subject matter insured. The insurer is entitled to the benefits of subrogation only to the extent of the amount he has paid to the insured as compensation. In contracts of indemnity, the insured cannot be allowed to make any profit from an insurance claim.

In some cases, there may be a possibility of the insurer getting something in addition to what he has received from the insurance company. The goods may have been partially damaged or the property may not have been fully destroyed. In such a case, the insured may try to obtain the value of the scrap in addition to the money received in the settlement of the claim. This will, however be contrary to the principle of indemnity because the insured will be able to get more than what he has really lost. Here, the doctrine of subrogation plays its part. The scrap or whatever is left of the damaged or the destroyed goods or property will automatically pass into the hands of the insurance company after the payment of the claim.

The main features of this principle are as follows:

a. The insurance company can get the benefit of this principle only after making compensation.
b. Insured with the help of the insurance company.
c. It applies only to contracts of indemnity.
d. The insurance company can file a suit in the court of law in the name of the insured.
e. The insurance company will have the same right that the insured had against the third party.
f. The insured will have to surrender all his rights and remedies in favour of the insurers, who have paid the claim, to the extent of the amount paid by the insurers.

5. Principles of contribution

The principle of contribution is a corollary of the doctrine of indemnity. The insured can take two or more than two policies of the same property but he shall not be entitled to claim from each insurer more than the rateable proportion of the loss to which one is liable.

Suppose 'A' insures his house for Rs 1 00 000 with insurer 'R' and for Rs 2 00 000 with insurer 'S'. A loss of Rs 1 20 000 occurs. The liability of R and S will be calculated as follows:

$$\text{Liability of R} = \frac{\text{Sum insured with R}}{\text{Total sum insured}} \times \text{loss}$$

$$= \frac{1\,00\,000 \times 1\,20\,000}{3\,00\,000}$$

$$= \text{Rs } 40\,000$$

$$\text{Liability of S} = \frac{\text{Sum insured with S}}{\text{Total sum insured}} \times \text{loss}$$

$$= \frac{2\,00\,000 \times 1\,20\,000}{3\,00\,000}$$

$$= \text{Rs } 80\,000$$

Thus all insurance companies are legally liable to contribute their proportionate share toward the payment of risk.

6. Mitigation of loss

The principle of mitigation emphasizes the responsibility of the insured to take all possible steps to minimize the loss or damage of the property, in case of mishap. For example, a warehouse catches fire; it is the duty of insured to do all that he would have done if the goods were not insured. The aim of this principle is that the insured person behaves like a responsible person.

7. Cause proximate

Cause proximate means the nearest cause. An insured person can recover the loss only when it is caused by any of the risks insured against it. Causes of loss may be of two kinds:

    a.   Insured perils
    b.   Excepted or uninsured perils

The insurer, in no case, is liable to compensate for the damages arising directly or indirectly or excepted perils. An insured may recover damages if the cause has been immediate or proximate to the loss.

TYPES OF INSURANCE

Insurance covers all types of risks. Insurance is divided into the following two categories:

1. Life insurance
2. General insurance

Life Insurance

Life insurance deals with life and its related mátters such as education and marriage of children, etc. Life insurance provides for payment of a stipulated sum of money to the insured person on expiry of a specified number of years or on his or her earlier death. The following schemes of life insurance are very popular.

1. Individual schemes
2. Group schemes

Individual schemes

The common individual life insurance policies are given below:

1. **Whole life policy:** This policy covers the risk as long as the policyholder is alive. There is no predecided period and the premium is payable throughout the life of the policyholder. There are also no survival benefits. The final lumpsum money including the bonus would be payable only to the nominee of the beneficiary upon death.
2. **Endowment policy:** This policy covers the death risk for a certain predecided period. The policyholder gets the sum assured plus bonus, if any, at the end of the period or death, whichever occurs first. Generally twenty years endowment policy is offered by many insurance companies.
3. **Term life policy:** This policy is a pure risk cover wherein the sum assured is payable only on death. If the policyholder survives the specified term, the risk cover comes to an end and no money is payable. The policy is available at a very nominal cost and takes care of the financial needs of the family or dependents in case anything happens to the insured.

4. **Joint life plan:** This policy is just like an endowment policy covering the risk for a specified period, but of two people simultaneously like husband and wife or business partners. LIC's Jeevan Saathi, a pure joint life plan that provides the sum assured to a surviving partner in case of death of one of the policyholders. The premium stops on the death or maturity and the full sum assured along with the bonus is paid back. If one or both the lives survive to the maturity date, the sum assured along with bonus is payable.

5. **Money back policy:** This policy is a blend of saving regular survival benefits after four to five years and life insurance. In this policy, the death claim comprises the sum assured plus any bonuses without the deduction of any survival benefit amount paid earlier.

6. **Children policy:** This policy provides benefits to a minor and takes care of his education, marriage and future needs. LIC has over a dozen policies for children like Komal Jeevan, Jeevan Sukanya, Jeevan Kishore, Jeevan Balya, Jeevan Chhaya, etc.

7. **Woman's policy:** This policy provides benefits to women and even covers diseases specific to women. Jeevan Bharti, LIC's money back plan, has been designed for women in the age group of eighteen to fifty years. This policy provides for accident benefit and disability benefit up to an overall limit of Rs 25 lakh and covers women specific diseases like cancer in the breast, ovarian, cervical and vaginal.

Group schemes

Group insurance schemes offers life insurance shield to the employees of a corporate sector and to partnership firms or professionals and people from economically weaker section. The following group schemes are available:

1. **Group superannuation plan:** This plan allows the employer and an employee to make a certain fixed regular contribution to a fund. The accumulated amount is utilized to provide various benefits on the retirement of the employee, on death or on withdrawal.

2. **Group term plan:** This plan provides for life cover to members of a group. The benefit is paid to the beneficiary nominated by the members on death.

3. **Group gratuity plan:** This plan helps the employers to fund their statutory gratuity obligation under the payment of the Gratuity Act. Every employer is under the obligation to pay half month salary for every completed year of service to each of his employee on their exit. At the end of the accumulation period, the policyholder has an option to choose pension for self only or pension for self and spouse.

General Insurance

General insurance deals with movable and immovable assets. It provides risk cover to houses, shops, factories, etc., (immovable assets) and goods stored in shops, godowns, goods in transit, vehicles (movable assets), etc. It is an important risk cover for businessmen. Almost all businessmen buy general insurance according to their needs. Following are some of the insurance covered under general insurance:

1. Fire insurance

Fire insurance is a contract under which the insurance company or the insurer, in consideration of the premium paid, undertakes to compensate the insured for any loss that may result due to the occurrence of fire. It is an yearly contract and automatically lapses at the end of the year, unless it

is renewed. The premium may be paid either in lumpsum or by way of instalments. The document of the contract is known as *fire insurance policy*. For taking out a fire policy, the owner of the goods or property has to fill a proposal form giving details of the property, its location, its contents, etc. The insurer then assesses the risk through the surveyors who may make on-the-spot enquiries about the property and determine the risks involved in its insurance against the risks of fire. After the acceptance of the proposal, the premium is required to be paid by the insured. The risk will commence only when the premium has been paid. The insurer issues a cover note that is in the nature of an interim protection note. Finally, a fire insurance policy duly stamped and containing the terms and conditions of insurance will be issued by the insurer to the insured.

Following types of fire policies are common:

a. Comprehensive policy: Such policies are issued to cover such risks as fire, explosion, lighting, thunderbolt, riot, strikes, burglary, etc. These are also called *all insurance policies*.

b. Blanket policy: It is issued to cover all assets, fixed as well as current, of the insured under one blanket.

c. Specific policy: In this policy, the risk for a specific sum is covered. In case of any loss to the property insured under such a policy, the insurer will pay the whole loss of the insured provided that it does not exceed the specified sum mentioned in the policy.

d. Floating policy: It covers one or several kinds of goods lying in different localities under one sum and for one premium.

e. Valued policy: In this policy, the value of the property is ascertained or agreed upon and the insurer undertakes to pay his agreed value in the event of the destruction of property by fire.

f. Reinstatement policy: In this policy, the insurer pays the amount that is required to reinstate the asset or property destroyed. While calculating the amount of claim, the depreciation is not deducted from the original value of the assets.

2. Marine insurance

In marine insurance, the risks covered are the loss or damage to the insured vessel, cargo or passengers during transportation on the high seas. Marine insurance is a contract under which the insurer undertakes to indemnity the insured against the losses incidental to marine adventure. Sea perils include risk of loss by piracy, capture, seizure, jettison, barbarry, etc. A marine policy may be taken for a particular period or for a particular voyage.

The following types of marine policies are common:

a. Time policy: This is a policy whereby the insurance is made for a specified period of time. It is suitable for hull insurance though it may be taken out also for movables and other goods when small quantities are involved.

b. Voyage policy: The policy is meant to insure the subject matter in transit from one place to another. The subject matter insured is generally cargo that is exposed to marine risks in the course of transit.

c. **Mixed policy:** It is also known as *time and voyage policy*. It seeks to insure the subject matter (hull or ship) on a particular voyage for a specific period of time.

d. Floating policy: It is used by the cargo owners, who make regular shipments of cargoes to insure the shipment expected to be made during a certain period of one policy. A policy may be taken for around amount. Whenever some cargo is shipped, the insured makes a declaration about the value of the shipment and the total value of the policy is reduced by that amount. Such declarations are made from time to time till the total value is exhausted and the policy is run off.

e. Blanket policy: It is taken for a certain amount but the premium is paid on the whole of it in the beginning of the policy and is readjusted at the end of the term of the policy in accordance with the actual amounts and the risk as shown by the records of the insured.

f. Fleet insurance policy: It is designed to insure a whole fleet of liners or steamers.

g. Port policy: It covers the ship when it is anchored in some port.

3. Mediclaim or medical insurance

Under this scheme companies pay for the insured's hospitalization, domiciliary hospitalization, intensive care, surgery and other related medical expenses.

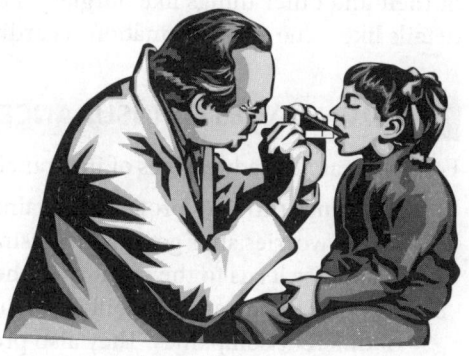

With a small annual premium, the insured can avail of all mediclaim benefits up to limits specified in the policy. The premium rates depend on the category and the scheme that has to be selected by the insured.

There are two schemes under mediclaim as discussed below:

Scheme A: Mediclaim with personal accident insurance.

Scheme B: Mediclaim without personal accident insurance.

The policy can be issued to all Indian citizens. The annual premium paid carries income tax benefits. The mediclaim policy is a boon to middle and lower income group families because it is difficult to meet the medical and surgical expenses of the hospital.

4. Miscellaneous Insurance

In addition to the above risk factors, there are some minor inherent risks also like theft, damage to the vehicle, recovery of loan, etc., so in order to cover these types of risk, the general insurance companies have introduced the following miscellaneous insurance policies:

Motor Insurance: A motor insurance covers the following risks.
1. Damage to the vehicle by fire or accident or theft.
2. Injury to the owner of the vehicle.
3. Injury or death of some other party due to an accident in which the vehicle of the insured is involves.

A policy covering all the above aspects is called as *comprehensive policy*.

Third party insurance: This policy covers the risk because of damage to the property of a third party in addition to that arising out of personal bodily injury caused to a third party, e.g. are house owner's liability to tenant's, etc.

Fidelity insurance: This policy is done by an owner of a business to cover the risks arising out of fraud and dishonesty by his employees. This is a type of precaution on the part of the owner to protect himself in case his employees cheat him of goods or cash.

Credit insurance: This policy consists of indemnifying the policyholder (a businessman) against the risks arising from the insolvency of a debtor. It implies that the insurer guarantees the credit worthiness and the solvency of the debtors.

Burglary, theft and robbery insurance: This is the policy, a comprehensive policy that covers the risks of theft and other things like burglary. For this type of policy, the insured has to provide the necessary details like value and information regarding the safe in which the valuables are kept, etc.

ADVANTAGES OF INSURANCE

Following are the advantages of insurance:

1. Insurance provides protection against the risk of loss. The businessman feels secured and free from all the worries after getting his business insured.
2. Insurance leads to the stability in the business, because it is free from all risks of loss and damage.
3. Insurance companies mobilize the savings of the public and invest them in the shares and debentures of different companies. They also provide financial assistance through underwriting activity.
4. Under life insurance, loan can be given to the insured on the basis of the paid up value of the policy. Hence, the insured person can easily get a loan against his insurance policy.
5. The insured person feels more safe, active and enterprising. Thus his efficiency increases.
6. Life insurance is a very good means of compulsory savings and deposits for old age and some bad days.
7. Insurance provides security against theft and burglary that are very common nowadays in new residential colonies.
8. It generates employment to the educated youth, interested to join as insurance agents.

Points to Ponder

1. Insurance is a means of shifting and dividing business risk of various types.
2. Some of the basic principles of insurance are
    a. Utmost good faith
    b. Insurable interest
    c. Indemnity
    d. Doctrine of Subrogation
    e. Principles of contribution
    f. Mitigation of loss
    g. Cause proximate
3. Insurance is divided into the following two categories:
    a. Life insurance
    b. General insurance.

Self-Assessment Exercises

1. Define the term *insurance*.
2. Name the different types of insurance.
3. Name the different principles of insurance.
4. Define the term *policy*.
5. Explain the term *premium*.
6. Write the advantages of insurance.
7. Explain the meaning of the contract of indemnity.
8. Write in brief about the doctrine of subrogation.
9. Discuss in brief the principle of contribution.
10. Write in brief about the different types of insurance.

Labour Welfare

WELFARE STATE

INTRODUCTION

Labour welfare can be defined as the creation of minimum required standards of the provision of facilities like health, food, clothing, housing, medical assistance, education, insurance, job security, recreation, etc., that enable the worker and his family to lead a good working life, family life and social life. Labour welfare is anything that is done for the intellectual, physical, moral and economic betterment of the workers by the employers or the government or other agencies over and above what is laid down by the law.

CHARACTERISTIC FEATURES OF LABOUR WELFARE

Following are the characteristics of labour welfare:

1. Welfare measures and amenities are provided not only to the employees but also to their family members.

2. There is a wide variation in the facilities and amenities provided that depend on the historical, cultural and societal conditions prevailing.
3. The contributors to labour welfare are the employers, government, trade unions and other outside agencies.
4. Labour welfare measures do not include those facilities that are statutory or obligatory under any contract between the employer and the employee. They are only optional and are voluntarily provided.

NEED FOR LABOUR WELFARE

India is a developing country that is aiming for rapid economical and social development. Hence, the concept of labour welfare is more important to our country. Labour welfare measures have immense beneficial effects on the workforce. The important benefits are as follows:

1. It has a humanistic approach that enables the workers to enjoy a fuller and a richer life.
2. It is economical as it improves the efficiency of the workers.
3. It has a civic approach in the sense that it develops a sense of responsibility and dignity among the workers.
4. It builds a stable workforce by reducing absenteeism.
5. It helps in winning the employees loyalty and to combat trade unionism.
6. It improves the morale of the workers and motivates them to work more.
7. It enhances the image of the organization and creates an atmosphere of goodwill between the labour and the management, and also between the management and the public.

OBJECTIVES OF LABOUR WELFARE

The following are the important objectives of labour welfare:

1. To provide a congenial working atmosphere where the workforce can excel.
2. To boost the morale of workers and to reduce a sense of frustration amongst them.
3. To relieve the workforce from their personal and family worries.
4. Helping the employees in maintaining good health.
5. To provide the employees means of self-expression and gratification.

PRINCIPLES OF LABOUR WELFARE

While formulating the objectives of labour welfare measures, the following principles to be kept in mind:

1. Right Spirit

The welfare activities should be undertaken in the right spirit. They are not substitutes for low wages and other allowances. Nor should they be provided to undermine the influence of the trade unions.

2. Should Serve the Real Need of the Workers

The scheme so formulated must serve the real need of the employees concerned. Special classes of workers require special type of welfare services. Depending on the nature of the work and the industry, the industrialist should assess the actual need of the workers and the priorities should be determined.

3. Cooperation of the Workers

No welfare scheme can succeed without the active support of the workers. The workers should be allowed to participate in the formulation and the administration of any welfare scheme to achieve the real objectives of the scheme.

4. No Compulsion

There should be no compulsion for workers to avail of these facilities. In other words, labour welfare should be voluntary and the workers should be free to take advantage of such facilities (However, some compulsion must be imposed on the employers).

TYPES OF LABOUR WELFARE

The labour welfare measures that are provided to the workforce can be broadly classified into the following categories:

Intramural Facilities

Facilities provided within the four walls of the organization or a factory. These facilities include canteen, provision of safety measures for the workers, good lighting conditions, first aid kit, etc. These facilities are required to be provided by law.

Extramural Facilities

Facilities offered to the workers outside the factory. They include accommodation, recreation facility, educational facility, sports facility, etc. These facilities are not obligatory but are provided by the organization for the general welfare of workers.

Statutory Facilities

These are the facilities that are to be provided under the provisions of law and labour legislation. These facilities may be either intramural or extramural facilities. They cannot be ignored as they are enforceable by law. For example, provision of potable drinking water, provision of clean latrines and bathrooms.

Mutual Facilities

These are the facilities that are not obligatory but done voluntarily by the workers themselves for their own interest. Hence, the management or the employer has no role in it.

Voluntary Facilities

The facilities provided by the organization on its own and which are not obligatory come under this category. These types of facilities boost the morale of the employees.

BENEFITS OF LABOUR WELFARE

Labour welfare measures provide several benefits for the development of workers. The important benefits are as follows:

Improvement in Morale

Welfare measures help in securing the willing cooperation of the workers that leads to a decrease in the antisocial and wrong activities on the part of the employees. Hence, this leads to increased morale and motivation.

Harmonious Industrial Relations

Strikes, *harthals*, conflicts by the workers are minimized and a feeling of oneness with the organization is created.

Improvement in the General Efficiency and Economy

Welfare measures will improve the efficiency and productivity of the employees because they are relieved from the domestic problems like poor housing, unsanitary conditions, etc.

Creation of Permanent Workforce

When the organization looks after the employees well by providing them all the necessary amenities and facilities, the employees will not look for a change and stick with the jobs for a longer period that helps in the stabilization of the workforce.

Social benefits

The increase in the efficiency of the workers leads to an increase in the production, rate of profit and the earnings of the organization. The increased earning leads to better salaries of the workers thus leading to their happiness. Hence, the standard of living of the society is raised.

LABOUR WELFARE IN INDIA

During the First and Second World War there were only isolated instances of labour welfare work in our country. In the postwar period and due to industrial revolution there was industrial expansion and the process of large scale production led to the rise of the working class as a source of power. After independence, more teeth were given to the Factories Act and the first two five year plans laid more emphasis on the effective implementation of various statutory provisions.

Agencies of Labour Welfare in India

Labour welfare work in India is usually carried out by four main agencies namely

1. The employers
2. The workers organization
3. The Central Government
4. The state government

Employers role in welfare work

The employer is in direct contact with the workforce. Hence he can play an important role in providing facilities required by the employees in addition to what is laid down by the law. Many organizations like Infosys, Satyam Computers, Tata Corp., Reliance are providing excellent benefits to the employees in the form of welfare measures. The important welfare amenities provided by them are educational facilities, crèches, housing facilities, sponsoring trips to the family abroad, gifts on the marriages of children, etc.

Labour welfare work by worker's associations

These are the activities provided by the unions for the benefit of their members by means of funds mobilized by them. Several unions have done a good deal of work in this regard. Some of them worth mentioning are Mazdoor Union, Textile Labour Association, etc. Welfare activities provided by these associations include schools, libraries, maternity homes, dispensaries, cooperative societies and free legal aid, etc.

Labour welfare work by the central government

The Central Government after independence has enacted several labour laws for the benefit of the workers. Some of the important acts are Factories Act, 1948, Coal Mines Labour Welfare Fund Act, 1947, etc. In the five year plans also, the Central Government has spent huge amounts towards labour welfare. For example in the first five year plan, Rs 29 crore; in second plan Rs 71.08 crore; and in the sixth five year plan Rs 350 crore.

Labour welfare work by the state governments

Several state governments and union territories have provided welfare centres that provide educational, recreational and health services to the workforce. These centres also provide library, gymnasium, training in handicrafts and tailoring classes for women workers, etc. The main sources of finances for these funds are realized from employees only in the form of fines, voluntary donations, unclaimed and forfeited sums in the provident fund account, and any fund transferred from any other sources.

Labour Welfare Under Factories Act, 1948

The Factories Act, 1948 contains the following provisions relating to labour welfare:

1. Washing facilities

In every factory
   1. adequate and suitable facilities shall be provided and maintained for the use of workers,
   2. separate and adequately screened facilities shall be provided for the use of male and female workers and
   3. such facilities shall be easily accessible and shall be kept clean.

2. Facilities for storing and drying clothing

In every factory provision a suitable place should exist for keeping clothing not worn during working hours and for the drying of wet clothing.

3. Facilities for sitting

In every factory, suitable arrangements for sitting shall be provided and maintained for all workers who are obliged to work in a standing position so that the workers may take advantage of any opportunity for rest that may occur in the course of work. If in any factory, workers can efficiently do their work in a sitting position, the chief inspector may require the occupier of the factory to provide such seating arrangements as may be practicable.

4. First aid appliance

Under the Act, the provision for first aid appliances are obligatory. At least one first aid box or cupboard with the prescribed contents should be maintained for every 150 workers. It should be readily accessible during all working hours. Each first aid box or cupboard shall be kept in the charge of a separate responsible person who holds a certificate in the first aid treatment recognized by the state government and who shall always be readily available during the working hours of the factory. In every factory wherein more than 500 workers are ordinarily employed there shall be provided and maintained an ambulance room of the prescribed size containing the prescribed equipment. The ambulance room shall be in the charge of properly qualified medical and nursing staff. These facilities shall always be made readily available during the working hours of the factory.

5. Canteens

In every factory employing more than 250 workers, the state government may make rules requiring that a canteen or canteens shall be provided for the use of workers. Such rules may provide for
1. the date by which the canteen shall be provided,
2. the standards in respect of construction, accommodation, furniture and other equipment of the canteen,
3. the eatables to be served therein and the charges that may be made thereof,
4. the constitution of a managing committee for the canteens and representation of the workers in the management of the canteen,
5. the items of expenditure in the running of a canteen that are not to be taken into account in fixing the cost of foodstuffs and that shall be borne by the employer and
6. the delegation to the chief inspector, of the power to make rules under clause (c).

6. Shelters, rest rooms and lunch rooms

In every factory where more than 150 workers are ordinarily employed, there shall be a provision for shelters, rest rooms and suitable lunch rooms where workers can eat meals brought by them with provision for drinking water. Where a lunch room exists, no worker shall eat any food in the work room. Such shelters or rest rooms or lunch rooms shall be sufficiently lighted and ventilated and shall be maintained in a cool and clean condition.

7. Crèches

In every factory where more than 30 women workers are ordinarily employed there shall be provided and maintained a suitable room or rooms for the use of children under the age of six years of such women. Such rooms shall provide adequate accommodation, shall be adequately lighted and ventilated, shall be maintained in clean and sanitary conditions and shall be under the charge of women trained in the care of children and infants.

The state government may make rules for the provision of additional facilities for the care of children belonging to women workers including suitable provision of facilities
1. for washing and changing their clothing,
2. of free milk or refreshment or both for the children and
3. for the mothers of children to feed them at the necessary intervals.

8. Welfare officers

In every factory wherein 500 or more workers are ordinarily employed, the occupier shall employ in the factory such number of welfare officers as may be prescribed under Sec. 49(1). The state government may prescribe the duties, qualifications and conditions of services of such officers.

Points to Ponder

1. Labour welfare can be defined as the creation of minimum required standards of the provision of facilities like health, food, clothing, housing, medical assistance, education, insurance, job security, recreation, etc., that enable the worker and his family to lead a good working life, family life and social life.
2. The various principles of Labour Welfare are
   a. Right spirit
   b. Should serve the real need of the workers
   c. Cooperation of the workers
   5. No compulsion

  **Self-Assessment Exercises**

1. Explain the provisions of the Indian Factories Act, 1948 with respect to the welfare of the workers?
2. Define the term *labour welfare*. Give a brief account of the welfare activities organized by different agencies in India.

Application of Computer in Accounting

Tally
Facts
MS Office
MS Excel
etc.

INTRODUCTION

Computer technology and its usage have registered a significant development during the last three decades. Historically, computers have been used effectively in science and technology to solve complex computational and logical problems. They have also been used for carrying out economic planning and forecasting processes. Recently, modern day computers have made their presence felt in the business and industry. The most important impact of computers has been on the manner in which data is stored and processed within an organization. Although manual data processing for Management Information System (MIS) has been quite common in the past, modern MIS would be nearly impossible without the use of computer systems. In this chapter we shall discuss the need for the use of computers in accounting, the nature of the accounting information systems and the types of accounting related MIS reports.

MEANING AND ELEMENTS OF COMPUTER SYSTEM

A computer is an electronic device that is capable of performing a variety of operations as directed by a set of instructions. This set of instructions is called a *computer programme*. A computer system is a combination of six elements as explained below:

1. Hardware

The hardware of a computer consists of the physical components such as a keyboard, mouse, monitor and a processor. These are electronic and electromechanical components.

2. Software

A set(s) of programmes that are used to work with such hardware is called its *software*. A coded set of instructions stored in the form of circuits is called *firmware*. There are six types of software as follows:

Operating system

An integrated set of specialized programmes that are meant to manage the resources of a computer and also facilitate its operations is called *operating system*. It creates a necessary interface that is an interactive link between the user and the computer hardware.

Utility programmes

These are a set of computer programmes that are designed to perform certain supporting operations such as a programme to format a disk, duplicate a disk or physically reorganize stored data and programmes.

Application software

These are user oriented programmes designed and developed for performing certain specified tasks such as payroll accounting, inventory accounting, financial accounting, etc.

Language processors

These are the software that checks for language syntax and eventually translate (or interpret) the source programme (that is a programme written in a computer language) into machine language (that is the language which the computer understands).

System software

These are a set of programmes that control such internal functions as reading data from input devices, transmitting processed data to output devices and also checking the system to ensure that its components are functioning properly.

Connectivity software

These are a set of programmes that create and control a connection between a computer and a server so that the computer is able to communicate and share the resources of the server and other connected computers.

3. People

People interacting with the computers are also called *liveware* of the computer system. They constitute the most important part of the computer systems as are discussed below:

a. *System analysts* are the people who design the data processing systems.
b. *Programmers* are the people who write programmes to implement the data processing system design.
c. *Operators* are the people who participate in operating the computers.
d. People who respond to the procedures instituted for executing the computer programmes are also a part of liveware.

4. Procedures

The procedure means a series of operations in a certain order or manner to achieve the desired results. There are three types of procedures that constitute part of the computer system: hardware oriented, software oriented and internal procedure. *Hardware oriented procedures* provide details about the components and their methods of operation. The *software oriented procedures* provide a set of instructions required for using the software of a computer system. *Internal procedure* is instituted to ensure a smooth flow of data to the computers by sequencing the operation of each subsystem of the overall computer system.

5. Data

These are facts and may consist of numbers, text, etc. These are gathered and entered into a computer system. The computer system in turn stores, retrieves, classifies, organizes and synthesizes the data to produce information according to a predetermined set of instructions. The data is, therefore, processed and organized to create information that is relevant and can be used for decision making.

6. Connectivity

It is being acknowledged as a sixth element of the computer system. The manner in which a particular computer system is connected to others, say through telephone lines, microwave transmissions, satellite links, etc., is the element of connectivity.

CAPABILITIES OF A COMPUTER SYSTEM

A computer system possesses some characteristics that in comparison to human beings turn out to be its capabilities. These are as follows:

1. Speed

It refers to the amount of time the computers take in accomplishing a task or completes an operation. Computers require far less time than human beings in performing a task. Normally, human beings take into account a second or minute as unit of time. But computers have such a fast operating capability that the relevant unit of time is fraction of a second. Most of the modern computers are capable of performing a 100 million calculations per second and that is why the industry has developed the Million Instructions per Second (MIPS) as the criterion to classify different computers according to speed.

2. Accuracy

It refers to the degree of exactness with which computations are made and operations are performed. One might spend years in detecting errors in computer calculations or updating a wrong record. Most of the errors in Computer Based Information System (CBIS) occur because of bad programming, errone-ous data and by deviation from procedures. These errors are caused by human beings. Errors attributable to hardware are normally detected and corrected by the computer system itself. The computers rarely commit errors and perform all types of complex operations accurately.

3. Reliability

It refers to the ability with which the computers remain functional to serve the user. Computers systems are well adapted to performing repetitive operations. They are immune to tiredness, boredom or fatigue. Therefore, they are more reliable than human beings. Yet there can be failures of computer systems due to internal and external reasons. Any failure of the computer in a highly automated industry is unac-ceptable. Therefore, the companies in such situations provide for backup facilities to swiftly take over operations without the loss of time.

4. Versatility

It refers to the ability of the computers to perform a variety of tasks, simple as well as complex. Comput-ers are usually versatile unless designed for a specific application. A general purpose computer is capable of being used in any area of application—business, industry, scientific, statistical, technological, commu-nications and so on. A general purpose computer system when installed can take over the jobs of several specialists because of being highly versatile. This further ensures fuller utilization of its capability.

5. Storage

It refers to the amount of data a computer system can store and access. The computer systems, besides having instant access to data, have huge capacity to store such data in a very small physical space. A CD-ROM with 4.7" of diameter is capable of storing a large number of books, each containing thousands of pages and yet leaving enough space for storing more such material. A typical mainframe computer system is capable of storing and providing online billion of characters and thousands of graphic images. It is clear from the above discussion that computer capabilities outperform the human capabilities. As a result, a computer, when used properly, will improve the efficiency of an organization.

LIMITATIONS OF A COMPUTER SYSTEM

In spite of possessing all the above capabilities, computers suffer from the following limitations:

1. Lack of Commonsense

Computer systems as on date do not possess any commonsense because no foolproof algorithm has been designed to programme commonsense. Since computers work according to a stored programme(s) they simply lack commonsense.

2. Zero IQ

Computers are dumb devices with zero Intelligence Quotient (IQ). They cannot visualize and think what exactly to do under a particular situation, unless they have been programmed to tackle that situation. Com-puters must be directed to perform each and every action, however, minute it may be.

3. Lack of Decision Making

Decision making is a complex process involving information, knowledge, intelligence, wisdom and the ability to judge. Computers cannot take decisions on their own because they do not possess all the essentials to take decisions. They can be programmed to take such decisions that are purely procedure-oriented. If a computer has not been programmed for a particular decision situation, it will not take the decision due to lack of wisdom and evaluating faculties. Human beings, on the other hand, possess this great power of decision making.

COMPONENTS OF COMPUTER

The functional components of a computer system consist of input unit, central processing system and output unit. The way these components are embedded in a computer may differ from one architectural design to another, yet all of them constitute the essential building blocks of a computer system. Diagrammatically, these components may be presented as follows:

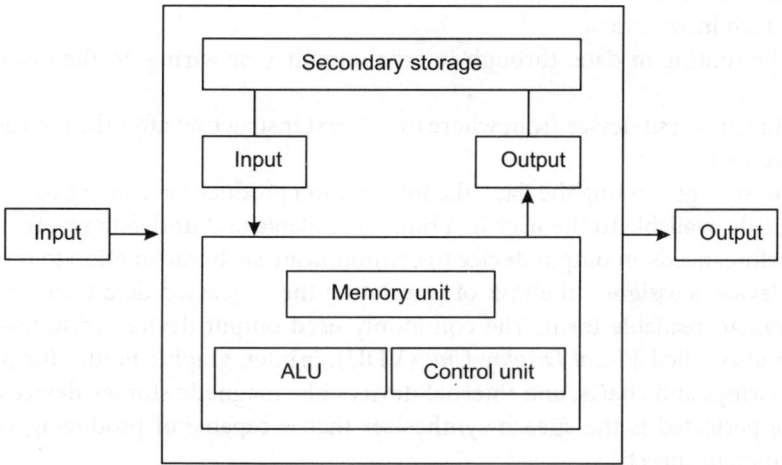

Figure 34.1. Block Diagram of Main Components of Computer

1. Input Unit

It controls various input devices that are used for entering data into the computer system. Keyboard and mouse, for instance, are the most commonly used input devices. Other such devices are magnetic tape, magnetic disk, light pen, optical scanner, Magnetic Ink Character (MICR) Recognition, Optical Character Recognition (OCR), bar code reader, smart card reader, etc. Besides, there are other devices that respond to voice and physical touch. A menu layout is displayed on a touch sensitive screen. Whenever a user touches a menu item on touch screen, the computer senses that a particular menu item has been touched and accordingly performs the operation associated with that menu item. Such touch screens have been installed at major railway stations for obtaining the online information about the arrival and departure of trains.

2. Central Processing Unit (CPU)

This is the main part of computer hardware that actually processes data according to the instructions it receives. It controls the flow of data by directing the data to enter the system, places the data into its memory, retrieves the same as and when needed and directs the output of data according to a set of stored instructions. It has three main units as described below:

a. **Arithmetic and logic unit (ALU):** It is responsible for performing all the arithmetic computations such as addition, subtraction, division, multiplication and exponentiation. In addition to this, it also performs logical operations involving comparisons among variables and data items.

b. **Memory unit:** In this unit, data is stored before being actually processed. The data so stored is accessed and processed according to a set of instructions that are also stored in the memory of the computer well before such data is transmitted to the memory from the input devices.

c. **Control unit:** This unit is entrusted with the responsibility of controlling and coordinating the activities of all other units of the computer system. Specifically, it performs the following functions:

    i.   Read instructions out of memory unit

    ii.   Decode such instructions

    iii. Set up the routing of data, through internal circuitry or wiring, to the desired place at right time

    iv. Determine the input device from where to get next instruction after the instruction in hand has been executed.

d. **Output unit:** After processing the data, the information produced according to a set of instructions need to be made available to the user in a human readable and understandable form. A computer system, therefore, needs an output device to communicate such information to the user. Essentially, the output device is assigned the task of translating the processed data from the machine coded form to a human readable form. The commonly used output devices include—external devices like monitor also called *Visual Display Unit* (VDU), printer, graphic plotter for producing graphs, technical drawings and charts, and internal devices like magnetic storage devices. Recently, a new device being perfected is the speech synthesizer that is capable of producing verbal output that sounds like human speech.

EVOLUTION OF COMPUTERIZED ACCOUNTING

Manual system of accounting has been traditionally the most popular method of keeping the records of financial transactions of an organization. Conventionally, the bookkeeper (or accountant) used to maintain books of accounts such as cash book, journal and ledger so as to prepare a summary of transactions and final accounts manually. The technological innovations led to the development of various machines capable of performing a variety of accounting functions. For example, the popular billing machine was designed to typewrite description of the transaction along with names and addresses of customers. This machine was capable of computing discounts; adding the net total and posting the requisite data to the relevant accounts. The customer's bill was generated automatically once the operator entered the necessary information. These machines combined the features of a typewriter and various kinds of calculators.

With a substantial increase in the number of transactions, the technology advanced further. With the exponential increase in speed, storage and processing capacity, newer versions of these machines evolved. A computer to which they were connected operated these machines. The success of a growing organization with complexity of transactions tended to depend on the resource optimization, quick decision making and control. As a result, the maintenance of the accounting data on a real time (or spontaneous) basis became almost essential. Such a system of maintaining the accounting records became convenient with the computerized accounting system.

INFORMATION AND DECISIONS

An organization is a collection of interdependent decision-making units that exist to pursue organizational objectives. As a system, every organization accepts inputs and transforms them into outputs. All organizational systems pursue certain objectives through a process of resource allocation that is accomplished through the process of managerial decision making. The information facilitates decisions regarding allocation of resources and thereby assists an organization in the pursuit of its objectives. Therefore, the information is the most important organizational resource. Every medium sized to large organization has a well-established information system that is meant to generate the information required for decision making.

With the increasing use of information systems in organizations, Transaction Processing Systems (TPS) have started playing a vital role in supporting the business operations. Every transaction processing system has three components: input, processing and output. Since Information Technology (IT) follows the GIGO principle (Garbage in–Garbage out), it is necessary that the input to the IT-based information system is accurate, complete and authorized. This is achieved by automating the input. A large number of devices are now available to automate the input process for a TPS.

TRANSACTION PROCESSING SYSTEMS

Transaction Processing Systems (TPS) are among the earliest computerized systems catering to the requirements of large business enterprises. The purpose of a typical TPS is to record, process, validate and store the transactions that occur in the various functional areas of a business for subsequent retrieval and usage. A transaction could be internal or external. When a department requisitions material supplies from the stores, an internal transaction is said to have occurred. However, when the purchase department purchases materials from a supplier, an external transaction takes place. The scope of financial accounting is confined to the external transactions only. TPS involves following the steps in processing a transaction. In order to understand these steps, let us consider a case wherein a customer withdraws money using the Automated Teller Machine (ATM) facility as described below:

1. Data entry

The action data must be entered into the system before it is processed. There are a number of input devices to enter data: keyboard, mouse, etc. For example, a bank customer operates an ATM facility to make a withdrawal. The actions taken by the customer constitutes data that is processed after validation by the computerized personal banking system.

2. Data validation

It ensures the accuracy and reliability of input data by comparing the same with some predetermined standards or known data. This validation is performed by error detection and by error correction procedures. The control mechanism, wherein the actual input is compared with the standard, is meant to detect errors while error correction procedures make suggestions for entering correct data input. The Personal Identification Number (PIN) of the customer is validated with the known data. If it is incorrect, a suggestion is made to indicate that the PIN is invalid. After validating the PIN (which is also a part of processing by TPS), the amount of withdrawal being made by the customer is also checked to ensure that it does not exceed a certain limit.

3. Processing and revalidation

The processing of data, representing actions of the ATM user, occurs almost instantaneously in case of the Online Transaction Processing (OLTP) system provided a valid data representing the actions of the user has been encountered. This called *check input validity*. Revalidation occurs to ensure that the transaction in terms of the delivery of money by the ATM has been completed. This is called *check output validity*.

4. Storage

Processed actions, as described above, culminate into financial transaction data that describes the withdrawal of money by a particular customer, are stored in transaction database of computerized personal banking system. This implies that only valid transactions are stored in the database.

5. Information

The stored data is processed using the query facility to produce the desired information. A database supported by DBMS is bound to have standard Structured Query Language (SQL) support.

6. Reporting

Finally, reports can be prepared on the basis of the required information content according to the decision usefulness of the report.

A simple computerized accounting system accepts the complete transaction data as input; stores such data in the computer storage media (say hard disk) and retrieves the accounting data for processing as and when required for generating an accounting report, as output. The input–process–output diagram shown below indicates how the accounting software translates data into information. This processing of data is accomplished either through batch processing or real-time processing.

Batch processing applies to large and voluminous data that is accumulated offline from various units, branches or departments. The entire accumulated data is processed in one shot to generate the desired reports according to decision requirement.

Real-time processing provides online outcome in the form of information and reports without any time lag between the transaction and its processing. The accounting reports are generated by a query language popularly called the *Structured Query Language* (SQL). It allows the user to retrieve the report relevant information that is capable of being laid out in predesigned accounting report. Accounting software may be structured with such components to provide for storage and processing of data pertaining to purchase, sales, inventory, payroll and other financial transactions.

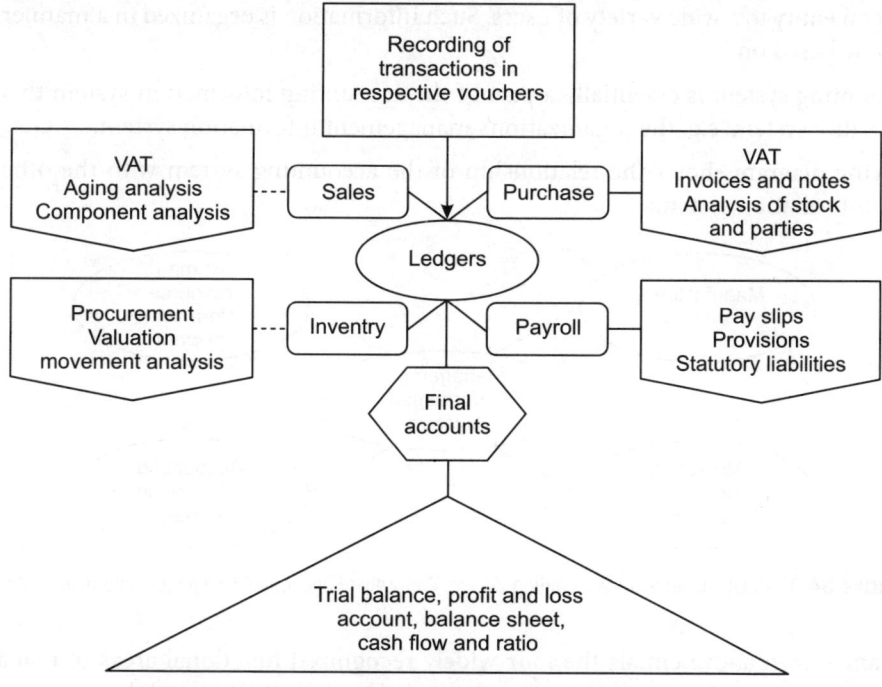

Figure 34.2. Components of Computerized Accounting Software System

COMPUTERIZED ACCOUNTING SYSTEM

Accounting software is used to implement a computerized accounting system. The computer accounting system is based on the concept of databases. It does away with the concept of creating and maintaining journals, ledger, etc., that are essential while working with the manual accounting system. Typically computerized accounting system offers the following features (Figure 34.2):

1. Online input and storage of accounting data.
2. Printout of purchase and sales invoices.
3. Logical scheme for codification of accounts and transactions. Every account and transaction is assigned a unique code.
4. Grouping of accounts is done from the very beginning.
5. Instant reports for management, e.g. aging statement, stock statement, trial balance, trading and profit and loss account, balance sheet, stock valuation, value added tax (VAT), returns, payroll report, etc.

MANAGEMENT INFORMATION SYSTEM AND ACCOUNTING

In order to remain competitive, organizations depend heavily on the information systems. Management Information System (MIS) is the most common form of information system being used. A management information system (MIS) is a system that provides the information necessary to take decisions and manage an organization effectively. MIS is supportive of the institution's long-term strategic goals and objectives. MIS is viewed and used at many levels by management—operational, tactical and strategic. Accounting Information System (AIS) identifies, collects, processes and communicates economic information about an entity to a wide variety of users. Such information is organized in a manner that correct decisions can be based on it.

Every accounting system is essentially a part of the accounting information system that in turn is a part of the broader system, e.g. the organization's management information system.

The following diagram shows the relationship of the accounting system with the other functional management information systems.

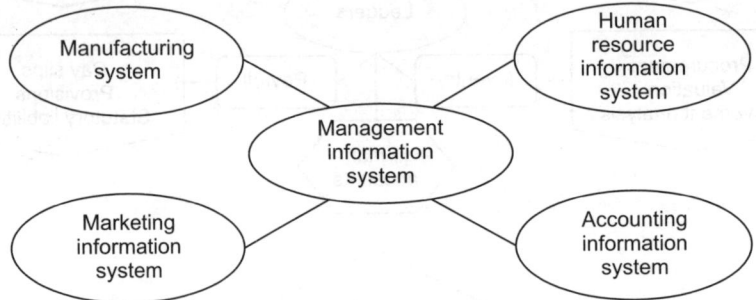

Figure 34.3. Relationship of the Accounting System With Other Functional Management Information System

The diagram shown above entails the four widely recognized functional areas of management. An organization operates in a given environment surrounded by the suppliers and the customers. The informational needs emerge from the business processes stratified into functional areas where accounting is one of them. The accounting information system receives and provides information to the various subsystems of the institutional or integrated MIS.

Accounting Information System (AIS) is a collection of resources (people and equipment) designed to transform financial and other data into information. This information is communicated to a wide variety of decision makers. Accounting information systems performs this transformation whether they are essentially manual systems or thoroughly computerized.

Conventionally MIS was also perceived as a day-to-day financial accounting system that is used to ensure that a basic control is maintained over financial record keeping activities, but now it is widely recognized as a broader concept. The accounting system is a subcomponent.

The reports generated by the accounting system are disseminated to the various users—internal and external to the organization. The external parties include the proprietors, investors, creditors, financiers, government suppliers and vendors, and the society at large. The reports used by these parties are more of a routine nature. However, the internal parties—the employees, managers, etc., use the accounting information for decision making and control.

Points to Ponder

1. The two major components of computer is Input unit and Central Processing Unit (CPU).
2. Transaction Processing Systems (TPS) are among the earliest computerized systems catering to the requirements of large business enterprises.
3. Automated Teller Machine (ATM) is useful for
   a. Data entry
   b. Data validation
   c. Processing and revalidation
   d. Storage
   e. Information
   f. Reporting

 Self-Assessment Exercises

1. State the different elements of a computer system.
2. List the distinctive advantages of a computer system over a manual system.
3. Draw a block diagram showing the main components of a computer.
4. Give three examples of a transaction processing system.
5. State the relationship between information and decision.
6. What is the Accounting Information System?
7. Write a short note on the application of computers in accounting.